SAINT THOMAS CHURCH FIFTH AVENUE

I. Exterior of the present (fourth) Saint Thomas Church, Fifth Avenue and Fifty-third, consecrated April 25, 1916 (architect, Ralph Adams Cram)

SAINT THOMAS CHURCH FIFTH AVENUE

BY *J. Robert Wright*

Published by
WILLIAM B. EERDMANS PUBLISHING COMPANY
and
SAINT THOMAS CHURCH FIFTH AVENUE
2001

© 2001 SAINT THOMAS CHURCH

All rights reserved

Published jointly 2001 by

WILLIAM B. EERDMANS PUBLISHING CO.

255 Jefferson Ave. S.E., Grand Rapids, Michigan 49503

P.O. Box 163, Cambridge CB3 9PU U.K.

www.eerdmans.com

and

SAINT THOMAS CHURCH FIFTH AVENUE

One West Fifty-third Street

New York, New York 10019-5496

www.saintthomaschurch.org

Design and typography by Jerry Kelly

Printed in the United States of America

05 04 03 02 01   7 6 5 4 3 2 1

ISBN 0-8028-3912-6

❧ FOREWORD

BY THE XIV BISHOP OF NEW YORK

I T GIVES ME GREAT PLEASURE to welcome the carefully detailed but at the same time clearly profound history of the first one hundred and seventy-five years of one of the truly great parishes of our diocese. This is the history of Saint Thomas Church, but it is not only about the church; much of the story focuses on the way in which Saint Thomas's congregation and its rectors responded to the unfolding events of history. Because of the importance of this parish, the history of Saint Thomas is much like a mirror in which we see reflected in an interesting way the life and times of the whole Episcopal Church. Also, what is abundantly clear in this story, and what all who enter her doors know to be true, is that Saint Thomas Church has a way of showing forth the "beauty of holiness." This is the church that has offered what so many thirst for, the experience of the transcendent.

I want to salute the rector, vestry, and parishioners of Saint Thomas for their accomplishments in the building up of God's Church under the Gospel of our Lord Jesus Christ and the patronage of Saint Thomas the Apostle. This is a parish known for strong leadership in both its clergy and its laity – a leadership that continues in the present. This bishop is grateful for the close connection between Saint Thomas and the diocese and its bishop.

I also wish to praise the work of Canon Wright, who has done a wonderful job of gathering this history from a number of sources and presenting it in a factual and interesting way. In undertaking this writing of their history, the rector, wardens, and vestry are to be congratulated along with Canon Wright, for such a work is not simply a preoccupation with the past, but a preparation to move forward in unison.

✠ THE RIGHT REVEREND RICHARD F. GREIN
XIV Bishop of New York

II. Exterior of the first Saint Thomas Church, consecrated February 23, 1826

❧ TABLE OF CONTENTS

1823-1827	Cornelius Roosevelt Duffie, first rector (from 17 February 1824).
12 October 1823	First church service in a room at Broome St. and Broadway.
9 January 1824	Date of incorporation as "St. Thomas Church in the City and County of New York."

First Church

27 July 1824	Laying of Cornerstone of first church, Broadway and Houston.
23 February 1826	Consecration of first church.
1828-1831	George Upfold, second rector.
1831-1843	Francis Lister Hawks, third rector.
1844-1851	Henry John Whitehouse, fourth rector.
2 March 1851	Fire destroys first church.

Second Church

3 April 1852	Consecration of second church, Broadway and Houston.
1852-1856	Edmund Neville, fifth rector.
1857-1888	William Ferdinand Morgan, sixth rector.
29 April 1866	Last service in second church.
6 May 1866 to *21 April 1867*	Services at Grace Church on Broadway.
21 April 1867	First service in temporary chapel, Fifth Avenue and Fifty-third Street.

Third Church

14 October 1868	Laying of Cornerstone of third church, Fifth Avenue and Fifty-third.
6 October 1870	First service in third church (architect, Richard Upjohn).
15 May 1883	Consecration of third church.
1888-1900	John Wesley Brown, seventh rector.
1901-1925	Ernest Milmore Stires, eighth rector.
8 August 1905	Fire destroys third church.

Fourth Church

21 November 1911	Laying of Cornerstone of fourth church, Fifth Avenue and Fifty-third.
4 October 1913	First service in fourth church (architect, Ralph Adams Cram).

III. Cornelius Roosevelt Duffie, First Rector 1823-1827

25 April 1916	Consecration of fourth church.
3 March 1919	Saint Thomas Choir School opened.
1926-1954	Roelif Hasbrouck Brooks, ninth rector.
1954-1972	Frederick Myers Morris, tenth rector.
19 November 1956	Arents Memorial Organ dedicated.
5 November 1961	All pew rentals terminated.
1965	Independence for Saint Thomas Chapel as All Saints Church.
23 November 1969	Loening Memorial Organ dedicated.
1972-1996	John Gerald Barton Andrew, eleventh rector.
14 March 1996	Loening/Hancock Organ rededicated.
1996-	Andrew Craig Mead, twelfth rector.

❧ INTRODUCTION

THE HISTORY OF THE GREAT PARISH of Saint Thomas
on Fifth Avenue in New York has previously received the attention of
two great historians of the Episcopal Church. The Rev. Dr. E. Clowes
Chorley, my distant predecessor as Historiographer of the Episcopal
Church, completed in 1943 a manuscript of some 570 pages that was still not
ready for the printer at the time of his death in 1949. This manuscript was
later updated but also shortened by Canon George E. DeMille and was finally published in 1958 as a book of 198 pages with very little annotation or
documentation. That volume recorded the history of Saint Thomas from its
beginnings in 1823 to the year 1954, which was the last year of the rectorship
of Dr. Roelif H. Brooks and the first year of that of Dr. Frederick M. Morris. Since that time there have been two more rectors, and the parish has celebrated its one hundred and seventy-fifth anniversary in October of 1998.
Shortly after Father Andrew C. Mead became rector in 1996, he and the
vestry invited me to undertake a thorough revision and extension of the book
that Canon DeMille published, in order to carry the story down to the year
of Father Mead's arrival; this project was intended to be published not too
long after the anniversary celebration in 1998. Our agreement was signed in
October of 1997, and the present volume is the response to that invitation.

Clearing away some previous commitments and beginning work on the
new volume in earnest, I soon realized that my mandate involved first of all
something of an archaeological expedition: retrieving significant portions of
the old Chorley manuscript that had been discarded by DeMille (possibly for
lack of space) and salvaging as much as possible of the DeMille book. It was
also necessary to correct several hundred factual errors found in the process. I
am grateful to the Historical Society of the Episcopal Church, original publishers of the DeMille book, for the freedom to claim that book as my own,
retaining those portions of it that I thought should be kept (even some concepts, sentences, and paragraphs) without the necessity of indicating them by
footnotes. The ultimate decisions about what to retain, to correct, to alter, and
to discard have of course been mine alone. I soon realized, however, that I was
not a solo author setting out afresh upon a project that had never before been
attempted. I have come to see my role in this undertaking as more like that of
the conductor of a symphony, for I have drawn upon the dominant scores already established but also tried to give them new life by correcting, refashion-
ing, annotating, extending, and expanding them. Moreover, this has been

done in collaboration with a group of assistants, and without their work the whole project would have taken many more years to complete. First in this regard I must record my greatest thanks to the Rev. Dr. Charles R. Henery, Professor of Church History at Nashotah House Seminary in Nashotah, Wisconsin, who has been my senior assistant, doing the lion's share of research in the Saint Thomas Archives and elsewhere and testing and substantiating or rejecting many assertions in the DeMille book. Since the time that Chorley and DeMille did their work, it is a sad fact that some of the documents they seem to have had at their disposal have been either temporarily or permanently lost, but it is also a happy fact that a number of other documents have surfaced since their days, with the result that on a number of important points Father Henery and I found much more that can now be said. With all these changes, with the old material to build upon, with so much new information, with several new chapters and appendices at the end, and with the hereby-acknowledged assistance of so many others, it has become possible to write a new and fully documented history of Saint Thomas.

In view of this expanding agenda, it became necessary to involve many others in the project, and I must therefore also express my thanks to Mr. Richard J. Mammana Jr., a student at Columbia University who served as my editorial assistant for an entire summer, and to Mr. Joseph Galvin, parishioner of Saint Thomas, who served as a volunteer research assistant, and to Dr. Gretchen Rehberg who did the beginning work on the index. For more specialized essays, I was also fortunate to be able to call upon a number of distinguished senior authorities intimately associated with the parish: Dr. Gerre Hancock on music; Mr. Kenneth A. Lohf on the Choir School; Canon Harry Krauss, the senior curate, on heraldry; and the present rector, Father Andrew Mead, for an epilogue. Thanks must also go to the parish history committee, consisting of Mrs. Otto Preminger, Mr. Louis Beal, Mr. Lohf, Father Mead, and Canon Krauss, who have collectively and individually been my advisors at every stage of the enterprise and whose preferences I have always followed whenever a choice had to be made. This book is therefore in a real sense their book also, the book they said they wanted me to write; they too have had prominent places in the symphony. The book has ended up being rather longer than was originally planned, but in the end it seemed desirable to create a new record that was, on the whole, more complete rather than less so. Still other voices who have contributed to this music, either through personal comments or interviews or through individual acts of research, include Father John Andrew (the previous rector), Mrs. Joan Hoffman, Mr. William Haas, Miss Claire Virginia Rouse, Mr. Sidney Stires, Mrs. Wolters Duffie Ledyard, Mrs. Patricia Ellerton Duffie, Professor John Atwater Duffie, the Rev. John Rawlinson, Miss Courtney Cowart,

Dr. Warren Platt, Sandra Hughes Boyd, Mr. Crosby Willet, Lee Whitley and the ever-helpful tour guides of Saint Thomas Parish, and probably others. I am also grateful to the staff of Saint Thomas Church who have been so patient in seeking answers to my questions: Douglas Robbe, James Marlow, Addison Keim, and Sharlene Shah. Finally, the manuscript at its last stages benefited immeasurably from the careful attention and helpful suggestions of some expert external readers in the persons of Professors Eric McKitrick and Kenneth Jackson of Columbia University, Professor Bruce Mullin of the General Theological Seminary, Professor Robert Prichard of the Virginia Theological Seminary, Dr. Mary Donovan, immediate past president of the Historical Society of the Episcopal Church, Dean Guy Lytle of the School of Theology of the University of the South, and Mr. Wayne Kempton, archivist of the Diocese of New York.

If every true history is a record of facts together with an interpretation thereof, then the history of Saint Thomas is, in a very particular way, the history of both a building and a people. It is the history of both building-stones and "living stones," intermingled over time to create a spiritual house to God's glory. It is the story of the worship that has been offered and of the service that has been rendered, as the vision of the "spiritual house" that is recorded in I Peter 2:4-5 has gradually, over the one hundred seventy-five years from 1823 to 1998, become a reality on the corner of Fifth Avenue and Fifty-third Street. This particular biblical theme seems to have been present at every major turning point of Saint Thomas's history. This is the interpretation, the common theme, that seems to give life to the facts so painstakingly recorded within these pages. It is a story of the interaction of silent building-stones with living, human stones, as God's Breath, God's Spirit, has given them life.

But if the factual history of Saint Thomas is best interpreted by the worship that has sustained it and the service to others inspired by that worship, then it is also true that the history of Saint Thomas is best told in terms of the rectors of the parish who have been the high priests of that worship and the instigators of that service. A certain constancy of stewardship and seriousness of intention has marked every one of them over the course of history. In a way that is rather peculiar to Saint Thomas, and endorsed by its parishioners over time and today as well, the history of this parish, the "symphony of Saint Thomas," is best orchestrated and told around the rectorships of the priests who have led it. For this very reason the chapters are largely constructed around them and the leadership they have given, with less emphasis placed upon their assisting clergy; much is said, however, about the activities of the congregation, the services of worship offered, and the visual memorials erected over time. Such a story does not proceed "from the bottom up" as some in the modern historical profession might prefer, but it is indeed the story that the surviving records indicate, and it is largely the way the parishioners today still understand themselves and the way they want to read their history. To that story we must now turn, for we have already entered it.

J. ROBERT WRIGHT

St. Mark's-in-the-Bowery Professor of Ecclesiastical History
in the General Theological Seminary,
and Historiographer of the Episcopal Church

New York City
January 6, 2001, The Feast of the Epiphany

IV. "Night-Fall, St. Thomas Church, Broadway, New York," c.1837, watercolor by George Harvey

NOTES ON STYLE: Original capitalizations, punctuations, and spellings have been retained within quotation marks. The title "Saint Thomas Church," official in the parish usage since 1923, has always been preferred over other variants outside of quotation marks. Clergy have been described by titles that are historically accurate, even though they vary over the years.

 SAINT THOMAS CHURCH FIFTH AVENUE

1. Cornelius Roosevelt Duffie, First Rector 1823-1827

CHAPTER 1

The First Stone of a Building

CORNELIUS ROOSEVELT DUFFIE
FIRST RECTOR, 1823-1827

"WE ARE ASSEMBLED TO LAY THE FIRST STONE of a building, intended, if God should prosper the undertaking, to be hereafter consecrated. . .exclusively to the duties of devotion," said Presiding Bishop William White of Pennsylvania at the laying of the cornerstone of the first Saint Thomas Church on Tuesday afternoon, July 27, 1824. Assisted by the prayers and presence of three other bishops (the diocesan, Bishop John Henry Hobart, being absent in England), Bishop White continued: "That the intended building may contribute eminently to. . .eternal interests, let us invoke the blessing of Almighty God." The first rector, the Reverend Cornelius Roosevelt Duffie (ill. 1), chose in his address to emphasize the relationship of building-stones to the living or spiritual stones who would worship there. He said: "Let us bethink ourselves; it is not enough to assist in rearing the altars and in building up the temples of the living God. We must ourselves be built up a spiritual house, an habitation of God through the Spirit."[1]

It has been more than 175 years since that infant congregation of Saint Thomas first met to worship in a simple room at the corner of Broome Street and Broadway on Sunday, October 12, 1823. The successive congregations of Saint Thomas have assembled and rendered their spiritual sacrifices, their worship of Almighty God, in successive generations. Saint Thomas is both a place and a people, and both place and people have histories that are intermingled and grown together into one. Their collective history is the subject of this book. It is the story of the response that Saint Thomas has made, of the worship its people have offered and the service they have rendered, to the God of their joy and gladness. Like every history, this is not only a record of facts, but also an interpretation thereof.

If one strains the ear it is just possible to hear the faint rumble of the subways below while attending the Choral Eucharist or Evensong at Saint Thomas

Church on Fifth Avenue. The heavenly songs of the Choir of Men and Boys are nonetheless dominant, as the worldly sounds of taxis, buses, cars, and masses of people on the street outside all gradually recede. Candle flames flicker more brightly as the vibrations subside. The presence of "the world" at all celebrations of the Sacred in this glorious church, however, is an undeniable fact. This church is both an oasis of the holy in the city as well as an integral part of the city. Without the city Saint Thomas would have neither a history to tell nor a congregation to offer worship and service in response to the Gospel preached there.

All this having been said, the roaring, polyglot metropolis that is New York today must disappear from our minds if we are to visualize the city in which Saint Thomas Church had its beginning. We must picture a smaller, much simpler city, a city in which the German tongue was as likely to be heard along with English on the streets as are Spanish and Chinese today. In 1823, as the parish was beginning, the population of New York was nearly 150,000, making it the largest city in the young nation, despite the fact that it had just recovered from the terrible scourge of Yellow Fever in 1822. While the walls of the first Saint Thomas Church were rising, Governor DeWitt Clinton led a parade down Broadway to celebrate the opening of the Erie Canal, that "Wedding of the Waters" which united Lake Erie with the Atlantic Ocean. This marked an epoch in the life of the city, since it was the canal which eventually solidified New York's status as the greatest port and largest city in the New World, eclipsing any claims of Boston, Philadelphia, or Baltimore to that distinction. The canal brought to New York the wealth and population for which it has subsequently been known so well throughout the world. It was this same prosperity that made possible, in time, the present Church of Saint Thomas.

The city had not then extended past the lower section of Manhattan Island, and one could conveniently walk to almost any point within it. Banks and other financial institutions centered on Wall Street. The leading merchants situated themselves on Front Street or nearby, and a few of the older, more conservative among them still lived above their stores and offices. The homes of the more substantial citizens were for the most part on the lower West Side below Canal Street, while St. John's Park, East Broadway from Bowling Green up to Chambers, and the area around City Hall Park were favorite residential neighborhoods. Greenwich Street, which paralleled the Hudson, was important, as was also the Battery, the city's premier park and promenade. Columbia College, the alma mater of Cornelius Roosevelt Duffie, Saint Thomas' first rector, stood on the site of the King's Farm at the foot of what is now Park Place. Greenwich Village was still, true to its name, a village. As yet there was little construction in the countryside north of

Fourteenth Street, and the rural hamlet of Chelsea, where the General Theological Seminary had just been situated, ran down to the wooded banks of the Hudson River. Conditions in the city in 1823 bordered on the primitive by modern standards. Not until 1835 was the first public water supply, drawn from the Croton River, in operation. Before then, those houses and public buildings that did enjoy the luxury of private water depended on rain collection in cisterns. Drinking water could be had for a penny a gallon. The poor drew theirs from contaminated wells, resulting in periodic epidemics. There were no railroads, and before 1830 there were no stages or street cars. New Yorkers traveled by foot, by private coach, or by canal boat.

Despite what now seems a lack of the essentials of civilization, the city was by no means devoid of culture. There were literary societies, libraries, a Museum of Natural History, an Academy of Fine Arts, and a Sacred Music Society. The Park Theatre, the American Theatre, Vauxhall Park, and, above all, Niblo's Garden, provided entertainment and society. The New York Public Library, much less the earlier Astor Library that it would incorporate, did not yet exist, but William Cullen Bryant and Edgar Allan Poe were living and writing in the city at the time. Washington Irving and James Fenimore Cooper paid periodic visits. Ample evidence indicates a populace whose cultural pursuits were healthy and active.

There were some 101 churches in New York City at this time, seventeen of them said to be Protestant Episcopal, and most of these were located in the heavily populated wards of the city within a one-mile radius of City Hall.[2] The Episcopal Church in New York was already old and strongly established, the New York diocese having been founded in 1785. Before the American Revolution, the Episcopal Church had, of course, enjoyed the dubious distinction of being viewed as "established" in its technical relations to the church and state in England. The revolution had dealt it a heavy blow, although recovery was now well on the way. Mother of all the churches in the city was, and still is, Trinity, then with its rounded porch and wooden steeple, but standing where it still does, at the head of Wall Street. Associated with it were its two chapels, St. John's and St. Paul's; the latter is the oldest public building and the oldest Episcopal church building in New York City in continuous use and still surviving today. St. George's, then in Beekman Street east of St. Paul's Chapel and near the old Brooklyn ferry slips, had originally also been a chapel of Trinity, but had by 1823 become an independent parish. Christ Church stood in Anthony Street, and Grace Church was at the corner of Rector Street and Broadway. St. Mark's-in-the-Bowery was situated at what is now East Tenth Street and Second Avenue in the East Village, today the oldest Manhattan location in continuous use for Christian worship. The French Huguenot Church of St.-Esprit, in 1803, had become

Episcopalian and had been consecrated by Bishop Benjamin Moore; it was there that the French translation of the English Prayer Book had recently been adapted to accord with the new American liturgy of 1789-90. Zion Church at Cross and Mott Streets, originally a Lutheran congregation, came into union with the diocese in 1810. St. Stephen's, St. Luke's, and Calvary Church were all situated within the lower limits of the island. Far in the north, remote from the city proper, were to be found St. Michael's, St. James', and St. Mary's in Manhattanville. Mention also must be made of St. Philip's, established in 1809 but, regrettably, excluded at that time from the diocese because of its ministry to the African-American community.[3] In all of these churches, there were in 1823 just over twenty-five hundred communicants.

The clergy of the city in 1823 constituted a notable group. First by far was the man with spiritual leadership and diocesan jurisdiction over the whole of the state of New York, the Rt. Rev. John Henry Hobart. Bishop Hobart is remembered as dynamic, quick-tempered, fearless, impulsive, and full of missionary zeal, but with sufficient greatness to recognize and repent of his own hastiness. He was in many ways the outstanding figure in the entire Episcopal Church at that time, and he remains the most famous of the Episcopalian Bishops of New York. His magnetic leadership did much to determine the churchmanship of the diocese. A staunch High Churchman himself, most of the diocese under him either acquired or maintained a decidedly High Church stamp. Benjamin T. Onderdonk, who would become Hobart's successor as bishop in 1830, was a less striking figure but nonetheless a hardworking priest who absorbed the best that Hobart had to offer. George Washington Doane, the future Bishop of New Jersey, was a scholar, poet, and creative thinker who in 1823 was still teaching in a classical school; like Hobart, he had a touch of genius. James Milnor, the rector of St. George's and a former member of Congress, was a militant Evangelical and a thorn in the bishop's side. Jonathan Wainwright and Manton Eastburn, both of whom were to become bishops themselves, now held positions in city churches. Before the end of 1824 there was to be added to this stellar collection the talent of Cornelius Roosevelt Duffie, the first rector of Saint Thomas.

The beginnings of Saint Thomas Church were humble rather than magnificent, a far cry from the vaulted roof, glorious stained glass, and towering reredos that now so impress worshipers and visitors alike. The first service of the congregation that would become Saint Thomas parish took place in a simple room at the corner of Broome Street and Broadway. It was heralded by an advertisement in the *New York Evening Post* of October 11, 1823, that read as follows:

Notice. – The large room (late Reading Room) on the corner of Broadway and Broome street, has been engaged for the purpose of divine worship according to the rites of the Protestant Episcopal Church.

The first service will take place on Sunday evening next, 12th inst. at half past 7 o'clock; after which, the regular services will be held on Sunday mornings, at half past 10; and on Sunday and Thursday evenings, at half past 7 o'clock.[4]

A small group of laymen, drawn from the parishioners of Trinity Church, Grace Church, and St. George's, sponsored this development. Their reason was obvious and practical: the city was creeping slowly north of Canal Street. Bankers like Isaac Lawrence (one of the first two wardens) and merchants like David Hadden (a member of the first vestry) now lived on Broadway (ill. 2). Others were moving into the neighborhood of what is now Fourteenth Street, and they naturally desired access to church services near their homes. The state of transportation being what it was, the distance between these addresses and the locales of the established churches was a greater hardship than it would be today. Moreover, with the exception of two churches, St. Luke's on Hudson Street and Calvary Church, no new parish had been created for several years. The existing churches were all near City Hall, and in the long stretch from St. Paul's Chapel to the village of Bloomingdale there was not a single Episcopal church.

Particulars of the beginning of Saint Thomas have been preserved in a pamphlet that has already been cited at the beginning of this chapter. Published at the request of the Wardens and Vestry of Saint Thomas in 1824 under the title *An Account Of The Ceremony Of Laying The Corner Stone Of St. Thomas' Church; Including The Addresses Delivered On That Occasion, Together with a Brief Statement Of The Rise Of That Church*, the pamphlet records that

2. Isaac Lawrence, Warden 1823-39, and David Hadden, Vestryman 1823 and Warden 1824-56

THE FIRST STONE OF A BUILDING

On Sunday evening, 12th October, 1823 (notice thereof having been previously given in some of the public papers) divine service, according to the rites of the Protestant Episcopal Church, was celebrated, for the first time, in the large room, No. 440 Broome-street, corner of Broadway, by the Rev. Dr. Wainwright, Rector of Grace Church; nearly all the Episcopal clergy of the city being present: after which a discourse was delivered by the Rev. Cornelius R. Duffie, from Psalm lxxxvii, 2.

Four days later, the Rev. Benjamin T. Onderdonk, then an assistant minister of Trinity Parish, wrote Bishop Hobart, who was in England: "Duffie made a beginning at the corner of Broome Street and Broadway last Sunday evening. It was a very full congregation, and everybody seems to think that his prospects are very good."[5]

Beginning with that first Sunday, services were held regularly. The next step was to give the incipient parish a formal organization. Accordingly, on December 4, 1823, a meeting "of persons friendly to the establishment of a Church in Communion with the Protestant Episcopal Church of the State of New York to be located above Canal Street" was held in the Broome Street room. The persons present were Isaac Lawrence, Charles King, Richard Oakley, William Beach Lawrence, John Slidell, David R. Lambert, John J. Lambert, Archibald McVickar, Dr. James Stewart, William Tripler, and Murray Hoffman. Isaac Lawrence was called to the chair, and Murray Hoffman acted as secretary. At this meeting, it was formally resolved "that the Reverend C.R. Duffie be requested to announce during Morning Service for two successive Sundays previous to the 25th December instant, that an Election would on that day be held, immediately after divine Service, at the Corner of Broadway and Broome Street, for choosing two Wardens, and eight Vestrymen."[6]

The required notice having been given, the election was duly held on Christmas Day. Isaac Lawrence and Thomas M. Huntington were elected wardens. David Hadden, William Beach Lawrence, John J. Lambert, Murray Hoffman, John Duer, Charles King, Richard Oakley, and William Backhouse Astor were chosen as vestrymen.[7] The parish, which then had twenty-three communicants, was incorporated under the title of "St. Thomas Church in the City and County of New York." Tuesday in Easter Week was fixed as the date for the annual election of wardens and vestrymen. The certificate of incorporation was formally acknowledged on January 9, 1824, before John T. Irving, First Judge of the Court of Common Pleas.[8] The parish was received into union with the convention of the Diocese of New York on October 19, 1824. The lay delegates who represented the parish at this convention were David Hadden, William B. Lawrence, Benjamin M. Brown, Richard Oakley, and John Duer.[9]

The first meeting of the newly constituted vestry was held on January 14,

1824, and Richard Oakley was elected treasurer with Murray Hoffman as clerk. It is worth pausing for a moment to observe what manner of men composed this first vestry. Their tenures were often long, for the custom at that time was to serve for life rather than for a limited term. Isaac Lawrence, warden, was a merchant and banker. He had served on the vestries of both Grace Church and St. George's Church and was one of the first trustees of the General Theological Seminary. David Hadden, who was to serve (first as a vestryman, later as a warden) for a total of thirty-three years, was born in Scotland and had become one of the leading merchants of New York. As chairman of the building committee which had oversight of the building of the first church, he rendered invaluable service, and he was throughout his life one of the most generous contributors to the support of the parish. For the first thirty years of the history of Saint Thomas, Hadden was probably its most useful layman, and of all the members of the original vestry, he was to have by far the longest tenure. Nevertheless, he was but one star in the original galaxy.

William Beach Lawrence was an eminent lawyer who later moved to Rhode Island and there became lieutenant governor. Charles King played many parts, all with distinction, in the life of the city of New York. Son of United States Senator Rufus King and brother of Governor John A. King, he was at first a merchant, then editor of the *New York American*. In 1849, he became president of Columbia College. John Duer was a lawyer who eventually became Chief Justice of the State Supreme Court. One of the ablest jurists in America, he was a notable figure in the stormy diocesan conventions of the forties. Murray Hoffman, likewise an eminent lawyer, was probably the first person in the United States to make a serious study of the canon law of the Episcopal Church. Two volumes written by him are still of historical interest: *A Treatise on the Law of the Protestant Episcopal Church in the United States* and *The Ritual Law of the Church*. He had graduated from Columbia in 1809, a classmate of Cornelius Roosevelt Duffie, Benjamin T. Onderdonk, and Jackson Kemper. The greatest fortune in this group was undoubtedly held by William Backhouse Astor, son of John Jacob Astor, the wealthiest man in the United States. William was sometimes known as the "landlord of New York," but he was more than just a landlord. Among other benefactions, he contributed half a million dollars to the Astor Library, which was one of the constituents of the present New York Public Library.[10] This was a very substantial group of leaders in the New York of their day, but also a very typical group of urban Episcopalian laymen of that time.

In the early part of the nineteenth century in New York, parishes were at times created to make a field for the display of the talents of a brilliant minister, or to extend the influence of an ecclesiastical party. Thus, when the friends of the Rev. Joseph Pilmore failed to secure his appointment as an assistant minister of Trinity Church, they built Christ Church as his sphere of influence. In like manner, the Church of the Ascension provided room for the distinctly evangelical tenets of the Rev. Manton Eastburn, a militant leader of his party and subsequently Bishop of Massachusetts.

There are some hints that similar motives may have contributed to the establishment of Saint Thomas parish. In 1823, party feeling ran high in the New York diocese. Under the aggressive leadership of Bishop Hobart, the apostle of "Evangelical truth and Apostolic order," the High Church movement was the dominant influence, though a few strong Evangelicals, entrenched in well-to-do city parishes, were managing to fight a good defensive action. There is every reason to believe that Cornelius Duffie, who had grown up at the feet of Hobart in Trinity Parish, was what was known in those days as a "Hobart Churchman." It may well be, therefore, that among the motives which led to the organization of Saint Thomas was not only the desire to find a place for Mr. Duffie, but also the intention to extend the influence of the Hobart school in the upper part of the growing city. It is certainly true that down to the end of the rectorship of John Wesley Brown, at the close of the century, the clergy of Saint Thomas were doctrinal High Churchmen.

At a meeting of the vestry held at the house of Isaac Lawrence on February 17, 1824, it was unanimously resolved "that the Reverend Cornelius R. Duffie be hereby called to be Rector of the parish of St. Thomas Church, and that the presiding Warden and the Secretary be a Committee to inform him of this Resolution, and to acquaint him with the present situation and future prospects of the congregation"[11] (pl. III).

The committee discharged this duty, and one week later presented to the vestry the following letter, written by Mr. Duffie under date of February 24, 1824:

Gentlemen,
In requesting you to report to the Vestry of St Thomas' my acceptance of the appointment of Rector, conferred by their Resolution of the 17th inst., and communicated through you, I pray you likewise to make known to the Board, the sense of obligation with which I have received that mark of their confidence. Of the great responsibility which I now assume, I am deeply conscious, and it shall be my uniform endeavor, by God's help, so to fulfil it, as shall advance the best Interests of the infant Congregation committed to our common charge.
With very great Respect, I am, Gentlemen,
Your Obdt. Servant,
Cornelius R. Duffie[12]

Mr. Duffie, who had accompanied his own letter, then took the chair and presided over his first vestry meeting. No mention is made in these communications of a stipend, but the following document in the parish archives sheds light on the issue:

We, the subscribers attached to St. Thomas Church, and frequenting the Room used as a Chapel for that Church, in Testimony of our respect and regard for our Rector, the Rev. Cornelius R. Duffie, agree to pay the sums set opposite our names respectively,

New York, 26 Decr. 1825

	DOLLARS		DOLLARS
Isaac Lawrence	50	Ch. Anthon	20
David Hadden	50	James Casey	20
Murray Hoffman	25	Ch. Bostwick	10
Rogers & Gracie	30	W. Langlen	25
W. B. Lawrence	25	Mrs. H. Robinson	20
Chas. King	25	T. J. Lambert	25
John Jas. Lambert	25	Jas. G. King	10
Richd. Oakley	20	C. Shirley	5
B. M. Brown	20	Mrs. Cox	10
J. Smyth Rogers	20	T. L. Smith	25
I. F. Cox	20	Morris Robinson	25
Mrs. Marx	20	Beverley Robinson	25
Mrs. Neilson	10	John Duer	20
Arch McVickar	20	Mrs. Gilliat	10

TOTAL $610

In addition to revealing how names were abbreviated at that time, this document indicates the way in which the Episcopal Church was financed throughout the first half of the nineteenth century. Parish budgets were unknown and, except for the occasional endowment and the pewrents that seemed inevitable at that time, parishes had no regular source of income. It was always easy to raise the money for projects, such as a new building or a new organ. But constantly recurring items like the rector's stipend, regular church expenses, or the coal bill were insoluble problems to the vestries of that day.[13]

Cornelius Roosevelt Duffie, the new rector of the new parish at the age of thirty-five, was born in New York City on March 31, 1789, the son of John Duffie and Maria Roosevelt. He was educated at the Episcopal Academy in Cheshire, Connecticut, and at Columbia College, where we learn from a contemporary that "he distinguished himself for the uniform propriety of his conduct, for the industry with which he acquitted himself at the private and public recitations."[14] This is no mere conventional commendation, and already the portrait of an individual begins to emerge. After graduating in 1809 he began the study of law, but the death of his father forced him to give this up and to enter his family's mercantile business. He succeeded in this enterprise for several years until economic reverses in the city's mercantile community forced him to abandon it. During the years from 1810 to 1818, which included the War of 1812, he also served as ensign and later captain in the New York State Militia. On April 16, 1816, at the age of twenty-seven, he married nineteen-year-old Helena Bache Bleecker, of a family already significant in New York history.[15] In 1821, about two months after her early death on August 17 of that year, Duffie wrote to Bishop Hobart: "A few years of practical acquaintance with the world [has shown] me that fortune and the fairest prospects were often vain and deceptive; and that even success and prosperity were less to be desired than feared, for their tendency to make men forgetful of themselves."[16]

Duffie had been brought up a Baptist, but like so many of his generation he revolted against the Calvinistic teaching to which the Baptists of the day were generally committed. His first movement toward Anglicanism, like those of some other converts, can be traced to a funeral he attended in an Episcopal church! He was so impressed with the service that he bought a copy of the Book of Common Prayer, studied it carefully, and then sought the advice of his college classmate, Benjamin T. Onderdonk. The result was that, at the age of twenty-six, he was baptized by this friend and advisor. He became a pew-holder in St. John's Chapel, coming into intimate contact with Bishop Hobart, who lived next door to the Chapel, and who later confirmed him in Trinity Church. Such was the confidence in Duffie's character and judgment that he was elected a member of the Trinity vestry in 1817 and served until 1822. During this period he also became a member and officer of the New York Protestant Episcopal Tract Society, an early and zealous promoter of Sunday schools in the city, and organizer of the New York Protestant Episcopal Sunday School Society, as well as an active founder of the Missionary Society.

It was in these days that his thoughts turned toward the ordained ministry of the Church, and after serious deliberation he determined at the ripe age of thirty-four to study for holy orders and to read theology under the direction of Bishop Hobart and Dr. Onderdonk. On August 6, 1823, he was ordained deacon by Bishop Hobart in Trinity Church. Three months later, he took charge of the services in the Broome Street room. On October 11, 1824, he was ordained priest in St. Luke's Church by Bishop John Croes of New Jersey, acting for Bishop Hobart who was then in Europe.[17]

The small beginnings of the new parish are reflected in its first parochial

Cornelius Roosevelt Duffie Jr.

Mr. Duffie's second son, Cornelius Roosevelt Duffie Jr., was born on August 6, 1821. Mr. Duffie's wife, Helena, died on August 17, 1821, within just a few weeks of that birth. Following in the footsteps of his father, the young Duffie became a candidate for holy orders from Saint Thomas Church, graduated from the General Theological Seminary in 1845, and was ordained deacon on June 29 of that year by Bishop Thomas C. Brownell of Connecticut. He served part of his diaconate at Trinity Church in New York, where his father had been a vestryman. On March 4, 1849, he was ordained priest in Trinity Church, New York, by Bishop William Rollinson Whittingham of Maryland. He was founder and first rector of the Church of St. John Baptist, located at Lexington Avenue and Thirty-fifth Street, which was organized in 1848 and erected its first building in 1849. It was consolidated with the Church of the Epiphany in 1893. For twenty-five years the younger Duffie was also chaplain of Columbia University. As Rector Emeritus of the Epiphany, he placed in its chancel a memorial window to his father. He died in 1900. The first rector also had two daughters, Helena and Maria, who did not marry.[25]

report to the Convention of the Diocese of New York. In less than its first full year, there had been five Baptisms, one marriage, four burials, and the parish reported twenty-three "communicants."[18]

For about three years, the parish continued to worship in the Broome Street room. Some insight into the life of the parish at this time is afforded by a letter addressed by Mr. Duffie to Bishop Hobart, who was still abroad:

New York 15 Nov. 1824

Right Reverend and Dear Sir,

I was made very happy today by the receipt of your letter of 17th Sept., and I thank you most sincerely for the kindness it manifested, and for the good wishes which it expressed. "The good Providence of God" is indeed upon Our Church throughout the State, and for the success which has attended my humble efforts to increase its prosperity, I in particular have great reason to be thankful. The infant congregation of St. Thomas' from a handful, has become a very respectable society of pious worshippers. Our Church is nearly ready to be enclosed, and thus far has given satisfaction both for its design and execution. The wishes which you have expressed respecting its interior arrangement agree entirely with our intentions and plans,[19] and I hope that upon your return, when it will be ready for consecration you will find it such as you would desire it to be.

While I have reason to rejoice in the goodness of God in respect to the undertaking, I have not been without a feeling of his chastening hand. My eldest child, my dear Charles, a fine boy of nearly eight years of age, and who since the death of his mother was becoming to me a most interesting companion, has been called to the house of a better Father. I pray He, who has given me submission to His will, would also give me grace worthily to improve this very trying dispensation. . . .

I have troubled you with a long letter, I will only add how sincere is my affection and respect, and how much I desire your paternal advice and direction in that new relation in which as yet I have been almost entirely debarred from enjoying it. That your protracted absence, the necessity of which we all so much lament, may be the means of completely restoring your health, and of giving to our Church the advantage of your valuable services, and to your numerous friends, the happiness of your society for many, many years is the earnest prayer of

Rt. Rev. and dear Sir
Your Servt. & Son in the Gospel,
Cornelius R. Duffie[20]

This intimate letter, with its revelation of heavy griefs patiently borne, helps to sketch a picture of this first rector of Saint Thomas. He is almost invariably characterized by contemporaries as "the gentle Duffie," and this is from all indications a well-deserved epithet. A quiet, simple, friendly soul, deeply religious, loyal to his superiors, rather over-gentle indeed for the hurly-burly of the secular world, he had suffered much in his comparatively short life but had learned how to turn that suffering into the means of saintliness. Such was the making of a good pastor.

Under his quiet sway, the infant parish continued to grow. Thomas N. Stanford, the church bookseller, remarked that "Mr. Duffie's people have organized under the name of St Thomas, and a most efficient and respectable vestry have been chosen. I attend the Sunday evening lectures with great pleasure and profit. He is a most beautiful and accomplished writer."[21]

Progress is indicated in Mr. Duffie's second report, to the diocesan convention of 1825:

Baptisms 12, marriages 5, burials 7. Communicants about 45. The collections required by the Canons[22] have not been made: it being thought more for the advantage of the respective funds that they should be delayed until they can be taken in the Church, which is now nearly completed. It is due to the enterprising spirit of the Vestry of this Church to state that, in addition to the house of worship which they have erected, they have commenced building a house on their grounds adjacent thereto, for the accommodation of the Rector, which will be ready for occupation in the ensuing Spring.[23]

The records of Mr. Duffie's official acts, which have been carefully preserved, shed light on the life of the parish in the Broome Street room. There "the Sacrament of the Lord's Supper" was administered for the first time on Sunday, March 14, 1824, by the Rev. Dr. William Berrian, an assisting minister of Trinity Church, assisted by Mr. Duffie, who was then in deacon's orders. Among the nineteen communicants at this service were John Duer and his wife, Dr. James Stewart, Leonard A. Bleecker, William Purcell the sexton, Mr. Beastall the parish clerk, Mary Adams, Mrs. Casey, Mrs. Scoles, Margaret Dunlap, Margaret and Cornelia Duffie (sisters of the rector who lived with him), Susan Lambert, and Miss Haines. These names make up the first communicant list of the parish. The collection, it was noted, was $7.40 – a rather meager sum considering the wealth and standing of the men who formed the backbone of the parish. But it must be remembered that in that day collections were a sort of optional extra, used for the relief of the poor, or for some diocesan or general Church purpose. They were in no way intended for the basic support of the parish.

The Rev. Dr. George Upfold, rector of St. Luke's, celebrated the Communion service on April 25, when there were twenty-four communicants. The next celebration was on June 27, with the Rev. Dr. John McVickar of Columbia College officiating, the offering then being $4.03. It is recorded that at this Communion service Richard Oakley, who had been a member of the vestry from the beginning, "united with the church for the first time." The Rev. Dr. William Harris, the president of Columbia College, celebrated on August 8, and Dr. Upfold again on September 26. Sunday, November 28, was a happy day both for rector and people, as Mr. Duffie, now ordained priest, celebrated the Holy Communion for the first time, which he did again on Christmas Day when "Mr. Charles Bostwick this day participated for the first time." On the following February 6, Mr. Brown was "added." The collection on Easter Day of 1825 was $5.82. At the Communion held on November 20, 1825, "Mrs. Col. Forbes and Mrs. Hubbard received the sacrament for the first time," and on Christmas Day Mrs. Wm. Dunlap was "added to the Communion." These notes seem both a clear indication of strong sacramental teaching on the part of the first rector and an indication that this teaching was beginning to bear fruit.

The records of the early Baptisms, marriages, and burials give some indication of the people who turned to the parish for pastoral service, and as firsts they deserve to be recorded. Mr. Duffie's first Baptism, on August 10, 1823, was that of Eliza Crolins Simmons. This took place in St. Paul's Chapel. The first to be baptized in Broome Street were William Brown, Caroline Brown, and Sidney Francis Cowell. It may be noted as an indication of Mr. Duffie's pastoral care and missionary zeal that on one Sunday he baptized twenty persons. His first marriage was that of Elisha Bloomer to Frances, daughter of John Moor, on August 15, 1824. His first burial was that of his eldest son, Charles William Duffie, who died on June 24, 1824. On September 28 he buried Sarah Maria, the wife of Thomas N. Stanford, the aforementioned church bookseller. This was the first public funeral in the new burial ground of Saint Thomas Church. In a ministry of just one month short of four years, the first rector of Saint Thomas baptized 102 people, buried 58, and officiated at 27 marriages. His first Confirmation class numbered 26 persons. His ministry was producing results.[24]

Notes

1 *An Account Of The Ceremony Of Laying The Corner Stone Of St. Thomas' Church; Including The Addresses Delivered On That Occasion, Together with a Brief Statement Of The Rise Of That Church*, pp. 7, 9, 15. This pamphlet was published by request of the Wardens and Vestry of Saint Thomas in 1824 and printed by T. and J. Swords, a New York City firm established in 1786 and later associated closely with Bishop Hobart and the Episcopal Church. It contains the addresses of both White and Duffie. Another account of the laying of the cornerstone is found in the appendix of *Memorials of S. Thomas's Church New York. Discourses by the Rev. Dr. W. F. Morgan, Rector of S. Thomas' Church, New York* (New York: Gilliss Brothers, 1882), pp. 87-95. Further accounts are found in *The Christian Journal and Literary Register* 8 (August 1824): 254-55 and 12 (December 1824): 358-62.

2 *The Evening Post* claimed that at the time of the organization of Saint Thomas Church and of St. Mary's in Manhattanville there were seventeen Episcopal churches in the city. See "New Episcopal Churches in New York," *The Christian Journal* 8 (March 1824): 95.

3 An early contact of Saint Thomas parish with St. Philip's took place in July of 1826 when Cornelius Roosevelt Duffie preached at the first ordination, conducted by Bishop Hobart, of the first minister of St. Philip's — the first ordination ever at that church. As reported in *The Christian Journal* 10:8 (August 1826): 253-54, the ordinand was "the Rev. Peter Williams, deacon, (a coloured man), minister of the said church." Both Williams and Duffie were followers of Hobart, and Williams was associated with the abolitionist movement and the Anti-Slavery Society, from which a later Bishop of New York (Onderdonk) would force him to resign. The ordination of

Williams was the first ordination of a black person in the New York diocese and the second in the country (after Absalom Jones). The reasons for the choice of Duffie as preacher are not known.

4 *The New-York Evening Post,* 11 October 1823, p. 3.

5 Morgan Dix et al., *A History of the Parish of Trinity Church in the City of New York* (New York: Putnam, 1898ff), vol. 3, p. 286. Duffie's discourse on Psalm 87:2, entitled "Public Worship," which was really his first sermon preached for Saint Thomas, is published in Cornelius Roosevelt Duffie, *Sermons, . . . to which is prefixed, a Memoir of the Author* (2 vols., New York: T. and J. Swords, 1829), vol. 2, pp. 283-95. For the details of that first service and the pamphlet that describes it, see *An Account of the Ceremony,* p. 5 (above, at note 1).

6 Saint Thomas Archives, Vestry Minutes, vol. 1, p. 1 (hereafter "VM 1:1," etc. with pagination always referring to the volumes that contain the typed copies of the manuscript originals), 4 December 1823. It was also resolved at this meeting that an "Incorporation of a Church" should be made at the time of the election.

7 VM 1:2 (25 December 1823).

8 VM 1:2-3 (25 December 1823). It was duly recorded in the County Register, Book 1 of *Religious Incorporations,* p. 122.

9 VM 1:22 (13 and 19 October 1824).

10 He served as a vestryman for only one year.

11 VM 1:4 (17 February 1824).

12 VM 1:6 (24 February 1824). A draft of this letter is in the Saint Thomas Archives, in which Mr. Duffie expresses his intention "to advance the best interests both temporal and spiritual of our infant congregation."

13 In 1826, the vestry fixed the salary of the rector at $1,200 a year together with the use of the rectory. At the time, it was resolved that "the wardens and vestry deeply regret that the present state of the finances deprive them of the power of offering to their Rector a more suitable compensation, and that they pledge themselves to raise the salary to the sum of two thousand dollars, with the parsonage, as soon as the funds of the Church will permit that increase." VM 1:46 (4 April 1826).

14 B. T. Onderdonk, "Memoir of the Rev. Cornelius R. Duffie," *The Church Register* 2:39 (29 September 1827): 305. Among his classmates was Jackson Kemper, later the first missionary bishop in the Episcopal Church and the inspirer of Nashotah House Seminary in Wisconsin.

15 Further on the history of the Duffie family, see Patricia Ellerton Duffie, *The Duffie Family* (Madison, WI: Dorsett, 1983), esp. pp. 320-21; some of the love-letters written by Cornelius to Helena in the year 1815 are transcribed on pp. 329-35.

16 Manuscript letter in the Saint Thomas Archives, dated 10 October 1821; full transcript printed in Patricia Ellerton Duffie, *The Duffie Family,* pp. 189-90.

17 Onderdonk, "Memoir," pp. 305-6. Dr. Onderdonk was the preacher on the occasion of Mr. Duffie's ordination to the priesthood, and the vestry of Saint Thomas requested that a copy of the sermon be furnished for publication in *The Christian Journal and Literary Register.* VM 1:27 (21 January 1825). The rector of St. Luke's at that time was the Rev. George Upfold, successor of Mr. Duffie at Saint Thomas Church.

18 This term was less clearly defined then than it is today, and the actual number of persons regularly attending and contributing may well have been more than the number given. *Journal of the Proceedings of the Convention of the Diocese of New York* (hereafter New York *Convention Journal),* 1824, p. 37; *Records of St. Thomas's Church and Register of Baptisms, Marriages, Funerals, etc., August 10, 1823 to December 3, 1831* [Not paginated].

19 Hobart had little use for the conventional interior arrangement of Episcopal churches inherited from the eighteenth century, in which the pulpit was the dominating element and the altar a little table tucked in behind it. By contrast, he aimed at restoring the focus of the church upon

the altar and the worship offered there; see *The Christian Journal* 11:5 (May 1827): 134-35 (including diagram). See also Arthur Lowndes, ed., *Hobart Correspondence (Archives of General Convention)* (6 vols., New York: 1911-12), vol. 2, pp. 511-19. This arrangement, which he promoted especially during the last four years of his episcopate, "had the merit," according to Lowndes, "when the priest went to the Holy Table to begin the Ante-Communion, of making him visible at that all-important and noblest part of the ordinary morning service" (p. 512).

20 Dix, *History of Trinity Parish*, vol. 3, pp. 366-67.

21 Dix, *History of Trinity Parish*, vol. 3, p. 322. See also Lawrence N. Crumb, "Stanford & Swords: Publishers to the Young Episcopal Church," *Publishing History* 42 (1997): 51-64.

22 New York *Convention Journal,* 1825, pp. 29-31, reports in that year no collections or contributions from the parish of Saint Thomas for the episcopal, missionary, and diocesan funds. Collections for these three funds had become required by the diocesan canons of 1821 (New York *Convention Journal,* 1821, pp. 70-72).

23 New York *Convention Journal,* 1825, p. 25; *Records of St. Thomas's Church . . . 1823 to 1831.*

24 *Records of St. Thomas's Church . . . 1823 to 1831.*

25 Patricia Ellerton Duffie, *The Duffie Family*, p. 183.

CHAPTER 2

Surely the Lord is in This Place

CORNELIUS ROOSEVELT DUFFIE
FIRST RECTOR 1823-1827

I

F GOD WAS TO BE APPROPRIATELY WORSHIPED
by this new congregation, there had to be a building adequate for that
purpose. The parish of Saint Thomas had begun to function in its
Broome Street room, but it was plain that this could not continue for
long. A permanent house of worship was needed. At the first meeting
of the vestry, held January 14, 1824, it was unanimously resolved "that it is expedient for this Corporation to make immediate arrangements for building
a church."[1] But where was the money to come from? Some of the members
of the parish had plenty, but, as is ever the case in churches, it was not too
easy to obtain. Trinity Church, with its large endowment and munificent
spirit, was looked upon as a sort of fairy godmother for all new beginnings of
the Episcopal Church in the state of New York. One of the reasons for the
phenomenal growth of the Episcopal Church in New York in the years immediately after the American Revolution, in fact, was the existence and attitude of Trinity Church, and it was therefore a natural recourse for the vestry
of the new parish to address to the vestry of Trinity a request for assistance in
the building of a new church. Time after time, Trinity had responded to the
multitudinous appeals that came to it, responded with a generosity that
could even threaten its own financial stability, but this time it felt unable to
help.[2]

Nonetheless, the effort went forward. A committee of the vestry was
charged with the vital tasks of reporting on "an eligible site for a church on
Broadway or elsewhere," and, after ascertaining the cost of the land, of reporting on a suitable plan for the building and the probable cost of the same.
In addition, the committee – consisting of chairman David Hadden,
Richard Oakley, and John Lambert[3] – was to devise the best means of obtaining the money and to make regulations for the sale of pews. It was a tall
order.

At a subsequent meeting of the vestry, the committee reported that they
had examined various sites from Broome to Bleecker Streets, and found that

the most suitable location was a lot on the north side of Prince Street, near Broadway. Unfortunately, upon investigation, they found that this lot could not be bought. The next best was one on Houston Street, near Broadway, and yet another was on Broome Street at the corner of Greene Street. The committee had shied away from building on Broadway itself, partly because the lots would be more expensive, but even more because "Broadway, being the great thoroughfare of the city, would consequently be very noisy – the congregation would thereby be disturbed in their devotions." However, the vestry did not concur with the committee's recommendation.[4]

The following week, on February 24, the vestry decided to locate the proposed church on the northwest corner of Broadway and Houston Street. The site comprised three lots on Broadway and, to the rear, two lots on Houston Street. It was just one block north and a few blocks west of the spot where the first St. Patrick's Cathedral, at Prince and Mott Streets, had been dedicated in the year 1815. These lots, which were each twenty-five feet wide and one hundred feet deep, were purchased in March for $11,000, and immediately mortgaged to the seller for their full price.[5] An additional lot was leased in April, which gave access to Mercer Street.[6]

The choice of this location was a venture of faith. Houston Street was so far removed from the center of the city's population that Mr. Duffie favored building farther south. The major Episcopal churches were in the lower wards, with St. Paul's Chapel being the nearest to the site selected for Saint Thomas. A graphic description of the new locale was later given in a sermon preached in 1865 by Dr. William F. Morgan, then rector of the parish:

> At that time, as some present may remember, this spot and the surrounding region was a rural suburb of the city below. Large open fields stretched off yonder to the southwest. Old country seats still held their place. Old mile-stones were still in requisition along what was then a turnpike, unpaved, and lined with modest footpaths. Brooks and running streams diversified the landscape. Groves of patriarchal trees were within sight. Gardens under tillage, and pastures enclosed with rails, and flocks and herds – yes! and hill and valley and bog were discernible, in almost every direction, especially to the north-east, and, although the city was growing up and encroaching here and there, still the rural aspect was altogether predominant at this very point; and when the corner-stone was laid, people wondered; and while its walls were going up they made excursions to visit the most notable specimen of Gothic architecture ever attempted upon this island: and it was said by many who are even now not much past meridian, "Here is a Church, but it is as useless as Melrose Abbey; for who are to fill it? Where is the congregation?"[7]

The site thus secured, it was now necessary to raise money to build the church. The vestry determined to seek donations "from such persons who may feel an interest in our undertaking," and the wardens and vestrymen were requested to head the list. The hope was that these donations might amount to $5,000.[8] But the vestry was too optimistic. When the final accounting had been made, it was found that these gifts amounted to only $625, and even in those days one could not build very much of a church with that sum. Then someone in the vestry had a bright idea. There was considerable open ground surrounding the projected church, and it was decided to utilize this for family burial vaults, each nine by eleven, and to offer them for sale at $225 each. Mr. Thomas. J. Swords, the Church bookseller and publisher on Pearl Street, allowed subscription lists for the purchase of pews and vaults to be displayed in his office.[9] As an immediate source of revenue, the plan had a measure of success. In three years, families of Saint Thomas purchased some eighteen plots, bringing in a capital sum of $2,700. The number eventually doubled to reach thirty-six plots.

The vestry now turned to serious thought on a suitable plan for a building. Indeed, the very same committee established to locate a site for the new church had been busy collecting possible building plans for some weeks. At a meeting held on April 6, 1824, the vestry resolved "that the order of the proposed Church be Gothic and that plans of a church of sixty-two by ninety feet, or thereabouts be procured from artists, with estimates of the expense."[10] This was an unprecedented step and a departure from the prevailing type of ecclesiastical architecture in New York and, indeed, in most of the Episcopal Church. In the city, Trinity, Christ Church, St. Michael's, and St. James' were plain wooden structures, while St. Paul's Chapel and St. Mark's-in-the-Bowery were reminiscent of Christopher Wren. St. Andrew's Church in Philadelphia, purportedly modeled after a temple of Bacchus, was said to have looked so much like a bank that strangers often went in during the week to have checks cashed.[11]

The plan eventually adopted for Saint Thomas has sometimes been ascribed to the Rev. Dr. John McVickar, a professor of political economy in Columbia College and a Gothic enthusiast of the day. The inscription on the cornerstone of the new church indeed bore such testimony. It is more likely, however, that Dr. McVickar acted as a consultant on the design of the building, as the minutes of the vestry clearly indicate that the architect was Josiah R. Brady.[12]

In any case, the plan submitted by Mr. Brady was to prove unprecedented, at least in the city. It called for a church to be built of stone, in the Gothic style, roughly according to the measurements approved by the vestry, and with two towers, projecting twelve feet from the front of the building (pl. II). The choice of Gothic, which in its very structure pointed beyond and upward, would effortlessly and inevitably orient the congregation of Saint Thomas toward a primary emphasis on worship that would be visibly written into the very fabric of its first permanent building. When completed,

Saint Thomas would help to establish Gothic as the favored ecclesiastical form in the city. One architectural historian notes:

> Though probably not the first building of the Gothic Revival in New York, St. Thomas Church was the first important one and for that reason alone should merit a prominent place in the architectural history of the metropolis. Designed inside and out along English Gothic lines, constructed of stone, with a wooden arched ceiling partly supported by brackets and partly suspended from a wooden truss, Brady's church is positively of the Gothic revival. The architect is consciously using the style as a whole rather than applying Gothic forms to a non-Gothic structure as had been done by his predecessors.[13]

A building committee, formally appointed on May 31, 1824, reported that the church as planned could be erected for $20,000, and that the subscriptions in hand would meet the payments to the builder until the church was enclosed. Fiscally speaking, this was an overly optimistic estimate. Contracts were made with Alexander Masterton and Francis Cochran, stone cutters; Joseph Tucker, mason; and Seth Geer and Osker Riley, carpenters. A "Mr. Wells" superintended the work. An additional loan of $9,000 having been obtained, the vestry authorized the committee to proceed with the building, and arrangements were made for the laying of the cornerstone.[14]

This ceremony was fixed for Tuesday afternoon, July 27, 1824, the same day as the commencement exercises of the General Theological Seminary. It was graced by the presence of Bishops James Kemp of Maryland, John Croes of New Jersey, and Thomas C. Brownell of Connecticut. In the absence of Bishop Hobart, who was in England, the venerable William White of Pennsylvania, Presiding Bishop of the Episcopal Church, conducted the service. At precisely six o'clock the procession moved from the Broome Street room to the new location in the following specified order:

> The Sexton, bearing a leaden box to be placed in the cornerstone
> The Building Committee
> Members of the Congregation
> Wardens and Vestrymen of other parishes
> Wardens and Vestry of Saint Thomas Church
> Students of the General Theological Seminary
> Professors of the same
> Clergy
> Bishops
> Officiating Bishop, accompanied by the Rector

A contemporary account of the ceremony tells us that "On arriving at the ground, the procession opened, and, the Bishops having passed through, took the seats prepared for them on an elevated platform, the clergy and others occupying the space evacuated for the foundation of the church, and a very respectable concourse of attentive spectators being ranged on the surrounding banks."

SURELY THE LORD IS IN THIS PLACE

After a short address by Bishop White, the Lord's Prayer and collects were said. Then the Presiding Bishop, saying "Other foundation can no man lay than that which is laid, which is Jesus Christ," struck the foundation stone three times: "In the Name of the Father and of the Son and of the Holy Ghost." The ceremony continued with an address by the rector, in which he stressed the importance to future generations of the act now taking place. Bishop White gave his blessing and the simple but significant ceremony ended. By resolution of the vestry, the proceedings of the day and the addresses delivered were published in pamphlet form.[15] Apart from printed copies of this pamphlet, the only tangible remainder that survives from that very day is a large silver flagon presented at that time which has survived all subsequent fires and is still used now on occasions.[16]

As the work of building progressed, certain modifications were made in the plans, the most notable being the lengthening of the church by some thirteen feet. In addition, the building committee called for plans and specifications for a three-story brick rectory, twenty-five feet by fifty, to stand on the corner of Mercer and Houston Streets. It was to be finished in a "neat but plain manner." Shortly afterward, the treasurer reported that the first payment to the stone cutters was due, and that, in spite of the optimism of the vestry, he had no money left and it was therefore necessary to borrow.[17] The insurance on the partly completed building was assigned to Dr. Bradhurst, from whom the land had been bought, as security for one loan. Four members of the building committee advanced an additional four thousand dollars, to be repaid from the sale of pews once there were pews to be sold.[18] And so in due course the work was completed and the congregation was ready for the adventure of moving. The total cost of land and building proved to be about $50,000.

On Sunday morning, February 10, 1826, the congregation gathered for the last time in the room on Broome Street. It was a service hallowed with sacred memories of the past and high hopes for the future. Taking his text from I Samuel 7:12, "hitherto hath the Lord helped us," Mr. Duffie depicted the "weak and feeble beginning" of the congregation in 1823. "Here," he said, "at least, in this unostentatious and retired place, we have realized the truth of his promise, 'where two or three are gathered together in my name, there am I in the midst of them. . . .' This lowly altar has been the scene where some have kneeled to receive for the first time the emblems of that body which was broken, and of that blood which was freely shed for their redemption." He reminded them how they had laid the foundation of a stately temple for the worship of God, but warned them wisely that however noble the temple might be, unless it were visited by the presence of God it could not be "compared with the humblest abode where the footsteps of his goodness and mercy had been manifested." He ended thus:

> And how can I better close my labors in this place, than by offering to him who
> hath hitherto helped us, the unfeigned and earnest prayer, that in like manner, as
> we now depart from hence, to meet in a better and more permanent sanctuary,
> so when our work on earth is finished, and we are called from thence, we may all
> be again assembled in a higher and more glorious temple of the new Jerusalem
> above, where, in the presence of our Almighty Father, we shall sing praises to
> him that loved us, and washed us from our sins in his own blood, and hath made
> us kings and priests unto God![19]

On Thursday morning, February 23, 1826, the first Saint Thomas
Church building was consecrated by Bishop Hobart.[20] It was a fine day at the
cobbled intersection of Broadway and Houston as the outdoor procession –
the congregation of the parish, vestrymen from other city churches, professors and students from General Theological Seminary, the vestry of Saint
Thomas, and the clergy and the bishop – made its way. The sentence of consecration was read by the Rev. Dr. Jonathan Wainwright, and Morning
Prayer was read by the Rev. William Creighton and the Rev. George Upfold.
The sermon, preached by the bishop from the text of Genesis 28:16, "Surely
the Lord is in this place," was a typical setting forth of the Hobartian and
Laudian principle of absolute ritual conformity. In ringing tones, the bishop
denounced "every mutilation of that liturgy which, in that awful presence, we
promised to preserve entire – every presumptuous introduction of our own
effusions into that full and impressive service by which the wisest and best of
men have deemed it an honor and a privilege to be regulated, and which the
most solemn obligation guards from this unhallowed freedom." Bishop Hobart went on to describe the Book of Common Prayer as "not only the best
manual of rational, sober and fervent devotion, but a most powerful guardian
of the distinguishing and fundamental doctrines of salvation, through the
merits and grace of a divine mediator." Knowing the mettle of Cornelius
Roosevelt Duffie, he concluded, "We hope, we are confident, that the Word
of God will here be proclaimed with fidelity, the worship devoutly performed, and His ministrations and ordinances duly celebrated by him who
has given such full confidence that he knows his high duties, and that
through God's grace, he will perform them."[21]

A second service took place in the evening, with the soft glow of the
hand-lit streetlamps in the background (pl. IV). Mr. Duffie preached a sermon on behalf of the Protestant Episcopal Tract Society, an organization
dedicated by Bishop Hobart to the dissemination of High Church ideals. An
offering was taken, which brought the society $149. It was a red-letter day for
Saint Thomas parish.

Even so, the church remained unpaid for. The expected donations had
almost entirely failed to materialize, and construction costs had been met

Total Cost of the First Church,[39] and the Financial Situation when the Building was Occupied

EXPENDITURES

The land	$11,000.00
Carpenters', Masons' and Stone Cutters' Contracts	30,169.79
Extra painting of pews in oak, walls, etc.	920.91
Marble aisles, extra iron work, superintendent's salary, making plans, drawings, etc.	1,857.01
Insurance on the church and interest paid on purchase money of ground until the church was finished	1,995.54
Also expended before and after consecration for iron fence in front	838.10
Stone coping and mason work	362.78
Carpets, cushions, hangings for desk etc.	403.33
Organ	500.00
Stoves and fixtures	381.34
Books for Desk and Altar	104.50
Lamps, branches, &c.	210.37
Bell	357.50
Wooden side fence, altering pews, &c.	689.17
Carpenter's work to Bell, &c.	549.08
Trees and mould for Yard	119.53
Making the Whole Cost of Church and Ground	$50,458.95

RECEIPTS

Pews sold, say 60	$21,475.00
Donations	625.00
Profit on 18 Vaults sold	2,700.00
Amount Received	$24,800.00

THE COMMITTEE FURTHER REPORTED THE FOLLOWING DEBTS:

Bond and Mortgage to Dr. Bradhurst	$20,000.00
Bond to Miss DePeyster	2,450.00
Note to John Rogers – Scholarship Society	555.50
Note to P. Hedl for Iron Railing	738.00
Due David Hadden, B. M. Brown, Richard Oakely for their Note lent to the church	1,500.00
Sundry small bills for church	666.36
Also for Rector's house and contract, including Bond to Miss Duffies[40]	5,400.00
Bond to Miss DePeyster, the same being used for House	2,850.00
Making the Whole Debt of the Church	$34,159.86

mainly through loans. The parish needed tangible means of support. In that age, the most reliable form of regular church income was derived from the sale or rent of pews. And now, Saint Thomas had pews to rent or sell. Accordingly, on February 27, 1826, a pew auction was conducted by Mr. Martin Hoffman.[22] There were 159 pews. Of these 7 were kept free so that there might be at least some provision for the poor to worship in the new church. The vestry had fixed a minimum price for the purchase of pews, the expectation being that most would be sold, and that the proceeds of the sale would roughly equal the cost of building and land. Furthermore, there was to be an annual rent on all pews unsold that would provide a steady income for the parish. The values of the pews, as set by the vestry, ranged from $800 down to a more affordable $60. However, at the auction it turned out that some pews were bought by Warden Isaac Lawrence for $1,000. In the end, the proceeds of the sale amounted to $21,400. The annual rental on unsold pews ranged from $50 to $15. It should be noted that under the Religious Corporations Act of 1813, the franchise at the annual election of wardens and vestrymen was held only by the owners or renters of pews.

A picture of this first Saint Thomas, in the context of early Gothic architecture in America, is provided through the eyes a young boy then living in New York City who had an artistic taste shaped by the Romantic movement of the time. This was Arthur Cleveland Coxe, later to become Bishop of Western New York. In his "Reminiscences," he gives a graphic description of the building as it appeared to his youthful eyes:

> This was the Gothic church, so called, and how magnificent it appeared to me. While it was going up on Broadway, just one mile from the City Hall – the first milestone stood just about a couple of rods to the south – I was struck by the

3. Interior of the first Saint Thomas Church, consecrated 1826; from a pencil drawing

SURELY THE LORD IS IN THIS PLACE

picturesque appearance; it looked like a sort of castle with its two towers and its stone walls. When finished, I imagined it a small Westminster Abbey. I first saw its interior on Christmas Day, and it affected me more than the great Cathedrals of Europe have ever affected me since. No galleries, and the woodwork of oak, the first oak-painted church I ever saw. The roof imitated an open roof very successfully, the great trusses between the bays being real, and ornamenting the walls with fine effect. The beautifully adorned pulpit hung upon the wall, with a gorgeous canopy and a niched doorway in the rear. Far up over it, a rose window, and occupying the triangle made by the open roof, was the organ loft, from which the music came down with sweet influence and fine effect.[23]

A modern architectural critic, looking at this first building of Saint Thomas, might not be quite so rapturous. It was really a great, barn-like auditorium (ill. 3), size 62 feet in width and 113 feet in length, the Gothicism of which consisted in its pointed windows, its stunted and battlemented towers, and the much-admired trussed roof. Above the main entrance was a large traceried window painted to imitate stained glass. Still, it was taken to be Gothic by the standards of its own day, and it marked that alliance between the parish and artistic excellence that has ever since distinguished the history and character of Saint Thomas.

In the interior of the building, six high-pointed windows on each side afforded the necessary light. A semi-circular communion rail sat about three feet higher than the nave. A marked departure from the prevailing custom in Episcopal churches, but in accordance with Bishop Hobart's tastes, was the placing of the reading desk – wide enough to accommodate two ministers – against the west wall, and the pulpit on the side wall, in order to allow greater prominence and visibility to the altar.[24] The large Bible and Prayer Book rested on a purple velvet cushion ornamented with gold braid. In front of the reading desk was the Communion table, carved and painted to represent oak. The pulpit, copied from the niche for a statue of Cardinal Wolsey in Christ Church Cathedral, Oxford, had a carved front and canopy. Preachers entered it by a flight of steps from the vestry room. The cushions for the pulpit and communion table were of purple silk. The chancel, covered with brussels carpet, had on both sides four large square pews. The font was on the gospel side and consisted of an oaken pedestal upon which was placed a silver bowl, and over it a canopy. Over the pulpit was a recessed gallery for organ and choir. The organ screen was copied from the monument of Henry VIII in Westminster Abbey. It was three feet, six inches high and surmounted by five pinnacles. The church was heated with long box-stoves in each corner of the building that burned cord-wood. From the hot ashes of these stoves, the sexton filled the square foot-stoves and placed them in the pews, for which service he expected a gratuity.[25]

The usual Sunday morning service consisted of Morning Prayer, the

Litany, and the Ante-Communion, the responses being led in a sonorous voice by the parish clerk. The Holy Communion was administered usually about once a quarter, but, in keeping with the High Church tradition of the diocese and the leanings of the parish, always on the feasts of Christmas, Easter, and Whitsun as well. Stoles and cassocks were still unknown and would be until the reverberations of the Oxford Movement began to reach American shores. The officiating minister wore a large, flowing surplice that reached down to the feet and a black scarf. During the hymn before the sermon, he went into the vestry room and emerged in a black preaching gown and white bands. It was customary, since the church was normally cold, for him to wear black silk gloves, with the fore-finger slit for convenience of turning the leaves of the manuscript sermon, which was invariably read. The officiant faced the congregation to read the offices. In celebrating the Holy Communion, he stood at the north end of the Holy Table.

On April 10, 1827, the building committee presented its final report to the vestry. The new church was now completed and occupied. Toward the total cost, donations had contributed practically nothing, but the sale of vaults and pews had produced nearly $30,000. There remained to be paid a debt of over $34,000. The committee added, "To pay the above we have one hundred pews on hand unsold, but it is presumed we cannot sell more than seventy-five which will produce at the prices affixed by the vestry, $22,500." They also had on hand two vaults paid for at $500 and vacant ground for twenty more.[26] At this heavy cost, the parish had obtained what was then, with the possible exception of St. John's Chapel, widely regarded as the finest Episcopal church in the city of New York. A contemporary guidebook to the city recorded its praise: "St. Thomas' is an elegant and stately edifice."[27]

The choice of a location, which had been such a matter of concern, was now proving to have been sound strategy. By the time the church was complete, many of the rural lanes surrounding it had become residential streets, inhabited by the kind of potential worshipers to whom Saint Thomas was especially attractive.[28] The congregation was steadily increasing. For almost the only time in its long history, Saint Thomas was a neighborhood church, where the rector could live in the midst of his people, making his parish calls on foot, building up a Christian community. For this work, for this particular kind of pastoral work, Mr. Duffie was eminently fitted. An acceptable preacher by the standards of his day, he was primarily neither preacher nor administrator, but pastor. Soon his work was bearing tangible as well as spiritual fruit.

The first Baptisms in the new church were those of Frederick Casey Oakley, son of Richard and Mary Oakley, and Oliver Hazard Perry, son of naval Lieutenant Matthew C. Perry, the pioneer who would open Japan to trade with the West. These occurred on February 26, 1826. On October 5 of the same year, Mr. Duffie wrote Bishop Hobart that he had about twenty persons ready for Confirmation, and asked the bishop to set a date for the administration of that rite. As it turned out, there were twenty-six persons in this first Confirmation class presented to the bishop just ten days later; included in the group was a future Bishop of New York.[29] The statistical growth of the parish is clearly reflected in the report the rector made to the diocesan convention of 1826:

> Baptisms, 32; marriages, 10; burials, *11*; communicants, 106; catechumens, 40. Since the last report, the church has been completed and consecrated, and the congregation now consists of about 130 families. The house erected by the Vestry, for the accommodation of the Rector, on their grounds adjacent to the church, has been finished. The congregation by their voluntary contributions, have purchased a valuable piece of communion plate.[30]

Saint Thomas was also earning a reputation for its liberal contributions to causes outside its own parish limits, a tradition that began already in Mr. Duffie's rectorship. The rector was deeply concerned with the problem of theological education and was well aware that many candidates for the ministry lacked the financial means to put themselves through seminary. He therefore organized "The Theological Scholarship Society of St. Thomas's Church," the object of which was to raise a capital sum of $2,500, the interest of which would then be applied to the assistance of some needy but deserving student at the General Theological Seminary. Naturally, preference was to be given to students from the parish. The scholarship thus formed was to be known as "The Scholarship of St. Thomas's Church in the City of New-York." The society was accordingly constituted with a rather elaborate apparatus of officers, managers, and life and annual subscribers. The fund was completed by 1832 and was handled by the parish until 1883, when the capital was handed over to the seminary authorities to constitute the "St. Thomas Scholarship."[31] One of the beneficiaries of this scholarship in later years would be the son of the first rector.

But now, just as everything was going so well for the infant congregation, fortune took a turn. On Sunday morning, August 2, 1827, Mr. Duffie preached what would turn out to be his last sermon, on the text from Hebrews 13:14: "Here we have no continuing city; but we seek one to come." It closed with the following words:

> God grant us grace that we may all so live, that we may not fear to die; so fix our treasures and our hearts in heaven, that we may hold lightly the things of earth; so confide in him who is the way, the truth and the life, and so be found in him, that when we pass from this perishing scene, we may be partakers of the kingdom prepared for the righteous from the foundation of the world![32]

The First Confirmation Class of Saint Thomas Parish

(Sunday, October 15, 1826)[41]

Ann Anderson
Mrs. Anwick
Margaret Aspinwall
Elizabeth C. Bailey
Rev. Bennet
Catharine Brown
Mary Ann Brown
Cornelia C. Cox
Rozina L. Cox
Jane Duer
Charity Fannington
Sarah Maria Francis
Victoria Geslain
Isabella Hadden
Mrs. O. H. Hicks
Maria Laing
John Meldrun
Matilda Nicholas
Richard Oakley
Mrs. Richard Oakley
Horatio Potter[42]
Anna D. Robinson
Catharine Robinson
Charity Shirley
Esther Stevens
Miss Stevens

A similar note runs through the last sermon he wrote, which he never delivered, on the text from Numbers 23:10: "Let me die the death of the righteous, and let my last end be like his."[33] These were foreboding words. Never a robust person, Mr. Duffie was seized by typhoid fever,[34] and on Monday, August 20, 1827, he died. The following evening, in the presence of a large congregation, he was laid to rest beneath the chancel of the church he had built, beside the bodies of his wife and young son, both of whom had predeceased him. There they would remain until the church was sold in 1865-66.[35]

Bishop Hobart reportedly burst into tears at the news of Mr. Duffie's death. In his address to the diocesan convention a few months later, the bishop noted the wide and strong expressions of grief over the unexpected and premature removal of this beloved clergyman as well as the numerous testimonies to his Christian virtues. He acknowledged his own particular reasons to lament the early death, at the age of thirty-eight, of one who was "congenial" with his own views "in all ecclesiastical concerns."[36]

The vestry indicated its attachment to the memory of the late rector in very tangible ways. At a meeting following his death, it was resolved that the parish would pay his funeral expenses and liquidate any debts he might have incurred. Afterward, a sum of $5,000 was set aside, $3,000 of which was to be invested for the benefit of his surviving children, and $2,000 to be given outright to his dependent sisters. It was further resolved to publish his sermons in two volumes and to give the proceeds from their sale to his remaining family members for their support.[37] Lastly, a monument to the revered pastor was commissioned, an ornamental work of oak with a marble slab to be placed in a niche of the church.[38] The pulpit and reading desk remained draped in mourning until Christmas.

Cornelius Roosevelt Duffie had launched the parish of Saint Thomas on its long voyage with solid ground on which to grow and an ample building that was conducive to worship and noble aspirations. The quality of his leadership would now be tested, and proven, once he had gone.

Notes

1 VM 1:3 (14 January 1824).

2 In August 1824 *The Christian Journal* (vol. 8, p. 254) reported that the people of Saint Thomas were "proceeding without any assistance or facilities, or the prospect of any, from the corporation of Trinity church, the present state of whose funds renders indispensable the painful duty of withholding all expenditures or responsibilities not connected with the parish itself." However, when circumstances improved, between the years 1828 and 1846, Trinity did give Saint Thomas $10,000 for maintenance, and $23,000 in additional loans and grants.

3 VM 1:3-4 (14 January 1824).

4 VM 1:4-5. The committee recommended building on a side street since the expense of property would be only one-third of that on Broadway. The vestry voted against this proposal with

the chairman of the committee alone dissenting.

5 VM 1:7 (24 February 1824), 1:8 (3 March 1824), 1:9 (10 March 1824). The seller of the lots was Dr. Samuel Bradhurst, a physician and apothecary in the city.

6 VM 1:9-10 (20 March 1824), 1:12 (12 April 1824). In this case the owner, the merchant George Lorillard, declined to sell the lot and so it was leased.

7 William F. Morgan, "Tokens of Decline. Anniversary Discourse at S. Thomas' Church, March 1865," in *Memorials of S. Thomas's Church New York. Discourses by the Rev. Dr. W. F. Morgan, Rector of S. Thomas' Church, New York* (New York: Gilliss Brothers, 1882), pp. 11- 12.

8 VM 1:5-6 (17 February 1824).

9 VM 1:10 (20 March 1824). The vestry requested Swords to place the subscription lists in his office.

10 VM 1:11 (6 April 1824). A new committee of three vestry members, the same three as before, was organized to procure "such plans and estimates."

11 Thomas March Clark, *Reminiscences*, 2nd ed. (New York: Thomas Whittaker, 1895), p. 40.

12 The inscription on the cornerstone is noted in *An Account Of The Ceremony Of Laying The Corner Stone Of St. Thomas' Church; Including The Addresses Delivered On That Occasion, Together with a Brief Statement Of The Rise Of That Church* (New York, T. and J. Swords, 1824), p. 11. McVickar was introduced to Gothic architecture on a visit to England in 1805, and on his return he drafted plans for a Gothic church at Hyde Park. He went on to become in 1847 a founder of the New York Ecclesiological Society, created to advance the science of church building and decoration. See John Brett Langstaff, *The Enterprising Life: John McVickar, 1787-1868* (New York: St. Martin's Press, 1961), pp. 356-65. On Josiah Brady, see also VM 1:5 (5 May 1824).

13 John Walden Myer, "The Gothic Revival in New York," *Museum of the City of New York Bulletin* 3:5 (April 1940): 52. According to Myer, Brady has not been given proper credit for introducing Gothic architecture to New York, "where in its maturity, it was to have, certainly in ecclesiastical work, its greatest flowering in the Western Hemisphere."

14 VM 1:16 (31 May 1824), 1:17-18 (7 July 1824). Dr. Bradhurst made the loan. The account and quotation that follow are taken from *An Account Of The Ceremony*, pp. 6-16.

15 A*n Account of the Ceremony Of Laying The Corner Stone Of St. Thomas' Church; Including The Addresses Delivered On That Occasion, Together with a Brief Statement Of The Rise Of That Church.* (New York: T. and J. Swords, 1924), from which the preceding quotations and details are taken. See also VM 1:20 (2 August 1824).

16 It is recorded in the *Insurance Appraisal of Property Belonging to St. Thomas Church*, completed by Christie's of New York and dated 10 June 1996, p. 42, no. 128, manuscript kept in Saint Thomas Archives.

17 VM 1:23 (16 November 1824). The minutes indicate a payment of $50 to Mr. Brady for his architectural plans.

18 VM 1:28 (14 March 1825), 1:35 (13 October 1825). The fire insurance policy was assigned to the building committee members as a security.

19 Cornelius Roosevelt Duffie, *Sermons, . . .to which is prefixed, a Memoir of the Author* (2 vols., New York: T. and J. Swords, 1829), vol. 2, pp. 69, 73-75, 79-80.

20 The canon requiring that a church must be free of debt before it may be consecrated was not passed until 1868. See *Digest of the Canons for the Government of the Protestant Episcopal Church in the United States of America, Passed and Adopted in the General Conventions of 1859, 1865, and 1868. Together with the Constitution.* (Printed for the Convention, 1869), p. 69. The same canon continues in the Episcopal Church today as Title II, canon 6.

21 *The Posthumous Works of the Late Right Reverend John Henry Hobart, D. D., . . . with a Memoir of His Life by the Rev. William Berrian, D.D.* (3 vols, New York: Swords, Stanford, and Co., 1832-33), vol. 2, pp. 37-42.

22 VM 1:38 (16 December 1825), 1:40 (15 February 1826). The latter is the date when the auction was authorized to be held on February 27.

23 "Reminiscences of Arthur Cleveland Coxe, Bishop of Western New York, 1865-1896," in *Historical Magazine of the Protestant Episcopal Church* 7:1 (March 1938): 88.

24 For a diagram and description, see *The Christian Journal and Literary Register* 11:5 (May 1827):134-35; see also Arthur Lowndes, ed., *Hobart Correspondence (Archives of General Convention)* (6 vols., New York: 1911-12), vol. 2, pp. 511-19. Lowndes concludes, "The 'splendors' of St. Thomas's, as they astonished Churchmen in 1826 with new conceptions of 'Gothic,' sealed the success of the new [i.e. Hobart's] plan" (p. 512).

25 This description of the interior is provided, in part, in a "Historical Sermon" preached by the Rev. John W. Brown on the occasion of the seventy-fifth anniversary of the parish and printed in the *St. Thomas Yearbook* for 1898.

26 VM 1:53, 55-56 (10 April 1827).

27 James Hardie, *The Description of the City of New York; Containing Its Population, Institutions, Commerce, Manufactures, Public Buildings, Courts of Justice, Places of Amusement, etc.* (New York: Samuel Marks, 1827), p. 178.

28 *The New York Evening Post* had welcomed the new church in anticipation that it would "be ornamental to that improving and beautiful part of our city." It was the duty, said the newspaper, "of persons interested in property in that vicinity, to aid in a plan by which it will be materially benefitted, besides adding another to the many beautiful edifices of which our city so justly boasts." Quoted in *The Christian Journal and Literary Register* 8 (March 1824): 95.

29 See note 42, later in this chapter.

30 New York *Convention Journal*, 1826, p. 54.

31 The first annual report of the society, approved on 5 June 1827, showed receipts amounting to $667.26. VM 4:1-2 (16 November 1883). See *First Annual Report of the Theological Scholarship Society of St. Thomas's Church, New York, Attached to the General Theological Seminary of the Protestant Episcopal Church in the United States of America.* (New York: T. and J. Swords, 1827).

32 Duffie, *Sermons*, vol. 2, p. 110. This was the last sermon he preached.

33 Duffie, *Sermons*, vol. 2, pp. 111-25.

34 Patricia Ellerton Duffie, *The Duffie Family* (Madison, WI: Dorsett, 1983), pp. 111, 118.

35 The remains of the rector and his family were removed to Green-Wood Cemetery in Brooklyn when the church at Broadway and Houston was sold, and it is probable that they still rest there, in Lot 4670. [Personal communication to the author from Professor John A. Duffie of Madison, WI, dated 2 December 1999; see also Patricia Ellerton Duffie, *The Duffie Family*, p. 229]. It was intended to translate the remains later to the new Saint Thomas and to inter them under the chancel or in the aisle. See manuscript letter of Archibald Duffie, the great-grandson of the first rector, dated 17 November 1967, in the Saint Thomas Archives.

36 New York *Convention Journal*, 1827, pp. 13-14.

37 The vestry allowed the family to occupy the rectory until the following spring: VM 1:64-65 (23 August 1827), 1:65-66 (28 August 1827), 1:66 (13 September 1827), 1:67 (11 October 1827).

38 The design for the monument was approved by Dr. John McVickar and executed by architect William Miller at a cost of $650. See VM 1:83 (20 May 1828), 1:88 (10 and 20 December 1828), 1:97 (29 October 1829). The monument was erected in 1829, and was later destroyed by the church fire of 1851. At the end of the century, this monument was described differently, by Mr. Duffie's son, as having been of granite, surmounted by a cross, with a richly carved canopy above: see *Year Book* 1898, p. xxxiv. In *Manuscript History of St. Thomas Church* (unpublished manuscript in Saint Thomas Archives, 1943; copy deposited in the St. Mark's Library of the General Theological Seminary, New York City), p. 97, E. Clowes Chorley describes the monument as having been of Irish granite and placed on the epistle side of the church. According to

Chorley, it bore the inscription "Mark the perfect man and behold the upright, for the end of that man is peace" (Psalm 37:37). Chorley also records (p. 232) that a portrait of Duffie, rescued from the fire, was placed in the custody of his sisters, at their request. The portrait may, however, have been destroyed in the fire: Patricia Ellerton Duffie, *The Duffie Family*, p. 112. In addition to the flagon described above at note 16, one other tangible connection to the first rector that does survive at Saint Thomas today, kept in the present rector's office, is a pair of American Renaissance Revival walnut side chairs, each with a Gothic pierced back and trapezoidal seat and each bearing a plaque inscribed "This chair belonged to the Reverend Cornelius R. Duffie, First Rector of St. Thomas Church, 1823-27." (*Insurance Appraisal* by Christie's [1996], p. 39, no. 122).

39 VM 1:53-56 (10 April 1827); spelling and punctuation retained from original manuscript.

40 Manuscript *sic*. The sisters of the first rector, who lived with their brother in the three-story brick rectory at Houston and Mercer Streets and helped with the care of his motherless children. Patricia Ellerton Duffie, *The Duffie Family*, p. 111.

41 *Records of St. Thomas's Church and Register of Baptisms, Marriages, Funerals, etc., August 10, 1823 to December 3, 1831* [Not paginated]. Spelling retained from original manuscript, but the confirmands are placed here in alphabetical order. See also New York *Convention Journal*, 1826, pp. 21-22.

42 At this time a student at the General Seminary, Horatio Potter (1802-1887) was to become Provisional Bishop of New York in 1854 and Diocesan Bishop in 1861, serving until his death in 1887. Due to illness, the Acting Bishop of New York from 1883 to 1887 was Henry Codman Potter, his namesake.

CHAPTER 3

The Golden Age at Broadway and Houston

GEORGE UPFOLD
SECOND RECTOR, 1828-1831

FRANCIS LISTER HAWKS
THIRD RECTOR, 1831-1843

THE WORSHIP CONTINUED, but no vacancy in a rector-ship is easy and, as it turned out, the total transition to a new era for Saint Thomas lasted over four years. During the vacancy, services in the new church were taken by several of the city clergy. The vestry's first attempt to secure a successor to Mr. Duffie was made on October 23, 1827, when it extended a call to the Rev. William Heathcote DeLancey, rector of St. Peter's Church, Philadelphia. The salary was to be $1,200 a year. Mr. DeLancey was one of the best of the younger men who followed the lead of Bishop Hobart, and he would eventually become the first Bishop of Western New York. He declined Saint Thomas, however, despite the vestry's urging him to reconsider.[1]

The call was next extended to the Rev. Henry Anthon, rector of Trinity Church, Utica, New York, the son of a family long connected with the Episcopal Church and with Columbia College. Although the offer was increased to $1,500, Mr. Anthon likewise declined on January 5, 1828.[2] A month later the Rev. Dr. George Upfold, from the neighboring St. Luke's on Hudson Street, was unanimously chosen rector, and he accepted (ill. 4). Not long before his selection by the vestry, Upfold had been invited to preach at Saint Thomas on behalf of the diocesan missionary society.[3]

Dr. Upfold was born in England, but came to this country with his parents at the age of six. His father taught school in Albany, New York, and was for several years warden of St. Peter's Church, the mother parish of that city. Young Upfold graduated from Union College in Schenectady and went on to receive a medical degree from the College of Physicians and Surgeons in New York City before reaching the age of twenty-one. His thoughts, however, soon turned to the ministry, and, like his predecessor at Saint Thomas, he

4. George Upfold, Second Rector
1828-1831

read for orders under the direction of Bishop Hobart. He was ordained deacon in 1818 and assumed charge of the churches upstate in Lansingburgh and Waterford. Two years later, he was ordained priest and returned to the city to organize a new parish, St. Luke's in Greenwich Village, as well as to serve as a temporary assistant minister in Trinity Church.

On March 6, 1828, the thirty-two-year-old George Upfold was formally instituted as the second rector of Saint Thomas Church. Bishop Hobart presided and preached the sermon for the occasion, taking for his text II Timothy 3:17: "That the man of God may be perfect, thoroughly furnished unto all good works." Among those present was Arthur Cleveland Coxe, then a small boy, who later remembered the event as

> a truly interesting occasion, when he preached a memorable sermon, and when I first saw him in his robes, was that of the Institution of Dr. Upfold, as the successor of my favorite Duffie, in St. Thomas'. This sermon did not please the low church brethren, but my venerated father, who was present, remarked that "it was the unquestionable doctrine of the Church of England, which, as bishop, he was consistently maintaining." It was on this occasion that I first heard of the "Apostolic Succession," which my father kindly explained to me as the groundwork of the bishop's argument.[4]

What had the great bishop said about that doctrine to make such an impression on the young Coxe? Almost certainly, it was the point at which the bishop had charged the people of Saint Thomas to

> Behold the man of God in the Sanctuary, exercising a divinely commissioned ministry – a ministry for which not all the mighty of the earth, powerful as they are in the gifts of temporal distinction, can give him a commission. . . . The man of God appears in the sanctuary, exercising divine functions. Divine power only can delegate him. And divine power does delegate him not only with the impress of holiness on the heart, but with the stamp of external authority – with a commission conveyed from the only source of spiritual power, even the Lord Jesus, the head of the mystical body over which he reigns – conveyed by a channel, traced to its divine source, through the same accredited records of historical fact by which the volume of inspiration is proved to have a divine origin. Thus commissioned, he stands forth in the sanctuary.[5]

If those of the "low church" persuasion did not like the sermon, the vestry of Saint Thomas clearly did, finding it "a lucid and correct exposition not only of ministerial duty, but of Christian doctrine and practice." Having thus taken a stand on the "higher" side of churchmanship as it was being discussed in that context, the vestry had it printed.

It is not altogether easy to estimate the character and achievement of Dr. Upfold. A man of undoubted ability, since he later became rector of Calvary Church, Pittsburgh, and was eventually elected first Bishop of Indiana, he must have seemed, after the exceptionally kind and gentle Duffie, rather stiff and unbending. Under Duffie, the vestry had things pretty much its own way. Upfold, however, was more inclined to stand on his rights. At first, all things went well. The parish continued to grow, reporting 170 communicants by 1829. The Theological Scholarship Society had increased its capital funds to $1,200. The parish was paying in full its promised contributions to the national, diocesan, and missionary funds. In those days, when parochialism ran rampant, this meant something. One hundred and four dollars was collected for the work of the Protestant Episcopal Missionary Society. About this time Sunday Schools for girls were started (in 1827) and soon after ones for boys were started as well,[6] and there was also a women's association that functioned as an auxiliary to the diocesan missionary society. Some additions and improvements were made to the church building. A marble font was installed, the gift of David Hadden. A gallery was built across the end of the church opposite the altar, and the organ was placed there. Lamps were hung down the center of the nave, and new chairs and carpet procured for the chancel which had been extended back to the wall. Nine new vaults were built in the churchyard, and ten additional ones authorized. In 1830, saddened by the sudden death of Bishop Hobart, the vestry ordered the church to be "strung in the customary mourning until the festival of Christmas" out of respect for his memory.[7]

Early in 1831, it began to be evident that all was not well with the parish. The trouble was mainly financial. It will be remembered that when Mr. Duffie died, there hung over the parish a debt of some $34,000. The land on which the church stood was mortgaged, the rectory was built with borrowed money, and interest charges continued to rise. In the autumn of 1827 the vestry had renewed its appeal to Trinity Church for help and in the following January received in return an outright gift of $3,000 and the promise of an annual grant of $600. But this was not enough.[8]

A new application for aid was made to the Trinity corporation in the summer of 1830.[9] While this was pending, a vestry committee was appointed in early January of 1831 to make a thorough examination of the state of the church's finances and to recommend measures of relief. The committee soon reported that the debt of the parish, come the first of next May, would reach $39,836, with interest at six percent of $2,390. The projected expenses for the ensuing year were estimated at $2,635 and the projected income at $3,850. "It must be obvious," the report said, "how rapidly such an increase of debt must lead of itself to utter bankruptcy."[10]

The report stressed the need for heroic measures. But the measures it proposed were largely a mere postponement of the day of reckoning. Either the rectory and adjoining lot had to be sold, which "would be injurious to the character, standing and prosperity of the church," or the rectory must be mortgaged. The committee remained hopeful that an appeal to Trinity for a further gift of $10,000 would be successful, and it was. The corporation of Trinity advanced a loan of $20,000 without interest, taking a mortgage on the church property for security.[11]

The committee also reported that Dr. Upfold had readily agreed to vacate the rectory in the interest of the parish. This offer was immediately accepted by the vestry and a yearly housing allowance of $400 for the rector was approved. On reconsideration, however, the vestry some three months later reversed itself and decided to mortgage the rectory for $4,000.[12]

The financial condition of the parish was an obvious concern and, naturally, an embarrassment to the rector. His relationship to the vestry appears to have been less than warm. Unlike his predecessor, or even his successor, Upfold was not referred to as "The Rector" in the vestry minutes, and, after the spring of 1831, his signature is not even found in the record. That summer he tendered his resignation to the vestry with "earnest prayers for the peace and prosperity of the congregation."[13]

The minutes of the vestry provide one insight into the uneasy relationship between the rector and that body, a strain which went beyond the financial straits they faced. The previous summer, in 1830, Dr. Upfold had informed the vestry that he had appointed a committee to "control the music of the church." The committee was composed of three ladies, Misses Barrell, Blackstock, and Jackson. This apparently irritated the vestry members and ten months later on May 19, 1831, the vestry proceeded to choose a new committee "to select *proper* persons to regulate the music of the church."[14] Those selected in their place were all men, although the sources give no indication of why this change was made. The action by the vestry may have prompted the rector to consider the future viability of his leadership. His intention to resign was made known to the vestry on the same day that it received the formal resignation of the music committee members appointed by him.[15]

After the removal of Dr. Upfold, a petition signed by eighty-five pewholders and members of the parish was handed to the vestry on October 4, 1831. This petition requested that the vestry extend a call to the Rev. Francis Lister Hawks (ill. 5), then rector of St. Stephen's Church at the corner of Broome and Chrystie Streets, one mile distant from Saint Thomas. The vestry assented and Dr. Hawks was called. The salary was fixed at $1,500, with a further sum "not exceeding $500 per annum as the income of the Church may enable the Vestry to allow."[16] Dr. Hawks declined the invitation, and Dr. Jonathan M. Wainwright, the rector of Grace Church, undertook the care of the parish for the time being. With the full approval of Bish-

5. Francis Lister Hawks, Third Rector 1831–1843

op Benjamin Onderdonk the call was renewed, and a special committee went to see Dr. Hawks. He thereupon reconsidered, accepted the election, and entered upon his new duties on December 17. Many of the people from St. Stephen's followed him, and a new era began for Saint Thomas.[17]

The new rector, at the age of thirty-three, was in many respects the ablest priest then resident in the city of New York. He was a man of astonishing versatility. A southerner by birth, he had first been a successful lawyer and had been elected to the legislature of his native state of North Carolina. Taking charge of a vacant parish as a lay reader, he had eventually determined to study for ordination under the direction of Bishop John Stark Ravenscroft of North Carolina, a militant Hobartian High Churchman who had himself entered the ministry after a considerable secular career. Dr. Hawks' rise in the ministry was rapid. He was ordained deacon in 1827 and seventeen months later was elected assistant minister of Trinity parish in New Haven, Connecticut. There he was ordained priest and earned a great reputation by his ability as a preacher. Then in rapid succession he became assistant to the venerable Bishop White at St. James' Church in Philadelphia, Professor of Divinity at Washington (now Trinity) College in Hartford, Connecticut, and rector of St. Stephen's Church in New York. Here his eloquent preaching attracted a large congregation, and people from all over the city flocked to his Bible classes and expository lectures. The initial call from Saint Thomas came after he had served only nine months as rector of the neighboring church.

At the time, the wardens of Saint Thomas were Isaac Lawrence and David Hadden; the vestrymen were Morris Robinson, William C. Rhinelander, William H. Jephson, John Duer, Robert Gracie, Oliver H. Hicks, Richard C. Auchmuty, and William Neilson. Hawks assumed the rectorship at a critical moment for the parish. As the vestry said to him in later years, "You found our church far from prosperous; few of our pews were sold, many of them not rented."[18] The annual income of the parish was $6,110.29 and the debt on the church was $23,905.29.

With the arrival of Dr. Hawks, things changed for the better with amazing speed. He was unquestionably a great pulpit orator, and eloquence in the pulpit was more important in the Episcopal Church then than now. Every pew was quickly sold or rented. So great were the crowds that within one month steps were taken to erect a gallery. At the next visitation of the bishop, sixty-three persons were presented for Confirmation. The attendance at the rector's Bible class averaged one hundred. His repute was expressed in an entry in the diary of Philip Hone, a former mayor of New York: "I went yesterday morning to St Thomas' where I heard from Dr. Hawks a glorious sermon."[19] Another contemporary tells us:

> His popularity as a Pulpit Orator has seldom been equalled, certainly never surpassed in the history of the American Church. Crowds flocked to hear him; nor was it a merely temporary reputation. Time, that severest of all tests, which tries charlatans and strips them of their borrowed garb, and exposes their pretentions, tried him; and still he stood forth, year after year, the peerless Preacher of the day.[20]

That shrewd observer, Bishop Thomas March Clark of Rhode Island, who heard Hawks in his prime, gives this graphic picture:

> To hear him preach was like listening to the harmonies of a grand organ with its various stops and solemn sub-bass and tremulous pathetic reeds. The rector of one of the Washington churches, where Daniel Webster was an attendant, told me that after Dr. Hawks had preached for him on a Sunday morning, Mr. Webster said that it was the greatest sermon he had ever heard.[21]

It is said that great orators are such by virtue of three gifts: a magnificent voice, a gift for the choice of words, and a magnetism that captivates the audience. Dr. Hawks seems to have had all three, but he was also more than an orator. He was one of the first to realize what the Episcopal Church as a whole has been slow to appreciate: the vital importance of Christian education. In his first parochial report, that for 1832, he noted that while the parish numbered only 180 communicants, there were 644 children in the Sunday School, 69 in the charity school, and 104 in the Bible class. The next year showed a gain of 41 communicants, but a Sunday School of 802 and a charity school of 170. A most significant fact is the mention of 50 pupils in a Sunday School for children of African descent[22] – an early indication that the parish was becoming aware of the divine commission to preach the Gospel to all, regardless of their differences.

Soon the vestry was proudly describing its Sunday School as "one of the largest and best arranged Sunday Schools ever collected in a church in this city."[23] Its success was due to the fact that Dr. Hawks was his own superintendent and supervised the school down to the minutest detail. By 1833, the church could no longer provide facilities for the children who flocked to it, and it was necessary to hold its sessions in the public school on Wooster Street. At the peak of its prosperity, in 1836, there were 1,400 children in the school, with 80 teachers. There were in addition 80 pupils in the school for children of African descent. The Sunday School library boasted over three thousand volumes.[24]

A small manuscript book entitled "Dr. Hawks' Sunday School, St. Thomas Church, New York," outlining the rules and regulations for the government of that mammoth institution, gave clear indication that Dr. Hawks was not content with mere numbers, and that he required quality from pupils and instructors alike. This book indicated that the teachers were required to

The Later Career of Dr. Hawks

After leaving Saint Thomas, Dr. Hawks moved to Holly Springs, Mississippi, where he became rector of that parish and again opened a school. At the diocesan convention of Mississippi held in May of 1844, he delivered the opening sermon, which so electrified the convention that he was unanimously elected first bishop of the diocese. This brought the confirmation of his election to the agenda of the stormy General Convention of 1844. Grave objections to the confirmation were raised by two clerical deputies from New York, one being the eminent Rev. Dr. William A. Muhlenberg. The reason for the objections was the failure of Saint Thomas' Hall at Flushing and the financial encumbrances that followed. There ensued a great debate, which occupied the time of the House of Deputies for several days. Dr. Hawks' defense of his conduct before that House was unquestionably one of the great speeches to which the House had listened. But it is doubtful whether it really did him much good. One of the shrewdest observers of the day, George Templeton Strong, was present during the debate, and recorded in his diary his impressions:

> Hawks's speech, by the way, was the ablest piece of Old Bailey eloquence, the cunningest web of crafty sophistry with its adroit *suppresiones veri* and its malicious *suggestiones falsissimi* (as against Muhlenberg, for example), its artistical blending of pathos and trenchant sarcasm with the conversational tone of a candid reasoner, its air of disinterested advocacy of jus-

tice, honest and humble admission of venial error and calm expostulation against hasty or prejudiced judgment, its occasional outbreak of something really like eloquent indignation, its cool shuffling aside of strong points and its triumphantly plausible attacks on weak ones altogether made it the greatest effort in that kind of dishonest word-mongering that folks call forensic eloquence I ever heard.[33]

Thomas March Clark, who was also present, discusses this speech in his *Reminiscences*. While his comments are less biting than those of Strong, he comes to the same conclusion – that the speech was a masterly piece of evasion.

The upshot of the debate was that while the House cleared Dr. Hawks of all moral guilt, it resolved that he ought not to be consecrated until the convention of Mississippi had again spoken. That convention expressed unabated confidence in him, but he eventually declined the election. In 1844, he became rector of Christ Church, New Orleans. Declining election as president of the College of William and Mary, he became in 1847 the first president of the newly formed University of Louisiana. In 1849, he returned to New York City as rector of Calvary Church. He held this office with conspicuous success until 1862. In 1852 he was elected to the episcopate in Rhode Island, but declined the office. In 1859 the chair of professor of history at the University of North Carolina was proffered him, but he declined this honor from his alma mater. At the outbreak of the Civil War he moved to

visit each child at home at least once a month and to attend teachers' meetings every two weeks. Every Sunday morning the session began at nine o'clock and continued until 10:15. At the latter hour, the entire school marched into church singing a metrical psalm, and the students remained for the service. In the afternoon, they met again, and were required to recite on the topic of the morning sermon in the church. Dr. Hawks also conducted a monitorial class, formed from those who had graduated from the senior class in the school, the purpose of this class being to train new teachers. On Saturday afternoons the rector publicly catechized the children.[25]

Dr. Hawks was not only a brilliantly successful rector of Saint Thomas; he was also one of the outstanding priests of the entire Episcopal Church. In 1832, he was assistant secretary to the House of Deputies of the General Convention, and from 1833 to 1835 he also served part-time as Professor of Ecclesiastical History and Pulpit Eloquence in the General Theological Seminary. Colorful but restless, he was also named secretary to the New York diocesan convention in 1834. He was one of the first persons to sense the importance of the study of the history of the Episcopal Church in the United States and made important contributions to it, such as the *Documentary History of the Protestant Episcopal Church* which he began to edit (1863-1864). The enthusiasm for history that he generated also led to the endowment of the St. Mark's Church-in-the-Bowery Chair of Ecclesiastical History at the General Seminary.

At the General Convention of 1835, Dr. Hawks addressed a letter to both houses, appealing for concerted action to collect and preserve material relating to the history of the Episcopal Church in this country, and offering the Convention a considerable number of periodicals from his own collection. The Convention responded by accepting the gift and appointing him "Conservator of all the books, pamphlets and manuscripts of this Church." Obtaining a year's leave of absence from the parish, he thereupon went to London, where he was able to copy from the records at Lambeth and Fulham palaces and from the mission archives of the Society for the Propagation of the Gospel a great number of important historical documents. He published two massive volumes from these efforts, one dealing with the early history of the Episcopal Church in Virginia, the other of the Episcopal Church in Maryland. Although criticized, these remain invaluable source books for the sections and periods they cover. As a reward for his industry and ability, Dr. Hawks was eventually named by the General Convention the second Historiographer of the Protestant Episcopal Church. Succeeding Samuel Farmer Jarvis, Hawks served as Historiographer from 1851 to 1866 and was himself succeeded by his associate William Stevens Perry.

His interest in history and its publication led him into a further enterprise. In 1837, in conjunction with the Rev. Caleb S. Henry, he founded the *New York Review*, intended as a counter-weight to the Unitarian-dominated *North American Review*. Ahead of its time, it continued for a few years to be among the best of the serious magazines published in this country. Later Hawks was instrumental in the establishment of *The Church Record* (1843), a weekly paper dedicated to Christian education, and *The Church Journal* (1853), a periodical of Anglo-Catholic perspective.

That Dr. Hawks' manifold activities did not involve any neglect of the parish is shown by its steady progress. By 1833, the work had grown to such an extent that the services of an assistant minister were necessary, and during the remainder of Dr. Hawks' rectorship there was always an assistant. The following year the rector's salary was increased to $3,000 and an additional sum of not less than $500 a year was also approved for his benefit. In 1841 the parish reported a communicant list of 452, a dramatic growth from its humble beginning, and representing in reality a congregation of at least 1,500 souls.[26]

It was to be expected that a man of Dr. Hawks' talents and brilliance would soon be considered a prospect for the House of Bishops. In 1835, a special convention of the clergy and laity from Louisiana, Mississippi, and Alabama elected him its first bishop. Nothing seems to have come of this, but at the General Convention of the same year he was elected to the newly-formed Missionary District of the Southwest, which was to include the state of Louisiana and the territories of Arkansas and Florida. He announced his willingness to accept "provided provision was made to his satisfaction for the support of his family." This was not forthcoming and he found it necessary to decline.[27]

The latter part of Dr. Hawks' rectorship was a stirring time in the history of the New York diocese and of the Episcopal Church as a whole. We have seen that when the parish was born, the Hobartian school of High Churchmen was dominant in the diocese. Hobart's views were obviously influential at Saint Thomas, even though during the 1830s there seems to have been a small and militantly Evangelical group called the "Association for Promoting Christianity" that gathered there under the influence of John Duer, a vestryman, and Evert Duyckinck, one of the group's leading spirits.[28] Hobart's successor as diocesan was Benjamin T. Onderdonk, a man lacking his brilliance, but nonetheless a sound and diligent bishop who held fast to his predecessor's principles. In 1839, during Onderdonk's episcopate, an invigorating but also unsettling influence began to be felt, as the first American edition of *Tracts for the Times* was published. The *Tracts*, which originated in England and the circle at Oxford that included John Henry Newman, John

Baltimore and became rector of Calvary parish in that city. With his friend and successor as Historiographer, William Stevens Perry, he edited in 1861 the *Journals of the General Conventions* from 1785 to 1853. In 1865 he returned to New York City and organized the new Chapel of the Holy Saviour on Twenty-fifth Street, as well as a Hispanic congregation, Iglesia de Santiago (where he preached and conducted services in Spanish, the translation of which he had earlier supervised).

He died the following year and was buried from Calvary Church. He had two brothers who were also priests: Cicero Stephens Hawks, who became Bishop of Missouri in 1844, and William Nassau Hawks, who became rector of Trinity Church in Columbus, Georgia, in 1855. Possessing wide-ranging interests, he was also a founder of the American Ethnological Society and of the American Geographical and Statistical Society, author of *Monuments of Egypt*, translator of a volume on *Peruvian Antiquities*, editor of the papers of Alexander Hamilton, and compiler of a narrative of the expedition of Commodore Perry to China and Japan.[34] At the time of his death in 1866 he had in his possession the major portion of the manuscript correspondence of Bishop William White, which he had borrowed and kept for over twenty-seven years, for settlement of which the bishop's descendants had to memorialize the House of Bishops at the General Convention of 1868.[35] After his death his extensive library was purchased from his family by Mr. William Niblo in 1867 and presented to the New-York Historical Society, of which he had been a very active member; its printed catalogue numbers over two thousand volumes.[36]

Saint Thomas' Hall

Saint Thomas' Hall was likely, in some sense, a competi-
tor to St. Paul's College, Dr.
William Augustus Muhlen-
berg's famous school, which
was also located in Flushing.
The prospectus of Saint
Thomas' Hall sets forth
clearly the principles it was
established to promote. It
was first of all a school centered in religion. "No system
of Education," declared Dr.
Hawks, its founder, "can be
right which does not, from
its commencement to its
close, include education for
eternity, as well as for time."
It was his conviction that a
boy's character is formed before he is fifteen, and that
mere academic instruction is
a relatively small part of true
education. The prospectus
clearly stated that "on the
subject of religion it is due to
candour distinctly to state
that, as the proprietor is
himself, on principle, a
Protestant Episcopalian, the
services of his chapel and the
religious training of those
under his direction will be in
conformity with the doc-
trines and worship of the
church to which he
belongs."[37]

The chapel was then
central in the life of the
school. Its chancel boasted,
according to one critical description,

a massive altar in the center – on one side a music
stand or lectern, on the
other a Gothic bronze
candlestick with seven
branches. . . . There was a
choir and a splendid
organ, and a gallery at the
back; the little boys, the
choristers, went into a
vestry room, each took
down his white surplice
from a peg, and ten or
twelve or fifteen entered
into the choir and chanted
the services of the
Church.[38]

In the 1840s this was "ritualism." The emphasis was certainly upon the primacy of
worship, an emphasis clearly
characteristic of Saint
Thomas parish itself.

Keble, and Edward Bouverie Pusey, at once became the center of a storm.
They were avidly read, especially by the younger clergy, who found in them
a warmth and vigor at times lacking in the teaching of the Hobartians.

The result was a division within the High Church party. And so, from
about 1840, we find in New York two schools of High Churchmen: the one,
Hobartian, old and well-established, perhaps a little stodgy; the other, young
and militant, sometimes casting longing eyes toward Rome and Roman
ways. Dr. Hawks and Saint Thomas were of the former persuasion, and
Hawks entered the controversy with a pamphlet directed against the contro-
versial confessional practices of Bishop Levi S. Ives of North Carolina, a
Tractarian partisan and, ironically, the son-in-law of the deceased Hobart.[29]
Ives would subsequently convert to Roman Catholicism, confirming the
fears of many that the Oxford Movement sought to "Romanize" the Episcopal Church.

Meanwhile, Dr. Hawks, always vitally interested in education but also
busy with many varied interests, tried his hand at a new venture in 1839. That
year he established at Flushing, Long Island, a boys' school which was
named Saint Thomas' Hall. Into this, as usual, he threw all his energy. Leaving the care of the parish largely in the hands of his capable assistant, the Rev.
Isaac Pardee, he erected a school building and a chapel at the cost of
$60,000. Catastrophe followed. Within three years, the school had failed,
and charges of financial mismanagement were rampant. As a result, Dr.
Hawks felt that his usefulness as a rector of Saint Thomas had been so im-
paired that the good of the parish demanded his withdrawal. Accordingly, on
October 21, 1843, he addressed to the vestry a letter of resignation. "I had expected to lay my bones beneath the chancel of St. Thomas," the letter read,
"but according to my best views of *duty* after much deliberation and prayer,
God seems to me to order otherwise." The rector added that he had "not the
smallest cause of complaint" and that over the years nothing but harmony
had existed between the vestry and himself, accompanied by "the tenderest
affections of the pastoral relation" with the congregation.[30]

The resignation came to the parish like a thunderclap, and immediately
a committee of the vestry was appointed to approach the rector to change his
mind. Several interviews ensued, but Dr. Hawks persisted in his resolve. At
length, the vestry reluctantly accepted his resignation. A substantial loan to
the rector was canceled and a grant of $1,000 was made to him. In a testimo-
nial the vestry summed up the achievements of his rectorate in these words:

During a connection with St Thomas Church for more than twelve years, we
have marked with the most sincere gratification the rapid increase of the Congregation under the very able and sound exposition you have ever given of the
doctrine and teachings of our Lord and Master. . . . You had scarcely com-

menced your pastorial [*sic*] care of us before we felt most sensibly its beneficial results. . . . Though we part with you with reluctance, we do so with the firm conviction that our separation is for the general good of the Church, that the Almighty has called you to make known His will, to plant His Gospel and administer His sacraments in a distant land in a Vineyard where the Soil though rank from want of culture is capable of, and willing to receive, the godly counsel and godly instruction which we feel assured it will receive at your hands.[31]

And so, a golden age came to an end. It had been a golden age made so by the preaching of a golden-mouthed rector, for Dr. Hawks had come to be known as "the Chrysostom of the American Church,"[32] and "golden-mouthed" was precisely what the Greek term "Chrysostom" meant when it was first applied to the most eloquent preacher of the early church, St. John Chrysostom. The comparison was appropriate.

Notes

1 VM 1:67 (11 October 1827), 1:68 (23 October 1827), 1:69 (5 November 1827).

2 Two years later, Anthon became rector of St. Stephen's Church, Manhattan, and in 1836 he assumed the rectorship of St. Mark's-in-the-Bowery. He was decidedly not of the Hobartian party. VM 1:71 (14 December 1827), 1:72 (4 and 11 January 1828).

3 VM 1:74-75 (5 and 12 February 1828). See also VM 1:71 (19 December 1827).

4 "Reminiscences of Arthur Cleveland Coxe, Bishop of Western New York, 1865-1896," in *Historical Magazine of the Protestant Episcopal Church* 7:1 (March 1938): 90-91.

5 *The Man of God: A Sermon, Preached in St. Thomas' Church, in the City of New-York, at the Institution of the Rev. George Upfold, M.D. into the Rectorship of the Said Church, on Thursday, the 6th of March, 1828. By John Henry Hobart, D.D.* (New York: T. and J. Swords, 1828), pp. 7-8. See also VM 1:77 (7 March 1828).

6 Already at the time of Duffie's death in August of 1827 the New York Protestant Episcopal Sunday School Society, which he had organized, memorialized him as "emphatically the children's friend" and one who "took a most lively interest in the mean[s] of promoting their temporal, spiritual, and eternal welfare, which is afforded in Sunday school instruction." *The Christian Journal* 12:8 (August 1828): 250-52.

7 VM 1:104 (15 September 1830).

8 VM 1:68 (23 October 1827), 1:73 (18 January 1828). The donation of $3,000 from Trinity Church was later directed by the vestry to be used for the fund to benefit the surviving children of Mr. Duffie; see VM 1:81 (10 April 1828).

9 VM 1:102 (2 July 1830).

10 VM 1:106 (12 January 1831), 1:108-9 (25 January 1831). The committee was composed of David Hadden, John Duer, and Murray Hoffman.

11 VM 1:109-12 (25 January 1831), 1:116 (13 April 1831). The vestry of Trinity "unanimously resolved to advance $20,000 for the purpose of satisfying the mortgage given by the Church to the estate of the late Dr. Bradhurst, the advance so made to be secured by either a new mortgage to be executed by this Church or by an assignment of the existing mortgage." The loan appears as a grant in a list of grants, gifts, and loans in Morgan Dix et al., *A History of the Parish of Trinity Church in the City of New York* (New York: Putnam, 1898ff), vol. 4, p. 549.

12 VM 1: 109, 112, 114 (25 January 1831), 1:116 (13 April 1831).

13 Upfold ceased to sign the vestry minutes on April 13, 1831. On July 1, he tendered his resignation to take effect on August 1 upon condition of payment of $2,500 "as a compensation for pecuniary loss which he must sustain by the change of his present situation." This was agreed to by the vestry. On August 5, the secretary informed Upfold that the vestry was ready to receive his formal resignation. VM 1:117 (13 April 1831), 1:119 (1 July 1831), 1:120 (3 August 1831).

14 VM 1:118 (19 May 1831). Italics added.

15 The vestry was undoubtedly displeased to learn that the new organ ran $750 over the projected cost and that the music committee requested the interest on this to be assumed by that body. On June 25, Upfold sent a letter to the vestry, the contents of which are unknown, and subsequently a committee was appointed "to confer with him on its subject." A member of this delegation was also one of those entrusted with appointing a new music committee. Following this interview, Upfold submitted his resignation. VM 1:118 (25 June 1831), 1:119 (1 July 1831).

16 VM 1:122 (4 October 1831). The salary was increased to $2,000 in February; see VM 1:127 (18 February 1832). E. Clowes Chorley, *Manuscript History of St. Thomas Church* (unpublished manuscript in Saint Thomas Archives, 1943; copy deposited in the St. Mark's Library of the General Theological Seminary, New York City), pp. 150-51.

17 VM 1:122 (7 October 1831), 1:125 (16 December 1831).

18 VM 1:164-65 (28 October 1843).

19 *The Diary of Philip Hone: 1828-1851*, ed. Allan Nevins, new edition (New York: Dodd, Mead and Co., 1936), p. 418. The entry is for 26 August 1839.

20 This estimate is found in a biographical sketch of Hawks published anonymously in *The American Quarterly Church Review and Ecclesiastical Register* 19:1 (April 1867): 9-10. The author was identified as the Rev. N.S. Richardson in a memorial volume published later in the same year: *A Tribute to the Memory of the Rev. Francis L. Hawks, D.D., LL.D.* (New York: 37 Bible House, 1867).

21 Thomas March Clark, *Reminiscences*, 2nd ed. (New York: Thomas Whittaker, 1895), p. 36.

22 New York *Convention Journal*, 1832, p. 61; 1833, p. 75. In his report of 1833, Hawks wrote: "There may be large pecuniary donations when there is but little of the Spirit of Christ, but it is no more than an act of justice to the Congregation of St. Thomas' to say, that while there is cause to lament the coldness of many, there is also much in the spiritual state of his charge to cheer the heart and stimulate the efforts of the Rector."

23 VM 1:164-65 (28 October 1843).

24 New York *Convention Journal*, 1834, p. 91; 1836, p. 81; 1837, p. 79; 1839, p. 79. In his report of 1837, Hawks noted: "In my Sunday school, all the children capable of learning it, are taught the catechism. I superintend the school myself, and every department of it I keep under my own supervision and control in all particulars."

25 The children met for catechism on Saturdays during the winter and spring months, and there was a Bible class for adults: New York *Convention Journal*, 1842, p. 90.

26 VM 1:136-37 (2 March 1833), VM 1:139 (18 January 1834).

27 *American Quarterly Church Review and Ecclesiastical Register* 19:1 (April 1867): 9-15.

28 James Elliott Lindsley, *This Planted Vine: A Narrative History of the Episcopal Diocese of New York* (New York: Harper and Row, 1984), p. 138.

29 The pamphlet, published in 1840, was entitled *Auricular Confession in the Protestant Episcopal Church*. Hawks was said to abhor extremes and "had little patience with the men who seemed to lower the Church to a level with either Romanism on the one hand, or Sectism on the other." *American Quarterly Church Review and Ecclesiastical Register* 19:1 (April 1867): 24. Both Ives and his wife converted to Roman Catholicism in 1853.

30 VM 1:161-62 (21 October 1843).

31 VM 1:163-65 (28 October 1834). Dr. Hawks' persistence in adhering to his resignation ap-

pears rather mysterious. At the time, however, imprisonment for debt was still legal in the state of New York, and it hung over him as a real threat. His friends and admirers later, upon his return to New York, removed the debt in the amount of $30,000.

32 *The Centennial History of the Protestant Episcopal Church in the Diocese of New York: 1785-1885*, ed. James Grant Wilson (New York: D. Appleton and Co., 1886), pp. 37-38.

33 *The Diary of George Templeton Strong: Young Man in New York, 1835-1849*, ed. Allan Nevins and Milton Halsey Thomas (New York: The Macmillan Company, 1952; 4 vols.), vol. 1, p. 247 [grammar *sic* in published text].

34 For a fuller sketch of Hawks' later life, see "Francis L. Hawks, D.D., LL.D." in *American Quarterly Church Review and Ecclesiastical Register* 19:1 (April 1867): 1-34.

35 *Journal of the General Convention*, 1868, p. 431.

36 Evert A. Duyckinck, *A Memorial of Francis L. Hawks, D.D., LL.D.* (New York: New-York Historical Society, 1871); the catalogue of Dr. Hawks' library extends from page 49 to page 166. Still another sketch of his life is given on pp. 9-40.

37 *Circular of St. Thomas' Hall, Flushing, L.I., Rev. F.L. Hawks, D.D., Proprietor and Rector* (1840), in Saint Thomas Archives.

38 The chapel was described in the debate at General Convention of 1844 as it was recorded in *The Protestant Churchman* 2 (26 October 1844): 45.

CHAPTER 4

Storm and Fire

HENRY JOHN WHITEHOUSE
FOURTH RECTOR, 1844-1851

EDMUND NEVILLE
FIFTH RECTOR, 1852-1856

I N SEEKING A SUCCESSOR TO DR. HAWKS, the vestry's first choice fell upon the Rev. Dr. Alonzo Potter, professor of Rhetoric and Moral Philosophy at Union College, Schenectady, New York, who later became a great bishop of Pennsylvania. He declined with regret however, the call to "a parish so long distinguished for its kindness and liberality," citing the claims of his present duties as well as health and family concerns.[1]

Less than two weeks later the vestry voted unanimously to invite the Rev. Dr. Henry John Whitehouse (ill. 6), the rector of St. Luke's Church, Rochester, to succeed Dr. Hawks. Dr. Whitehouse delayed a formal decision until after visiting New York City and allowing the parish an opportunity to see and hear him. He viewed it, in his words, "of great importance that all precaution should be taken to prevent disappointed expectation on either side." After officiating on two Sundays in Saint Thomas and coming away with "a higher sense than ever before of its great relative importance to the Church at large," Dr. Whitehouse accepted the call to be its fourth rector on January 30, 1844. He did so, the wardens were informed, with the conviction that "I may presume upon a full unanimity in the congregation, and their confidence, and of a useful and successful ministry."[2]

Dr. Whitehouse was born at Park Place, New York City, on August 19, 1803. His parents had emigrated to the city from England, and his father went on to become a prominent merchant. Young Whitehouse graduated from Columbia College at the age of eighteen, and then entered the newly established General Theological Seminary. He was ordained to the diaconate in 1824 but not to the priesthood until three years later, when he reached the required canonical age of twenty-four. His first parish was Christ Church in Reading, Pennsylvania. In 1829 he moved to Rochester, and in his first two years as rector of the parish there the number of communi-

6. Henry John Whitehouse, Fourth Rector 1844-1851

cants more than doubled. In 1835 he was elected the first bishop of Michigan, but declined the office.

Now, at the age of forty-one, Dr. Whitehouse was an intellectual and an accomplished linguist: a master of Hebrew, Greek, Latin, French, Italian, and, to a lesser degree, German. His avocations included the study of law and medicine. In churchmanship, he was of the strict Hobartian variety. In personality, however, he was a complete contrast to his predecessor. Lacking entirely in Dr. Hawks' magnetism, Dr. Whitehouse was rigid, very much inclined to stand upon his rights and dignity, and something of a martinet. This independence was increased by the fact that he had his own financial means on which to draw. He seems to have taken a certain delight in battle throughout his career.

In the three-month interim before the new rector assumed his duties, the vestry invited the Rev. John Henry Hobart, son of the late bishop, to officiate.[3] During this period the vestry itself was undergoing changes. Dr. Jeremiah Van Rensselaer had just become treasurer, and Peter Lorillard Jr., Samuel I. Bebee, Charles M. Leupp, Luther C. Carter, Walter Rutherford, and William Burgoyne were new names on the list. Of the original group which had participated in the incorporation of the parish, only David Hadden was left.

The parish was in debt to the sisters of the first rector for bonds of the corporation held by them. To adjust the basis of this debt, which totaled $5,492 with accumulated interest, the vestry resolved to apply to the Court of Chancery for leave to mortgage the rectory and lot at the corner of Houston and Mercer Streets to the two sisters. This was shortly accomplished.[4]

At the first vestry meeting over which Dr. Whitehouse presided, on May 24, 1844, it was made plain that the parish still faced financial trouble. A committee was appointed "to examine into the affairs of St. Thomas Church and report its liabilities and some plan of reducing the same." The report, issued at the next meeting, recommended that a permanent committee of two be established to procure all church supplies, such as fuel, lights, and stationery, and directed that the accounts be audited by the standing committee of the vestry, a group charged with general oversight. This proposal was adopted. However, a recommendation for the immediate sale of the rectory and "the settlement of all liabilities against the Corporation so that it may be entirely free from debt" was postponed.[5]

The report further advised that a special committee be appointed to examine whether alterations and repairs in the church building were needed and to give estimates of the probable costs, together with suggestions on raising the necessary funds. A committee on repairs was assigned and soon announced the need for a thorough cleaning and repair, and for "sundry alterations . . . highly expedient for the greater convenience and beauty of the building." Having consulted with Richard Upjohn, the architect of the new

Trinity Church, the committee proposed that the arched ceiling should be flattened and paneled, the galleries lowered by two feet, and the vestry room and vestibule thrust into the body of the church. This would permit the recessing of the chancel, the suitable re-location of pulpit and desk, continuance of the galleries, and the addition of pews in the gallery and nave. The sale of the new pews was valued at $10,000 and was expected to add an annual income of $700. It was also proposed to introduce gas lighting for the building and to install basement furnaces. These changes, in addition to physical improvement, were considered to offer "some important advantages in a pecuniary point of view."[6]

There was considerable difference of opinion within the vestry as to the wisdom of such a step. The committee was instructed to secure more accurate estimates of the expenses and to inquire whether the necessary funds could be raised on the security of the projected new pews. A motion to employ Mr. Upjohn was carried only by the casting vote of the rector, and he was afterward retained on a percentage of the outlay.[7]

An effort to postpone action for several months was defeated. Instead, the committee on repairs, now constituted as a building committee, was authorized to proceed with the proposed alterations and repairs as soon as a "subscription list for $9,000 be filled and the money paid or secured." The specific repairs and alterations carried out in the summer of 1844 are not clear, but they appear to have been minimal. Indeed, the vestry minutes simply record "that $500 be placed to the credit of the Rector for the purpose of varnishing pews and having new trimmings for the pulpit, altar and carpets." It was also resolved to raise $1,000 by subscription to install gas lighting in the church. The following winter essential repairs were made to the rectory, along with the introduction of plumbing with water from the Croton Aqueduct.[8]

Within two years, however, the vestry again faced the troublesome problem of alterations to the church. A new committee, in consultation with Mr. Upjohn, recommended a list of "necessary and desirable" improvements estimated to cost nearly $14,000. Among the interior proposals were adding rib tracery to the ceiling, eliminating a rear partition and moving the pulpit, desk, and chancel back six feet with an ornamental screen behind, installing leaded stained glass, enlarging the pew seating, and buying all new pews. The list included as well the earlier proposal for basement furnaces.

The vestry approved these ambitious plans unanimously in late March of 1846, on the condition that the required funds be raised without increasing the debt of the church. The vestry allowed at the same time that no changes were to be made to the pews until a majority of the pewholders consented to the proposed plans and the related assessments. It soon became evident, though, that the only way to finance the alterations would involve an additional mortgage on the church property, and that this would entail an application to Trinity parish to waive the priority of its existing lien. This action was endorsed by the vestry, but "a large number of parishioners" were discovered to be "entirely opposed" to raising the necessary funds by mortgage.[9] It also became known that a paper expressing dissatisfaction with any alterations – entitled *Report of the Committee of Investigation of St. Thomas Church to the Congregation* – had been circulated and signed by "a large number of the most respectable of the Congregation."[10]

In the wake of this fractious and formidable opposition, the vestry retreated. A more modest plan was then determined upon, addressing only the most needful repairs while leaving aside the major interior alterations. The new expense was estimated at $3,000. The concern was that no funds existed in the church treasury to cover even this expenditure and the annual income of the parish would not permit any claim. In the meantime, certain repairs could not be ignored and a special appeal was made to cover emergency expenses of $429. As the repairs were "all made by individuals who are dependent upon their labor for their daily support," the building committee urged that they be paid promptly.[11]

The financial state of the church had by this point weakened considerably. The vestry, meeting in March 1847, could no longer avoid the need for a new mortgage to defray "the expenses of the necessary repairs and debts of the Church." This measure still required that application be made to Trinity Church to waive its first lien on the property of Saint Thomas to the amount of $3,000. To this request the vestry of the Wall Street parish acquiesced in part, releasing its priority of lien on the property to Thomas Morris and William H. Harison, trustees of the estate of John C. Van den Heuvel, for the sum of $2,800 and one year's interest on the same for the term of three years. In turn, the vestry of Saint Thomas borrowed from Morris and Harison the sum of $2,800 on the bond of the parish with seven percent interest per annum, together with a mortgage on the Broadway and Houston Street lots.[12]

The vestry now proceeded to authorize overdue repairs and improvements. No charge for any portion of the work was to be levied on current income, nor any debt created on the corporate property. It was "expressly understood" that the expenses were to be covered by the sale of proposed new pews and donations. Alterations were made in the chancel to provide six new pews, furnaces were installed, and the church interior painted. In addition to these, the building committee later reported having been able to extend the improvements to include adding stained glass in the windows, ribbing and paneling the ceiling, carpeting the chancel and vestry, and re-bronzing the gas fixtures and providing new ones for the chancel "with such subordinate refrains as the edifice appeared to require." The total cost came to $4,276, of which all but $1,000 was satisfied by the sale of the new pews and the balance met through contributions, including that of the rector.[13]

The recent years of financial strain had taken a heavy toll on the life of the parish. Relationships between the rector, some members of the vestry, and parts of the congregation were, at best, stressful. In the spring of 1849 Dr. Whitehouse, taking note of the parish's accumulating deficit in income, offered to donate $1,000 of his salary and the same amount for each successive year of his rectorship to the vestry. This offer was referred to a committee with instructions to report on the present finances and prospective revenue of the church. The situation, as reported, was serious. Even private pledges to the church were judged inadequate and could not be expected to be sustained for more than a year. The vestry therefore accepted the rector's donation toward current expenses, with thanks for his generosity, but informed him that "after examination of the income of the church [it] cannot promise the rector a salary of more than $1,500 per annum and the House." No mention was made of the fact that the rector's salary was already in arrears of over $2,000.[14]

The following April, in 1850, the vestry appointed a new committee to examine the financial health of the church. A report, endorsed by a majority of the five committee members, revealed that the current debts of the parish amounted to $3,644, to which had to be added a mortgage of $2,800 that would soon be due. These liabilities, it was believed, had grown out of the ordinary expenses of the church during the last five to six years; they were thus independent of the repair costs which had been entirely defrayed by private contributions and the sale of new pews. The only regular income of the parish came from the sale and rental of pews. In both these items there had been a progressive decline. In 1845 sixty-three pews were rented; by 1849 the number had been reduced to twenty-two. The income from the rentals declined from $1,790 to $629.

The majority report[15] undertook to trace the reasons for the present state of affairs. It began with an expression of affection "for the Rector and the high estimation in which we hold his talents and acquirements as a Theologian and a Scholar, and his character as a Christian Minister." However, it continued, "It is not to be denied, that soon after the Rector had entered upon his duties at St Thomas' Church, feelings of dissatisfaction were evinced by some members of the congregation, which gradually increased and strengthened till they assumed the form of a faction and determined opposition." Even so, it was noted that "on all such occasions the Rector received the determined support of the Vestry." Yet other factors, such as the new Grace Church nearby on Broadway, the removal of many families uptown, and the recent return of Dr. Hawks to the city as rector of Calvary Church, "presented ready occasions" for leaving Saint Thomas and these "were embraced by many members of the congregation." There also had been the general expectation that in consequence of the alterations made to Saint Thomas in 1847 "the church would speedily fill up, its declining condition be retrieved, and its finances once more placed in a state of increasing prosperity." This sadly had not been the case. The future appeared bleak. Unless the "downward course" could be reversed, observed the majority of the committee members, there promised to be "a heavy accumulation of debt, which must eventuate in the congregation falling to pieces and finally in a sale of the church." The only remedy was a still further "retrenchment of the yearly expenses of the church, so as to bring the same within its ascertained and known yearly means and resources."

A minority report, signed by John Zimmerman and Mark Spencer, sought to pour oil on troubled waters. It took exception with the views expressed by the majority concerning the past and called for the putting aside of "unpleasant feeling" between the rector and some members of the vestry. Creating harmony, it asserted, would remove "any spirit of disaffection that may still lurk in the congregation" and would lead to improved financial conditions. The revival of good feelings and confidence in the future welfare of the church, the minority report proposed, might well be inspired "if the Rector would consent to receive in lieu of salary, what income there may be over and above all other necessary expenditures, until such times as the finances may have been adequately retrieved." In making this proposal, the two members acknowledged an "injustice . . . in expecting from the Rector greater sacrifices than he has already generously tendered." In return, though, it was further proposed that the vestry would be "bound to provide by subscription or otherwise for the arrears due to him."[16]

The minority proposal commended itself to both the rector and the vestry, but a conference between the parties was deemed necessary. A committee appointed by the vestry waited upon the rector, who requested that a meeting be scheduled in which the accounts of the parish might be examined afresh. In this meeting the rector pointed out certain expenditures that had been in his opinion unjustly charged to the ordinary income of the parish and should have been regarded as liabilities. Due to this, salaries had not been paid. Indeed, the rector properly pointed out that his salary had always been in arrears since shortly after the time that he had accepted the call, that the amount had ranged from one to three thousand dollars, and that he had therefore been obliged to borrow to meet his personal needs, paying interest on these loans. As to other considerations related to the financial state of the parish, the rector attributed the diminution in new pew rents to the departure of the popular Dr. Hawks and to the establishment in the more immediate neighborhood of such parishes as Calvary, Holy Communion, and Grace Church. Families had steadily been moving north, and the uptown parishes proved attractive and more convenient. Still, with respect to new members, there had been during his incumbency as rector an average yearly addition of twenty new families and in the last year the number had increased to twenty-five.

On hearing the rector and re-examining the financial records, the vestry committee offered its own perspective. The committee reported that, in fact, owing to the arrears in his salary for most of his rectorship, Dr. Whitehouse had been the creditor to the church, providing "virtually a constant loan" without interest, and that this had posed a serious personal inconvenience. The committee concurred with the other extenuating factors cited by the rector, and believed that the parish's "present spiritual condition is probably larger than ever before, and the schools connected with it are useful and vigorous." In addition, admission was made that the financial deficit was owing to "interest on existent liabilities and extraordinary expenditures for repairs . . . and other matters foreign to the current expenses." With respect to the decline in pew rents, the committee attributed this to the re-selling of pews at a moderate rate to newer members. "Few churches," the committee said, "are able to sustain from Pew Rents alone their current expenses for successive years without paying interest on any debt. The state of St. Thomas' in comparison with the other churches, is neither peculiar, nor grievous."[17] The findings of the committee were ordered placed in the minutes of the vestry. A resolution was at once adopted whereby Dr. Whitehouse would agree "to accept the net income of the church in lieu of salary for one year," provided payment be made on the arrears owed him by the sale of bonds. The rector thought it inappropriate to have the debt due to him raised by contributions from the congregation. This being agreed, harmony was restored and maintained.[18]

The same could not be said of the ecclesiastical world of New York at that time, in which the controversies surrounding the *Tracts for the Times*, those treatises of the 1830s and 1840s that signaled the High Church revival in England known as the Oxford Movement, were beginning to have repercussions in other areas of church life. The ordination by Bishop Benjamin Onderdonk of Arthur Carey, a General Seminary graduate suspected of Romish sentiments, aroused great furor in 1843. The following year, the General Convention ordered a committee of bishops to investigate Tractarian influences at the institution on Chelsea Square. The climax – or debacle, as the case may be – came in 1845 when Bishop Onderdonk was accused of "acts of immorality" by three other bishops. An episcopal court afterward suspended the New York diocesan from the office of bishop. This, in turn, set up a new division within the diocese between supporters and opponents of the bishop.

It was impossible for the parish of Saint Thomas to avoid becoming embroiled in all these events. Dr. Whitehouse held a prominent place in the diocese, and it was he who proposed to the diocesan convention of 1849 that it "earnestly and affectionately beg the Rt. Rev. Bishop Onderdonk to resign" in his own interest as well as that of the church. Later, after a canon was adopted permitting the election of a "Provisional Bishop" for the diocese, Dr. Whitehouse, on the first ballot, received the second highest vote in both the clerical and lay orders, but then withdrew his name.[19]

It was against this ecclesiastical background that Saint Thomas encountered a new crisis. At about midnight on Sunday, March 2, 1851, a fire, apparently originating in the basement's newly installed furnaces, broke out in Saint Thomas Church. The following graphic description of the scene appeared in *The New York Herald*:

> When first discovered . . . the flames were fiercely making their way up to the ceiling, behind the altar to the roof of the building. In a very few minutes the roof was in one sheet of flame, which rose with majestic grandeur, and might have been seen the entire length of that part of Broadway lying between Union Square and the Bowling Green. It was a magnificent sight. The surging flames rolled and hissed in their frenzy, and not only bade defiance to every attempt to arrest their wild career, but menaced destruction to the adjoining edifices. The embers showered on the roofs like hail, and the houses on the north side of the church . . . were in imminent danger. . . . Owing to the immense quantity of massive oak in the interior, the fire continued to burn steadily, and with great fury. . . . The bell in the southern tower fell with a tremendous crash when the framework gave way. The organ, too, came down like a thunder clap. The walls of the fine stone edifice, which was built like a fortress, are still good, with the exception of the north tower, which is cracked considerably. . . . [A]t half past three o'clock, after the roof fell in, the fire began to languish, but it continued to burn till after daylight; and during the forenoon, yesterday, smoke issued from the embers and smouldering ruins.

Recalling the beauty of the church and the splendor of its worship, the newspaper lamented the destruction of one of the city's treasures: "Its solid masonry, its gothic structure; its two towers, its finely carved oak, and rich furniture, combined to render it unsurpassed by any other church in New York for beauty and grandeur."[20]

Other Episcopal churches immediately offered the use of their buildings. The vestry, hoping to keep the congregation together in a location as near as possible to the burned church, accepted instead the courtesy of the Dutch Reformed Church at the corner of Greene and Houston Streets. It was arranged to use that building for early morning service on Sundays and in the afternoon, and during the week for Lenten services. Later, Saint Thomas leased a lecture room of the Stuyvesant Institute for services, and the vestry presented to the Dutch Church a handsome folio Bible in gratitude for its ready hospitality in a time of need.[21]

The unsettled state of the parish was further disturbed in 1851, when the Diocese of Illinois began its search for an assistant bishop to the venerable Philander Chase. The choice fell upon Dr. Whitehouse, and on November 20, 1851, he was consecrated to the episcopate in St. George's Church, New York City. In a letter to the vestry tendering his resignation as rector, Dr. Whitehouse acknowledged that "the seven years of my ministry among you have been in some respects less successful than my anticipations." He continued: "But all remembrance of struggle and pain is lost in the consciousness of my own deficiency." In reply, the vestry expressed respect, affection, and gratitude. Since it was to be some time before Dr. Whitehouse entered upon

The Later Career of Dr. Whitehouse

Dr. Whitehouse's life as Bishop of Illinois was almost as stormy as his time at Saint Thomas Church. Since the diocese furnished neither stipend nor residence, Bishop Whitehouse spent the first nine years of his episcopate living in New York City, making only periodic visits to Illinois. He took up residence in Chicago only after the diocese demanded it and the House of Bishops urged him to do so.

Not long into his episcopate, Whitehouse returned to his original theological position as an old fashioned High Churchman, and he was soon engaged in active controversy with two priests of his diocese, Dr. Charles Cheney and Dr. G. D. Cummins. In 1871, Cheney stopped using the terms "regenerate" and "regeneration" in the baptismal office. Bishop Whitehouse first admonished him, but finding him obdurate he proceeded to deposition. This was one of the actions which precipitated the Reformed Episcopal schism of 1873, a schism in which Cheney, Cummins, and W.R. Nicholson (the latter two having been called by Saint Thomas as potential rectors) joined the new church body.

Bishop Whitehouse was an influential proponent of the extension of the cathedral system in the Episcopal Church. In 1861 he purchased the Church of the Atonement in Chicago and converted it into the Cathedral of St. Peter and St. Paul. Earlier he submitted a cathedral plan for New York City to Professor John McVickar.

The Illinois prelate was also a prominent participant in the first Lambeth Conference of Anglican bishops in 1867, at which he preached the opening sermon. Both Oxford and Cambridge Universities awarded him honorary doctorates. He died on August 9, 1874 and was buried in the family vault on Long Island, eulogized as "A Warrior Bishop: Defender of the Faith."[40]

his new field of ministry, the vestry invited him to fill the pulpit of Saint Thomas and to render the benefit of his counsel during the rebuilding of the church. This he did, attending the vestry meetings in an unofficial capacity.[22]

The rebuilding of the church was now the parish's major challenge. Twenty-four hours after the destruction of the building, a special meeting of the vestry had convened to consider what should be done to provide a permanent place of worship for the bereft congregation. Fortunately, the building, including the organ, had been insured for $29,000. A committee was appointed to collect the insurance, and another to make a careful examination of what remained of the structure, under expert supervision. It was found that the walls were intact. There was a large crack over the east window, and the south tower was so badly damaged that it would have to be taken down. The interior was of course completely gutted.[23]

A committee consisting of the acting rector and the wardens was charged with the responsibility of reporting on the possible disposition of the property and all others matters pertaining to the future of the structure. At a subsequent vestry meeting, the treasurer reported that the insurance had been paid in full. After due consideration, it was determined to use part of this money to discharge all debts and mortgages standing against the property, and thus to start anew with a clean sheet. The debts, amounting to a little over $11,000, were duly paid off. Thus for the first time in its history Saint Thomas was free of debt, save for the mortgage held by Trinity Church.[24]

The report of the committee on the possible disposition of the church property was a long and careful document. It took into consideration the vital fact that the location of the church, so venturesome in 1823, so completely satisfactory in 1840, was now thoroughly bad. The completion of the Erie Canal had made the city of New York the greatest seaport of the United States. The potato famine in Ireland and the political troubles in Germany, both in the 1840s, had brought to that port a torrential flood of immigrants, many of whom had remained in the city. The result had been an extraordinary growth of population. The comparatively small, compact New York of 1823 had multiplied its population by three; in 1851, it contained over half a million residents.[25] The pleasant country site on which the first building of Saint Thomas Church had been erected was no longer that at all. The city had reached up to Saint Thomas and grown far past it; now the ruined church stood in an area that was partly a business district, partly a roaring slum. The committee therefore recommended that the church be moved to a better location farther uptown. After careful consideration of this report, the vestry determined, with only one negative vote, to follow the recommendation and to sell the entire property, making some sort of settlement with the owners of the vaults, and to find a site for a new building. During the interim, it was determined to erect a small chapel on the present church grounds as a means of holding the congregation together.[26]

But before this sensible decision could be carried into effect, a new factor altered the situation. Mr. Gerard Stuyvesant, who lived next door to the church, had already made various communications to the vestry regarding aid in rebuilding on that spot, and the vestry now resolved that the committee on property should begin negotiation with him. It was determined that if $15,000 in additional funds could be raised it would be expedient to rebuild on the old site. Mr. Stuyvesant offered to donate $13,000 toward the cost of rebuilding the church on the condition that the space between it and his house should remain open for a period of twenty years. Since this offer was the line of least resistance, and since serious difficulties had arisen regarding the plan to move the vaults, the vestry and Dr. Whitehouse determined to accept the offer.[27]

The architectural firm of Wills and Dudley, specialists in Gothic Revival churches, was engaged to draw the plans. The exterior was to be restored substantially as it had been in the beginning. The internal arrangement of the former structure was to be followed, except that the organ was now to be located at the east end. And so, at a cost of about $28,000, the old church was rebuilt (ill. 7). Fortunately, enough money was available at once to pay for the whole reconstruction, and when completed it was ready for consecration. On March 31, 1852, there was a sale of pews. On April 3, the Rt. Rev. Carleton

7. Exterior of the second Saint Thomas Church at Broadway and Houston, rebuilt after the fire of March 2, 1851, and consecrated on April 3, 1852

The consecration of the partly newly-erected St. Thomas' Church, Broadway, took place yesterday morning before a crowded and fashionable assembly. A little after half past ten o'-clock, Bishop Chase [of New Hampshire], the consecrating bishop, entered the church through the middle aisle, reciting the usual benediction, followed by the Rev. Dr. Vinton of Brooklyn, Mr. Halsey, Dr. Haight of Trinity Church, Dr. Schroeder, Mr. Eigenbrodt of All Saints Church, Dr. Lewis of the Holy Trinity Church, Brooklyn, Mr. Abercrombie, Mr. Johnson of the Theological Seminary, Mr. Eaton of St. Clement's Church, and about twenty other clergymen attired in their surplices, and ten unattired.

The Rev. Mr. Halsey read the Instrument of Donation upon which the title to the church was founded; and the Rev. Mr. Haight the sentence of consecration.

The first part of Morning Prayer was read by Dr. Schroeder, the first lesson by Mr. Eigenbrodt, and the second lesson by Dr. Lewis; and the morning portion was concluded by the Rev. Mr. Johnson. Dr. Haight gave out the Psalms, and the communion service was read by the consecrating Bishop, assisted by Mr. Abercrombie who also read the Gospel. Mr. Eaton read the Epistle, and the choir was presided over by Dr. Hodges of the Trinity Church choir.

The Rev. Dr. Vinton of Brooklyn preached the con-

Chase, Bishop of New Hampshire, acting in the vacancy caused by the suspension of Bishop Onderdonk, consecrated the second Saint Thomas Church.[28]

Finally, in May of 1852, Dr. Whitehouse departed for his new see. The vestry bade him farewell in a most complimentary letter, one paragraph of which indicates the position of the vestry, if not of the whole congregation, in the churchmanship difficulties of the day:

> In the days of your ministry among us, when the Protestant character of our Church has been sorely assailed by foes from within, and the apostasy of many of her ministers has made her laity jealous to remark and prompt to resent the slightest attack on the doctrines of the Reformation, your testimony has been unwavering against these "novelties which disturb our peace."[29]

It is notable that, in the midst of the challenge of rebuilding, the vestry was able as early as January of 1852 to issue a call to a new rector. The invitation, unanimously adopted, went to the Rev. Dr. Alexander H. Vinton, rector of St. Paul's Church, Boston. Dr. Vinton was one of the great preachers of the day. He was also a strong Evangelical and his call is clear evidence of how far the parish, or at least the vestry, was tempted to abandon its Hobartian moorings, perhaps in reaction against the perceived "novelties" that were coming to New York from Oxford. The vestry offered Dr. Vinton a stipend of $3,500. He seemed inclined to accept the call, even inquiring about vacation leave during the summer, but his Boston congregation urged him to remain, offering to build new galleries to accommodate the crowds who wished to hear him there. Dr. Vinton notified the vestry of his inability to accept its invitation on February 17.[30]

A few weeks later, on March 8, the vestry tried again, calling now the Rev. Dr. Edmund Neville, rector of Christ Church, New Orleans (ill. 8). The salary was set at $3,000, with a moving allowance of $500. The vestry expressed its regret that the financial condition of the parish did not permit the provision for a house, the rectory then being leased. Dr. Neville accepted the call with the assurance "that with God's help I will endeavor to put things on a better footing."[31]

At the time of his election, Dr. Neville was forty-seven years old. English-born, he had been ordained in this country in 1839 following service as an ensign with the East India Company in Bombay. He had successfully held parishes in Massachusetts and in Philadelphia before going to New Orleans. While in New Orleans, he had developed a plan, unheard of in those days, whereby "a committee of the vestry should wait upon all the members of the congregation in January of each year to solicit contributions for parish support." This attempt to widen the base of church support was plainly an anticipation of the present Every Member Canvass, born some seventy years ahead of its time.

Dr. Neville commenced his ministry at Saint Thomas on June 1, 1852. When he took over, the parish had two services every Sunday, morning and evening, with a monthly celebration of the Holy Communion. Communicants numbered 168. In the Sunday School, there were just over 200 pupils. Both these figures indicate a great decline from the flourishing days of Dr. Hawks. Especially to be noted is the dramatic depletion of the mammoth Sunday School that Dr. Hawks had organized. Even so, the financial picture was not so bad. Pew rents brought in an income of just over $6,000 a year, the rent of the rectory an additional $900. Sunday collections were, as usual at the time, devoted to special causes, such as missionary work and the relief of the poor.[32] The largest item of expenditure, apart from the salary of the rector, was one of $1,200 a year for music – an indication that the parish was already striving to excel in that respect.

It is almost impossible to determine what manner of man Dr. Neville was. After such pronounced personalities as Hawks and Whitehouse, Neville flits through the parish records like a shadow. Nevertheless, he was apparently proving satisfactory or better, since within six months of his arrival the vestry had increased his salary to $4,000 and appropriated an additional $500 to pay an assistant. Closer to the Hobartian middle than Alexander Vinton would likely have been, Dr. Neville even seems to have manifested a faint ritualistic tinge, since he was granted permission by the vestry "to cover the communion table with an altar cloth." At the same time, one of the vestry presented the church with a set of Prayer Books, kneeling benches for the chancel, and a crimson altar cloth on which were embroidered the words, "This do, in remembrance of Me." David Hadden also gave a carpet for the chancel. In one sense such adornments were but the outward and visible signs of the worship they embellished, but in a deeper sense they indicated a spirit of devotion that was struggling to grow in those troubled years.

In 1854, the vestry began to compare its income from pew rents with the figures of other parishes, such as Grace, Calvary, and Ascension. Determining from this comparison that the pew rents at Saint Thomas were too low, it resolved to increase them by ten percent. At the same time, it also resolved that in 1855, in addition to his stipend of $4,000, the rector should receive any surplus income after current expenses had been met. In 1856, the salary was formally raised to $5,250 – a very tidy sum in those days.

There is, in one of the few surviving literary remains of his own composition, a sermon extant by Dr. Neville that indicates a remarkable social conscience for an Episcopal priest of his means at this time. In "The Duty of Remembering the Poor," which he preached at Saint Thomas Church "in behalf of the Protestant Episcopal Brotherhood of New York" on the evening of February 11, 1855, Dr. Neville delivered an eloquent plea for "domiciliary visitation" of the poor in New York City "at their houses, their rooms, their cellars" to be organized by "our various parishes in this city" on the basis of a mapping or districting

secrating sermon. He took for his text Hebrews, 9th chapter, 24th verse: "For Christ is not entered into holy places made with hands, which are the figures of the true, but into heaven." &c.

The reverend Doctor's discourse was very brief, and of a spiritual and admonitory character.

...The Old Hundredth Psalm was then sung, and a benediction pronounced.

After the conclusion of the services, the consecrating Bishop, assisted by Drs. Haight and Vinton, administered the holy communion, and thus this interesting affair terminated.

8. Edmund Neville, Fifth Rector 1852-1856

that had apparently already been done. Grounding his call upon the theological maxim that "God makes the cause of the poor His own cause in the Bible," he pointed forcefully to the fact that

> the great body of the poor in New York . . . receive no religious visit, hear no Gospel invitations, have no one to care for their souls. The Gospel should be communicated to them by domiciliary visitation. Missionaries should be employed in going daily from house to house, reading the Scriptures in families, and by the sick-bed; explaining the Scriptures, exhorting and praying with the poor. It is manifest that this most imperative and urgent duty is not performed by existing machinery of religious effort. And it is as manifest that it ought to be performed, and that with very little difficulty it may be performed.[33]

Neville's outlook was a brief anticipation, in a rectorate that would soon be all too short and about which very little is known, of the same spirit of mission and outreach that two years later would blossom under his successor Dr. Morgan and in the founding of the Free Chapel of Saint Thomas. It reflected a stirring of concern that was already present in the early development of the Episcopal City Mission Society.

Meanwhile, Saint Thomas had its own financial concerns. Back in 1831, Trinity Church had loaned Saint Thomas $20,000, secured by a mortgage on the property. Some twenty-five years later, in 1856, the corporation of Trinity Church requested the vestry of Saint Thomas to renew the bond. Although no interest had been paid or asked on this mortgage, the vestry resented this request and passed a resolution, rather impertinent in its wording, asking Trinity to cancel the mortgage outright. The impertinence would seem undue, given the great consideration and generosity with which the Wall Street church had treated the parish over the years. It was, after all, a fact that the loan of 1831 had saved Saint Thomas from almost certain extinction. Trinity did not comply in 1856. The eventual renewal of the mortgage without interest was a protection to the corporation of Trinity in the event of the sale of the property.[34]

Dr. Neville was apparently doing well as rector, the financial difficulties were diminishing, attendance was increasing (augmented by visitors from two new hotels nearby), and the future of Saint Thomas looked bright. Then occurred one of the stranger episodes in the history of the parish. In May, 1856, the rector asked the vestry to grant him four months' leave of absence to attend to certain family affairs in England. The vestry agreed to his request. Then in August, about one month before his leave of absence was to terminate, the vestry received a letter from Dr. Neville asking it to accept his resignation. What lay behind this request, there is now no means of telling. A committee was appointed to approach the rector on his return, hoping to induce him to change his mind, but its efforts were unavailing, and in the same month, August, his rectorship ended. So far as the records go, there was no official expression of esteem or regret.[35] Subsequently, Dr. Neville served in other parishes less well known, and eventually died in July of 1871.

While the rector was absent in England and before his letter of resignation had been received, the parish suffered another great loss in the death of David Hadden, who had been a member of the first vestry and had become warden in 1824. Other men of greater secular eminence had been members of the vestry at that time – Astor, Hoffman, Duer – but they had all gone, and Hadden had remained for thirty-three dedicated years. In every parish activity, he had been foremost; he had served on virtually every important committee; he had been liberal in his contributions to the parish; he had been in the truest sense a pillar of the church. And now he was removed by death. It was resolved that on the Sunday following Hadden's passing, Dr. Hawks should be asked to preach a commemorative sermon. To this request he complied with his usual eloquence.

Deprived of Mr. Hadden's wisdom and experience, the vestry again set about the task of calling a rector. The first choice was an extraordinary one. On November 10, 1856, the vestry unanimously resolved to call the Rev. Dr. George David Cummins, rector of Trinity Church, Washington, setting the stipend at $4,000. In its letter of call, the vestry pictured the parish in the most rosy tones, stating that "Dr. Neville has left us in a condition of general prosperity. . . .St. Thomas' occupies a prominent site on Broadway, and has been recently rebuilt."[36] This call is remarkable because Dr. Cummins, although a man of undoubted ability, was an extreme Evangelical of the stripe of James Milnor and Stephen Tyng. His call is evidence that opposition to the Tractarian movement was still active in the parish. Considerable pressure from outside was brought upon Dr. Cummins to accept the offer. His fellow Evangelicals saw in this a golden opportunity to capture a strategic location in the center of Hobartian churchmanship. After some correspondence with the vestry, however, Dr. Cummins declined; he soon moved to Chicago, and the following year was elected Assistant Bishop of Kentucky. A call was then issued to the Rev. Dr. W. R. Nicholson of Cincinnati, who also declined.[37] It should be noted that both of these men subsequently joined the Reformed Episcopal Church – a nineteenth-century group that broke with the Episcopal Church over alleged excesses in Tractarian teaching and practice. Dr. Cummins became its first bishop.

The vestry then seems to have fallen into a kind of panic. Again it approached Dr. Vinton of Boston, who had already declined in 1852. It offered him $5,000 as an enticement to accept, but this did not succeed. Following that rejection, the vestry took the odd step of attempting to induce Dr. Neville to return, but a committee appointed to communicate with him reported that "negotiations for the return of Dr. Neville would not be practicable."[38] Dr. Abram N. Littlejohn of New Haven, later to become first Bishop of Long Island, now came under consideration, but on a motion to extend a call to him the vestry divided evenly. At length, on January 23, 1857, the following statement appeared in the minutes: "On a motion proceeded to a ballot for Rector, Mr. Hance and Mr. Cutting were appointed tellers. Eight votes were reported, five for the Rev. W. F. Morgan of Norwich, Connecticut, three for the Rev. A. N. Littlejohn. Whereupon the chair declared Mr. Morgan duly elected."[39]

Conflict and conflagration, storm and fire, had disturbed the peace of Saint Thomas Church in the two middle decades of the nineteenth century, but by the beginning of 1857 the long and difficult search for another rector was at an end.

Notes

1 The vestry issued the call to Dr. Potter on 6 December 1843, nearly six weeks after its acceptance of Dr. Hawks' resignation. Potter's brother Horatio was in the first Confirmation class of Saint Thomas Church. VM 1:167 (6 December 1843), 1:168 (15 December 1843).

2 VM 1:169 (27 December 1843), 1:170 (10 January 1844), 1:171-73 (30 January 1844).

3 VM 1:173 (13 February 1844).

4 VM 1:174-75 (20 March 1844).

5 VM 1:177 (24 May 1844), 1:177-78 (4 June 1844).

6 VM 1:178 (4 June 1844), 1:182-83 (20 June 1844).

7 VM 1:184-88 (20 June 1844), 1:188 (19 July 1844). Mr. Upjohn was to receive five percent of the outlay in exchange for his services as superintendent of the works.

8 VM 1:188 (19 July 1844), 1:190 (17 September 1844), 1:191 (7 November 1844), 1:191-92 (25 November 1844), 1:192 (8 February 1845), 1:193 (22 March 1845).

9 VM 2:2-4 (31 March 1846), 2:12 (21 May 1846), 2:13 (1 June 1846).

10 *Report of the Committee of Investigation, of St. Thomas' Church, To The Congregation* (New York: Herald Book and Job Office, 1846), pp. 1-16.

11 VM 2:13 (1 June 1846), 2:15 (3 June 1846), 2:17 (22 July 1846), 2:20-21 (19 November 1846).

12 VM 2:25 (16 March 1847), 2:26 (1 April 1847), 2:32-33 (30 June 1847). Harison was a vestryman and comptroller of Trinity Church.

13 VM 2:33 (30 June 1847), 2:33-36 (9 July 1847), 2:39-40 (24 April 1848).

14 VM 2:50-51 (14 May 1849), 2:51-54 (21 May 1849), 2:62 (5 April 1850).

15 VM 2:63 (5 April 1850), 2:64-69 (19 April 1850).

16 VM 2:69-71 (19 April 1850).

17 VM 2:71-72 (19 April 1850), 2:73-74 (26 April 1850), 2:74-84 (30 April 1850).

18 VM 2:85-86 (30 April 1850). Four months later it was reported that the arrears due to the rector had been paid in full; see VM 2:89 (17 September 1850).

19 There is no evidence that Dr. Whitehouse's attitude toward Onderdonk contributed to the withdrawal of funds from Trinity Church in 1846, despite that parish's status as a strong supporter of the suspended bishop. Whitehouse, in fact, believed that the bishop, following his resignation, should be restored to the full functions of his office as allowed. The expense of building its new church led the Trinity vestry to be less liberal in its aid, and yet Dr. Whitehouse was invited to participate in the consecration of the new Trinity Church in 1846. See Morgan Dix et al., *A History of the Parish of Trinity Church in the City of New York* (New York: Putnam, 1898ff), vol. 4, pp. 263-64, 283. William Creighton declined election as Provisional Bishop of New York in 1851, and it was not until the next year that Jonathan Wainwright, assistant minister of Trini-

ty Church, was elected to the same position on the ninth ballot. New York *Convention Journal*, 1849, pp. 54-57; 1850, pp. 36-37; 1851, pp. 84-90; 1852, pp. 51-52, 70-71, 96-99.

20 "City Intelligence. Fires on Saturday Night and Sunday Morning – The Destruction of St. Thomas's Church," *The New York Herald* 16:61 (3 March 1851): 4. The firemen succeeded in saving the altar and the marble font; the font was subsequently restored to the rebuilt church.

21 VM 2:96-97 (10 March 1851), 2:125 (17 June 1851), 2:128 (1 July 1851).

22 VM 2:132-35 (10 November 1851). An anonymous and undated ten-page pamphlet, actually published in May of 1851 and entitled *To the Corporators of St. Thomas' Church. A Few Facts. Causes and Effects*, states that in 1850 five out of seven vestry members, alarmed by the financial condition of the parish, had requested Dr. Whitehouse to resign as rector. The request was ignored, as was a second, and now four of the five petitioners had deliberately not been re-elected. The pamphlet also charges that the rector had been privately searching for a new site for the church at the same time that he was professing from the pulpit his desire to rebuild on the same location. The author, who signs as "A Lover of Plain Speaking, Plain Dealing, and Plain Preaching," calls upon the congregation to elect a new vestry that will force a resignation, noting that "It has been done before now in St. Thomas', and with less cause." The latter is clearly an allusion to the resignation of Dr. Upfold in 1831. Adding that if church law will not aid in this matter then civil redress should be sought, the author asserts that some people have left Saint Thomas "because of the abstract, or obstruse or metaphysical nature of the Sabbath discourses, or for other reasons." A copy of this pamphlet in the St. Mark's Library of the General Theological Seminary is signed "Rev. Dr. Whitehouse, the Rector" on its first page.

23 VM 2:95 (3 March 1851), 2:98-99 (10 March 1851).

24 VM 2:99, 101-2 (10 March 1851).

25 The population of New York City grew from 123,706 in 1820 to 515,547 in 1850. See *The Encyclopedia of New York City*, ed. Kenneth T. Jackson (New Haven: Yale University Press, 1995), p. 922; Ira Rosenwaike, *Population History of New York City* (Syracuse: Syracuse University Press, 1972), p. 36.

26 VM 2:102-9 (10 March 1851). A letter of inquiry was sent to Trinity Church asking that corporation whether it might consider a grant of $25,000 to Saint Thomas Church for rebuilding on the old site. Trinity declined to make the grant. See VM 2:118-19 (15 May 1851).

27 VM 2:120 (22 May 1851), 2:121-25 (30 May 1851).

28 Some thirty-five pew holders and others who attended Saint Thomas sent a petition on 16 January 1852 to the wardens and vestry objecting to the proposed consecration of the new church on the grounds that it was unnecessary. The petition observed that "in these times of innovation, when the use of so-called harmless ceremonies has caused much discord & secession in the Prot. Episcopal Church, it appears to us that no ceremonies, except such as are not only canonical & necessary but also customary, ought to be indulged in; and least of all in a Congregation which has hitherto avoided novelties." Another letter to the senior warden, dated 13 February 1852, stated further that, in the view of the petitioners, "the first consecration is still in full force and validity." No response being forthcoming from the vestry, copies of these documents and a covering letter were forwarded to the Standing Committee of the diocese for its attention. The letter, dated 1 March 1852, informed the Standing Committee that the desire for "reconsecration" of the church by members of the vestry was motivated by the desire of attracting a crowd and thereby promoting the sale of pews and also by "the amiable wish to gratify Bishop Whitehouse, who is expected to perform the ceremony." [Bishop Whitehouse, however, did not do so]. The author of the letter to the Standing Committee, Matthew Maury, reported that he was aware of only "two instances of reconsecration in this City where the old walls were used." [Archives of the Diocese of New York, Saint Thomas Parish File Box]. For an account of the consecration, see sidebar on p. 55.

29 It is worth noting that the old silver bowl that served as a baptismal font was inscribed and presented to Whitehouse along with a plate of dinner service in the time following his final leave of the parish. The phrase "novelties which disturb our peace" was the title of a published series

of letters addressed to the bishops, clergy, and laity of the Episcopal Church in 1844 by Bishop John Henry Hopkins of Vermont, taking exception to certain Tractarian views. Hopkins was of the old High Church Hobartian school, some of whom later in life embraced the new ritualism inspired by the Tractarians.

30 VM 2:136-39 (5 January 1852), 2:139 (20 February 1852).

31 VM 2:141 (8 March 1852). In response to the vestry call, Dr. Neville requested a $1,000 moving allowance, provision for a rectory, six weeks of summer leave, and $1,000 in advance on his salary for home furnishings. The vestry informed him that it was unable to comply with his wishes except for the matter of vacation. On 5 April, Dr. Neville telegraphed the vestry to give notification of his acceptance. See VM 2:143-44 (27 March 1852), 2:156-57 (16 April 1852).

32 The parish received its first legacy in 1852 from the estate of James E. Boisseau in the sum of $2,000 directed for the benefit of the poor. See VM 2:137 (5 January 1852), 2:159-60 (26 July 1852).

33 Edmund Neville, *Remember the Poor: A Sermon Delivered in Behalf of the Prot. Episcopal Brotherhood of New-York at St. Thomas's Church, Feb. 11, 1855* (New York: John A. Gray, 1855), pp. 17-18, 22.

34 VM 2:186-87 (28 March 1856). In 1837 the vestry asked Trinity Church to cancel its obligation against Saint Thomas, but to no avail: VM 1:148 (24 March 1837). In 1846, Trinity informed the vestry of Saint Thomas: "We consider the money lent to St. Thomas' Church, as an obligation due the Trinity, and before the expiration of the twenty years, we shall call for a nominal part of the principal, to preserve our legal rights": *Report of the Committee of Investigation*, p. 14.

35 VM 2:189-90 (12 August 1856).

36 VM 2:192 (10 November 1856). The letter of call is not found in the vestry minutes, but is printed, with other related correspondence, in Alexandrine Cummins, *Memoir of George D. Cummins, D. D., First Bishop of the Reformed Episcopal Church* (New York: Dodd, Mead and Co., 1878), pp. 112-13.

37 VM 2:193 (24 November 1856), 2:194 (22 December 1856).

38 VM 2:194 (22 December 1856), 2:194-95 (29 December 1856).

39 VM 2:195-96 (12 January 1857).

40 Two good sources of information on Dr. Whitehouse are Percy V. Norwood, "Bishop Whitehouse and the Church in Illinois," *Historical Magazine of the Protestant Episcopal Church* 16:2 (June 1947): 167-80; and John Brett Langstaff, *The Enterprising Life: John McVickar, 1787-1868* (New York: St. Martin's Press, 1961), p. 364.

41 As reported in *The New York Herald* 18:94 (4 April 1852): 2.

CHAPTER 5

An Altar and a Spiritual Home

WILLIAM FERDINAND MORGAN
SIXTH RECTOR, 1857-1888

9. William Ferdinand Morgan, Sixth Rector 1857-1888

WILLIAM FERDINAND MORGAN (ill. 9) was forty-one years old at the time of his acceptance of the call from Saint Thomas Church. Born in 1816 and a graduate of Union College and of the General Theological Seminary, he had been assistant minister at Trinity Church, New Haven, under that stalwart old High Churchman, the Rev. Harry Croswell. Since then, until called to Saint Thomas in 1857, he had been for fourteen years rector of Christ Church, Norwich, Connecticut. Under his able pastoral care, that parish had grown steadily and peacefully. The crown of his labors there had been the erection of a noble church edifice designed by Richard Upjohn. In 1849, Trinity College, Hartford, had made him a Doctor of Divinity. He was already well situated, and an obvious priest to be considered for the vacancy at Saint Thomas.

In extending the call to him, the vestry did not disguise the total situation of the parish, financial and otherwise. Dr. Morgan himself later stated that "the excellent gentlemen who, acting on your behalf, invited me to this position, eight years ago, were candid enough to say to me that the parish was moribund – ready to die: and at the beginning of my ministry, I thought it was even so; and considering all things, I think so still."[1]

The rapid expansion of the city to the north had left Saint Thomas stranded. Some of the old families had died or moved to the upper part of the city. The brownstone mansions, once abodes of respectability, had been turned into boarding houses filled with immigrants. And no longer was Saint Thomas *the* Gothic church of the city. Upjohn's Trinity at the head of Wall Street and James Renwick's Grace Church on Broadway far outshone the old Saint Thomas, with its dark, unventilated interior and neglected grounds. The crowds which had filled the galleries in the palmy days of Dr. Hawks had drifted away. The divisions in parish and vestry under Dr. Whitehouse, the recurring financial crises, the sudden and unexplained departure of Dr.

Neville, and the long vacancy, during which "a large number of influential families withdrew" and "the tokens of sudden decline were painful and mortifying," had brought the parish to the verge of extinction.[2] Knowing all this and coming into the situation with eyes wide open, Dr. Morgan saw in the call a challenge rather than the awarding of an ecclesiastical plum. His letter of acceptance, dated March 4, 1857, stated his intention "to commence my ministry among you at as early a day as may be practicable."[3]

On the first Sunday in March in the same year, he began his memorable ministry of thirty-one years at Saint Thomas, the longest rectorship in the history of the parish.[4] It was an exemplary demonstration of the fact that in the life of a parish brilliance is often of less significance than stability. The coming of Dr. Morgan was also a reversion to the original churchmanship of the parish. Born and bred in the Connecticut tradition inherited from Bishop Samuel Seabury, Dr. Morgan brought back to Saint Thomas the traditional High Churchmanship in which it had been grounded in the days of Duffie and Hawks, and from which it had wandered at the beginning of the Tractarian movement. In the course of a sermon preached some years after his arrival, Dr. Morgan articulated the standards of Saint Thomas in his own words:

> In its pastoral administration, in the celebration of divine worship, in the tone of its pulpit ministrations, there has been a sober and dignified adherence to the old paths of the Church, to her wisest and safest traditions, and to those doctrinal standards which lie above the entanglements of sections, and parties, and extremes, in the clear light of accepted Catholic truth. Novelties have found no favor in this sanctuary, either in service or discourse; nor any of those startling exaggerations which, without altering a word of the Liturgy, make it altogether a different thing in its spirit and effect to the sober-minded Churchman.[5]

Changes in the character of the population around the church had made the old rectory seem an unfit location, and already for ten years it had been rented. Dr. Morgan therefore took a house in West Fourth Street, on the south side of Washington Square, where he lived for five years. When, during the Civil War, the Square was turned into a drilling ground, he moved with his growing family to Astoria, Long Island. But the distance that this interposed between him and his charge involved no neglect of the pastoral oversight of the parish; in fact, results soon appeared as people responded to his careful ministrations. At the end of his first full year as rector, Dr. Morgan reported to the convention of the diocese that during the preceding year there had been 75 Confirmations, that the parish now had 250 communicants coming from about 200 families, and that its total constituency numbered about 1,200. He reported that the Holy Communion was celebrated monthly and on the greater festivals, and that services were held during Lent on Wednesdays and Fridays, as well as on every day in Holy Week, and even on

Thursday evenings during a portion of the year.[6] This degree of attention to liturgical worship was not at all common for that period, although it might not impress Episcopalians today as being unusual.

Up until this time, the parish had not made adequate provision for housing its Sunday School. The large school of Dr. Hawks' day had been forced to meet in a nearby public school. Later, much diminished in numbers, it met in the galleries of the church. Early in Dr. Morgan's term of office, a committee was appointed to report on the feasibility of erecting a Sunday School building in the rear of the churchyard on Houston Street in order to remedy the situation. The committee estimated that such a building would cost $3,500. Though this was no excessive sum for the rapidly recovering parish to raise, the subject was tabled.[7] This is only one of a number of indications making it abundantly clear that from the day he became rector, Dr. Morgan had quietly determined that the parish had no future on Houston Street. It was characteristic of his method of work that he made no great public announcement of this determination, but merely went on in an unobtrusive fashion to lay the groundwork for the inevitable move through smaller actions. Despite the handicap of its location, however, it was no part of Dr. Morgan's plan that the parish should merely mark time or that it should abandon the less fortunate population of its immediate neighborhood. In 1858, as we shall see, an important initiative was taken with the opening of "The Free Chapel of Saint Thomas Church."

Directly after Dr. Morgan assumed the rectorate, however, financial catastrophe struck the country and the parish. The year 1857 has been called one of panic, depression, and recession; all three terms indicate the same symptoms. Banks and businesses failed, stock values plunged, factories closed, construction ceased, jobs vanished, bread lines formed, and the finances of Saint Thomas parish, in a critical state for over a decade, now became even worse. Within six months of Dr. Morgan's arrival, the vestry applied again to Trinity Church, which already held a considerable mortgage on the property, asking to borrow an additional $2,000 for building improvements.[8] Current expenses also began to show a deficit. In 1861, a second mortgage of $3,000 was placed on the property, and a few weeks later $2,000 more was borrowed. Desiring to share the burden of the parish, the rector wrote the vestry in November, suggesting that his salary be reduced by $100 a month, although unlike Dr. Whitehouse he was not a man of private means.[9] This forced the vestry to give serious consideration once more to the growing necessity of a change of location.

At a special meeting of the vestry held on February 5, 1859, the first official act toward such a removal was made. A committee consisting of Messrs. Willett, Mix, and Gillespie was appointed "to collect information in reference to the value of the church property, the canceling of the rights of the vault owners, the state of the outstanding scrip, and other matters affecting the condition of the church at present, in reference to a possible sale of the premises and the removal of the church to a new location." On November 5 the vestry, having heard the report of this committee, voted that "the removal of the church was expedient."[10] At last it was committed to a forward step.

The disposal of the vaults was the crucial difficulty in any proposed sale of the property. It will be remembered that in order to raise money for the building of the first church in 1824, the vestry had sold lots to be used for burials in the rear of the church. The deeds under which these were sold protected the rights of the vault owners for the duration of the corporation. Obviously, the property as a whole could not be sold unless the vault owners would agree to surrender their rights or to sell the land back to the corporation. The committee of the vestry appointed for the purpose reported that while a majority of the vault owners had so agreed, several refused absolutely to give their consent. Even one dissenting owner could block the sale. The only recourse was to take the matter to court.[11]

Three-fourths of the congregation having voted to take this action, the vestry applied to the Supreme Court of the state, attesting "that it was their purpose to go further uptown and to provide the congregation with a more commodious place of worship.... The present building was too small to hold the congregation and the public desiring to attend there. It was believed that the proceeds of the proposed sale would erect a large building and leave a large surplus on hand for the benefit of the church in other matters." This petition was opposed by twenty-three of the vault owners, who alleged that the majority of the congregation resided below Fourteenth Street. After due consideration, Justice Bonney ordered that the property (which included the vaults) be sold for not less than $300,000, that a stipulation should be made as to the disposition of this sum, and that some indemnity clause be inserted to protect the rights of the vault owners. The amount of $300,000 was set so that the church could respond to any action taken by the vault holders. Beyond the fact that the court had given permission for the sale of the property, however, this decision was far from clearing the way for the move.[12]

Nevertheless, Dr. Morgan reported to the next diocesan convention that by unanimous action of the vestry and the general consent of the congregation, measures were then under way for the removal of Saint Thomas to a more suitable location. Never deviating from his conviction that a move was necessary for the continuing life of the parish, the rector kept up a steady pressure on vestry and congregation to act in accordance with this decision.

In the month of March, 1865, at the beginning of the ninth year of his rectorate, Dr. Morgan preached a sermon, notable in the annals of the parish, on "Tokens of Decline," using as his text II Corinthians 12:13, "For what is it, wherein ye were inferior to other churches?" In this sermon, he summed up in a masterful manner the past history of the parish, pointed out the obvious truth that ever since the days of Dr. Hawks the parish had been on the downgrade, and stressed how bad the present location had become. With compelling logic, Dr. Morgan continued:

> We are now planted in the centre of the worst neighborhood in this city – the most degraded and the most completely surrendered to the purposes of crime; crime which we cannot and do not mitigate in the least; crime which runs riot on all sides around us, unchecked, unabated, uncared for, while we are saying our prayers and listening to the preached Word. And sure am I, that if the denizens of this immediate vicinity were to resolve upon a better observance of Sunday, and enter this church, you would forsake it at once, and in a body.[13]

Turning to the pastoral side of parish life, the rector spoke of the increasing distance of its families "whose continuance with us is essential to our very life." Further, the matter of distance, he said, affected the order and decency of the church services. On Sundays when the Holy Communion was celebrated, at least one half of the communicants left before the others received. On Sunday afternoons the church was deserted, and during the week for an evening or occasional service it would be the same. So scattered, disunited, and without any local ties was the congregation that "the pastor is cut off from all contact with the collective body of his people, except on one-half day of the week."[14]

This forceful plea from a devoted pastor who longed for closer contact with the people committed to his charge really marked the beginning of the end of the old church. The vestry was now ready to act. In June of 1865 the two lots at the corner of Broadway and Houston Streets, which included the church and rectory but not the vaults, were sold for $175,000. The purchaser, a large clothing house, was at liberty to take down the church and build a store there after the first of May following. In the interim, the parish agreed to pay a rental of $12,000 for the use of the church until the time expired. It likewise retained for itself the organ and chancel fixtures and the stained glass windows.[15] The rector and wardens of Saint Thomas also approached the vestry of Trinity Church and requested once more that the mortgage from 1831 be released. Finally, in 1865, this was granted by Trinity Church.[16]

But this did not dispose of the problem of the vaults. The vestry continued to make every honorable effort to meet the demands of the owners, but settlements were difficult to reach. An offer to refund the original purchase price and to pay the cost of the removal of the bodies to new vaults provided by the vestry in Trinity, Green-Wood, or Woodlawn Cemeteries was refused. The vestry then offered to do all this and pay for each lot a premium of $500. This was likewise turned down. One prominent churchman refused an offer of $1,000 for a vault which had originally cost him one quarter of that amount. Some vault holders did transfer their contents to other places; the remains of the Astors, for example, were removed to Trinity Cemetery. In the final settlement, the vestry was compelled to pay $48,550 for the twenty-eight vaults. They had proved to be, for their owners, a tidy little speculation in New York real estate.[17] About the same time, on September 18, 1865, the rector and vestry, obviously anticipating their new building, made an offer to the son of the first rector to have the remains of his father, the Rev. Cornelius Roosevelt Duffie, "interred under the aisle or Chancel of the new Church," but this was never done.[18]

Now at last Dr. Morgan was able to announce that the final service in the church on Houston Street would be held on Sunday, April 29, 1866, although the impending move was not without its objectors. A bitter editorial appeared in the pages of *The Church Journal*, proceeding from the pen of a brilliant and outspoken clerical critic, John Henry Hopkins Jr. With a criticism that would surface even more stridently in the voices of inner-city advocates within the Episcopal Church of the mid- and later twentieth century, Hopkins denounced the whole project to move the church as a means of denying the obligation to preach the Gospel to the poor. In spite of assurances to make provision for church services in the deserted neighborhood, he said, the money that would go from the sale of the old church "to the chapel for the poor will be nothing to boast of. . . . the rich will suck the orange, and then fling the rind to the poor."[19]

Notwithstanding such concerns, on Easter Day, 1866, the last service was held in old Saint Thomas Church. There is always something saddening about the end of an institution that has had its great days, even if it is a structure whose spirit and substance will surely continue elsewhere. Dr. Morgan, in spite of his determination that the church should move, realized this, and his sermon was well suited to the occasion. He declared:

> There is no virtue in consecrated walls – none whatever – when a higher interest for God or man can be advanced by their downfall. The sentence of consecration, though repeated every year, cannot save a building from the fluctuations of time, or the movements and recessions of human society. . . . I have as much veneration for holy places as any other man, but I utterly repudiate and deny that superstitious fancy which would attach inherent sacredness to stone and wood because they have once been dedicated to the service of Almighty God. . . . I thank God that we are permitted to remove before utter disintegration and death have overtaken us, before the ancient glory of this temple has been utterly despoiled. . . . I would not have it die, but live; I would not see it fall, but rise; I would not cherish it as a landmark or nurse it as a ruin, or surrender it to uncertain ends; but, by the blessing of God and the co-operation of my vestry and people, I would renew its strength upon other and broader foundations, and give

it the opportunity and a power for good, which, if it yield a needful benefit to the rich, shall yield a larger benefit to the poor, in manifold ways. In a word, beloved, were my prayer granted, this building from which we mournfully retire today, should be replaced by another, majestic in its aspect, noble in architecture, capacious, convenient, well equipped, solid, which for ages should bear the name of the disciple, St. Thomas, and for ages bring honor to the name of Christ, his Master and ours.[20]

And now, for the space of a year, Saint Thomas was to be without a permanent home. Just when it looked as if the congregation would be reduced to worshiping in some hall, however, a golden opportunity was offered. The venerable Dr. Thomas House Taylor, rector of Grace Church, was to be absent in Europe for twelve months. The vestry of Grace Church therefore invited the homeless congregation to worship with them. Dr. Morgan was to have temporary charge of both congregations. The offer was gratefully accepted and the arrangement proved to be highly satisfactory to both groups.[21] The congregation of Saint Thomas now had the opportunity of worshiping in a notably beautiful building, the work of James Renwick, Gothic of a very different order from that of their abandoned structure. And the congregation of Grace Church had the advantage, no small one, of having Dr. Morgan as their pastor. Although there is no mention of it in the official records of either parish, there seems good reason for believing that on the death of Dr. Taylor, which occurred within the year, the rectorship of Grace Church was offered to Dr. Morgan. It must have been a tempting offer, since it would have given him a stable congregation housed in a noble building. He would have been freed from the onerous task of organizing what amounted to a new church in a new neighborhood. But Dr. Morgan understandably concluded that since he had been the prime mover in the change of location, it was his job to carry through with the plan.

Naturally, the location of the new church was a matter of deep concern to rector, vestry, and congregation. From the beginning, the minds of the rector and the vestry had turned to what was then the upper part of Fifth Avenue. Messrs. Willett, Williams, and Collins were appointed to a committee to inquire concerning the purchase of the Colored Orphan Asylum property on Fifth Avenue; certain lots owned by Columbia College on Fiftieth and Fifty-first Streets were also considered. Eventually the committee decided on lots consisting of 100 feet of frontage on Fifth Avenue at the corner of Fifty-third Street and of 235 feet on Fifty-third Street itself. They were procured for $115,000.[22] It was a neighborhood where many families of great wealth and fortune were already beginning to locate their homes.

The selection of this site was, like that of the first church in 1824, something of an act of faith, since Fifty-third Street was then far uptown. But Dr. Morgan was above all a man of supremely good judgment. He stated thus the advantage of the new site:

> It is a spot beautiful for situation, and, in many respects, resembling that on which the foundations of the first St. Thomas were reared. . . . In like manner do we commence the foundations of the second church, at a point somewhat open and unoccupied. We see on every hand traces of suburban peacefulness and beauty. Only the ripples of an advancing population are as yet playing around us. But soon the mountain surge will come, and the last vestige of ancient farms and homesteads will disappear. Even before the top stone of our temple can possibly be brought and laid with shoutings, our range of observation and prospect will be utterly cut off. Walls of domestic architecture will hem us in on every side; swarming and compact life will be upon us, and around us, and pressing eagerly beyond us."[23]

Dr. Morgan would have been surprised at the extent to which his prophecy was to be fulfilled. It was indeed a strategic time for the move. The Civil War had just ended and the United States had entered the Gilded Age. It was the time of transcontinental railroads and the settling of the far West. It was an era for unparalleled industrial development. It was the period of corporations and the growth of great American fortunes. Carnegie and Vanderbilt and Rockefeller and Morgan were abroad in the land. The center of all this great new development was New York City, which had become the financial capital of the country. Of the wealth that now flowed into the city of golden dreams, Saint Thomas was to have its good share.

The moving spirit in the planning for the new building was of course the rector, aided by a building committee of which George C. Collins was the chairman. Dr. Morgan had very definite ideas as to what the new church ought to be. It should be a monument of beauty exceeding anything in ecclesiastical architecture the city could show. Thus he stated his ideal for the new Saint Thomas:

> I would enrich such a building, and adorn it with goodly stones, and bring to it the costliest gifts; but not merely for man's approval, or to inflate his pride; but because our best gifts belong to God; because we have no right to offer Him of that which costs us nothing; because we deserve rebuke when we dwell in our ceiled houses – we sinners, we pensioners – and cheapen His Houses and make His courts poor and contemptible. No greater insult could be offered to Him, especially at the hands of those who are shortly expecting, by His Grace, to be received into that upper Temple, whose walls are jasper, and whose very gates are pearl.[24]

In the minutes of the vestry, there is, strangely, no mention of the formal engagement of an architect, but on October 30, 1865, it is stated that "plans for the new church and rectory of Mr. Upjohn were exhibited by the rector." These plans would not be finally approved and adopted until May of 1867. The selection of Richard Upjohn must have commended itself for several reasons, at least in the mind of Dr. Morgan. Upjohn had been the architect of the church at Norwich that was built when Dr. Morgan was rector there.

10. Exterior of the third Saint Thomas Church, at Fifth Avenue and Fifty-third, consecrated May 15, 1883 (architect, Richard Upjohn)

A Note on Some Memorials in the Saint Thomas Church of 1870 [39]

1. The marble font given by David Hadden to the first church in 1831. It was in use again after being rescued from the fire of 1851.

2. The chancel reredos and murals, given by Mr. Charles H. Housman in memory of his mother.

3. The carved Gothic oak lectern with the full-length figure of an angel in bold relief, given by Cora and Myra Moffatt in memory of their father.

4. A clock formerly in old St. George's Church on Beekman Street, given by Mr. Thomas P. Cumings.

5. A bust of Francis Lister Hawks, former rector, given by his wife and placed in the chancel.

6. A white woolen Easter cloth from Mrs. W. F. Morgan, the rector's wife, and a white silk altar cloth and pulpit hanging from Mrs. William Bond, both made by the Clewer sisters in England.

7. A complete set of green silk hangings and cloths, also made at Clewer, presented on the twenty-fifth anniversary of Dr. Morgan as rector by his three daughters.

8. A cedar-lined chest for the altar cloths, given by Dr. Morgan himself.

9. The altar in the Lenten Chapel (on the north side of the church), its main panel depicting the first miracle at Cana of Galilee, and matching reredos of richly carved oak, depicting

The completion under Upjohn's planning of Trinity Church, New York, had made him the foremost church architect in the United States, for that design demonstrated that he was probably the first man in this country able to produce genuine beauty of construction through the Gothic form. The architecture of the Ascension and the Holy Communion, both churches in the city, would also have come to mind. Moreover – and this undoubtedly had weight with Dr. Morgan – Upjohn was a devout churchman, strongly influenced by the Oxford Movement, and he designed churches that were not

an angel with the heads
of cherubs, given by Mr.
Joseph Harper.

10. Five windows in the
same chapel, the gift of
Edward Willett in mem-
ory of his family.

11. In the gallery over the
Lenten chapel, a three-
light window given by
Dr. Morgan and his
brother in memory of
their mother.

12. Somewhat later, a
chime of twenty-one
bells was hung in the
tower, given by Thomas
H. Walton and his sister
Harriet in memory of
their mother.

merely auditoriums for the hearing of sermons, but structures manifestly planned for liturgical worship.[25]

Anticipating the time when services with Grace Church would end and desiring to preserve the unity of the Saint Thomas congregation, the building committee began to consider other arrangements. The expedience of renting a hall was considered and found to be doubtful, if not impracticable. The conviction then arose that the costly lots on Fifth Avenue should be put to some use at once. After several interviews with Mr. Upjohn, the building committee recommended that a temporary chapel be erected in that portion of the architectural design embraced in the nave of the proposed church. It was determined that the chapel would seat six hundred people, "be church-like and symmetrical in form and convenient in arrangement," and not exceed $25,000 in cost.[26]

The last united service was held in Grace Church on Sunday, April 14, 1867. The following Sunday, Easter Day, the Saint Thomas family, broken in numbers but united in heart, met for worship in its own chapel and on its own ground. The building, *The Church Journal* reported, "consists of what will be the nave of the complete new church, and is by no means imposing in its present condition." However, the new Saint Thomas when finished, the church paper promised, would "be one of the most original and remarkable of the designs of Mr. Upjohn."[27]

Just one year had elapsed since the last service in the old church at Broadway and Houston Streets. With this happy renewal of parish life, Dr. Morgan was able to report to the next diocesan convention that "seventy families of the downtown Congregation formed a nucleus for the new organization, and with additions from the neighborhood, at once filled the Chapel."[28] Messrs. George C. Collins, John S. Williams, and Daniel T. Hoag were now appointed a permanent building committee, and were authorized to proceed at once with building the foundation of the church, and to prepare for the laying of the cornerstone. The finance committee was empowered to borrow money as needed. Mr. Upjohn estimated that the cost of the building, including the tower and the rectory, would be $255,391.[29] This was over five times what the first church had cost.

On October 14, 1868, the cornerstone of the third Saint Thomas Church was laid. Unfavorable weather rendered the congregation rather small, with "fully one-half being ladies," as *The New York Herald* reported. The procession, however, was imposing, having among its ranks representatives from other parishes and churches, along with students and faculty of the General Theological Seminary, members of the Church Union, and delegates to the General Convention who happened to be meeting in the city. Among the vested clergy were the Dean of Nova Scotia and the bishops of Tennessee,

Minnesota, and Colorado. The officiant for the ceremony was naturally the Bishop of New York, Horatio Potter, who as a young student from the General Seminary had been a member of the first Confirmation class at Saint Thomas in 1826.

Dr. Morgan, at one point in the proceedings, read a list of the contents of the leaden box that was to be placed within the cornerstone. The several items included a Bible "in token that this church is built on the truth revealed by God," a Prayer Book "as a testimony that this church is built on a pure faith and a spiritual worship," pastoral letters of the House of Bishops and charges of the Bishop of New York "in acknowledgment of the Apostolic Ministry on which this church is built," and three sermons by the rector on the history of Saint Thomas. Dr. Morgan also announced that the old cornerstone of 1823 was to be re-laid and embedded with the new, "thus blending the memories and associations of the past with the living interests of the present."[30]

As the building of the church progressed, it of course became necessary to vacate the temporary chapel. For about a year and half, the services of the parish were held in the Church of the Resurrection, which had recently moved to the corner of Madison Avenue and Forty-seventh Street. (At that time the name of the present Church of the Resurrection on east Seventy-fourth Street was the Church of the Holy Sepulchre.)

Finally on Thursday, October 6, 1870, came the culmination of the hopes and plans of Dr. Morgan and his people. The third Saint Thomas Church was solemnly opened for divine worship (ill. 10). Since it was still in debt, it could not be consecrated, a stipulation that had been introduced to the national canons of the Episcopal Church in 1868,[31] but the service was what Dr. Morgan happily described as a "partial hallowing." It was conducted by the bishop of the diocese, who was accompanied by Bishop Littlejohn of Long Island and Bishop Talbot of Indiana. Beginning with the hymn "Blessed City, Heavenly Salem," the opening sentences of Morning Prayer were read by the Rev. Dr. Francis Vinton of the General Theological Seminary; the first lesson by Dr. Henry Codman Potter, the recently-instituted rector of Grace Church; and the second lesson by Dr. H. E. Montgomery of the Church of the Incarnation. Dr. William Rudder, the rector of St. Stephen's Church in Philadelphia, led the Creed and Dr. Samuel Osgood the prayers following. The celebrant of the Eucharist was Bishop Potter, assisted by his other episcopal brethren and Dr. Morgan Dix, rector of Trinity Church, as well as Dr. Joseph H. Price of St. Stephen's parish in the city. Over five hundred persons received Communion.[32]

The sermon for the occasion was preached by Dr. Morgan, taking for his text John 1:39, "They came and saw where He dwelt." There was much left to be done, the rector observed, before all the elements of the new church, from the top-stone of the tower to every tuneful key of the organ, "shall unite in the jubilee of thanksgiving over a worthy offering, and a finished work!" Nonetheless, the day was one of blessing. "After a dependent and unsettled life of nearly five years," he reminded his listeners, "we come within the borders of the promised land today. We stand within our own parochial limits. We have an Altar and a Spiritual Home." From this time forward they would assemble "as a household and one family" in the Lord, and be able to say, "Master, it is good to be here."

In closing his sermon, Dr. Morgan paid a special and splendid tribute to the sixty-eight-year- old Richard Upjohn:

> To the architect of this church, I am glad to tender the thanks and the unqualified satisfaction of those I represent this day. As if premonished that it might be the last great work of his advanced and venerable years, he has given to it the ripest and best considered studies of his life. He has surrendered himself to this structure – his genius, his supervision, his careful direction, both of the massive and the minute, of the solid and the decorative, have been thoroughly concentrated here, and have brought out a result which utters his praises and confirms his eminent reputation, a thousand-fold louder than the Preacher's voice.[33]

The neo-Gothic building well deserved the praise lavished on it. *The Evening Post* hailed it as "a notable addition" to American church architecture. "In this spacious and commodious structure," the paper related, "the aesthetic and the practical are combined with a skill rarely equalled." The outward appearance offered "the magnificence of a cathedral," and the interior arrangements promised to claim "the title of the model parochial church." The new church, it was declared, set a precedent for vestries "who may wish to avail themselves of the best results of modern ecclesiology."[34] Later in 1898, its total seating capacity was described by the rector then, Dr. Brown, as "2000 sittings available for the congregation."[35]

The last important work of its designer, and regarded by him (but not by all) as his masterpiece, the new Saint Thomas Church was to some extent a departure from the characteristic simplicity of Upjohn's style. The great feature of the exterior was the corner tower, solid, with severe simplicity in its two lower stories, the second with its added middle buttresses acting as a transition to the belfry. Atop this rose an octagonal level adorned with a little spire. For decades it dominated this area on Fifth Avenue, complemented by a spacious and beautiful rectory built in 1872-73 and also designed by Upjohn.

The church itself was cruciform, but the crossing (ill. 11), instead of being a simple intersection of nave and transepts, was widened out into a spacious octagon. One side of this octagon was occupied by the polygonal apse, which was not cluttered by choir seats, these being located on a platform under the crossing. The diagonal faces flanking the apse were smaller semi-apses containing the great four-manual Roosevelt organ, installed in 1881. Over such a crossing one might have expected to find, as at Ely Cathedral, a great lantern, but no such construction was ever planned, its place being taken by a rather inadequate flèche.

The glass used in the windows was manufactured primarily in Metz, France. It was crafted into variegated windows and stained by Alphonse Friedrick of Brooklyn. By his work on Saint Thomas Friedrick was said to have "easily placed himself at the head of the glass-stainers in this country."[36]

In the decoration of the chancel, there came to be a wedding of all the arts. The reredos, a bas-relief of plaster but finished in old gold, representing the "Adoration of the Cross by Angels and Cherubs," was fashioned by Augustus Saint-Gaudens. This was flanked on either side by illusionistic murals painted by John La Farge that depicted "Christ Appearing to Mary Magdalene" and "The Angel at the Tomb" on the left and "The Arrival of the Three Marys at the Tomb of Christ" on the right.[37] La Farge also executed, for the arched recesses above the organ, a series of angels with musical instruments in the manner of Fra Angelico. The reredos and chancel murals were installed shortly before the death of Richard Upjohn in 1878. The combination of all this art together is said to have represented the first collaboration in

11. Interior of the third Saint Thomas Church, consecrated 1883

America of a great architect, a great sculptor, and a great painter, all for the glory of God.[38]

This collaboration was, for Saint Thomas Church, but an extension and continuance of its determination to worship "decently and in order" (I Corinthians 14:40) for the edification of God's people and the right rendering of praise to God. It had been Dr. Morgan's stated goal to "enrich such a building, and adorn it with goodly stones, and bring to it the costliest gifts," and that goal was now achieved.

Notes

1 *Memorials of S. Thomas's Church New York. Discourses by the Rev. Dr. W. F. Morgan, Rector of S. Thomas' Church, New York* (New York: Gilliss Brothers, 1882) [Hereafter: Morgan, *Memorials*], p. 18. Dr. Morgan was the first rector of Saint Thomas not to receive the unanimous call of the vestry.

2 Morgan, *Memorials*, p. 17.

3 VM 2:197 (4 March 1857).

4 The vestry now consisted of Mark Spencer and Lyman Denison as wardens, with Edward M. Willett, George C. Collins, Elihu L. Mix, Evert A. Duyckinck, Revo C. Hance, Fulton Cutting, George D. H. Gillespie, and C. A. Berrian as vestrymen.

5 Morgan, *Memorials*, p. 41. These remarks were delivered in his "Closing Discourse" preached at Broadway and Houston on 29 April 1866.

6 New York *Convention Journal*, 1858, p. 174.

7 VM 2:202 (22 September 1857), 2:203 (29 September 1857).

8 VM 2:202-3 (22 September 1857), 2:203 (29 September and 22 November 1857).

9 VM 2:227 (7 October 1861), 2:228 (23 October 1861), 2:229 (16 December 1861). Dr. Morgan noted that the burden of providing a house kept him from increasing the amount. "I think, he added, "we shall have a full and outwardly prosperous Church, but not a profitable one in the pecuniary sense."

10 VM 2:213 (5 February 1859), 2:216 (5 November 1859).

11 VM 2:217 (15 December 1859).

12 "New York," *The Church Journal* 8 (25 July 1860): 210; VM 2:221 (7 September 1860).

13 Morgan, *Memorials*, p. 21.

14 Morgan, *Memorials*, pp. 22-23.

15 VM 2:253-54 (18 May 1865), 2:255 (21 June 1865), 2:256-57 (26 June 1865); *The New York Times*, 2 August 1865.

16 VM 2:257-58 (26 June 1865), 2:258 (2 August 1865).

17 VM 2:263-64 (30 October 1865), 2:266-67 (29 December 1865), 2:301-2 (16 February 1868), 2:302-3 (11 March 1868), 2:312 (3 June 1868).

18 Saint Thomas Archives, Letter of Archibald D. Duffie, great-grandson of the first rector, to the Rev. Frederick M. Morris, dated 17 November 1967; see above, chapter 2, note 35.

19 "St. Thomas's, New York," *The Church Journal* 14 (25 April 1866):116.

20 Morgan, *Memorials*, pp. 37-38, 41-42.

21 VM 2:268-69 (29 March 1866), 2:273-74 (13 April 1866).

22 VM 2:250-51 (3 January 1865), 2:259 (2 August 1865), 2:259-60 (25 August 1865), 2:260-61 (19 September 1865), 2:262 (27 September 1865), 2:263 (30 October 1865).

23 Morgan, *Memorials*, pp. 50-51.

24 Morgan, *Memorials*, p. 55.

25 VM 2:264 (30 October 1865), 2:265 (5 December 1865), 2:297 (9 May 1867). Upjohn had also designed the Chapel of St. Mary the Virgin at Nashotah House Theological Seminary, Wisconsin, in 1859-60, and his grandson would graduate from that same institution in 1887.

26 VM 2:277 (30 May 1866), 2:278-82 (12 June 1866), 2:278-86 (20 June 1866). The building committee's report of 12 June 1866 indicates that while Upjohn had been asked to submit plans for the new church, there was as yet no commitment to engage him as architect.

27 "New York," *The Church Journal* 15 (24 April 1867): 114. The editor, John Henry Hopkins Jr., who earlier castigated the parish for moving uptown, remarked at the same time that the Upjohn design would "if anything could – make Churchmen forgive and forget the desertion." See "St. Thomas's, New York," *The Church Journal* 14 (25 April 1866): 116.

28 New York *Convention Journal*, 1867, p. 218.

29 VM 2:283-85 (12 June 1866), 2:297-98 (9 May 1867).

30 Full list in Morgan, *Memorials*, pp. 96-97. See also "Laying the Corner Stone of St. Thomas' Church," *The New York Herald* 33:289 (15 October 1868): 7. The descriptions of the Bible and Prayer Book that Dr. Morgan read were the same as those used for the contents of the first cornerstone in 1823: *An Account of the Ceremony Of Laying The Corner Stone Of St. Thomas' Church; Including The Addresses Delivered On That Occasion, Together with a Brief Statement Of The Rise Of That Church* (New York: T. and J. Swords, 1824), p. 7.

31 See above, chapter 2, note 20.

32 A full account of the opening of Saint Thomas, with excerpts of newspaper coverage, occupied the front page of *The Church Journal*. See "Opening of the New St. Thomas's Church," *The Church Journal* 18 (12 October 1870): 325.

33 W. F. Morgan, "The Dwelling-Place of Jesus," *Sermon Preached at the Opening of the New St. Thomas' Church, Cor. of 5th Ave and 53D St., October 6th, 1870. By William F. Morgan, D.D., Rector* (New York: American Church Press Co., 1870), pp. 6, 11, 20.

34 "Opening of the New St. Thomas's Church," *The Church Journal* 18 (12 October 1870):325, which quotes from *The Evening Post* of 5 October 1870. For further details of ecclesiology, see *The Centennial History of the Protestant Episcopal Church in the Diocese of New York: 1785- 1885*, ed. James Grant Wilson (New York: D. Appleton and Co., 1886), pp. 259-61. The word "ecclesiology" in Anglican usage at this time still meant primarily something like "the science and study of the building of churches," rather than its modern meaning of "theological reflection about the nature of the Church itself."

35 *Year Book* 1898, p. xxvii; E. Clowes Chorley, *Manuscript History of St. Thomas Church* (unpublished manuscript in Saint Thomas Archives, 1943; copy deposited in the St. Mark's Library of the General Theological Seminary, New York City), chapter 13, p. 7; see also "Opening of the New St. Thomas's Church," *The Church Journal* 18 (12 October 1870), which quotes from *The Evening Post* of 5 October 1870: "will accommodate 2000 persons."

36 "Opening of the New St. Thomas's Church," *The Church Journal* 18 (12 October 1870).

37 H. Barbara Weinberg, "John La Farge: Pioneer of the American Mural Movement," in Henry Adams, et al., *John La Farge* (Pittsburgh: Carnegie Museum of Art, 1987), pp. 172-73. These are now understood to be the correct titles of the La Farge murals, and not "Christ Healing the Sick" and "The Resurrection" as has at times been erroneously asserted.

38 "Opening of the New St. Thomas's Church," *The Church Journal* 18 (12 October 1870). See also Everard M. Upjohn, *Richard Upjohn: Architect and Churchman* (New York: Columbia University Press, 1939), pp. 178-80.

39 Chorley, *Manuscript History*, pp. 361-64.

CHAPTER 6

Mission in the City: The Free Chapel

WILLIAM FERDINAND MORGAN
SIXTH RECTOR, 1857-1888

RALPH HOYT, FREDERICK SILL, JOHN J. ROBERTS, ROBERT C. LOWRY
VICARS OF THE CHAPEL

B Y THE MIDDLE OF THE NINETEENTH century, the older New York families included the leading bankers, lawyers, and prosperous merchants, largely Dutch or British by descent, generally well educated, refined, and comparatively well-to-do. Such persons constituted the backbone of the Episcopal Church as well as of the Dutch Reformed and Presbyterian bodies. Although there was also a middle class occupied in smaller trades or as artisans, clerks, and domestic servants, the fact remained that nearly half the city's population were recent immigrants, wretchedly poor, often on the verge of starvation, with only rags to protect them. They were housed by the thousands in dark rear tenements devoid of even elementary sanitation. Whole families were crowded in cellars and garrets reeking with foul air; they had no social outlets save the saloons. These people had little hope, whether material or spiritual; their sense of God's love was little developed, and the Gospel had seldom if ever been preached to them.

It is a painful fact that the ministry of the Episcopal Church, indeed of most churches at this time, was directed to the socially privileged. Saint Thomas was no exception. Pews were sold at public auction, openly advertised in the papers and sold to the highest bidders, who often paid considerable sums. Unsold pews were also rented at substantial figures. When the income from these sources proved inadequate to meet regular current expenses, pew owners and pew renters were assessed to meet the deficit. After the fire of 1851, the pews in Saint Thomas were publicly auctioned, a set price having been fixed by the vestry, and none were sold below that price – which ran around $500. It was estimated that the sale value of all the pews in the rebuilt church of 1852 was $67,670, and that the annual rental was $5,429.[1] Obviously, the effect of all this was to shut out completely the middle and lower classes from the regular ministrations of the Church.

Bishop Benjamin T. Onderdonk, who in 1830 had succeeded Bishop Hobart, called pointed attention in his very first convention address to "the vast increase in this city of the number of those who are totally unable to provide themselves with the ministrations of religion, including many of our own communion, and of our sister Churches of England and Ireland, and the immense numbers among us who are the proper objects of that highest of Christian charities which cares for the souls of those who care not for their own."[2] Stirred by the bishop's words, the "New York Protestant Episcopal City Mission Society" had been created and incorporated under that name in 1831. Its purpose was "to provide, by building, purchase, hiring, or otherwise, at different points in the city of New York, churches in which the seats shall be free, and mission-houses for the poor and afflicted."[3] Within a year or two, three churches had been established by the society to carry out its intent. But still the bishop felt that only the surface had been scratched. Reporting on the consecration of these three churches, he took occasion to utter some plain but unpalatable truths:

> Thousands still wander through our streets, to whom the Gospel – its word and its Church – are as strange as if there were a broad wall of adamant between it and them. Our ordinary churches, so far from inviting, virtually exclude them. Let them, then, indulge me, when I say that, easy as they may feel in the enjoyment of those spiritual privileges for which they liberally pay in their well furnished places of worship, there rests upon them a heavy burden of responsibility touching the poor against whom these places are virtually barred.[4]

These were strong words and they had their effect. In 1832, St. Mary's, far up in the rural reaches of Manhattanville, declared itself a "free church." In 1844, the Rev. Dr. William Augustus Muhlenberg, a pioneer in so many directions, established in the heart of the city the Church of the Holy Communion where, from the first, all pews were free of rent or purchase. These two churches, together with the three city mission churches, went far to meet the spiritual needs of such persons as artisans, mechanics, and clerks.[5] There still remained, however, the very poor, the outcasts. It is quite remarkable that within three months of the beginning of his rectorship, there is evidence that Dr. Morgan was already deeply moved by the conditions among the dense population on the lower East Side of the city. Whether he was aware of the urgent and similar plea made from the pulpit of Saint Thomas back in 1855 by his predecessor Edmund Neville is unknown. Nevertheless, whatever the motivation, determined that something must be done, Dr. Morgan laid out his moves like a general planning a military campaign. The first step was to assess the actual conditions, and he therefore decided on a survey. To assist him, he chose the Rev. Ralph Hoyt (ill. 12).

Born in New York City, Mr. Hoyt had left school at the age of fourteen and worked for a time as a printer and then as a cabinet maker. He married

12. Ralph Hoyt, first Vicar of the Chapel 1858-59

when nineteen years old and passed through a variety of other occupations before answering a call to the ministry that he had long entertained. For five arduous years, he read privately for holy orders, supporting himself and his family by teaching and writing for various periodicals. His only recreation was poetry and his compositions eventually brought him some notoriety, with Edgar Allan Poe numbering among his intimates.[6]

From the day of his ordination to the diaconate at the age of thirty-five, Hoyt knew himself called to work among the poor. In 1846, he had established the Church of the Good Shepherd, situated in a very poor and neglected part of the city known as the Five Points district, a notorious haunt of vice and crime. His only assured support was a grant of $200 per year from Trinity Church. The place of worship was initially located on the second floor of a shabby structure that advertised a saloon on its street level. Within a short time, the congregation had grown sufficiently that it was received as a parish of the diocese. Over the next few years services were held from one rented hall to another in the neighborhood.

Meanwhile, Mr. Hoyt moved his growing family to Fort Lee, New Jersey, constrained by their health and the high rents of the city. Here he discovered another opportunity for missionary work and immediately set about organizing yet another new congregation, even building a small church largely with his own hands and furnishing it with the cast-offs of more opulent parishes. He named it the Church of the Good Shepherd, after his Five Points congregation, where his work had never ceased during all this time.

Such was the man whom Dr. Morgan now chose to assist him in the proposed survey. The survey took place through a period of five months and was made with great thoroughness. Its avowed purpose was to "ascertain the condition of the poor, bring children to Sunday school and adults to church, and to afford such temporal aid as circumstances might require or means allow." In making his report Mr. Hoyt described part of the district as "revealing a long succession of such mournful pictures of debased and suffering humanity as might well make angels weep, and Christians tremble under a sense of their responsibility." Through the aid of Dr. Morgan and the women of the parish, Mr. Hoyt was able to dispense food and medicine so that at least "a few families were saved from utter destitution and despair; a few children rescued from the paths of ruin."[7]

The scene of another neighboring area was pictured in these moving words:

The section comprises some 300 families, nearly all residing in rear buildings, in streets running from Grand to Bleecker Street. The history of the whole affords a painful prolongation of the same sad tale of sin, sorrow, and destitution, as those presented in the instances where you have made a personal inspection with your visitor. Estimating your district by the portion thus far examined, it will probably be found that there are 20,000 persons living in rear tenements, garrets, and cellars within its limits; and your own observation in many of these wretched abodes will, no doubt, justify the presumption, that more than half of this great number will need the helping hand of charity this Winter, to prevent their perishing by starvation.[8]

Mr. Hoyt described the appalling conditions found as a challenge. "There are great encouragements and great duties," he observed, "for St. Thomas's Church." He continued: "All those instances, of daily occurrence, in which the Rector or his representative, is enabled to befriend the stranger, minister to the widow, and the fatherless, breathe the sweet consolations of the Gospel at the bedside of the sick, or place a child under the benign influences of the Sunday school; all these are great compensations for untiring zeal even in this sterile field."[9]

After a careful study of the survey, Dr. Morgan concluded that it would be impossible to induce such people to attend in any appreciable number the services of the parish church. Likewise, he realized that Saint Thomas had no provision whatever for the large numbers of children who might flock to a Sunday school. He was therefore convinced, as was Mr. Hoyt, that "a system of parochial ragged schools, and the establishment of numerous free chapels for public worship, would alone afford the means of adequately meeting these imperative demands of humanity, morals, and religion."[10]

The rector thereupon proposed that Saint Thomas Church undertake to found a "Free Mission Chapel." The district surrounding the parish location at Broadway and Houston, he told the vestry, "has greatly changed in the character of its population within a few years past and now in many of its streets, lanes and other localities presents a legitimate and most inviting field for missionary effort." The task involved relieving the "spiritual destitution" and reclaiming or improving "a neighborhood now very generally surrendered to vice and irreligion." With enthusiasm the rector issued his call, and with enthusiasm the vestry responded, even though the parish itself faced a diminishing congregation and a deficit in current accounts. A resolution passed by the vestry on April 9, 1858, stated: "That the Rector, Wardens and Vestry of St. Thomas' Church, strongly impressed with the desirableness and urgency of such missionary work, will, of ourselves and according to our ability, contribute and will exert our influence that the Congregation of St. Thomas shall contribute to the prosecution of this work."[11]

A committee, consisting of the rector, one warden, and Messrs. George Gillespie, George Duyckinck, and John Tappan, was appointed to care for the finances of the project. It was further determined that four collections should be taken every year in the parish church to pay for the expenses of the chapel. It was hoped that these collections would be enough to pay the stipends of the missionary, the organist, and the sexton.[12]

In a noble sermon preached at the very time that it began to look to him and to others that a change in location for the parish itself was inevitable, Dr. Morgan presented to his congregation the solemn duty that remained:

> I stand before you this day, beloved, to utter a plea for Jesus Christ, and His flock scattered through the lower wards of this city, "as sheep having no shepherd." . . . In Christ's name, I ask you to recognize, watch over and sustain The Free Chapel of St. Thomas's Church. . . . There is a stirring and emotional Christianity sometimes to be witnessed in cultivated circles and perfumed boudoirs, which weeps plentifully over the hardships and sacrifices of missionary life in far off latitudes, while the ignorant and neglected, and the comfortless of its own neighborhood are anything but objects of pathetic interest; nay, are suffered remorselessly to live and die in a darkness more dense than that of heathendom. . . . [While] Pastors and churches are rapidly deserting the lower wards of the city and thereby surrendering tens of thousands to spiritual neglect. . . . The question is, can *we afford to leave any portion of our vast Metropolis Churchless and Christless*; can we afford to migrate and leave behind neither messengers, nor means of grace? We think not. Remove as far up as you will. Build your mansions and your temples as far beyond the reach of uproar and secularity, as the limits of this island will permit, but unless you plant the torch lights of religious truth and knowledge in the sections you desert, then the surges of ignorance and impiety and insurrection will overtake you, wherever you are.[13]

The response to Dr. Morgan's appeal was immediate, not merely in the realm of financial aid but also in personal service, another tradition that would be maintained throughout the years to come. At the corner of Prince and Thompson Streets, there stood a church building formerly occupied by the Church of the Annunciation. When that institution had moved to Fourteenth Street, its building was for a time used by the short-lived Emmanuel Church. It was now at the point of being transformed into a stable. In 1858, Dr. Morgan rented the building as a place to start his projected Free Chapel (ill. 13). The Corporation of Trinity Church, now as always generous in assuming extra-parochial responsibilities, agreed to contribute $800 a year toward the rent.[14] Dr. Morgan now invited Mr. Hoyt to take on the charge of that chapel also, at a stipend of $600 a year, more than he had ever before received in his ministry.[15] The following notice accordingly appeared in the church press:

> This Chapel will be open for Divine Service, on Sunday next in the morning, at half-past 10, and in the afternoon at half-past 3. The sessions of the Sunday School will be at 9 A.M. and half-past 2 P.M. The seats in this Chapel are FREE, and all persons in the neighborhood, and others interested in the success of this religious enterprise, are affectionately invited to attend. The Rev. Ralph Hoyt, will for the present officiate at the Chapel, as assistant to the Rector.
>
> William F. Morgan, D.D.,
>
> Rector of S. Thomas's church[16]

On Sunday, May 2, 1858, the chapel was duly opened for public worship. From the first, the venture was a success. "It certainly can no longer be said that the Church in this city is unmindful of its duty to the poor," declared a church periodical in reporting on the chapel at the end of the year. The "quiet but energetic and unceasing devotion" of the rector and the members of the Saint Thomas congregation to "practical Christianity" was praised.[17] Mr. Hoyt gave of himself unsparingly. His annual report indicated clearly the principles governing the operation of the chapel:

1. The full services of the Church on Sunday, Wednesdays, Fridays, and the Festivals, with regular preaching of the Gospel and due enforcement of Christian truth: each celebration being attended by increasing congregations, many of whom have heretofore been neglectful of all religious duty. It is indeed an important feature of a Church Mission, properly conducted, that it attracts by its open doors, and liberal disinterestedness, many who would never enter a more restricted place of worship. Every shade of New York life and character is thus represented at the service of St. Thomas's Chapel; – from persons of the highest respectability, education and refinement, down to those whom ignorance, poverty and dissipation have driven beyond all hope, save that declared by Him whose mercy is thus extended even to the outcasts of the world.

2. The daily visitations of a minister of Christ around the district, bearing divine

13. The first Free Chapel of Saint Thomas, Prince and Thompson Streets (1858)

consolation, instruction, reproof, and temporal aid where needed; always ready for an errand of mercy, yet never obtrusive; dispensing freely, yet demanding nothing: sympathy for the poor; hope for the desponding; prayer for the sick; consolation for the dying; and Christian burial for the dead.

3. *The Sunday School.* – Here are gathered companies of little ones from many homes where destitution and evil example would soon, but for this counteracting effort, give them that fatal moral misdirection which leads inevitably to crime and death. Much good has already been effected in this department of the chapel work, by the active faithfulness of the Superintendent, and the assistant teachers.

4. The labors and liberality of ladies of St. Thomas's Church, in devoting much time and expense in preparing garments for the destitute; by which means a large number of persons have been comfortably clad and enabled to attend the chapel services during the inclement seasons of the year. This diligent exertion has been unmentioned by themselves; but the results have gladdened many a sad heart, and they entitle the "Ladies Society" to our sincerest thanks and highest commendation.

5. *An Industrial School* is now commenced, for the purpose of gathering children into working classes, and training them to habits of industry; while they will also be taught useful lessons in morals and religion.[18]

It must be borne in mind that Mr. Hoyt was at this time involved in mission work in three distinct areas: Fort Lee, the city mission, and now the Free Chapel. This proved too much for even his superabundant energies and, in June of 1859, he resigned the Free Chapel. He was succeeded by the Rev. Frederick Sill, who, like himself, was esteemed for his "pastoral fidelity." This concern was highlighted in an article in *The Church Journal* describing a Christmas service in 1859 for the poor of the chapel and of the parish church. "Churchmen have seldom witnessed a sight equal to that which was enjoyed at the Mission Rooms of S. Thomas's chapel, on Saturday noon last," declared the periodical. It reported, in the language of that era, that Mr. Sill briefly spoke of "the great affection which the Church has for all her members, both of high and low degree," and then, after a few prayers, invited each of those present to come forward to receive a Christmas gift. When a name was called, "the Ladies filled his or her basket" with chickens, bread, tea, cakes of soap, and, in some cases, a pair of shoes. Some seventy families in attendance enjoyed this Christmas favor and several baskets were sent out to others who were unable to attend. Among those gathered for the occasion was "one bright little boy," readers were told, "whose great grandfather was organist to Bishop White for 40 years." It was this Bishop William White who had presided at the laying of the cornerstone of the first Saint Thomas Church back in 1824.[19]

Building on the foundation so well laid by Mr. Hoyt, Mr. Sill was able to report a gradual and healthy increase both in numbers and in interest. In 1860, the chapel had 88 communicants, more than the mother parish counted at the beginning. The following year, in 1861, the number of communicants increased to 151; a total of 45 had been presented for Confirmation, and 112 had been baptized. The chapel was evidently reaching the children of the slums. The financial statement for 1861 reveals that out of their poverty the people of the Free Chapel were already making some contribution to missionary work beyond their own limits. In 1864, Mr. Sill noted with satisfaction the addition of 17 communicants from the Church of England, evidence that the chapel was successful in attracting immigrants. Mr. Sill summed up the total results of five years of ministry in the district, reporting the baptisms of 68 adults and 485 children, the confirmations of 215 persons, the addition of 417 communicants, and the performance of 154 marriages and 403 burials.[20]

It is plain from this report that already the chapel was fulfilling exactly the mission and ministry that Dr. Morgan and the vestry of Saint Thomas had intended for it. But now history took a different course. In 1864, the chapel building, which the parish had heretofore rented, was ordered by the courts to be sold. The property was purchased by Henry Weil who, in turn, sold it to Mr. Sill at a reduced price, but on condition of an advance of $1,000. This sum was made up by supporters of the chapel in the course of a week and the remaining balance was paid at an annual interest of six percent by a member of the vestry, Mr. George C. Collins, who now held the property in his name on behalf of the chapel congregation. His timely offer, together with the earlier contributions of friends, saved the mission for the present.[21]

However, as it turned out, Mr. Sill had other plans. He had already determined to purchase the chapel building and to organize an independent congregation with funds gathered for that purpose. Eventually, in order to avoid unseemly controversy and litigation, it was agreed that the property should be conveyed to the congregation on payment of the cost incurred by Mr. Collins.[22] A new parish was incorporated with this action in 1867, with Mr. Sill as its rector and no longer nurtured by Saint Thomas. It took the name of St. Ambrose and continued to function until 1885, when it was taken over by the City Mission Society.

The way to the second building of the Free Chapel of Saint Thomas was now already facilitated by its very first missioner, Mr. Hoyt. His effort to maintain a free church in the Five Points area had not been successful. He had therefore sought another section of the city in which to establish a mission, and found it uptown in 1855 in the neighborhood of East Fifty-fourth Street between Second and Third Avenues. Mr. Hoyt described it at the time as "a frontier garrison, situated in an uninviting, hostile neighborhood, and almost surrounded by breweries and manufactories." There he secured a plot of ground one hundred feet square, on which he was determined "with the divine blessing to erect a free church where all may benefit as well for the body as the soul."[23] The project had the approval of Bishop Horatio Potter, who was as deeply concerned as his predecessor Bishop Onderdonk that the Episcopal Church should extend its reach. For several years this new Good Shepherd Free Church struggled along under the watchful care of Mr. Hoyt, bearing the same name as his other congregations. Finally, in 1868, Mr. Hoyt suggested that Saint Thomas lease this chapel.[24]

Had Dr. Morgan been a man of less faith and vision, his response would undoubtedly have been negative. It was a difficult time in the life of the parish. Nearly two years before, the old church at Houston Street and Broadway had been closed. The financial collapse of 1857 was still fresh in memory. The twelve months during which the parish had enjoyed the hospitality of Grace Church had come to an end. When Mr. Hoyt advanced his proposition, the congregation itself was meeting in the temporary chapel erected within the incomplete walls of the new Fifth Avenue church. But the rector was quick to sense the opportunity of linking the parish in its new home with mission work in that part of the upper East Side which lay between Fifth Avenue and the East River. His people were about to take possession of a church of exceptional beauty, adorned with all the adjuncts of splendid worship. He fully realized the ever-present danger that the parish could become self-centered, made up of respectable people comfortable in their religion. Such danger would be lessened by the creation of new mission work among the poor, within the confines of the parish, for which the people of the parish would make themselves responsible.

Early in 1868, therefore, the parish took over this Church of the Good Shepherd and renamed it Saint Thomas Chapel. The first service under the new auspices was held on Sunday evening, March 29, 1868, and was conducted by the Rev. J. F. Butterworth, assistant at the parish church, and the Rev. J. B. C. Beaubien, who was to be in charge of the work of the chapel. The sermon was preached by Dr. Morgan from the text, "Bear ye one another's burdens, and so fulfill the law of Christ" (Galatians 6:2). In this sermon, Dr. Morgan paid high and deserved tribute to the pioneer work of the Rev. Ralph Hoyt. "The prospects of the Mission are very inspiring," reported the church press. "It has been undertaken with the warm approval of the Bishop, and with the intention, on the part of S. Thomas's parish, of making it a centre of earnest Missionary and Church work."[25]

So began the life of the second free chapel. As its activities expanded, Dr. Morgan had one of his flashes of strategic genius. The continuance and success of the work depended upon the interest taken in it by the laity of Saint Thomas who, after all, had to provide the funds. As far back as April 30, 1863, Dr. Morgan had organized the younger men of the parish into a society, the aim of which was to contribute to the support of patients in St. Luke's Hospital. Now Dr. Morgan invited this same group to sponsor the work of this mission chapel. The name of the group was accordingly changed to the "St. Thomas' Association for Parish Work." Its first president was William I. Peake. The devoted work of these men constitutes one of the brightest chapters in the history of the parish. Not only were they successful in raising funds for the chapel; they also and more importantly took an active part in its work, giving their time and interest to its manifold activities of worship and outreach. The Association was represented at every service held in the chapel; its members conducted Bible classes, superintended the Sunday School, organized clubs for men, and assisted the vicar in his house-to-house visitations. It proved one of the best moves for practical Christianity Dr. Morgan ever made.[26]

Mr. Beaubien's stay as minister there was brief. In October of his first year at the second chapel, the very month that the cornerstone of the new Saint Thomas was being laid, Mr. Beaubien left and was succeeded by the Rev. John J. Roberts. Soon Dr. Morgan was able to report that the work at the chapel was flourishing, with large congregations attending the services and with a threefold increase of pupils in the Sunday School. Mr. Roberts was diligent in his pastoral visitations and contributed much to the success of the plan by the cottage meetings he developed. "The Mission is deemed eminently prosperous," the readers of *The Church Journal* were informed, "and its advance is attributed chiefly, under God, to the plan adopted of preaching from house to house." Such efforts, it was reported, "appear to have been crowned with success."[27]

In 1871, however, the lease of the property occupied by the chapel expired and the property was sold by the owner. As temporary measures, the use of the public school on East Fifty-first Street was secured for the Sunday School, with Brevoort Hall on East Fifty-fourth Street for the morning services. Evening services were held in the Lenten Chapel of the new parish church.[28]

The Association immediately began to lay plans for some better provision. In December of that year, vestryman George Kemp offered to donate $15,000 for the purchase of three lots on East Sixtieth Street, between Second and Third Avenues. The offer was accepted, the Association set about raising funds, and on October 4, 1872, Bishop Horatio Potter laid the cornerstone of this, the third Free Chapel of Saint Thomas. Construction proceeded and, at a total cost for land and building of about $33,500, the building was completed (ill. 14). This money had been raised almost entirely by the efforts of the men of the Association.[29]

On Saturday, December 21, 1872, the feast of Saint Thomas, the new chapel was consecrated by Bishop Potter with appropriate ceremonies. In his

14. The third Free Chapel of Saint Thomas, East Sixtieth Street between Second and Third Avenues (consecrated 1872)

sermon on the occasion, the bishop pointed out that, in the absence of the visible presence of Christ, we have "His visible Church – His mystical Body, filled with His Spirit . . . His ministers, bearing His commission, and in His name dispensing the Word of God and His holy sacraments." The bishop therefore explained that "the worship and work of this Chapel is for the creating and supporting of Faith in the unseen Lord." The "poor, weary, anxious soul" who passes through its doors will find time and time again "the secret emotions of love, of desire, of sorrow for sin, of thanksgiving, breathe out in whispers, 'My Lord and My God'." The purpose of the chapel, he asserted, "is to do for thousands in this neighborhood what the visible presence of our Lord did for Saint Thomas: awaken a living, operative, purifying faith in the risen, all merciful-Saviour!"[30]

This new chapel was a building of no architectural pretensions, but it was adequate for its purpose, with a seating capacity of six hundred and a room that could accommodate two hundred children for the Sunday School. The Association presented the vestry of the church with a deed of the lots and the building, declaring it to be the mind of the donors that the property be maintained as a free mission chapel, and stating clearly that if it should ever seem desirable to sell the property, the proceeds should be invested in one or more mission churches in the city of New York.[31] In December of 1873, Mr. Roberts was succeeded by the Rev. Robert C. Lowry, under whom the work of the chapel was to see further expansion.

Thus Saint Thomas Church, in its new home since 1870, was now able to raise this considerable sum for a purely missionary venture. The Free Chapel of Saint Thomas had become a stable institution, an integral part of the life of the parish. That this was so is evidence of the spirit of charity and missionary enterprise that pervaded the parish, and of the foresight and spiritual leadership of William Ferdinand Morgan. It was a vision, a spirit of mission and outreach, that, once secured, the parish would never lose.

Notes

1 VM 2:131-32 (3 November 1851), 2:142 (22 March 1852), 2:171-72 (13 April 1854); E. Clowes Chorley, *Manuscript History of St. Thomas Church* (unpublished manuscript in Saint Thomas Archives, 1943; copy deposited in the St. Mark's Library of the General Theological Seminary,

New York City), pp. 303-4.

2 New York *Convention Journal*, 1831, p. 33.

3 *The Centennial History of the Protestant Episcopal Church in the Diocese of New York: 1785-1885*, ed. James Grant Wilson (New York: D. Appleton and Co., 1886), pp. 389-92.

4 New York *Convention Journal*, 1834, pp. 30-31. The word "adamant" originally denoted a hard, impenetrable substance, and often referred to the diamond.

5 The free city missions were the Churches of the Epiphany, the Holy Evangelists, and St. Matthew.

6 See, for example, Ralph Hoyt, *Echoes of Memory and Emotion* (New York: A. D. F. Randolph, 1861), of which there is a copy in the New-York Historical Society.

7 "Report from the Rev. Mr. Hoyt," *The Church Journal* 5 (4 November 1857): 322; *The Church Journal* 6 (3 March 1858): 42. Mr. Hoyt was not a stranger to the parish. His city mission had received earlier a contribution from the vestry and in the interim after the resignation of Dr. Neville he had taken occasional services in Saint Thomas: VM 2:193 (17 November 1856); 2:198 (4 March 1857).

8 "New York," *The Church Journal* 5 (2 December 1857): 354.

9 "New York," *The Church Journal* 5 (2 December 1857): 354.

10 "Report from the Rev. Mr. Hoyt," *The Church Journal* 6 (3 March 1858): 42.

11 VM 2:207-8 (9 April 1858).

12 VM 2:207-8 (9 April 1858).

13 "The Messengers of the Churches," *Sermon Preached in St. Thomas' Church, On the First Sunday After Trinity, June 6, 1858. By the Rector* (New York: E.B. Clayton's Sons, 1858), pp. 3-4, 8, 11, 14. The number of churches open and ministering in the lower wards of New York City had decreased strikingly between the years 1825 and 1857. By the latter year, the lower six wards of the city sheltered a population of about 100,000 people; in the same districts were to be found 2,000 places selling liquor and 400 houses of ill repute.

14 VM 2:208 (9 April 1858), 2:208-9 (7 May 1858). Trinity Church responded to an appeal from the Saint Thomas vestry for aid in its mission work.

15 VM 2:209 (7 May 1858).

16 "New York," *The Church Journal* 6 (5 May 1858): 113.

17 "New York," *The Church Journal* 6 (29 December 1858): 386.

18 "New York, Report of the Rev. Ralph Hoyt, April 30, 1859," *The Church Journal* 7 (11 May 1859): 122.

19 VM 2:215 (25 June 1859); "New York," *The Church Journal* 7 (12 July 1859): 195; "New York," *The Church Journal* 7 (28 December 1859): 386.

20 "New York," *The Church Journal* 8 (4 November 1860): 337; "New York," *The Church Journal* 9 (24 July 1861): 209; "New York," *The Church Journal* 12 (27 July 1864): 218.

21 "New York," *The Church Journal* 12 (27 July 1864): 219; "New York," *The Church Journal* 14 (5 December 1866): 370.

22 VM 2:276 (18 May 1866), 2:290 (10 November 1866). The eighth ward in which the new parish was located numbered some 40,000 inhabitants in 1867, and Mr. Sill was almost the only clergyman resident in the area; see "New York," *The Church Journal* 15 (24 July 1867): 216.

23 Chorley, *Manuscript History*, p. 377.

24 VM 2:300-1 (8 February 1868), 2:302 (16 February 1868).

25 "New York," *The Church Journal* 16 (15 April 1868): 105.

26 A printed pamphlet of 1868, kept in the Saint Thomas Archives, contains the constitution

and by-laws of the Association, the object of which was "to perform such work in the Parish as may from time to time be required from the lay members."

27 "St. Thomas's Mission of 'The Good Shepherd'," *The Church Journal* 17 (17 February 1869): 50; New York *Convention Journal*, 1868, p. 204; 1870, p. 155. In his chapel report for 1870, Mr. Roberts reported: "The morning congregations are large – the Sunday School has been well attended; and the results of the work quite visible in the neighborhood of the Chapel."

28 "St. Thomas's Chapel of the Good Shepherd," *The Church Journal* 19 (8 March 1871): 75. The vicar of the chapel reported that Brevoort Hall "is not popular as a place of worship. The worshippers in general and the communicants are not as numerous as when I made my last report." Cf. New York *Convention Journal*, 1871, p. 162.

29 VM 3:49-50 (8 May 1872); "City News," *The Church Journal* 20 (10 October 1872): 439.

30 "Faith in the Seen and in the Unseen." *A Sermon Preached at the Consecration of St. Thomas' Chapel, New York, On the Feast of St. Thomas the Apostle, Saturday, December 21, 1872, By Horatio Potter, D.D., LL.D, D.C.L., Bishop of New York* (New York: St. Thomas Association for Parish Work, 1873), pp. 17, 19-20. Bishop Potter also noted (p. 7): "The faith and courage with which this work was conceived and undertaken, and the vigor with which it has been carried on to its completion, speak well for the spirit of the young men and their co-workers in St. Thomas' Church."

31 "Consecration of St. Thomas's Chapel," *The Church Journal and Gospel Messenger* [formerly *The Church Journal*] 20 (26 December 1872): 567. Dr. Morgan reported in 1872: "The charities of the Parish have been well sustained, and very liberal contributions given to objects beyond. Thirty-two thousand and five hundred dollars have been pledged and nearly paid, by members of the Parish, toward the erection of a new Mission Chapel on East 60th Street": New York *Convention Journal*, 1872, p. 162.

❧ CHAPTER 7

The Second Golden Age

WILLIAM FERDINAND MORGAN
SIXTH RECTOR, 1857-1888

HOUSED IN A MAGNIFICENT new church at one of the most strategic locations in New York, Saint Thomas was now to enter upon a second and even greater golden age. Fresh life soon filled the building, and the beauty of holiness now permeated the worship. From the very beginning the most careful attention was given to the ordering of the services, with, according to Dr. Morgan, "a view to greater impressiveness."[1] In this was set a tradition, from which the parish has seldom if ever deviated, of offering the Prayer Book service at its best. With the encouragement of Dr. Morgan, as the parish entered a new era in a new building, particular attention also began to be paid to music, and the finest music possible was sought for God's service.

Up until the opening of the third church at Fifth Avenue and Fifty-third, published comments about music at Saint Thomas do not indicate much out of the ordinary, even though by the 1850s about one-fifth of the annual budget was being spent for that purpose. But at the opening of the new Saint Thomas Church, on October 6, 1870, *The Evening Mail* jubilantly declared that "the music, to say the least, was superb."[2] This was the first service at which George William Warren officiated as organist, and it marked the beginning of a stellar thirty years of music at the church. From this point on, music became a particularly outstanding feature of the services.

George William Warren was born in Albany in 1828. In 1870, therefore, he was in the prime of life. Largely self-taught in music, he had been successively organist at St. Peter's and St. Paul's churches in Albany. During the decade from 1860 to 1870, he was at Holy Trinity, Brooklyn, where he made for himself a great reputation. His call to Saint Thomas was an indication that the rector and vestry had determined to have in their new church the best music available. The old Hall and Labagh organ had been completely rebuilt by Hilbourne Roosevelt, resulting in a four-manual instrument that was considered one of the largest and best in the United States at the time.

In its coverage of the opening service, *The Evening Mail* had this to say:

They were very careful and particular in the selection of voices, as it was fully determined that the music of St. Thomas' should not be excelled by any in the city or vicinity, and they have met with complete success. The choir consists of a quartette of soloists. . . . In addition to these singers, there is a volunteer chorus of ladies, gentlemen and boys, twenty-five in all – and all selected voices. Mr. Warren is also assisted at the organ by Mr. P. Auguste Schnecker, deputy organist; and on the occasion of these opening services by Mr. Toulmin, harpist to the New York Philharmonic Society. . . . The places for the choir being in the choir proper on either side of the chancel, the members can enjoy the services and privileges of the pulpit and enter into their part of the service with a fervor that the ordinary isolation of the organ-loft rarely inspires. They were not, and will not be surpliced.[3]

Though the latter statement that the choir "will not be surpliced" would subsequently bear emendation, the liturgical importance of music would never be neglected at Saint Thomas in the able hands of Dr. Warren. Testimony agrees that Dr. Warren was a person of sterling character, to whom music was essentially a religious vocation. He was an accomplished organist and an excellent organizer of choirs and trainer of voices, and under his direction the music was superbly rendered. In the selection of that music, however, he was perhaps less gifted. The dominant school in church music of that day was the flamboyant school of Dudley Buck and George F. Le Jeune, and to that school Dr. Warren belonged. This no doubt assured more popularity than if he had followed a more severely classical tradition. "Colorful and popular," says one historian, "but devoid of taste."[4]

Dr. Warren was not unfamiliar with composition. For the Jubilee Service of the parish in 1873, he composed a *Te Deum Laudamus* and *Benedictus* dedicated to the rector, wardens, and vestry. A newspaper reported that the music on this occasion was "of the highest excellence" and that "the choir certainly has not only ample material and finish, but also delicate and rich expression."[5] In 1888, Harper and Brothers published a volume called *Hymns and Tunes as Sung at St. Thomas's Church, New York*, the music of which was composed and adapted by Dr. Warren. Of Warren's various tunes, only one, the setting to "God of Our Fathers, Whose Almighty Hand," survives in modern hymnals. The trumpet fanfares, which were its original glory, have been restored to it in the Episcopal Church's *Hymnal 1982*, where it still appears, under his name, as number 718.[6]

The enhancement of the musical program was paralleled by augmentations of other kinds. Already from 1856 on, the parish had enjoyed the services of an assistant minister. The congregation had grown steadily since the parish moved to Fifth Avenue, however, and an increasing number of young people were being attracted to its services. By 1876, Dr. Morgan felt that an assistant of mature experience and a preacher of distinction was now needed. He accordingly invited the Rev. Frederick Courtney, a priest of the Church of England and vicar of St. Jude's Church in Glasgow, Scotland, to visit New York. As a result of that visit, Mr. Courtney was invited to become assistant minister of the parish. Dr. Morgan, with his accustomed unselfishness and eye for strategy, surrendered $2,000 of his stipend to make the position of assistant attractive to a man of such quality.[7]

Mr. Courtney's special charge became the Sunday afternoon service. Gifted with a melodious voice, and master of a pure English style, he was an unusually attractive preacher. And so it became something of the vogue to attend Evening Prayer at Saint Thomas. Every seat in the church was occupied, and crowds often stood in the aisles and around the doors. This highly successful ministry continued until Easter of 1880, when Mr. Courtney left to become rector of the Church of St. James in Chicago. He was afterwards elected fifth Bishop of Nova Scotia.[8]

In 1875, the parish suffered a considerable loss in the death of George C. Collins, who had been a member of the vestry since 1852, who had served as chairman of the building committee and as parish treasurer, and whose liberality to the parish was admirable. "Few have walked before God more unblamably," the vestry said in grateful tribute, "or have sought more conscientiously to adorn the doctrine of God their Saviour in all things."[9]

Thirteen years elapsed between the completion of the church and its consecration. At the time of its completion, there remained a debt of $300,000, which was gradually reduced to $130,000. In 1882, Dr. Morgan and the vestry set out to raise the remaining sum and to free the church for consecration. At the beginning of 1883 there still existed a mortgage for $60,000 held by the Manhattan Life Insurance Company. On Palm Sunday of that year, a new effort was made to pay off this debt, and by Sunday, May 6, nearly the whole amount had been raised, with two hundred members of the congregation subscribing toward the fund. This in itself is evidence of the great change in parish finances which the move to Fifth Avenue had effected. A few years earlier the raising of such a sum by the parish would have been inconceivable.[10]

The day appointed for the consecration of the third church was Tuesday, May 15, 1883. In the absence of the venerable Bishop Horatio Potter from the infirmities of old age, the Rt. Rev. Henry Adams Neely, Bishop of Maine and former vicar of Trinity Chapel, New York, acted as consecrator, assisted by the Rt. Rev. John Scarborough, Bishop of New Jersey. Among the distinguished clergy present in the sanctuary were Henry Codman Potter of Grace Church, Morgan Dix of Trinity, Samuel Cooke of St. Bartholomew's, and Henry Yates Satterlee of Calvary, all representing parishes which had historic connections with Saint Thomas Church. Two former assistants of the parish, Frederick Courtney and Frank L. Norton, were present. With Dr.

Morgan were his assistant, Alexander Mackay-Smith, and two of the chapel clergy, Robert Lowry and Roland E. Grueber.

The bishops and clergy moved up the center aisle, reciting Psalm 122. Morning Prayer was said by the Rev. Drs. Cooke, Courtney, Potter, and Dix. Bishop Scarborough commenced the Communion Service. The Instrument of Donation was read by Mr. John H. Watson, clerk of the vestry; the Sentence of Consecration by Dr. Morgan. The sermon, preached by the Rt. Rev. William Bacon Stevens, Bishop of Pennsylvania, touched upon the past, the building, the people, and the future. Of the past, he said: "Nearly sixty years ago the first Bishop of Pennsylvania, the venerable Bishop White, laid the cornerstone of your first edifice at the corner of Broadway and Houston Street in what was then a rural suburb of the city; and now again another Bishop of Pennsylvania preaches the Consecration Sermon on the completion of this magnificent pile of buildings." Of the building, he said: "It is strong, and it is beautiful, as the work of a human architect. What we want now, is, that the life within these walls, the living stones, may be built by the Divine Architect, the Holy Ghost, into a living temple." Of the people, he said: "The devout people who worship here ever rejoice in God's goodness and shout aloud his praises and the beauty of holiness; and may this edifice prove to many successive generations of worshipers as they pass in long procession through these courts none other but the house of God and the very gate of heaven." And of the future, he concluded by predicting that "the next three score years will witness changes and growth in Church life and Church work and Church power which will far outstrip what has been done between 1823 and 1883."[11] A veritable "gate of heaven" had been established. The offering that day was designated for the missionary work of the parish.

The origins of the famous "Easter Parade" were associated with the new Saint Thomas Church of the mid-1880s, as the well-dressed and affluent began the custom of strolling along Fifth Avenue in their Easter finery to carry the altar flowers to the sick at St. Luke's Hospital one block to the north.[12] The practical Christian duty to less privileged members of society also continued to be a prominent feature of parish life as evidenced by the active labors of Saint Thomas Chapel. In December of 1873, Mr. Roberts had resigned as vicar, and was succeeded by the Rev. Robert C. Lowry, who gave the chapel a stability of administration which had been somewhat lacking. At the time of his arrival, the district for which the chapel was responsible extended from Fifth Avenue to the East River, and from Fiftieth to Seventy-second Streets. Mr. Lowry noted that there were only three or four families of wealth in the congregation, while one-third of them came from "very humble walks of life, and two-thirds were dependent on daily labor for support." The ministry of this chapel, *The Church Journal* announced in 1875, was the only "religious instruction" many of the residents of the East Side ever received. "*St. Thomas' Church,*" the periodical observed, "cannot be classed among the parishes which exist but to provide the wealthy fashionable with Church architecture, music and oratory after the best style. It is abundant in good works."[13] In the previous year, Dr. Morgan had reported that the Sunday School of the chapel was "ranked among the largest in the city," numbering 319 pupils.[14]

The social ministry of Saint Thomas was greatly dependent upon the energetic support of the women of the parish. In 1872 the Ladies' Employment Society was founded by Mrs. W. F. Morgan, the wife of the rector, "to help the industrious poor, and save them from being paupers, by supplying them with work." The Industrial School was organized by Mrs. Annie Rutherford Dahlgren in 1876 and met on Saturday mornings, teaching poor young girls to sew and training them to be self-supporting. Three years later, the "Helping Hand Association" was established to provide for the spiritual wants of women and to offer counsel, sponsoring mothers' meetings and a maternity society. In its first year an average of sixty women from the East Side participated in the organization's activities and several mothers were confirmed in the church; the same period saw the baptisms of seventeen children. This organization was inspired by Mrs. T. P. Cummings and Miss Harriet Fellowes, and took an important role under the leadership of Mrs. Elizabeth H. Cullum. The last two of these organizations alone, according to the Rev. Mr. Lowry, were responsible for making the location and services of the chapel widely known and also for increasing the enrollment of the Sunday School to the limit of its capacity. The appointment of a "Parish Visitor" for Saint Thomas Chapel in 1878, a lay woman named Miss Lisa Lovell, also proved indispensable to the mission work. Each week the Visitor made personal calls among the neighborhood population, bringing to Mr. Lowry's attention "cases of destitution, children who were unbaptized, and families neglecting Church Services." He, in turn, followed up these weekly reports with his own visitations, conducting in one year nearly nine hundred parochial and sick visits. Over the next forty-seven years a select company of women faithfully ministered in the important post of Parish Visitor, taking the initiative on behalf of Saint Thomas to offer a ministry of the Gospel in a city that sorely needed their gifts and help.[15]

At the close of nearly a decade on Fifth Avenue, Dr. Morgan could only express gratitude for the parish's growth and outreach,[16] and this was well illustrated in the foundation of Saint Thomas House. So great was the increase of the Sunday School at the chapel that additional room had become imperative. Again the Saint Thomas Association took the lead and authorized Dr. Morgan to purchase lots in the rear of the chapel for $8,000. Mr.

James Fargo, a member of the vestry, contributed half of this in memory of his mother, and the balance was to be raised by subscription.[17]

The problem of the actual cost of the building was met in a beautiful way. Henry Keep Flower, a young man of brilliant promise, had recently died at the age of fifteen. His parents, Roswell and Sara Flower, were members of the parish (and Roswell, it is interesting to note, later became the governor of New York). They communicated to Dr. Morgan their desire to erect a building, to be known as Saint Thomas House, as a memorial to their son, making an initial contribution for this purpose of $35,000, and, when this proved insufficient, making up the deficit. The couple had also already given $5,000 in bonds, to be known as the "Henry Keep Flower Memorial Fund," the interest of which was to be spent by the minister of the chapel for the benefit of the worthy poor who were worshipers there or were connected with its charitable agencies.[18]

The architect of Saint Thomas House was Mr. Charles C. Haight, a member of Trinity Parish and of a family great in the ecclesiastical annals of New York. The quality of his architecture is evidenced in the Chapel of the Good Shepherd at the General Theological Seminary, which can still be seen inside the Close of Chelsea Square. The house he now designed for Saint Thomas at 229 East Fifty-ninth Street was a brownstone structure of four floors with basement. Within it, full provision was made for the expanding social and religious activities. It contained a lecture hall, a reading room, a library, rooms for the Sunday School and for the various charitable organizations, and a day school for poor children. The building was described as "a noble structure, solid and capacious," the ultimate cost of land and building being nearly $50,000. It was dedicated by Dr. Morgan at a service held on Thursday, December 14, 1882, and a tablet commemorating the Flower Memorial was placed in the vestibule.[19]

In these years, the neighborhood of the chapel was inhabited for the most part by an immigrant population, largely German and mostly laborers. Therefore, in 1882, the Rev. Roland E. Grueber, a priest of German descent able to minister in German, was added to the chapel staff to work especially with this group. In official publications of the parish, he was called the "German Pastor." Five years later, he reported 77 German-speaking communicants and a Sunday School of 120 pupils. Initially, the mission made use of a neighboring hall on Sunday mornings, and later Saint Thomas House was designated especially for the use of the German congregation.[20]

In the spring of 1884, some members of the Young Ladies' Foreign Missionary Society of the parish church determined to establish a school for the Chinese who were beginning to move into the vicinity of the chapel. The project had been first suggested nine years earlier, but now the time appeared ripe for the endeavor. As a result, a Chinese Sunday School began on Sunday the fourth of May of that year.[21] It started with five teachers, only some of whom already had experience in such teaching, and three pupils, the number of which eventually rose to an average of nineteen. The sessions were held in Saint Thomas House where each of the pupils had a personal teacher, whose job was first of all to teach spoken and written English. After this, the students learned the Lord's Prayer, the Creed, and the Ten Commandments. The first head of the school was Mr. Francis Lister Hawks Pott, a grandson and namesake of the third rector of Saint Thomas and a candidate for ordination. His work here was the beginning of a notable career, since he later became a missionary to China, and finally president of St. John's University in Shanghai, the outstanding Christian institution of higher education in China and one of the Episcopal Church's greatest missionary undertakings.[22]

A later development of foreign work at the chapel was the establishment of a service and Sunday school for the Czech-Slovak population which followed Germans and Chinese into the area. The Helping Hand Association was again active in this mission. In 1885, the Association also organized a day nursery to care for babies while their mothers were at work. This work grew until it had its own quarters, a small wooden building next to Saint Thomas House. There as many as fourteen thousand children were cared for in one year. In addition, a diet kitchen was supported by the Helping Hand to provide nourishing food for the poor and sick on the East Side.[23]

In 1888, Dr. Morgan reached his seventy-second year. For thirty-one years he had served as rector of the parish, and he was quite pleased with its life and productivity. "So many and varied channels of parochial activity are offered," he observed, "that a pleasureable choice is easily afforded according to inclination and ability."[24] This choice included, besides those organizations previously mentioned, the Association for the Employment of the Industrious Poor, the Girls' Friendly Society, the Workingmen's Club, the Ministering Children's League, the Boys' Guild, St. Thomas' Guild, the Good-Will Society, the Fresh Air Fund,[25] St. Andrew's Brotherhood, and the Choir Guild. The general missionary outreach of the parish beyond the city was undertaken by the various branches of the Ladies' Missionary Association and its companion organization, the Young Ladies' Missionary Society.[26]

The diocese had long ago demonstrated its recognition of Dr. Morgan's work. For years he had been elected to the Standing Committee, and at one time he was the only person to serve on both the Standing Committee and the powerful Missionary Committee. Strangely enough, he never appears to have been considered for the episcopate, though his strategic vision and his clarity of purpose were just the qualities often sought. But now the years of unceasing activity were beginning to take their toll. Dr. Morgan was slowing down. Out of deep affection for him, Bishop Henry Codman Potter, former rector of Grace Church and now assistant to his uncle Bishop Horatio Potter in the see of New York, volunteered to assist in the services at Saint Thomas and to preach from November of 1885 to Easter of 1886, so far as his diocesan duties would permit. This offer was gratefully accepted.[27] Afterward, a number of assistant ministers were appointed for varied periods to aid the rector in the administration of the parish.

Then, in February of 1888, Dr. Morgan called a special vestry meeting to hear a report from a committee appointed to select an associate rector. The committee, of which the rector was chairman, had traveled recently to Providence, Rhode Island, to hear the Rev. Dr. David H. Greer of that city's Grace Church preach. The result was that the committee, so far as it was able to determine from listening to Dr. Greer preach only twice, "believed he would give satisfaction" to Saint Thomas.

Dr. Morgan, however, added that Bishop Henry Codman Potter, who had become the new diocesan in 1887, had stated in a conversation that he did not regard "Dr. Greer as a very thorough theologian," although he did consider him "an earnest worker, and a talented preacher." Dr. Morgan also reported that Potter did not believe Greer's "churchmanship and theology were entirely in harmony with the tradition of St. Thomas' Church." Bishop Potter had suggested instead that he himself should preach once a month at Saint Thomas and ultimately make Saint Thomas parish the pro-cathedral of the diocese! Dr. Morgan, despite his friendship with Bishop Potter, was not sympathetic to this idea, and expressed "his opinion that St. Thomas' should continue an independent parish and always remain so."[28]

The rector informed the vestry that he was willing to call Dr. Greer although, having spent most of his life in the service of Saint Thomas parish, he "would be sorry to have the wrong man accepted." To this, Mr. George M. Miller, the Junior Warden, offered additional information respecting Dr. Greer, believed by him to be reliable; if so, then the candidate would "outrank all others in the church."[29] After some discussion, it was resolved that Dr. Morgan should secure the services of Dr. Greer, already known as a leader of the Broad Church party, provided that after correspondence and other contact the rector be satisfied that he "is in every way qualified, suitable, and desirable for such association." Six days later, on February 24, 1888, Dr. Greer was unanimously elected associate rector with right of succession to the rectorship. Dr. Morgan then expressed his intention to transfer to the associate the full administration of the parish the following October.[30]

It was known at the time that another prominent parish in New York City, St. Bartholomew's, was also seeking the services of Dr. Greer. There is, curiously, no mention of the Providence rector's response to the call from

Saint Thomas in the vestry minutes. It is, however, recorded elsewhere that when a friend asked Dr. Greer which call he would accept, he replied: "St. Thomas' has its pews full, has a large congregation and does an active work. At St. Bartholomew's half the pews are vacant, its congregation is small, and its resources undeveloped. I shall have more to do at St. Bartholomew's." So, in the belief that he would have "to work harder," Dr. Greer went to St Bartholomew's, and later became Bishop of New York.[31]

In April, Dr. Morgan then suggested that a deputation representing both the vestry and the congregation should visit St. Paul's in Buffalo, to hear the Rev. Dr. John Wesley Brown preach, with a view to his being called to the rectorship. The deputation went, reported favorably, and Dr. Morgan warmly approved. Dr. Brown intimated his willingness to entertain a call,[32] and Dr. Morgan on April 22 tendered his resignation to take effect on the first of June.[33]

The resignation was accepted by the vestry with expressions of profound and sincere regret. Dr. Morgan was designated Rector Emeritus, and given a life annuity of $7,500 a year by the vestry.[34] On Sunday morning, May 6, 1888, Dr. Morgan preached what proved to be his last sermon in the church he had built. It is recorded that in the Holy Communion service that morning "he departed from his custom and administered both the bread and the wine to an unusually large number of communicants."[35] On the following Thursday, he was taken ill, and on Saturday, May 19, he died. The Burial Office was said in the church on Wednesday, May 23, in the presence of a sorrowing congregation of more than two thousand people. Bishop Potter officiated, assisted by Dr. Brown, the rector-elect. The Rev. Dr. Samuel Cooke of St. Bartholomew's read the Lesson. Dr. Morgan Dix led the recitation of the Creed. The Committal was said by Bishop William C. Doane of Albany, and the music was rendered by the full choir under the direction of Dr. Warren.

Dr. Morgan's body was taken to Newport, Rhode Island, where he had a summer home. The Rev. Dr. George J. Magill, rector of Trinity Church in that city, officiated at the grave in the burial ground of St. Mary's Church, South Portsmouth. There Dr. Morgan was laid by the side of his wife, who had died in 1882. Over his grave was erected a granite cross patterned after that marking the grave of the saintly John Keble in Hursley churchyard, England. "We loved and revered him during his life-time for his staunch and manly fidelity to the everlasting Gospel," wrote Morgan Dix of his old friend, "and for his loyalty to the Church from which he had the grace of his baptism and his priesthood; and we honor him in his death, as one who 'kept the faith once delivered to the saints'." He was and is "our father departed," Dix continued, and his best monument was his great work, "his noble and prosperous parish . . . a living power for good among us, and in the Church."

Now that parish was "to be administered by the hands of one to whom he, dying, resigned it."[36]

The tradition of Saint Thomas was now established firmly on Fifth Avenue, and a second golden age had clearly been the legacy of William Ferdinand Morgan. All the buildings in use by the parish at the time of his death had been constructed during his rectorship. In 1943, the distinguished church historian E. Clowes Chorley would hail him as "the first presbyter in the diocese of New York to recognize the responsibility of the privileged for the outcast and the poor."[37] A bronze bust of Dr. Morgan by Olin Levy Warner (ill. 15) that would later survive the great fire of 1905 still remains in the ambulatory of the present church, across from the organ console. His rectorship of thirty-one years from 1857 to 1888 remains the longest in the history of the parish.

15. Bust of Dr. Morgan by Olin Levy Warner that survived the fire of 1905

THE SECOND GOLDEN AGE

Notes

1 New York *Convention Journal*, 1871, p. 161.

2 "Opening of the New St. Thomas's Church," *The Church Journal* 18 (12 October 1870): 325.

3 "Opening of the New St. Thomas's Church," *The Church Journal* 18 (12 October 1870): 325. The white flowing robe called a surplice was at that time a mark of higher Anglican churchmanship. The choir began to be vested in 1902; see below, page 120.

4 Leonard Ellinwood, *The History of American Church Music* (New York: Morehouse-Gorham Company, 1953), p. 237.

5 E. Clowes Chorley, *Manuscript History of St. Thomas Church* (unpublished manuscript in Saint Thomas Archives, 1943; copy deposited in the St. Mark's Library of the General Theological Seminary, New York City), pp. 365-66.

6 Dr. Morgan, in his introduction to the 1888 volume, wrote: "It need scarcely be said that its welcome is assured, or that it will become at once a cherished possession, not only to members of the parish, but to thousands from every part of the country who, in attending the services of St. Thomas's Church, whether at morning or evening prayer, have shared in the quickening power of its music." The tune for number 718 in the *Hymnal 1982* was composed by Warren in 1892 for the centennial of the adoption of the Constitution of the United States and was used at Saint Thomas for the Columbia celebration on 8 October 1892. The tune initially was named "America." Number 718 has been called "the only hymn of ecumenical acceptance that features an accompaniment with trumpet fanfares in the organ": *The Hymnal 1982 Companion*, ed. Raymond F. Glover (New York: The Church Hymnal Corporation, 1994), vol. 3B, p. 1335.

7 VM 3:99 (27 October 1875), 3:101-3 (19 January 1876), 3:104-5 (26 January 1876). Dr. Morgan may have met Mr. Courtney while visiting Europe in 1875. The salary of the assistant was $5,500.

8 At the time of his election to the episcopate, Mr. Courtney was rector of St. Paul's Church, Boston. On resigning his see after 16 years, he returned to New York to become rector of St. James' Church on Madison Avenue (1904-15).

9 VM 3:81 (12 February 1875).

10 VM 3:234 (13 April 1881), 3:240-41 (16 March 1882), 3:273 (5 December 1882), 3:282-83 (11 May 1883). See also an unidentified newspaper article entitled "St. Thomas's Church. Ceremonies at the Consecration of the Edifice Yesterday," pasted on the back page of the *Register of Baptisms, Marriages, Funerals, etc., 1867-1888, April 21, 1867 to August 20, 1888*, in the Saint Thomas Archives.

11 William Bacon Stevens, *A Sermon Delivered at the Consecration of St. Thomas' Church, New York, on WhitSun-Tuesday, May 15ᵗʰ, 1883* (Philadelphia: McCalla and Stavely Printers, 1883), pp. 17-18, 19.

12 *The Encyclopedia of New York City*, ed. Kenneth T. Jackson (New Haven: Yale University Press, 1995), pp. 356, 1038. The Easter Parade's origins, however, may have been a bit earlier than this and not linked exclusively to Saint Thomas Church. See *Fifth Avenue* (New York: Fifth Avenue Bank of New York, 1915), p. 61; Robert J. Myers with The Editors of Hallmark Cards, *Celebrations: The Complete Book of American Holidays* (New York: Doubleday and Company, Inc., 1972), p. 109. Later, at least in the 1960s once Saint Thomas had a choir school, it became necessary to warn the choristers solemnly on Easter Day that they were under no circumstances to laugh at any hat they might see! William Self, organist and choirmaster at Saint Thomas from 1954 to 1971, records this stricture in his autobiography, *Mine Eyes Have Seen the Glory* (Worcester, MA: Worcester Chapter of the American Guild of Organists, 1990), p. 198.

13 "New York," *The Church Journal and Gospel Messenger* 23 (23 December 1875), 802; Chorley, *Manuscript History*, p. 401.

14 New York *Convention Journal*, 1874, p. 150.

15 "Report of the Minister-in-Charge, St. Thomas' Chapel," *Annual Record* 1879, pp. 14-16; "Reports of Organizations in St. Thomas Parish," *Annual Record* 1879, pp. 21-72. The *Annual Record*

was instituted by Dr. Morgan in 1876 to report on the yearly life and work of the parish. Its exterior cover and its title page both continued to be entitled *Annual Record* until 1891. In that year the exterior cover was re-titled *Year Book*, but the title page continued to be entitled *Annual Record*. Beginning in 1901, both the exterior cover and title page were entitled *Year Book*. In 1978 the latter two words were combined to become *Yearbook*. The earliest copy of the *Annual Record* in the Saint Thomas Archives dates from 1879. See also "Parochial Notes" found on the back page of the *Register of Baptisms, Marriages, Funerals, etc., 1867-1888, April 21, 1867 to August 20, 1888*, in the Saint Thomas Archives.

16 "Note by Rector," *Annual Record* 1879, p. 2. See also "Seventy-Fifth Anniversary of St. Thomas's Church," *Year Book of Saint Thomas's Parish, A.D., 1899*, p. xiii.

17 VM 3:194-95 (28 January 1880), 3:199 (25 March 1880).

18 VM 3:220-22 (23 February 1881), 3:225-26, 3:231-32 (13 April 1881).

19 VM 3:235 (13 April 1881), 3:255 (5 December 1882). For a good description of the parish house and its work, see "The Helping Hand Association of St. Thomas's Mission, New York," *The Churchman* 32 (18 June 1898): 891-92.

20 *Annual Record* 1887, pp. 55-56.

21 Already in May of 1869 there was a Chinese Sunday School at the Church of the Advent in San Francisco; see Lionel U. Ridout, "The Church, The Chinese, and The Negroes in California, 1849-1893," *Historical Magazine of the Protestant Episcopal Church* 28:2 (June 1959): 127.

22 "Report of the Minister-in-Charge, St. Thomas's Chapel," *Annual Record* 1884, pp. 51-52; *The Church Eclectic* 22:10 (January 1895): 951.

23 *Annual Record* 1887, p. 73.

24 *Annual Record* 1887, p. 2.

25 This Fresh Air Fund, founded in 1877, is the same which continues today to send children from New York City to suburban and rural destinations every summer for two-week vacations. By the mid-1990s, it had provided this service to more than 1.6 million city youth.

26 *Annual Record* 1889, pp. 2-6. The multiplication of organized activities, social institutions, and charitable enterprises at Saint Thomas under Dr. Morgan had its parallels in other New York churches of the later nineteenth century, such as Holy Communion under William Augustus Muhlenberg, Grace under Henry Codman Potter, and St. George's under W.S. Rainsford.

27 VM 4:45 (13 October 1885).

28 VM 4:94-95 (18 February 1888). The conversation reported with Bishop Henry Codman Potter was ordered, on motion, expunged from the vestry minutes. Although pencilled out, it remains readable. Bishop Horatio Potter had spoken of the need for a cathedral for the diocese in his address to the diocesan convention of 1872, which had given its unanimous approval to move ahead. The following year a charter of incorporation was granted by the state legislature, but the financial panic of 1873 had intervened and a site was not chosen until 1887. Bishop Horatio Potter had earlier been known to favor a location not "too high up town or too far west of the Fifth Avenue": James Elliott Lindsley, *This Planted Vine: A Narrative History of the Episcopal Diocese of New York* (New York: Harper and Row, 1984), pp.202-3. See also George Hodges, *Henry Codman Potter: Seventh Bishop of New York* (New York: The MacMillan Company, 1915), chapter 14, for that bishop's thoughts about "The Cathedral Idea."

29 VM 4:96 (18 February 1888).

30 VM 4:96-97 (18 February 1888), 4:99-100 (24 February 1888).

31 E. Clowes Chorley, *The Centennial History of Saint Bartholomew's Church in the City of New York, 1835-1935* (New York: privately printed, 1935), p. 140.

32 VM 4:111-12 (13 April 1888), 4:113-14 (21 April 1888).

33 VM 4:115-16 (23 April 1888).

34 VM 4: 116-22 (23 April 1888).

35 Chorley, *Manuscript History*, p. 422.

36 The "Memorial Tribute" by Dix is printed on pp. 22-25 of *Sermon Preached on All Saints' Day, 1888 by the Rev. John Wesley Brown, D.D. In Memory of the Rev. William F. Morgan, D.D. For Thirty-one Years Rector of St. Thomas' Church New York* (privately printed without date or publisher or place). Text also in *The Churchman* 57 (2 June 1888): 658.

37 Chorley, *Manuscript History*, p. 401.

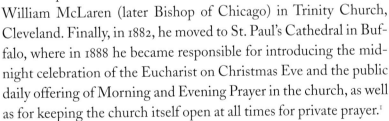

CHAPTER 8

Developing the Spiritual Life

JOHN WESLEY BROWN
SEVENTH RECTOR, 1888-1900

A N INTENSIFICATION OF THE SPIRITUAL
LIFE of Saint Thomas parish was inaugurated on June 1, 1888,
when the Rev. John Wesley Brown (ill. 16) became its seventh
rector at the age of fifty-one. Born in Baltimore in 1837, and a
graduate of Dickinson College with a degree in civil engineering, he then spent two years in the United States Coast Survey. At the age of
twenty he entered the Methodist ministry, where he served with distinction
for five years. Coming under the influence of that pillar of nineteenth-century Anglican Catholicism, Bishop William Rollinson Whittingham of
Maryland, he determined to seek credentials of ordination that would rest
upon a more catholic and apostolic foundation. In 1866, he was ordained
deacon in the Episcopal Church and appointed assistant minister of Emmanuel Church in his native city. Within a short time he was called to be rector of St. Anne's Church, Middletown, Delaware, and there was ordained to
the priesthood in the summer of 1866 by Bishop Alfred Lee. After a period
as rector of Trinity Church, Philadelphia, Brown succeeded Benjamin Pad-
dock (later Bishop of Massachusetts) in Christ Church, Detroit, and then

16. John Wesley Brown, Seventh
Rector 1888-1900

William McLaren (later Bishop of Chicago) in Trinity Church,
Cleveland. Finally, in 1882, he moved to St. Paul's Cathedral in Buffalo, where in 1888 he became responsible for introducing the midnight celebration of the Eucharist on Christmas Eve and the public
daily offering of Morning and Evening Prayer in the church, as well
as for keeping the church itself open at all times for private prayer.[1]

Saint Thomas, which called him that same year, numbered then
857 communicants in the parish church, 434 at the chapel, and another 98 in the German Mission.[2] Coming to Saint Thomas, Dr.
Brown understood that he inherited a parish tradition dedicated
alike to the dignity of worship and the benefit of humankind. He
fully intended to honor both. From the start of his rectorship he
made it clear that first consideration was to be given to the fostering
and nurturing of the spiritual life, and this now emerged as a domi-

103

nant theme in the annals of the parish. Growth and progress in that life, he firmly believed, came from a due appreciation and use of the sacraments of the Church as a means of grace. Accordingly, Dr. Brown increased the celebrations of Holy Communion in the parish, from twice a month at the end of his predecessor's tenure to twice a Sunday by the end of his first year as rector. In addition to the greater festivals of the Church year, he instituted a morning celebration of the Holy Communion on "all Holy Days."

The new rector's first annual report took care to explain and underscore the benefit of weekly Communion. "The Celebration of the Holy Communion every Lord's day," he pointed out, "offers an opportunity for all devoutly disposed persons to receive that 'most comfortable Sacrament' not only on the first Sunday of the month, but on any or every Sunday." The early Sunday morning celebration in particular, his report suggested, should be seen as "a blessed sanctification" of all the services of that day. Spiritual solace, the report further added, was available outside the regular weekly services. Indeed, "at no time can the Services of the Church and her Minister be more valuable than in times of sorrow and sickness." The rector, parishioners were informed, stood ready "to respond to your calls, and begs not only to have the opportunity to express his sympathy on such occasions, but to administer consolation in the name of the Lord."[3]

Within six months of Dr. Brown's tenure, the vestry approved his recommendation to employ for parish work a woman named "Sister Julia," whose identity has not been established with certainty and who may have been a Deaconess or possibly a member of a women's religious order. Initially, she was employed at the modest stipend of $50 a month, but in 1891 this was increased to $1,000 a year.[4] In the summer of 1892 it was reported that she had collected 254 pieces of wearing apparel from twenty parishioners, as well as the sum of $876, for distribution among the poor.[5]

In 1891 the vestry minutes record their first reference to the spiritual life and condition of the parish. In keeping with his theological view that practical charity flows from devotion, the rector is said to have expressed his desire for "an active and more intensified interest in Church work, treating the Church, the Chapel and all the outlying posts as one field," and the junior warden, in turn, allowed that he was "in favor of having the Services in the Church during the week multiplied."[6]

The weekday services became now more numerous than at any previous time. The office of Morning Prayer was instituted on Wednesdays and a lecture was featured at the Evening office. On Fridays there was the Litany and an address in the morning, and Evening Prayer in the late afternoon, with a Rector's Bible Class from Advent season to Good Friday. In addition, Morning and Evening Prayer were said daily during Advent and Lent, and in the latter season there was a brief address every day in the afternoon. On Good Friday a service and sermon had been introduced in the morning. In that afternoon there was a three-hour service with meditations on the Seven Last Words from the Cross, and on Easter Even and Rogation Days there were appointed offices. Other liturgical enrichments included Choral Evensong with a sermon on Sunday afternoons, and a parish anniversary commemoration on the Sunday nearest the feast of Saint Thomas. Worshipers were thus given greatly expanded opportunities for corporate worship in the best of the Anglican tradition.

In the scheduling of the liturgical life of the parish, pastoral and missionary concerns also received equal attention from Dr. Brown. Parishioners were encouraged to see the rector and other clergy in the vestry room after any service, as well as daily during certain announced hours or at any other notice. Religious literature was made available on distributing desks in the vestibule of the church. An additional feature was the annual Lenten lectures sponsored by the Church Club of New York, held at Saint Thomas beginning in 1889, the series that year being on "The Church in the British Isles: Sketches of its Continuous History from the Earliest Times to the Restoration."[7] Goodwill offerings were carefully designated to various missions and charitable endeavors. In Advent a special collection was set aside for domestic missions, and in Epiphany for foreign missions; the Lenten season supported diocesan, "Indian," and "Colored" missions. In Eastertide the Fresh Air Fund was a major recipient, and in Trinity season there were the "Indian" and Mexican missions as well as the City Mission. The first Sunday in each month the offering went to the poor of the parish. The fund for the chapel benefited from the offerings at nearly every season of the year.[8]

The concern for missions, even those far abroad, was to receive a special boost later in Dr. Brown's tenure when, on June 14, 1893, in Saint Thomas Church, the Rt. Rev. John McKim was consecrated as Missionary Bishop of Tokyo (formerly Edo or Yeddo), Japan, and the Rt. Rev. Frederick Rogers Graves was consecrated as Missionary Bishop of Shanghai, China. In addition to the three canonical co-consecrators there were a number of other bishops participating in the service, including the former Primate of Australia and Bishop of Sydney, Dr. Alfred Barry. The event was certainly a public, sacramental, and even exciting statement of the church's obligation to proclaim the Gospel beyond its own borders.[9]

Enthusiasm for this revival of parish life under Dr. Brown is implied in the vestry's action to grant the new rector and his family a three-month vacation, with advance in salary, to visit Europe at the end of his very first year. Two years later the vestry voted to take out a life-insurance policy for the rector and recorded its "appreciation of his Churchly bearing, his earnest and

17. The Morgan Memorial Altar, installed 1896 and destroyed by fire 1905, together with the present Altar Cross that survived the same fire, surrounded by the La Farge murals and the Saint-Gaudens reredos that were also destroyed.

powerful efforts, as a preacher of the Gospel, to accomplish great and good results for the spiritual welfare of all those who come under his preaching."[10]

A major challenge to Dr. Brown's high ideals came after he had been rector for less than a year. He had inherited a venerable but crusty old sexton named Benjamin Williams, since 1858 an employee of the church but not a member of it, whose particular animosity to Dr. Brown will probably never be adequately explained. It seems that Williams was interviewed by *The New*

York Sun about the question of whether or not strangers were welcome at Saint Thomas, and that his contentious reply was reported in that paper as follows:

> We haven't any room in our church for people who haven't paid for their seats. Our trouble is not to find places for strangers, but to keep them out. We don't ask them to come, and we don't want them. If they come, they are in the way, and we have hard work to get them out of the way; but we manage to do it nevertheless. We have to watch them, but sometimes they elude us and contrive to find seats somewhere. Then we have to tell them very plainly to get up and go out. And we make them do it.[11]

Needless to say, a controversy ensued from this report, with leading members of the parish all rejecting the sexton's comments, but it was still necessary for Dr. Brown himself to articulate the official reply, which he did in moving terms. He said:

> I have always sincerely wished that in all my church work I could go on trying to do good, and doing good without anything getting into the papers. But since this unpleasant notoriety has been created, I want to have the opportunity to declare most emphatically that the rector and the wardens and vestrymen of St. Thomas's Church do not regard the presence of strangers as undesirable. We do want them. The Church of St. Thomas is the house of God. It is not a social club, not a body of rich men selfishly organized for comfortable worship.[12]

In this public and unequivocal response by the rector, one senses something of the depth of his spirituality and the catholicity of his theology.

Dr. Brown sought to build on the strong foundations left by his eminent predecessor, for whom he had profound admiration. This esteem was reflected in a sermon he preached on All Saints' Day in 1888 commemorating the life and work of Dr. Morgan. In the sermon Dr. Brown described the former rector as "the faithful Pastor and dutiful Priest" and praised him for "all his foresight and wisdom." "Today this magnificent church building," he exclaimed, "stands with its noble accessories for worship and religious usefulness as one of the works which has followed him in testimony to his Christian bravery – his trust in God – and his zeal for the Master."[13]

It seemed to Dr. Brown that a most fitting memorial to Dr. Morgan would be the erection of a marble altar in the parish church to replace the Communion table. This purpose he urged upon the vestry in 1891, although it encountered opposition from some who were concerned, no doubt, about advanced ritualistic practices. At length, though, in 1896, a splendid marble altar in memory of the late rector was placed in the sanctuary (ill. 17), the cost of which had been met by subscription. Designed by C. R. Lamb, its style was Italian Gothic, harmonizing with the Gothic arches and vaulted ceiling of the church, as well as with the decorative details of the reredos and chancel by Saint-Gaudens and La Farge. Of white marble, it was decorated in mosaic of Venetian and oxidized gold, and approached by three steps. The retable screen and canopy, with a niche to hold the altar cross, were arranged in pyramidal form with a background of iridescent mosaic and mother-of-pearl. The new altar, together with a white marble rail and credence table also given as memorials, was consecrated by Bishop Potter on the feast of Saint Thomas. The altar was "set apart for a sacred and august use, first of all, in this our catholic and apostolic worship," the bishop observed in his sermon on the occasion, and then as a loving memorial of one who "stood for so many years in this pulpit, and both here and there, in yonder sanctuary, broke to you the bread of life." The people of Saint Thomas were to be congratulated, he said, that the memory of their former rector was to be perpetuated

Benjamin Williams, the Sexton

In 1908, Benjamin W. Williams completed fifty years of service as "Sexton and Collector" of Saint Thomas Church. He had begun in the old church at the corner of Houston Street and Broadway under Dr. Morgan on February 22, 1858, and he died on February 17, 1914, at the age of eighty-seven. He rented the pews, collected fees, and supervised repairs to the buildings. During his long period of service, he became a well-known character in New York, and much of the following reminiscences about him are found in the writing of the Rev. William Owen, an assistant minister of Saint Thomas from 1901 to 1908.[28]

Williams was born in Lancashire, England, in 1827, and it is believed that his parents were Quakers. He ran away to sea when a boy, and as a young man found his way to New York where he engaged in the real estate business. Nearly six feet in height, he was stocky in build and weighed not less than two hundred pounds. He walked with a peculiar gait, impossible to describe, and seemed to be a bit flat-footed, more so in one foot than in the other. He had a very high-pitched voice and long flowing white hair. By the people of the parish he was either much loved and respected or cordially disliked. He himself had strong likings and equally strong aversions. He had a profound respect for Dr. Morgan and viewed him as his ideal of a Christian and a gentleman. That regard, however, was not extended to Dr. Morgan's successor, to whom he usually referred simply as "Brown." Stories about him were the stuff of legend.

18. The Vanderbilt wedding, November 6, 1895

in such a "sacred and beautiful structure."[14]

Understandably, the Fifth Avenue church was also gaining notoriety as a favored place for society weddings. The most famous of these was the marriage of Miss Consuelo Vanderbilt to the ninth Duke of Marlborough on November 6, 1895 (ill. 18). The wedding, according to *The New York Times*, was "the most magnificent ever celebrated in this country." An organ solo by Dr. Warren preceded the ceremony. There was also a sixty-member symphony orchestra under the direction of Walter Damrosch. The bishops of New York and Long Island officiated. A fashionable congregation filled the pews in a church extravagantly decorated with floral arrangements. One of the many simpler weddings took place the following spring when former President Benjamin Harrison married Mary Scott Dimmick (ill. 19). Although the hour of that ceremony had been kept secret, advance notice of the event in a newspaper brought a large crowd that remained outside the church throughout the day.[15]

The year 1897 was marked by the beginning of the parish endowment fund. The call for this fund came from Dr. Brown, who stressed its importance to the parish in "securing for all time the ministration of the Word of God and the Holy Sacraments, independent of the changes of residential population or business prosperity." What was wanted, the rector said, was not a full endowment, for that would lead to decay, but rather "a sufficient amount, permanently invested to provide against all contingencies, . . .to be

19. The Harrison wedding, April 6, 1896

DEVELOPING THE SPIRITUAL LIFE

secured in behalf of this Parish, which will soon be known as a down-town Church." The vestry agreed and accordingly resolved that ten percent of all pew rents should in future be set apart and held in trust as a permanent endowment fund. This indicates both the lavish scale on which the parish now operated, and the fact that income was exceeding expenses. On December 19, 1898, the treasurer reported that $7,551.46 had been set apart as the beginning of the endowment.[16]

On Christmas Day of 1898, the parish observed the seventy-fifth anniversary of its incorporation by beginning a series of services that continued throughout the octave. At eight o'clock in the morning, there was a celebration of the Holy Communion with carols, one of which, "Hosanna to Our King," was written by Dr. Brown. At the later festal Eucharist, the rector preached an anniversary sermon on the text "Glory to God in the highest, and on earth peace, good will towards men." The truth expressed by this text, he said, had been the charter of Saint Thomas parish since its beginning, and it referred both to the "Dignity of Worship and to the Benefit of Mankind." The passing years had seen "progress to a higher, larger and grander Ritual" in the liturgical life of the parish, but "under, through and with all the richness of the Service the truly devotional spirit prevails." There was "a home-feeling for the Soul in the Services of St Thomas's Church," as both stranger and parishioner often commented. At the same time, "there has been always the discharge of practical Christian Duty in works of Charity." The labors and liberality of the parish had also been extended "in every direction and through every channel of Church work." Dr. Brown also noted his particular pleasure in "the growth and yearly progress of the Spiritual life of the Parish" through the influence of the sacraments. "If this Church has not stood for the begetting and the developing of the spiritual life," he exclaimed, "it has proven untrue to the intention of its founding and unworthy of continuance. But we rejoice that the known lives of individuals and families, in the experience of the Pastorate for these seventy-five years agone, is indisputable evidence of its worthiness and life."[17]

The following Sunday morning, Dr. Brown preached a sermon that evaluated the parish's recent history. In surveying the last decade that he had served as rector, he expressed gratitude for continued prosperity. The church, owing to its "abundant revenue," was free of debt and had been "fully repaired, refurnished and redecorated." Electricity had been introduced "for lighting, ventilation and power for the great Organ." Inside the church there were signs "of a gracious liberality in memorial and loving gifts," as seen in the Lenten chapel or "chantry" with "a most attractive Altar, Reredos, and all things necessary to a becoming worship." The establishment of new churches and parishes in the last ten years to the north of Saint Thomas, he noted, confirmed the wisdom of its location and made it "once more a down-town Church."[18]

Among the featured speakers during the anniversary commemoration was the Rev. Dr. William Reed Huntington, the distinguished rector of Grace Church on Broadway and eminent author of works on ecumenism, liturgy, and the nature of the Church. In his address, Dr. Huntington recalled the time over thirty years earlier when the two congregations had worshiped together under one roof at Grace Church. In spite of the controversy at that time over the move to a new home uptown, congratulations were now due, he said, to the rector of Saint Thomas upon the opportunities this move afforded. "No minister of Christ in these United States has a better vantage ground from which to speak for God." The Fifth Avenue parish "should be accounted spiritually as well as literally a city set on a hill; about its stately tower might be inscribed the Psalmist's word, 'I have ordained a lantern for mine Anointed'" (Psalm 132:17). Then, in conclusion, the Broadway rector directed his listeners' attention to the patron saint of the parish, Saint Thomas. This apostle deserved to be remembered, he urged, as "the one who was courageous in the face of doubt." People now found themselves living "in anxious times," especially anxious times religiously, and many within and without the church were asking who would show them what Christianity had to offer. The great need at present, he argued, was for parishes of "the temper of St. Thomas," full of individuals "who in the face of discouragement and notwithstanding the besetting doubt, are bold to go ahead." In sacred art, Dr. Huntington pointed out, the symbol of Saint Thomas is the builder's rule. This is a good sign, for what is wanted in any parish is construction, which means people who know how to build up rather than to pull down. "So then all honor to St. Thomas with his brave heart and his builder's rule," declared the rector of Grace Church, "and many a Happy New Year to St. Thomas his Church."[19]

Dr. Brown took a deep and personal interest in the work of Saint Thomas Chapel on the East Side. With regret he accepted the resignation in 1889 of the Rev. Robert Lowry, who, after serving for fifteen years as vicar of the chapel, had accepted a new call to become superintendent of the "Orphan's Home and Asylum of the Protestant Episcopal Church in New York." He was succeeded as vicar by the Rev. William Hawks Pott, Ph.D., another grandson of the third rector and son of the church publisher James Pott, who continued throughout the remainder of Dr. Brown's rectorate. Under him, the Sunday school increased by leaps and bounds. In 1900, it had 1,165 pupils and 98 teachers, a number worthy of comparison with the enormous church school of Dr. Hawks.[20]

An important move was made in 1893. Dr. Brown had long been concerned with the welfare of East Side children during the hot summer months, when the climate of New York City could become almost unbearable. A generous gift of Miss Grace Scoville made it possible for the parish to buy some sixty acres of land on the shore of the Sound at East Marion, Long Island, and there a chapel and other buildings were erected where the children of the tenements could draw long breaths of fresh air. By the second summer of operation nearly four hundred children had been guests of the Children's Home there. Eventually, the facility was named the John Wesley Brown Summer Home (ill. 20) of Saint Thomas Parish.[21] It was finally closed in 1925, in the face of expensive new state regulations.

The Helping Hand Association had been organized to give daytime care to children whose mothers were forced to work outside their homes. This had now grown to such an extent that new facilities were needed. Therefore, in 1897, Mrs. Frederick Halsey, a niece of New York Governor Roswell Flower (whose earlier generosity had made possible the building of Saint Thomas House and who by 1883 had become a member of the vestry), gave the money to erect a new and capacious building for this purpose, a structure which bore the name of the "Halsey Day Nursery" (ill. 21). It was the finest of its kind in that day. It contained a laundry facility, a children's dining

20. The John Wesley Brown Summer Home (camp) at East Marion, Long Island (1893-1925)

room, and rooms for a kindergarten. There was a roof garden, fenced and fitted with hammocks for babies. Food was supplied from a well-equipped
kitchen. The building was so compact that it could be adequately staffed by
three nurses, a matron, a cook, and a laundress. The cost of caring for one
baby was fifteen cents a day. The mothers, when able, paid five cents of this;
the balance was made up by the board of managers of the home.[22]

In 1893, after the lapse of twenty-one years, it was found that the chapel
itself stood in need of extensive and costly repairs. After careful consideration, it was determined to tear it down and rebuild completely on the same
site. In 1894, Mrs. A. A. Linsley offered to contribute $18,000 for this pur-
pose as a memorial to her son, Richard Jessup Morgan. The vestry found the
additional funds that were necessary, and the chapel was accordingly built
anew from the designs of Mr. C. E. Miller. On the Sunday after Easter in
1894, the new chapel was consecrated (ill. 22) by the Rt. Rev. Henry Codman
Potter, Bishop of New York. The total cost of the building was about
$30,000. It was described as "one of the most cheerful and well arranged
churches in the city," featuring a beautiful chancel with distinctive windows
executed from the designs of Holman Hunt.[23]

22. The fourth Saint Thomas Chapel, consecrated 1894

Among his outside duties, Dr. Brown had served as a trustee of the Cathedral of St. John the Divine since 1895. In 1898, although at the age of sixty-one he was by no means an old man, his health definitely began to fail. The vestry granted him a leave of absence, hoping that a long vacation might restore him to health, but the hope was in vain. On Saturday, November 10, 1900, he died in the rectory, aged sixty-three years. The following Tuesday his body was taken into the church and during the night members of the Parish Association kept vigil. In the presence of a vast congregation the next morning, the burial office was said by Bishop Potter, assisted by the bishops of New Jersey and Nebraska and other clergy of the city and diocese.

Many were the tributes of respect. First and foremost among them was that of the vestry of the parish he had served so faithfully. The memorial reads, in part:

> The Vestry of St. Thomas' Church with a deep sense of the loss which the Parish have sustained in the death of their Rector the Rev. John Wesley Brown, D.D. desire to put upon record, and to express to his family their high appreciation of his character and eminent services, his faithful labors, his never-failing testimony to the Gospel, his loving sympathy, and care for the poor, not only in, but outside of the Parish, and his unceasing endeavor to establish works which should succor and comfort them in generations to come.[24]

The vestry went on to cite Dr. Brown's efforts in rebuilding the chapel on the East Side, the establishment of the summer home for children and the day nursery, and the erection of the Morgan memorial altar in the chancel of the parish church. Finally, the vestry's memorial testified "to Dr. Brown's uniform kindness, courtesy and gentleness, and above all to his devotion to the spiritual interests of the Parish."

Also moving was the tribute of the Parish Association, witnessing as it did to Dr. Brown's great love for the poor and his abiding interest in the chapel. The late rector, said the Association, "was a man of large heart and broad sympathy which found a field in constant acts of self-denial, of charity to the poor, of comfort to the afflicted, of succor to the distressed, winning the hearts of all to whom he ministered by his kind and affable manner."[25]

When Dr. Brown had assumed the rectorship in 1888, the parish numbered 800 communicants, with an additional 376 at the chapel. In his last year the number of communicants in the parish had grown to 1,368 and in the chapel to 697. The baptized membership in the parish grew from 1,600 in 1888 to 2,615 in 1900, the year of his death; and that in the chapel from 810 to 1,800.[26] Dr. Brown had, in his own words, fostered "a higher, larger, and grander ritual" at Saint Thomas, but he had done it for the sake of, as he put it, "the growth and progress of the spiritual life," from which, he was convinced, the parish's "discharge of practical Christian duty in works of charity" would be augmented accordingly. His line of reasoning had proven itself well founded.

A committee consisting of the two wardens, Daniel Taylor Hoag and George McCulloch Miller, together with James C. Fargo, was now appointed to recommend an appropriate successor. After due consideration, they nominated the Very Rev. Wilford Lash Robbins, dean of the Cathedral of All Saints, Albany. Dean Robbins, who later became dean of the General Theological Seminary, was an "Albany Churchman" – that is, a Hobartian with a strong dash of ritualism. But he declined the offer. On May 6, 1901, the committee presented to the vestry the name of the Rev. Ernest Milmore Stires, rector of Grace Church, Chicago, who was unanimously called. He accepted, to take office on the first of September.[27] A new era at Saint Thomas was about to begin.

Notes

1 George E. DeMille, *St. Paul's Cathedral Buffalo 1817-1967: A Brief History* (Buffalo: St. Paul's Church, 1966), pp. 79-80.

2 E. Clowes Chorley, *Manuscript History of St. Thomas Church* (unpublished manuscript in Saint Thomas Archives, 1943; copy deposited in the St. Mark's Library of the General Theological Seminary, New York City), p. 428.

3 *Annual Record* 1890, pp. 4-5.

4 VM 4:140 (18 November 1888), 4:235 (18 December 1891). It has proved impossible to trace with certainty the identity of this "Sister Julia," the name of her order, where she came from prior to Saint Thomas, or where she later went. Nor is there any evidence that would identify her as a Deaconess. Her salary could have been paid to her order.

5 *The Living Church* 15:16 (16 July 1892): 260. Sister Julia's services were discontinued in June of 1893 in order to employ a second assistant to the rector: VM 4:268 (21 April 1893).

6 VM 4:211 (25 March 1891).

7 James Elliott Lindsley, *The Church Club of New York: The First Hundred Years.* (New York: The Church Club of New York, 1994), pp. 15-17.

8 Schedules of services and special offerings are found in the *Annual Record* or *Year Book.*

9 *The Living Church* 16:12 (17 June 1893): 207; 16:13 (24 June 1893): 228; *The American Church Clergy and Parish Directory for 1905*, ed. Frederic E. J. Lloyd (Uniontown, PA: Frederic E. J. Lloyd, 1905), pp. 132, 191. Barry was not a representative of the narrowly evangelical cast of churchmanship for which Sydney is so well known.

10 VM 4:156 (26 April 1889), 4:211 (25 March 1891).

11 "Are Strangers Welcome?" in *The Christian Union* 39:8 (21 February 1889); I owe this reference to my colleague Professor Bruce Mullin.

12 "Are Strangers Welcome?" in *The Christian Union* 39:8 (21 February 1889).

13 *Year Book* 1888, pp. 3-12; *Sermon Preached on All Saints' Day, 1888 by the Rev. John Wesley Brown, D.D. In Memory of the Rev. William F. Morgan, D.D. For Thirty-one Years Rector of St. Thomas' Church New York* (privately printed without date or publisher or place).

14 VM 4:219 (25 April 1891), 4:13 (14 April 1897), *Year Book* 1897, p. 4.

15 *The New York Times*, 7 November 1895, pp. 1-2; 7 April 1896, p. 1. For a later discussion in the year 1926 about the validity of the Marlborough-Vanderbilt marriage, which had ended in divorce in 1920, see James Elliott Lindsley, *This Planted Vine: A Narrative History of the Episcopal Diocese of New York* (New York: Harper and Row, 1984), p. 276.

16 *Year Book* 1897, pp. 3-4; VM 5:20 (5 May 1897), 5:23 (6 December 1897), 5:26 (6 April 1898), 5:48 (19 December 1898).

17 *Year Book* 1898, pp. xi-xviii.

18 *Year Book* 1898, pp. xxix-xxxii.

19 *Year Book* 1898, pp. xxxv-xxxviii.

20 *Year Book* 1900, p. 89; *The Church Eclectic* 22:10 (January 1895): 951.

21 VM 4:270 (20 June 1893), 5:63-64 (29 November 1899); *Year Book* 1896, pp. 92-93. Initially a house and land were donated to Saint Thomas Church at Sag Harbor, but the vestry later declined the offer in preference for a closer location within the diocese.

22 "The Helping Hand Association of St. Thomas's Mission, New York," *The Churchman* 77:25 (18 June 1898): 891-92.

23 *The Churchman* 77:25 (18 June 1898): 891-92; VM 4:283 (21 March 1894), 4:291-93 (15 April 1894).

24 VM 5:83 (14 November 1900).

25 Chorley, *Manuscript History*, p. 447.

26 *Year Book* 1888, pp. 104-5; *Year Book* 1900, pp. 88-89.

27 VM 5:77 (25 February 1901), 5:92-93 (6 May 1901), 5:95-96 (5 June 1901). Of interest is a letter, dated 5 June 1901, from the vestry to Dean F. W. Farrar of Canterbury expressing appreciation for his willingness to suggest English candidates for the Saint Thomas rectorship and notifying him of the call issued to Dr. Stires.

28 William H. Owen, *I Remember* (privately printed), pp. 41-44.

CHAPTER 9

Still Loftier Ideals in Great Aspiring Arches

ERNEST MILMORE STIRES
EIGHTH RECTOR, 1901-1925

O N SEPTEMBER 1, 1901, the Rev. Dr. Ernest Milmore Stires (ill. 23) became rector of Saint Thomas Church. He was indeed a new rector for a new century. Born in Norfolk, Virginia, in 1866, he was at the time of his call only thirty-four years old, which made him the youngest rector in the history of the parish. Educated at the University of Virginia and the Virginia Theological Seminary, he was ordained to the diaconate in 1891 by Bishop Francis McNeece Whittle of Virginia and to the priesthood the following year by Bishop Alfred Magill Randolph of Southern Virginia. His first charge was at St. John's Church, West Point, Virginia, a rural parish of less than one hundred communicants. In 1892 he became rector of the Church of the Good Shepherd, Augusta, Georgia, and from there a year later moved to a curacy at Grace Church in Chicago. During a leave of absence granted the rector, he had administered Grace Church with such conspicuous success that, upon the resignation of the rector, he had been invited to succeed to that position, despite being only twenty-seven years old. There he remained eight years, making the reputation which earned him the call to Saint Thomas. Theologically, he belonged to the new school of Liberal Evangelicals, but with much more emphasis on Evangelical than Liberal. He brought to Saint Thomas the old and strong loyalties to the doctrine, discipline, and worship of the Episcopal Church that had characterized his predecessors, but he imparted to them a new warmth and fervor.

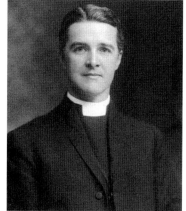

23. Ernest Milmore Stires, Eighth Rector 1901-1925

Dr. Stires inherited a parish that was strong and vibrant despite the passing just before his arrival of John Hall Watson, vestryman for thirty-three years, and of Daniel Taylor Hoag, warden for twenty-one years. The present wardens were George McCulloch Miller and James C. Fargo, and the vestrymen were Anson R. Flower, Henry H. Cook, John T. Atterbury, Harris C. Fahnestock, W. Seward Webb, James T. Woodward, Clarence M. Hyde, Alexander M. Hadden (grandson of the David Hadden who had been a member of the first vestry), Darius Ogden Mills, and Charles H. Stout. The assistant ministers at the parish church were DeWitt L. Pelston and William H. Owen Jr., both of whom afterwards became rectors of other large parishes in the city. The Rev. Robert Claiborne was vicar of the chapel; his assistant was the Rev. Robert W. Cochrane. Mr. Will Macfarlane had been organist of the parish church since 1900, with Mr. Gordon Darlington Richards as his assistant. The venerable Dr. George W. Warren, who had recently retired, was "honorary organist," and Alfred Toulmin continued as harpist and bell chimer, a post he had now held for some thirty years.

The church to which Dr. Stires came in the new century was a changed Saint Thomas in a changed New York. The comfortable little city of 1823, numbering nearly 150,000, had by now grown to a great metropolis of nearly three and one-half million people. The city of 1823 had been mainly Anglo-Saxon in race, but successive waves of immigration – first Irish and German, then Italian, Greek, Jewish, and Slav, as well as scattered groups of nearly every people on the face of the globe – had wholly changed the composition of the city's population and its social and cultural atmosphere.

Not just the city had changed; the nation and world had as well. The United States had just emerged from the Spanish-American War and found itself, to its own amazement, an imperialistic world power. London, so long the financial capital of the world, was slowly yielding place to New York. This was the age of the trusts – Standard Oil, United States Steel, American Tobacco, New York Central – and they and their sort dominated the American scene. It was the age of massive fortunes. The great names of the age were Morgan and Rockefeller and Harriman and Carnegie. They all lived in New York, some of them in grandiose mansions along Fifth Avenue not far from Saint Thomas. It has been suggested that at no time in history was corporate wealth so influential in the government of the United States as during the administration of President William McKinley. Hardly had Dr. Stires become rector of Saint Thomas, however, than McKinley died, assassinated by an anarchist. McKinley would be succeeded by Theodore Roosevelt, a child of old New York himself, who was to be the herald of a new age.

In the preface to the first *Year Book* issued under his rectorship (1901), Dr. Stires set out a clear-cut objective for the future of Saint Thomas parish. He boldly wrote:

> Each parish, because of its location, or other conditions, has a mission more or less peculiar and distinct. What is the mission of St. Thomas's? "To the poor," I can hear many reply. The answer is good, but not exact. The mission of St. Thomas's is to the well-to-do, for their own sake, and for the sake of those who are not well-to-do. Things are unequally distributed in this world, and it may be that in another world "one star differeth from another star in glory." At any rate, many suffer here from having too little, and many from having too much. One

class is unable to get the relief it needs, and the other has not learned to give the relief in its power. All must suffer until the relief is given. The mission of St. Thomas's is to help us to save ourselves by saving others; to regard all our successes, our influence, our money, as worth nothing in themselves, but worth much when devoted to elevating humanity. The pursuit of wealth for selfish ends is morally criminal; to make money for the purpose of making men is to do our duty to God, to our fellows, and to ourselves.

In this effort to help our brother man and sister woman, we dare not in any narrow fashion limit our sympathies. Of course, St. Thomas's Chapel, that interesting and lovable child of this Parish, will ever be the object of its generous care. But our hearts and hands must be quick to aid the suffering anywhere, to help God's cause everywhere. The mission work of the Church in this land must be more liberally sustained than ever before, for the needs and opportunities were never so great, nor has there been a time at which the King seemed so clearly to remind his followers of His final, explicit command to "go and teach all nations." These are the Church's marching orders from the Commander: "to doubt would be disloyalty, to falter would be sin."[1]

Regarding the chapel on the East Side, Dr. Stires asked $27,000 for the maintenance of this important ministry among the poor. The congregation responded with an offering of $30,000. Among the many organizations at the chapel there would soon be such groups as the Girl and Boy Scouts, the Athletic Club, and even a gymnasium with its own Physical Director. Contributions for domestic missions increased from $7,150 in 1901 to $25,308 in 1902, not insignificant sums in that day. The funds for foreign missions jumped from a meager $1,978 to $7,978. In 1901 the parish gave for various diocesan projects $5,881; in 1902 this figure had risen to $19,960.[2]

The parish itself was responding to new and dynamic leadership. Old organizations took on new life, and new ones, such as the Altar Guild and the Ushers' Committee, sprang into being.[3] Fifty new families were added in the first year of the new rectorship, and seventy-five persons were presented for confirmation.[4] The liturgical life of the parish likewise experienced notable change. The weekly Sunday Communion services instituted by Dr. Brown were continued at the early service, but at the second service Communion was now limited to twice monthly, on the first and third Sundays. Morning Prayer preceded the celebration on the third Sunday. On the second and fourth Sundays, clergy and people joined in Morning Prayer and the Litany. Evensong was introduced on Tuesdays and Thursdays during the week, but Evening Prayer on Wednesdays and Fridays was eliminated. The Daily Office was also eliminated during the season of Advent, though it remained during Lent.[5] There was also a service of the Holy Communion in Japanese, on Sundays at 9 a.m., at least in the later years of Dr. Stires' rectorate.[6] The choir of men and boys began to wear vestments in the year 1902 under Dr. Warren's successor, William C. Macfarlane. In an important proposal that synthesized the primacy of worship with the strategic location of the parish church, the new rector announced his conviction that the church should be open daily to the public and recommended to the vestry that such arrangements be made. This proposal met with approval and it was resolved that "St. Thomas' Church be kept open daily, Sundays, week-days and holidays from 8 AM to 5 PM."[7]

On March 16, 1902, George William Warren died at the age of seventy-four, having earlier retired in the year 1900. His thirty years of service to Saint Thomas Church had made him memorable, not only as a skilled master of music, but also as a deeply religious man. He had exercised a profound spiritual influence, especially on the young people's choir which he organized for Lent and weekday services, and his personal interest in the work of Saint Thomas Chapel was also notable. It was "his unique distinction," said Dr. Stires, to be remembered "most of all for purity of character, conscientious performance of duty, the joyful use of every chance to do good, resulting in perfect self-sacrifice."[8] Hundreds of people attended Dr. Warren's funeral, which was conducted by Bishop Potter assisted by the rectors of Trinity Church, St. Bartholomew's, Grace Church, and, of course, Saint Thomas. Among the honorary pall-bearers was the mayor of the city and former president of Columbia, Seth Low. It was decided that the service would be without music, so the organ was silent and no choristers were seated in the stalls.[9]

At the end of his first year as rector of Saint Thomas, Dr. Stires, energized by the progress made, wrote to his parishioners: "Let us say to the Church that we are daring to hope that soon we shall demand of ourselves a measure of service larger than that which the Church has ever asked from us." In his pastoral relations, he expressed pleasure that so many people were "disposed to consult him in times of distress and anxiety, and that they so cordially receive his sympathy in hours of pain or sorrow." Parishes today are "small dioceses," he remarked in an observation at least true for Saint Thomas, and "a well organized parish is not unlike a great business corporation." Still, it was his "desire to see and know his people in their homes, to develop that strong, sweet pastoral relation which years ago was not uncommon."[10]

Two years later, in 1904, Dr. Stires heralded the advent of an unordained ministry for women heretofore unknown in the annals of Saint Thomas, unless the elusive "Sister Julia" at the end of the previous century may be considered one of their number. This was the addition of Deaconesses in the work of the chapel and the opportunities opened for their services. "The uniform or habit of the Deaconess," he observed, "undoubtedly gives much of the Church's authority and consolation to the advice and ministrations which these devoted women take to many homes." The following year, owing to a generous bequest from Miss Evelina Dortic, a building adjacent to the chapel was purchased as a Deaconess House. It was intended, said the rector, to be "a

STILL LOFTIER IDEALS

house of sympathy and help for the distressed women of the East Side, a veritable city of refuge for young girls who can go to our kindly Deaconesses for counsel and comfort."[11] At least six Deaconesses are known to have worked in Saint Thomas parish, all of them within the rectorate of Dr. Stires, and he himself was elected in 1911 or 1912 as a member of the Board of Trustees of the New York Training School for Deaconesses, serving until 1915.[12]

Saint Thomas Church was only beginning, in the view of the rector, to come into its own and to fulfill its intended purpose when it met with a major catastrophe. In the summer of 1905, many members of the congregation had as usual scattered to the mountains or the seashore. The rector and his family were at Lake George, and the parish was temporarily in the charge of the Rev. James B. Wasson, an assistant. On Sunday morning, August 6, the Feast of the Transfiguration, Mr. Wasson conducted what proved to be the last service in that church. At five o'clock the next afternoon the sexton locked up the building and went home, and in less than twenty-four hours the church was a smoking ruin (ill. 24).

It was at about six o'clock on Tuesday morning August 8 that the caretaker at the rectory perceived the windows of the apse to be brightly illuminated. Soon smoke was pouring out of the great chancel windows. After some delay in reporting the alarm, and even though fifty fire companies eventually arrived on the scene, the fire was completely out of control. Within half-an-hour of the outbreak, the roof crashed, the chime of bells fell with a thunderous clang, and the whole interior was a blazing furnace. By nighttime the third Saint Thomas Church resembled an ancient Gothic ruin. Of the church proper, the tower alone was left standing; only the rectory and the parish house were saved. The walls of the apse and the nave stood like gaunt skeletons. A few fragments of charred mosaic were the only reminders of the magnificent Morgan memorial altar. The priceless La Farge murals, the statuary and reredos of Saint-Gaudens (which, collapsing in the heat, had protected the altar cross), the decorations of the chancel, a memorial bust of Dr. Brown, the superb stained glass, the new organ – all had disappeared in the flames. A short in the organ's wiring may have caused the fire. Of the interior furnishings only the bust of Dr. Morgan and the large gilt altar cross survived; the former can be seen in the present ambulatory across from the organ console (ill. 15), and the latter still adorns the high altar[13] (ill. 17, pl. VI). Also surviving – and also still in use today – were an engraved silver ewer dating from the time of the first church; the high altar communion plate of 1890 consisting of two chalices, two cruets, and a paten inlaid with a 1799 ten-dollar gold piece; and a precious chalice and paten of sterling silver-gilt that had been presented as recently as All Saints' Day of 1904. Beauty old, therefore, did survive in part, to wait its day to blend in time with beauty new.

When Dr. Stires arrived from Lake George later that afternoon, streams of water were still being cast upon the smouldering ruins. He was naturally shocked by the scene, but one who stood by said, "I was everlastingly impressed by our rector. He set a grand example of a strong man under duress. In speech and manner he was entirely calm, but I could see all the same the deep-down anguish of his soul."[14] Taking immediate command of the situation, Dr. Stires soon announced that a new church would forthwith be erected on the site of the old edifice, and informed the press: "It is most gratifying to find that the congregation takes the burning as merely a setback to our work. I have received many telegrams and telephone messages promising me the fullest support for anything the vestry decides upon. One parishioner has already offered $50,000 for the work."[15]

Asked if he had any particular plans for rebuilding, Dr. Stires answered:

It will take two years at least to rebuild, and I know nothing at present of the size or character of the church that will be erected save that it will be of Gothic architecture and design. Whether the present tower can be utilized is a question for the architects to decide. In the meantime our church work will go on, and for our own needs of worship we hardly need a place until October, although we have always kept St. Thomas' open during the summer months.[16]

24. The Great Fire of 1905

Dr. Stires went on to tell the people of New York that they could "be quite sure that the congregation of St. Thomas' will put up a church worthy in every way of the city and the site. I think I may say it will be Gothic, and that no pains will be spared to make it of the purest architecture, for, to my mind, there is no style so fitting for divine worship."[17]

The morning after the fire, the rector and such members of the vestry as were available met in conference to devise a plan for carrying on the services. Emergency meetings of the vestry were held at the new St. Regis Hotel, nearby, for two or three days in a row.[18] Several churches, not all Episcopal, had offered the use of their buildings. It was, however, the desire of the parish authorities to keep the congregation functioning together as near its accustomed place as possible rather than in a neighboring church or hall.[19] A plan was therefore devised. It was decided to erect a temporary chapel within the shell of the burned church. Competent builders, having certified that such a plan was quite feasible, were therefore instructed to remove the debris and to build a frame structure on the same location. It was to be completed by November 1, 1905.

In an eloquent letter addressed to all his parishioners, the thirty-eight year old rector outlined the situation and the prospects for the future:

> At seven thirty o'clock on the morning of August eighth, when the fire was at its height, I called, over the long distance telephone, a meeting of the Vestry. I reached New York while the engines were still throwing powerful streams upon the ruins of the noble structure. That night the Rector and certain members of the Vestry discussed the problems with which we were confronted. On the following morning other Vestrymen reached town, and then, within twenty-four hours after the fire, authorization was given for the removal of the debris and the construction of a temporary building within the walls of our present church – to be completed not later than November first. The plan for the temporary building is now before me. As I write, a large force of workmen is busy within the walls of the church, and I have good reason to expect that by November first you will be summoned by the same chime of bells, now dearer to us than ever, ringing out from our beautiful tower – which is practically uninjured – and you will enter, through the same splendid doorway, a temporary structure which will seat fourteen hundred persons and over which the new church will be built. Will not all this mitigate our sorrow a little?
>
> Work has been begun on everything. The chime is being repaired, plans for a new organ are being drawn (our fine instrument was fully insured) and I have some hope that within a year from this Fall, St. Thomas's will be restored so far as the skill and energy of workmen can make this possible.
>
> The Rectory and Parish Rooms show few traces of the fire. Our regular work will continue. Yesterday there was a service with a short address at eight o'clock in the Parish Rooms, and this will be maintained every Sunday until November first, when we hope to enter our temporary building.
>
> The insurance amounts to $200,000, and I have every reason to expect that the companies will allow our claims in full. It is estimated that we shall require over $300,000 more than our insurance to rebuild. Please God, we shall try to

meet the need in a manner worthy of Him, and ourselves.

Your grief I can well understand and I beg to offer my affectionate sympathy. But you will let me ask you to try, with God's help, to see a vision of the new temple we shall build for His glory and the blessing of mankind. Fix your minds and hearts upon the future and make it worthy of our noble past.

Many telegrams, cablegrams, and hundreds of letters, testify the loyal devotion of our people, and the tender sympathy of the Church in all parts of the country, and of the multitudes outside our own communion. One of our Bishops writes: "This baptism of fire will draw you and your people closer in a most tender and sacramental relationship." Help me to make this true.[20]

The parish responded nobly to this courageous appeal, which demonstrated how fortunate the parish was in having a rector still in the resilience of youth. Furthermore, the parish found useful friends outside its own borders. Messrs. J. and R. Lamb, furnishers of church equipment, volunteered to supply an altar and chancel furnishings. The Hutchins Organ Company lent an organ. By the time the congregation had returned from summer vacation, the temporary chapel was ready for use. It was opened for services on All Saints' Day with a congregation of five hundred.[21]

Parish activities were not only maintained during this time of trial; they were in fact expanded. Three weeks after the congregation began to use the temporary chapel, an offering of $20,000 was collected for work on the East Side. The annual collection on Hospital Sunday was double that of the previous year. For work inside the diocese, the parish contributed within the year $40,000; for the missionary work of the Church at large, over $39,000. These amounts, together with gifts for theological education, brought the giving of the parish that year for non-parochial purposes to $89,769.21. And all this was done, it must be remembered, while the congregation was facing an unknown financial burden for rebuilding. "Our people have been loyal, patient, more deeply devoted than ever," the rector proudly observed, adding: "The destruction of the church's body made the immortality of its spirit the more evident."[22]

The first question facing the rector and vestry was to determine whether or not to build a new church around the surviving tower, so well known as a hallmark of Saint Thomas Church. That plan would make use of such parts of the apse and nave as still stood. To do so would have been to resurrect the Upjohn church. At a meeting of the vestry held on September 19, 1905, a committee on "plan and scope" was appointed and given authority to take counsel with the best architectural experts available. This committee consisted of John T. Atterbury, Clarence M. Hyde, James T. Woodward, Harris C. Fahnestock, and the rector. Mr. George B. Post was retained as consulting architect. After minute examination, Mr. Post reported that the tower, with a portion of the apse and the north wall of the nave, was the only thing left of value. He estimated that the church, without furniture or decoration, could be restored for about $300,000. An entirely new church of more durable material and fireproof construction would, in his estimation, cost twice that amount. Mr. Post also expressed the opinion that the brown sandstone of which the previous church had been constructed was not a suitable material in the climate of New York. Moreover, it is quite evident that Mr. Post did not subscribe to the praises that had been lavished on the Upjohn design of 1870. Indeed, he stated very plainly:

> I have always regarded the old church as the least satisfactory and interesting of all designs of the late Richard Upjohn, who was a very great architect. The tower, its best feature, now stands almost intact, but though graceful in proportion and detail, it is singularly small in scale of design and consequently appears insignificant in contrast with the buildings on Fifth Avenue. Except for considerations of sentiment and for economy it is certainly not worth preserving.[23]

After due consideration of this report, the Committee on Plan and Scope came to the unanimous opinion that an entirely new church should be built.[24] It is abundantly clear from the records that the rector and the vestry saw that a unique opportunity now lay before them.

Dr. Stires, rising to the challenge which history had presented, set forth his own vision for the new building in the parish's *Year Book* of 1905. What could be finer, he asked his parishioners, than "to see a parish rise from the ashes," courageously offering to God "a worthy dwelling place," as they erected a building wherein "the architect's skill and the sculptor's art," as in the past, should give them "still loftier ideals in great aspiring arches, more eloquent 'sermons in stones'." People expected the new Saint Thomas to be an inspiration, a noble church. They were not to be disappointed. "We shall have a church which, for its beauty and reverent appropriateness," the rector declared, "will be almost as worthy of visiting, and of thoughtful study, as the famous parish churches of England." It would be a building, "in beauty and impressiveness," that would also "fairly challenge the costly secular structures in which our city abounds."[25]

The decision to discard entirely the work of Upjohn raised the secondary but vexing question of whether to remain on the same site. Earlier, slums had swallowed up the first location. Now, by 1905, business was already encroaching upon the residential section of Fifth Avenue, and it was evident that this trend would continue and would also spread to the side streets near the church. The University Club at Fifty-fourth Street and Fifth Avenue had been completed in 1899, and early in the twentieth century no less than three hotels were going up nearby. Not a few parishioners were themselves starting to move still farther uptown, and there was the distinct possibility that Saint Thomas would be left as a sort of oasis in a desert of bustling com-

The Response of Dr. Stires to Unitarian Criticisms[55]

The Rev. Ernest M. Stires, rector of St. Thomas's Episcopal Church, replied yesterday to the criticism of the erection of the Cathedral of St. John the Divine expressed by the Rev. Dr. John Haynes Holmes at the dinner of the Unitarian Club on Wednesday night. Dr. Holmes had said:

"What will the people of this city think of the Church of God which will spend millions for that tomb of marble on Morningside Heights when people are dying because the Society for the Prevention of Tuberculosis is in need of funds; when the iniquity of child labor exists, and so much remains to be done?"

"It occurs to me," said Dr. Stires yesterday, "that the argument in support of the point of view which Dr. Holmes has advanced was first voiced about nineteen centuries ago and came from the lips of Judas Iscariot. When Mary broke the alabaster box of ointment in order to anoint the Master's feet, Judas exclaimed, you remember: 'Might not this ointment have been sold for more than three hundred pence and given to the poor?'

"All about us here we see the rise of magnificent temples to Mammon – the great new Public Library at Forty-second Street, serving the intellectual side of man; the wonderful new hosteleries springing up all about to minister to the body of man and his comfort. Is it then right and fitting that the house of God should move into a side street?

"It was this feeling that prompted St. Thomas's Church to remain where it was, although, after the fire, this plot could have been sold for $2,500,000, and we could have saved much money by moving uptown. We stayed here because we believed that a church should have as conspicuous a site and as nearly perfect a building as that new library or those hotels.

"Just so it is with the new cathedral. It is but right that in this city the great finger should rise on Morningside Heights, as the steeple of old Trinity does at the head of Wall Street, to remind men that all things of worth are not those of the material world.

"I question another side of this Unitarian argument. I question the propriety of such a criticism as has been made, without some proofs of what the Unitarians themselves have done. It must be remembered that the very people who are building this great cathedral are the people who have given most largely to the poor; the people of the church, which does, perhaps, without the exception of any other denomination, the widest and greatest work among the needy – in the East Side, in the hospitals, in the sections of the city which are not fashionable. And I ask, What is there to show on the other side? What hospitals do the Unitarians support? What sacrifices are they making for the poor? What proportion of their goods are their people giving for charity's sake?

"It is seemly that they should look to themselves before they criticise."

merce. It is therefore by no means surprising that some members of the vestry and of the congregation felt that the church should join the steady exodus of the city's northward growth. There was also the troubling feeling that the site of the burned church, which Dr. Stires a few years later said could have been sold for $2,500,000, was too valuable to be retained for Christian worship.[26] At one stage of the planning, the vestry practically committed itself to the proposition that the new church should be located at the northeast corner of Fifth Avenue and Sixty-third Street. Fortunately, in retrospect, the purchase of this site proved impossible.[27]

Dr. Stires never wavered from his conviction that the new church should be built on the old site. In his view, no site was too costly for a great house of worship that would stand in the midst of fashion and commerce, an enduring witness to the faith and truth of the Gospel. This view was shared by Dr. Greer, the Bishop of New York. Dr. Stires later referred to this location as "the strategic center of Manhattan Island."[28] Looking into the future, he may have envisioned three enduring strategic points for the work of the Episcopal Church there: Trinity far downtown in the financial district, the Cathedral of St. John the Divine on the heights near Columbia University, and Saint Thomas at the center.[29] Regardless of population changes, these three would have a perpetual function of witness because of their geographic situation. It was decided to build on the old site.

The committee had already decided upon certain general specifications. The plans were to include a church, a parish house, and a rectory. The style was to be Gothic. In obtaining designs, it was determined to hold a competition. Mr. William Aiken, architect of New York City, was retained as an advisor in this matter. He, in turn, recommended that Mr. Frank Miles Day of Philadelphia, president of the American Institute of Architects, and Mr. R. Clipston Sturgis of Boston, both recognized authorities on Gothic architecture, be asked to assist the committee in its selection. Invitations to compete in the contest went out to ten of the leading architects of the country.

The results, however, were disappointing, and all the entries were rejected.[30] The committee felt compelled to report to the vestry that "none of the designs is consistent with the high ideals entertained by the Committee of the dignity and importance of the opportunity." The expert advisors concurred in these drastic judgments. One of the competitors, however, had given encouraging evidence of an ability to address the challenge. Even though his submission was not approved, his design did indicate a "thorough appreciation and understanding of the truest form and expression of Gothic art as applied to Church architecture." The committee, therefore, observing that the competition had been for the selection of an architect and not necessarily for the adoption of any one design, reported that it felt justified in

127   STILL LOFTIER IDEALS

25. Ralph Adams Cram (left) and Bertram Grosvenor Goodhue (right)

negotiating with that architect for another plan, and the vestry recommended that the committee proceed along the lines suggested.[31]

Just as the vestry minutes of the later 1860s had made no mention of the formal engagement of Richard Upjohn to be the architect of the Saint Thomas Church of 1870, so the later vestry minutes record no formal appointment of the architect for the new Saint Thomas even though it is clear that Cram, Goodhue and Ferguson was the firm with whom they were proceeding. The minutes do state that at a vestry meeting on May 16, 1907, "the plans for the new church were presented and the details thoroughly explained by Mr. Cram," and that eleven days later general approval was given to "Plan R," submitted by the firm of Cram, Goodhue and Ferguson, who were requested to obtain estimates of the probable cost.[32] In the following January, *The Plans and Elevations for St. Thomas' Church made by Cram, Goodhue and Ferguson . . .* were published in a beautiful booklet printed by D. B. Updike and the Merrymount Press.[33] This firm's attention to the purity and nuances of the Gothic style appealed especially to Dr. Stires, who had regarded the old Upjohn building as rather Victorian and gloomy,[34] and who already knew the Gothic work of the Cram firm from the new chapel at West Point, where he had been a member of the Board of Visitors.

Ralph Adams Cram was then in his early forties, and had only begun to earn a national reputation as a church architect. As designer of All Saints Church, Ashmont (Dorchester), Massachusetts, and Calvary Church, Pittsburgh, he had shown outstanding ability in his career thus far. And in his early volume called *Church Building*, first published in 1899/1900, he had made very clear his intentions and direction. Convinced that the "natural process of development" of Gothic, indeed of Christian, architecture had been "stopped" early in the reign of Henry VIII,[35] he believed that "modern Gothicists should 'go back to the 16th century not to endeavor to build churches that shall pre-

Statement by Dr. Ralph Adams Cram on the Plan and Construction of the Fourth Church[56]

In many respects, St. Thomas Church will represent a departure from the ordinary ideals and methods of church building in this country. Our prime intention is the construction of a parish church which in its design, its construction and its decoration should represent, so far as we are able to produce this result, a model of ecclesiastical architecture conceived in the great spirit of the Middle Ages, adapted in every essential part to contemporary conditions and requirements, and expressing in every respect the ministry of beauty in divine worship.

Just because of this high ideal, St. Thomas Church will be, in all probability, the most expensive church per square foot built thus far in the United States, but this expense follows less from elaboration in richness of detail than from massiveness and honesty of construction. Throughout, it will be a piece of absolutely direct and honest masonry construction. There will be no steel columns masked by applied stone, no girders doing the work supposed to be accomplished by vaults and arches, no thin curtain walls, no subterfuges of any sort. From footings to crestings, it will be of such masonry as may be found in the most majestic buildings of the Middle Ages.

Outside and inside, the church will be entirely constructed of stone from quarries in Kentucky, the exterior being of a silvery limestone, the interior of a warm golden sandstone. In the church itself, there will be no plaster. All the wall surfaces will be of masonry and the high vault as well, which are made of Guastavino tiles, especially designed in color, texture and shape for this particular place.

Not the least interesting aspect of the church is the manner of its construction. After the fire, a temporary wooden church was erected within the ruined walls. When work was begun on the new fabric, the old church and rectory were removed and the choir and parish house built to the height of the latter. Then the temporary church was removed and its material stored. An enormous force of workmen entered on the premises, the foundations for the entire church were built, and when the floor had been completed, the old temporary church was reassembled and set up within the nave walls of the new. This temporary church will be occupied for the future while the construction of the new work is carried forward without intermission. In the spring, holes will be cut through the roof of the temporary church and the piers of the nave built through, and thereafter the work will continue uninterruptedly until the new church is completed, the parish still continuing to use the temporary church until such time as it can be removed, when the completed fabric will reveal itself in its entirety.[57] (ill. 26)

27. Stone being hoisted onto main tower in construction, 1913

26. Interior of the Temporary Church, 1911-12

tend to have been built in that century,' but, rather, in order that [they] might then 'work steadily and seriously towards something more consistent with our temper and the times in which we live'."[36] A vigorous Anglo-Catholic, and a founder of the Medieval Academy of America, he regarded church architecture as a sublime manifestation of religious faith. In his constructions, he would allow no sham, no meaningless battlements, no windows painted to imitate stained glass, no concealed steel beams, nothing covered over to look like stone that was not. A church building must show clearly of what it was made. He was an uncompromising advocate of the Gothic, not of the "neo-

Gothic." Such a man, such a touch of genius, such a determination, though difficult to deal with, does produce results of unique quality.

Joined with Cram was a partner whose artistry complemented his own; they were already at work on the chapel at West Point on the Hudson when the Saint Thomas project came their way. While Cram dealt with plan and design, with mass and proportion, Bertram Grosvenor Goodhue could produce those refinements of detail which distinguish a particular Gothic building and energize its effect[37] (pl. VII). Saint Thomas was "the last, and I think the best, of the projects on which we worked together in complete unity," Cram was later to say. The masonry would be traditional, without the aid of structural steel, although steel later had to be added to keep the north wall from collapsing.[38] The vaulting was to be conventionally quadripartite. A tower, at a height of some fifteen stories far stronger and more massive than Upjohn's admired construction, was planned for the southeast corner – planned in such a way that it not only would dominate Fifth Avenue as it presently existed, but could also not be threatened by the taller secular buildings that would inevitably rise in its vicinity. And within this house of God, everything would lead up to the magnificent reredos or altar-screen at the (geographical) west end, reminiscent of that in Winchester Cathedral but continuing the appearance and central theme (the Adoration of the Cross) of the Saint-Gaudens reredos from the old church; it would be entirely the design of Goodhue, in collaboration with the sculptor Lee Lawrie.[39] The rather shallow aisle chapel to the south along Fifty-third Street, eighteen feet wide with the lateral side gallery over it and the church offices to the west opening to the street, was an innovation unique to Cram, of which he continued to remain "rather inordinately proud."[40] This arrangement did create an asymmetrical interior on the east-west axis, placed off center by about ten yards to the north (to the right as one enters), but this in no way lessened the evocative or emotional effect of the interior as a whole. It has rightly been said that Cram and Goodhue (ill. 25) "clearly understood the power that well-known architectural images have over the mind."[41]

For three years after Cram's appointment as architect, he and the vestry committee labored mightily over the details of the plans, which had already been first published in January of 1908. In all they were thoroughly revised some twelve times. At length, in 1910, the paperwork was complete. The architectural plan proper, that is, the size, proportions, and mass, was the product of Cram's mind; indeed, there seems to be evidence that Goodhue himself had submitted an entirely different scheme for the whole church, which the Building Committee rejected.[42] The innumerable details of beauty, however, were subsequently contributed by Goodhue; indeed, they were probably drawn up, or at least finalized, from late 1912 to mid-1913 in Goodhue's

Even then it makes no attempt to challenge its neighbors by its height, but it holds the admiration of all by its incomparable grace and charm and by its four crowning turrets of unequal measurements.

The whole exterior is massive and varied in silhouette and extremely fine in proportion. The plain base of the tower, the severe simplicity of the buttresses, and the flat wall of the parish house are cleverly offset by the exquisite lacework of carving and the picturesque turrets that soften the building against the sky, as well as by the remarkably lovely rose window and the splendid doorway.

The interior is as beautiful in effect as the exterior. The wide and lofty nave impresses the visitor by its dignity and reserve. The straight, strong ribs rise from the pavement in aspiring lines that lead the soul of the worshiper heavenward with them in simplicity and truth. The rushing world is left without. The mere sight-seer entering the church forgets to criticize or compare. It is beautiful, uplifting – spiritual – and he is awed by the presence of an indescribable something. The impression of truth and sincerity has been gained by the use of no less powerful agents than absolute truth and sincerity in themselves. There is not a sham in the whole building. (ill. 27)

top-floor penthouse studio at 2 West Forty-seventh Street, where the arms of all three partners of the firm can still be seen on the mantel above the fireplace today.[43] The Committee on Plan and Scope, which had labored so long and so well, was discharged with thanks, and a small Building Committee was set up to work with the architects. The cost far exceeded anything that anyone had anticipated; Cram did not believe in sparing costs and would be content with nothing second best.[44] Whatever may have been the extent of rivalry or competition between Cram and Goodhue, it was their collaboration that made Saint Thomas Church possible, and it was only later in 1914, after the major construction of Saint Thomas was finished, that the firm of Cram, Goodhue and Ferguson was dissolved.[45]

The parish's financial resources had already been taxed by the donation of a significant sum to aid the victims of the great earthquake that struck the city of San Francisco in April of 1906. To raise funds for the new building, Dr. Stires now proposed to the vestry a plan to invite certain parishioners to the church parlors to examine the architectural drawings and to solicit subscriptions. This was unanimously adopted by the vestry in February of 1910. Three months later the rector reported that two-thirds of the cost of the new church, estimated at $1,079,000, had already been subscribed. It was as though an "angel of generosity" was directing the parish finances throughout these years, for in 1908 it had already been reported that the parish was giving to others almost five dollars for every one dollar it spent on itself, and in February of 1912 it was reported that, ever since the church burned in 1905, Saint Thomas had given to charity and to missions more money than it had set aside for its own rebuilding.[46]

The construction contract had been awarded to the Norcross Brothers of Worcester, Massachusetts, in June of 1910, and all work on the new church was to be completed on or before June 1, 1913, with the material and labor to cost $929,000.[47] The exterior was to be of Kentucky limestone (quarried in Bowling Green and cut in New York), and the interior of South Carrollton sandstone (slightly warmer and deeper in color). The reredos, to be completed somewhat later, and upon whose face the whole panorama of church history was to be displayed, would be of "Dunville" stone, a texture between limestone and sandstone. At one time this stone was thought to come from Danville, Ohio, but in 1971 it was discovered to be from Downsville, Wisconsin.[48]

On November 21, 1911, the cornerstone of the fourth Saint Thomas Church was laid by Bishop Greer. Two days previously, on Sunday, Dr. Stires anticipated the event in his sermon. "Before very long," he told his people, "we shall have our impressive new church, more beautiful and more firmly established than ever, in the center of Manhattan Island." The social troubles of the day, however, from domestic problems nearby and across the country

STILL LOFTIER IDEALS

to the armaments race abroad, could not be ignored. "These and other similar problems," he declared, "the new St. Thomas's must face with intelligence, sympathy and courage." A "greater future" was summoning the parish "to press forward for God and His people."[49] Under the new cornerstone[50] – upon which the inscription "Anno Domini MDCCCCXI" can still today be seen outside to the left of the main entrance near "the Bride's Door" – there were placed also the cornerstones of the two previous churches of Saint Thomas. It is worthy of note that among the congregation gathered on that day were Bishop Whitehouse's son and a daughter of Dr. Morgan – two living links with past rectors. The parish house was also completed in 1911.

The first service in the new church was held on October 4, 1913. Since the General Convention of the Episcopal Church was then meeting in New York, advantage was taken of that event to hold, on Saturday evening October 11, a special service largely attended by the bishops, clergy, and lay deputies present at the Convention. The principal address was given by the Rt. Rev. Daniel Sylvester Tuttle, Presiding Bishop of the Episcopal Church, whose memories of Saint Thomas while he was a college student and seminarian went back to the church on Houston Street; soon he would become the sole living person sculpted in the new reredos.[51] Another to speak briefly at that time was the Rt. Rev. William F. Nichols, Bishop of California, who "generously acknowledged the practical sympathy of St. Thomas parish with the church in San Francisco at the time of the earthquake and devastating fire."[52]

One of those who watched with interest the rising fabric of the new Saint Thomas was Henry Holt, a prominent New York publisher and author. He confessed to not being able to walk past the structure "in the morning without tracing his steps and studying it afresh from several angles of observation." He believed that the church "would do much toward lifting the whole ideal of church architecture in this country." With this view a correspondent to *The Churchman* heartily concurred, confidently predicting that "this last creation in stone of this firm of architects will stand when completed unrivaled among the parish churches of America."[53] And so it has for many. To the remarkable leadership of Ernest Milmore Stires, to the wisdom and judgment of the vestry, and to the generosity and patience of the congregation, endless gratitude was due for giving to the world, as a contemporary architect remarked, a church "clothed with a mantle of inspiration, a masterpiece of craftsmanship, a work of genius."[54]

Notes

1 *Year Book* 1901, pp. 5-6.

2 *Year Book* 1901, p. 125; *Year Book* 1902, pp. 8, 158.

3 VM 5:118 (23 April 1902).

4 *Year Book* 1902, p. 157.

5 *Year Book* 1901, pp. 18-19.

6 *Year Book* 1922, p. 25.

7 VM 5:126 (1 December 1902).

8 *Year Book* 1902, pp. 8-9. For twenty of the thirty years that he served as organist and choirmaster, Dr. Warren paid for the music used in the church out of his own stipend.

9 *The Churchman* 85 (5 April 1902): 448.

10 *Year Book* 1902, pp. 7-10.

11 *Year Book* 1904, p. 9; VM 5:156-57 (19 May 1905); *Year Book* 1905, pp. 7-8.

12 Their names and dates, culled from the *Year Books* of his time, are as follows: Josephine A. Lyon (1902-1903), Eugenia Collins (1903-1904, 1906-1907), Minnie A. Crosby (1903-1910), Mary Palmer (1904-1905), Ellen Adwen (1904-1906), and Louise Schodts (1912-1925). Deaconess Crosby, who also served as a nurse at Saint Thomas Chapel over the years 1900-1910, was set apart as a Deaconess at Saint Thomas Church on 17 May 1903, with Bishop Henry Codman Potter officiating and Dr. Stires giving the address. There is much additional information about all these Deaconesses in the Archives of the Diocese of New York and elsewhere, although very little of it pertains to their activities at Saint Thomas Church.

13 It had been given at Easter of 1891 in memory of John Hopson Schoenberger, as its inscription reveals.

14 E. Clowes Chorley, *Manuscript History of St. Thomas Church* (unpublished manuscript in Saint Thomas Archives, 1943; copy deposited in the St. Mark's Library of the General Theological Seminary, New York City), p. 474.

15 "Flames Destroy Old St. Thomas'," *The New York Herald,* 9 August 1905, p. 3.

16 "Flames Destroy Old St. Thomas'," p. 3.

17 "Flames Destroy Old St. Thomas'," p. 3. See also *The New York Times* 54:17364 (9 August 1905): 3; *The New York Daily Tribune* 65:21451 (9 August 1905): 4.

18 Personal recollection of Mr. Sidney Stires, former Senior Warden of Saint Thomas and grandson of the Rev. Dr. Ernest M. Stires, communicated to the author on 12 December 1999.

19 VM 5:161 (11 September 1905).

20 Original letter of E. M. Stires to parishioners, 14 August 1905, in Saint Thomas Archives.

21 *Year Book* 1905, p. 9.

22 *Year Book* 1905, p. 9.

23 VM 5:177 (19 September 1905), VM 5:179-83 (15 November 1905).

24 VM 5:179-81 (15 November 1905).

25 *Year Book* 1905, pp. 10-12.

26 See sidebar on p. 127.

27 VM 5:214-15 (3 December 1906: evidence that a site on Fifty-second Street was being considered), 6:33 (8 April 1909: evidence for consideration of a site at Sixty-third Street), 6:43 (29 November 1909), 6:70-75 (6 June 1910).

28 *Year Book* 1914, pp. 13-14.

29 Sidebar on p. 127; Chorley, *Manuscript History*, chapter 14, p. 4.

30 Nine of them were published in *Architecture* 13 (15 May 1906): 68-98.

31 VM 5:205-8 (9 April 1906).

32 VM 6:6 (16 May 1907), 6:7-8 (27 May 1907). The firm of Cram, Goodhue and Ferguson had submitted four months earlier "a bill for $7,500 on account of their compensation for work already performed," although the nature of the work is not specified; see VM 6:2-3 (28 January 1907).

33 Copy in the Saint Thomas Archives.

34 Personal interview 13 November 1998 with Mr. Sidney Stires, former Senior Warden of Saint Thomas and grandson of the Rev. Dr. Ernest M. Stires.

35 Ralph Adams Cram, *Church Building* (Boston: Small, Maynard & Company; second edition, 1914), pp. 264, 269. Rejoicing in the "power of achievement" given to ecclesiastical art by "the Oxford Movement, which aimed at the restoration to Ecclesia Anglicana of her catholic heritage," the "Retrospect" added by Cram to the second edition of this book opens with a full-page photograph of the new Saint Thomas Church (pp. 239, 240). Cram seems to have used the terms "Gothic" and "Christian" somewhat interchangeably; cf. p. 239: "Gothic or Christian."

36 Douglass Shand-Tucci, *Ralph Adams Cram: American Medievalist* (Boston: Boston Public Library, 1975), p. 17, quoting from Cram's remarks about the construction of All Saints Church in Ashmont (Dorchester), Massachusetts, that were published in 1892 and 1899.

37 Further on Goodhue, see Richard Oliver, *Bertram Grosvenor Goodhue* (New York: The Architectural History Foundation; Cambridge, Massachusetts, and London, England: The MIT Press; American Monograph Series; 1983), and Christine Smith, *St. Bartholomew's Church in the City of New York* (New York: Oxford University Press, 1988), chapter 2. Goodhue was also the designer of the Churches of the Intercession and of St. Vincent Ferrer, as well as of St. Bartholomew's (Smith, *St. Bartholomew's Church*, p. 39) and the Grolier Club. Within a glass case in the north nave aisle of the present Saint Thomas Church, there is displayed the very fine printing of the 1892 Book of Common Prayer that was published in 1893 by D. B. Updike and the De Vinne Press, bound in vellum in limited edition, the covers and borders of which were designed by Goodhue himself. Another unique example of Goodhue's work that still survives is the very elaborate "Saint Thomas Bible" (pl. VII), designed under his supervision by Clarence S. Stein, bound in pigskin, decorated in copper gilt and carved ivory, printed by Oxford University Press, and presented as a thank-offering by Miss Florence S. Sullivan on All Saints' Day of 1916 (*Insurance Appraisal of Property Belonging to St. Thomas Church*, completed by Christie's of New York and dated 10 June 1996, p. 60, no. 216. Manuscript kept in Saint Thomas Archives). For full description and picture, see [Frank Le G. Gilliss], *A Short Description of the Reredos, Wood Carvings and Other Objects of Interest in Saint Thomas Church New York City* (New York: Gilliss Press, 1927), pp. 61-63.

38 Gerald Allen in *Dimensions: Space, Shape & Scale in Architecture* (New York: Architectural Record Books, 1976), p. 29. See also sidebar on p. 128.

39 The word "reredos," meaning "back," refers to any decoration behind and above an altar. Cram used the Winchester reredos as the frontispiece for the second edition of his *Church Building*. See also Allen, *Dimensions*, p. 33. The magnificence of the reredos was desired and endorsed by Dr. Stires, even at the large sum, for that day, of $60,000. (Personal interview 13 November 1998 with Mr. Sidney Stires). Goodhue was responsible for the scheme and positioning of the figures, Lawrie for their design and expression in stone, and the firm of Ardolino Brothers for their actual cutting and carving; the collective inscription of gratitude by all of them is incised in Latin on the sanctuary wall to the right of their work. Lawrie, who lived from 1877 to 1962, had been a pupil of Saint-Gaudens. Further see Hanna Tachau, "Lee Lawrie – Architectural Sculptor" in the August 1922 issue of *International Studio*. Chorley, *Manuscript History*, chapter 15, p. 38, gives the total final cost for the "Reredos, Altar, and the windows and certain other features" as amounting to just under $110,000. The similarity of the Great Reredos of Saint Thomas to that of the chapel of All Souls College in Oxford is also noteworthy. The "Doors of the Angels" at either side of the Saint Thomas Reredos were to depict, on the right, traditional angelic symbols, and, on the left, modern persons who serve as angels (such as a nurse, a soldier, a sailor). The covers for their keyholes, indicating Goodhue's skill at detail, replicate in miniature the outline of the reredos. Later elsewhere, and in very different styles, Lawrie in 1925 designed the magnificent pulpit of St. Bartholomew's Church on Park Avenue (Smith, *St. Bartholomew's Church*, pp. 138-40), and in 1937 he sculpted the great figure of Atlas at the entrance to Rockefeller Center, 630 Fifth Avenue.

40 Ralph Adams Cram, *My Life in Architecture* (Boston: Little, Brown, and Company, 1936), pp. 79, 116.

41 Allen, *Dimensions*, p. 27.

42 Shand-Tucci, *Ralph Adams Cram*, pp. 30, 35.

43 Oliver, *Bertram Grosvenor Goodhue*, pp. 171-73; *The New York Times,* Sunday, 16 April 2000, p. 9. I thank Mr. Martin Hutner for assisting me to see the former Goodhue studio.

44 VM 6:10 (29 November 1907), 6:16-17 (10 February 1908), 6:37 (12 May 1909), 6:43 (29 November 1909), 6:51 (26 January 1910), 6:57 (21 March 1910), 6:58 (15 April 1910), 6:60-61 (26 May 1910). It is interesting to note that by following strictly the idea of developed Gothic, Cram had made a perfectly fireproof building.

45 Allen, *Dimensions*, p. 29. Positive experience with Cram and Ferguson at Saint Thomas may well have brought them the contract for the Cathedral of St. John the Divine in 1911, where Dr. Stires and warden George M. Miller were trustees at that time. On the former's defense of the cost involved in the cathedral's construction, see sidebar on p. 126.

46 As reported in *The New York Times* for 17 January 1908 and 12 February 1912. The former story also reported that the parish's "total income" for 1907 was $271,000, second in New York only to St. Bartholomew's of $316,000, and its "membership" a total of 3000, the same as that of St. Bartholomew's.

47 VM 6:55-56 (18 February 1910), 6:60-61 (26 May 1910), 6:69 (31 May 1910), 6:70-75 (6 June 1910).

48 Further see chapter 12, note 36.

49 *Year Book* 1911, pp. 14-16.

50 For the list of its contents, see *Year Book* 1911, pp. 203-4. The trowel from this ceremony, of Gorham silver, is still in the possession of the parish (*Insurance Appraisal* by Christie's [1996], p. 51, no. 177).

51 The figure of Bishop Tuttle appears in the present reredos. He had been born in Windham, New York, in 1837, and graduated, like so many nineteenth-century Episcopalian clergy, from both Columbia University and the General Theological Seminary. He was consecrated first missionary bishop of Montana, Idaho, and Utah at the age of thirty in 1867. He became third bishop of Missouri in 1886. When he was sixty-six years old he became the Presiding Bishop of the Episcopal Church by virtue of seniority in consecration. He died on 17 April 1923, and is the only person who was living at the time whose figure was placed in the reredos.

52 Chorley, *Manuscript History*, chapter 14, p. 22.

53 *Year Book* 1913, pp. 189-90.

54 *Year Book* 1913, p. 189. The architect/author was George B. Ford.

55 As reported in *The New York Times* of 27 January 1911, p. 4. See also the issues of January 26, p. 18, and January 28, p. 10.

56 Statement issued by Dr. Cram after the cornerstone ceremony on 21 November 1911; text supplied from Chorley, *Manuscript History*, chapter 14, pp. 17-18.

57 It must be added that, eleven years after the completion of the church, it was unfortunately discovered that the unbuttressed north wall of the building was bulging dangerously. It was therefore necessary, contrary to Cram's principles, to resort to steel beams for reinforcement. These were placed, at enormous expense, across every pair of columns above the ceiling. Later, as the subway under and across Fifty-third Street was being drilled, it was also thought wise to place a steel beam under the high altar and reredos, which remains there. Nonetheless, the support for the church's roof still comes basically from its pillars, not its walls, and the great Gothic edifice still conveys the appearance, as well as the reality, of something that is permanent and enduring. See below, page 158.

58 H. L. Bottomley, "The Story of St. Thomas' Church," *The Architectural Record* 35:2 (February 1914): 120, 122, 126. Also quoted in Chorley, *Manuscript History*, chapter 14, pp. 29-31.

28. Exterior of the present (fourth) Saint Thomas Church, Fifth Avenue and Fifty-third, consecrated April 25, 1916 (architect, Ralph Adams Cram)

CHAPTER 10

Like a City Set on a Hill

ERNEST MILMORE STIRES
EIGHTH RECTOR, 1901-1925

IN 1914, DR. STIRES DETERMINED to eradicate the debt of $150,000 remaining on the church. By the time of the outbreak of World War I in Europe, about $80,000 of this had been contributed.[1] Early in 1916, he was able to announce that the remaining amount had been pledged, and that the church could be consecrated shortly after Easter of that year (ill. 28). The total cost of the building had been $1,171,906.44.[2] And the building had taken place at a most propitious time. It has been remarked that, a few years later, a comparable building would have cost four times as much, and that a few years later still, financial depression and rising income taxes would have made the raising of the necessary funds four times as difficult. But it was not only financial temporalities that made the date of the building so fortunate; a Ralph Adams Cram does not exist in every generation.

In these very same years that he was so concerned with building and finance, Dr. Stires also took steps to organize the parish for outreach by constituting a Men's Association that would work through eight committees. The first was to be concerned with Saint Thomas Chapel, the second with missions in the city, the diocese, and beyond, and the other six with areas of civic life: city administration (police and fire), city institutions (jails and workhouses), city improvement (streets and parks), industrial problems (unemployment and strikes), social problems (poverty, vice, crime, disease), and legislation.[3]

On Tuesday in Easter Week, April 25, 1916, the present and fourth church was consecrated. The service, which was marked by great dignity, was the consummation of eleven years of patient and devoted work by rector, vestry, and congregation. To the stirring strains of the traditional dedication hymn, *Christ is Made the Sure Foundation*, the long procession – consisting of some 150 vested clergy, the members of the Standing Committee of the diocese, the two architects, and nine bishops – moved from the parish house to the front entrance of the church. It would have pleased them greatly to see above them over the doorways the outlined images in gilded wood of all four of the Saint

137

Thomas Church buildings with their dates.⁴ Here Bishop Greer of New York, the consecrator, was met by the wardens and vestrymen and given the keys of the fourth church. As the procession advanced up the aisle, Psalm 24 was recited. The Instrument of Donation was read by George McCulloch Miller, now for over fifty years an officer of the parish. The Sentence of Consecration was read by Bishop Charles S. Burch, Suffragan of the diocese.

The sermon was preached by Bishop Greer. He took for his text James 1:22, "Be ye doers of the Word, and not hearers only." The Christian church, the bishop told the congregation, faced the challenge of taking "its old historic creed" and making it alive in every aspect of life, not merely the personal but the social, the national, and the worldwide. Only in this way would the church regain "its own distinctive work and mission," one "that will differentiate it at once and by a leap from every other social organization on the face of the earth." The church, Bishop Greer maintained, was intended to be "an incarnation in the world, the incarnation of God, and so continue in the world the Incarnate Jesus Christ."

The people of Saint Thomas were thus entrusted with a particular role of leadership. "Your building is great, your membership is great, your resourcefulness is great," exclaimed the bishop, "and, situated as you are, on one of the great thoroughfares of this community and this country, like a city set on a hill, your example cannot be, in its reach and scope otherwise than great." More importantly, though, "you have, and have shown, in your parish life, a great potential energy, a great spiritual and vital force," which in the face of adversity "still held you together in one great corporate life, unbroken and unimpaired." To a large extent this was owing, he said, "to the brave, indomitable and indefatigable leadership of your Rector."⁵

On the following Sunday Dr. Stires gave his own interpretation. More significant than any other event in any other building in society, he said, is the consecration of a church, for it alone "humanizes science, moralizes knowledge, spiritualizes wealth, and inspires the highest patriotism." Yet the true consecration of a church is "the consecration of the people who built it and will worship there, for they constitute its soul." He observed: "We are living in the greatest of all ages. For a century science has been weaving its magic spell about the earth, drawing us nearer and nearer. It must mean that the earth is preparing to hear the voice of God in the midst of the life of today; and it means that we are commissioned to deliver His message and to re-value all things in terms of character and of the endless life."⁶

Hardly had the new church been completed when World War I broke out. Even before the United States entered the conflict, in 1917, the war was a very present fact in the daily life of New York City. As the greatest seaport of the country, it had always been aware of Europe in a way that the interior of the nation was not. Now its streets were thronged by sailors of the Allied Powers. When the United States declared war, to these foreign troops were added hundreds of American soldiers and sailors who often were unable to find decent lodging in the strange metropolis. Under the leadership of Dr. Stires, the parish resolutely tackled this problem. Arrangements were made to shelter as many of these men as possible in the parish house, where they received breakfast every morning. A house situated at 8 West Fifty-third Street was fitted up as a club for soldiers and sailors, and largely frequented by them. There was always an aggregate of uniformed personnel at the services of the church. "The considerable number of men in uniform attending our services," Dr. Stires suggested to the congregation, "have contributed much to the reality and deepening of our worship as we have come to our divine Leader for forgiveness, for orders, for blessing." Paying tribute to the contribution that women had made, he also declared: "American womanhood stood the test; over there, and over here."[7]

Like the rest of the nation, the parish too began to pour its young men into the armed forces. The service flag displayed outside the church had 325 stars; eventually fourteen of these were gold stars – symbols of men who had died in service. In addition to these, fourteen women of the parish were enlisted as YWCA workers, nurses, and persons in other spheres of war activity. Included in the list of servicemen was the rector himself. The vestry having granted him leave of absence, he volunteered as a chaplain, was accepted, and saw service for six months on the front lines in France.[8]

On November 14, 1917, vestryman George McCulloch Miller died. He had served in that capacity for forty years, and as senior warden for sixteen. His services to the church had extended far beyond the confines of the parish. For many years he had been a trustee of St. Luke's Hospital, and he finally became president of that venerable institution. He had founded the Hospital Saturday and Sunday Association, now known as the United Hospital Fund, and had shared with Francis Lynde Stetson the distinction of being the outstanding layman at many diocesan conventions. One of the original trustees of the Cathedral of St. John the Divine, he was secretary of the board from 1873 until his death. A devoted servant of Saint Thomas parish, of the diocese, and of the city of New York, he passed to his eternal reward at the ripe age of eighty-five.

Back in 1912, after fifteen years of service, Mr. William Macfarlane had resigned as organist and choirmaster to become municipal organist of the city of Portland, Maine, the first position of the kind to be created in the nation. Saint Thomas Church said farewell to its gifted master of music with great regret. During his tenure he had been a founder of the American Guild of Organists and had enjoyed a reputation as the most popular organist in the city. Crowded congregations attended his special musical services, and many frequented his recitals after Evensong.[9]

The vestry then cast about for a suitable successor. At this time T. Tertius Noble (ill. 29), the acclaimed organist of York Minster and already an honorary fellow of the Royal College of Organists, was in the United States for a series of organ recitals. The vestry made contact with him, and invited him to become organist of Saint Thomas. He accepted, and arrived to take up his duties in May of 1913. In his acceptance letter, Dr. Noble pledged to do "everything in my power to make the service of the Church as devotional and beautiful as possible." He trusted that "all will help me in my work to stamp out anything which is not worthy of such a beautiful place of worship."[10]

29. T. Tertius Noble, Organist and Choirmaster 1913-1943

Dr. Noble had already, as his position in England would indicate, won recognition as one of the great organists and choirmasters of his day. Born at Bath on May 6, 1867, he had begun his musical career at an early age, and later graduated from the Royal College of Music, London, in 1889. He was successively organist of Trinity College in Cambridge University, of Ely Cathedral, and from 1898 of York Minster. His coming brought to Saint Thomas a rich experience of the finest Anglican musical traditions. And it brought to the United States one of the most heralded composers of church music of the day. He became a member of the Joint Commission on the Hymnal in 1916, the Joint Commission on Church Music until 1943, and the Musical Committee of the Hymnal of 1940. Such anthems as "Souls of the righteous" (voted the single most popular anthem in a survey of leading choirmasters taken in 1923)[11] and service music like the *Magnificat* and *Nunc Dimittis* in B Minor placed him in distinguished company. In the Episcopal Church's Hymnal of 1982, his musical settings survive as numbers S38 (an Anglican chant for the *Venite*), 383 ("Fairest Lord Jesus"), and 541 ("Come, labor on"). In the *Year Book* of the parish for 1915, Dr. Stires was able to remark with sincerity: "Our music is a constantly increasing stimulus and joy. In the choir, in the organ recitals, in St. Thomas's Choral Society, Mr. Noble is rendering service beyond our power adequately to praise. His ability, his fine spirit and the beauty of his compositions have endeared him to the Parish."[12] Another feature of Dr. Noble's tenure at the organ bench in Saint Thomas was the recitals given for many years on Sunday evenings at eight o'clock. These recitals were completely devoid of parade. Concert-goers came in, received a little printed program from an usher, and found a place in the dimly-lighted church. There was, of course, no applause; listeners left when they pleased; they never even saw the performer. But for a glorious hour the great soaring arches of Cram resounded to the best of organ music, superbly rendered.

Such an organist, called to a great new church, required a great organ.

On January 3, 1913, the vestry signed a contract with Ernest M. Skinner, one of the most renowned American organ builders of the day, for the erection of a new organ at a cost of $25,000. The specifications, which had been originally done under the oversight of Mr. Macfarlane, were two years being drawn up.[13] Dr. Noble arrived in time to make some revisions to these and added some of the best features he knew from the organ of York Minster, which was regarded as the finest in England. The organ filled four bays in the chancel, the pipes showing only in one bay, with the others hidden by a richly carved screen. This superior instrument was the gift of Mrs. Georgie B. de Heredia and Mrs. Marianne C. McDougall, in memory of their parents, Henry H. and Mary McKay Cook. The gift was singularly appropriate as Mr. Cook had been the donor of the previous organ, installed in 1903 and so quickly destroyed in the fire of 1905.

Only one thing was now lacking to make the music of Saint Thomas truly great: a choir school.[14] As far back as 1902, when the boy choir was first established, Mr. Macfarlane had expressed the hope that the parish might some day have a choir school where the boys would be under constant supervision. Such a school would of course ensure regular attendance at rehearsals and services. The fire of 1905 had of necessity postponed such a project, but the idea was never forgotten. In 1913, Dr. Stires pointed out that both the Cathedral of St. John the Divine and Grace Church had established choir schools much to the advantage of their worship and music. Dr. Noble likewise felt the increasing necessity of such a step. The boys who made up the choir came from Staten Island, from Long Island, and from New Jersey. To gather them for rehearsals became every year more difficult. In fact, Dr. Noble had to resort to the heroic expedient of individual rehearsals for some of the boys if they were to be rehearsed at all.

The rector and three members of the music committee were appointed at a meeting of the vestry held on April 30, 1918, to investigate the possibility of establishing a choir school. They suggested that thirty parishioners might be found, each of whom would be willing to provide a scholarship of $500 a year for five years. If this could be accomplished, the vestry was ready to assume responsibility for the rent of a suitable house to contain the school. By the end of the year nearly two-thirds of the required funds had been pledged by twenty subscribers, "warranting, in the judgment of the Committee, the leasing of a house and the starting of the undertaking." This was done and, on March 3, 1919, the Saint Thomas Choir School was opened at 123 West Fifty-fifth Street, with twenty-one boys, fourteen of whom were boarding pupils.[15] This was of course a tremendous help to Dr. Noble, who bore testimony to its value in the next issue of the *Year Book*. "I need not say," he observed, "what an enormous advantage it is to our music in having this school, for I am able to teach these children daily, and I find that the more they sing, the more they love it. Thus our daily rehearsal is not looked upon as lessons, but as an hour of joy to all concerned." The rector reported that the boys had "all become more and more a part of the Church family, regarding the privileges of attending services as a reward rather than a duty to be performed."[16] The house was large enough to accommodate thirty boys; the committee therefore expressed the hope that additional scholarships might soon be provided to care for ten more boys, giving the choir the full complement required for effectiveness in a church the size of Saint Thomas.[17]

30. Charles Steele, Vestryman 1905-15, Warden 1915-39, Patron and Benefactor of the Choir School

At a vestry meeting held on December 15, 1922, the rector reported that Mr. Charles Steele (ill. 30), warden of the parish and chairman of the music committee, an astute railroad lawyer and business associate of J. P. Morgan, had bought and presented to the parish two houses, the one already in use at 123 West Fifty-fifth Street and its neighbor at number 121 (ill. 31). To make this property fully effective, it was necessary to do some remodeling. This work Mr. Steele underwrote for an amount up to $30,000. He likewise guaranteed the ten additional scholarships needed to bring the choir up to full quota. When he had done all this, it was found that he had given the choir in all $160,000, the largest single gift that had been made to the parish up to this time. Yet he did not stop even there. To assure the permanence of the school, Mr. Steele wrote the vestry in 1925 to state that he was donating to the institution securities to the value of $275,000 as an endowment fund. This was accepted and appropriately named "The Charles Steele Foundation."[18]

And thus was continued that marriage of the arts in the service of the church that Saint Thomas had already established, especially under Dr. Morgan. A glorious new building, noble stained glass, fine sculpture, an eloquent rector, beautiful music – all these were combined to make the services at Saint Thomas an offering worthy of rendering to Almighty God.

The new church's structure itself was now complete: 214 feet long, 100 feet wide, the width of the nave between the columns 43 feet, the height from the pavement to the crown of the vault being 95 feet. The published plans, in fact, indicated a church of greater width and height than any cathedral in England.[19] Because of the scarcity of lateral space there were no transepts, and the demarcation between the seven-bay nave and the two-bay chancel was minimal. That division was marked, however, by "the parapet," the low wall that separates the nave from the chancel or choir, containing eight mosaics of unpolished colored stone surrounded by ceramic tile.[20] Beginning at the far left, there were placed on the parapet four panels symbolic of the church, depicting it as 1) a ship on stormy waters (the traditional arms of Saint Thomas upon its sail); 2) a lighthouse (Christ himself being the light); 3) a city of refuge (showing the gateway of a walled city with a young man knocking at its entrance); and 4) the tree of knowledge (with birds resting on its branches and animals beneath, such as a lion and lamb reclining together).[21] Beginning at the far right and moving toward the center, there were placed four historical panels depicting 1) the first celebration of the Holy Communion in the new world at Jamestown, Virginia, in 1607; 2) the American Revolution and Independence Hall in Philadelphia; 3) the Capitol in Washington as symbolic of the reunification of North and South at the end of the Civil War (with the words of President Ulysses S. Grant, "Let us have peace"); and 4) Rheims Cathedral, so badly damaged in World War I and located near the area where Dr. Stires had served in the war. This last panel was even made of stones that he had brought from Rheims and other war-ravaged European cathedrals.[22]

31. Home of the Choir School from 1922-87 at 121-23 West Fifty-fifth Street

Related symbolically to the parapet, the floor of the chancel was constructed to incorporate five quatrefoil mosaics of polished stone and colored tile representing at the right the arms of the state and city of New York, and at the left the arms of the diocese (founded 1785) and the former arms of the parish (inscribed "Let us also go that we may die with him," the words of Saint Thomas in John 11:16). In the center was placed the Great Seal of the United States.[23] The ceramic tiles in the floors of both chancel and sanctuary (as well as of the Chantry) were executed under the supervision of Henry Chapman Mercer at the Moravian Pottery and Tile Works in Doylestown, Pennsylvania.[24] Moving onward and symbolically heavenward toward the high altar, in front of its rail were placed the symbols of the seven sacraments (with slight variations): Penitence (substituted for "Penance," the traditional term), Holy Orders, Baptism, Holy Communion (in the center), Confirmation, Holy Matrimony, and Prayer (replacing "Unction," which would have been customary). Communicants were hereby boldly reminded that it is by the seven sacraments of the Church that the Gate of Heaven is approached.

The seating capacity was estimated then at about seventeen hundred places[25] for the worshipers who would soon throng to complete and fill this new house of God (pl. VIII). Included was a transverse gallery in the easternmost bay of the nave, covering the narthex, as well as another gallery along the south side. The walls themselves were divided into the three levels of arcade, triforium (without windows), and clerestory. There was still much more to be done to the interior, as stained glass windows, altar and reredos, altar rail, font, and choir stalls, many of them to be memorials, had yet to be supplied, not to mention the niches on the façade that had to be filled.

The spectacular reredos (pl. V, ill. 32), some forty-three feet wide and eighty feet high and containing over eighty figures, was soon to be a memorial to Mr. and Mrs. Harris C. Fahnestock given by their children (ill. 33).[26] This altar-screen would easily compensate for the architectural inability to erect any great window at the far end because of the property line that excluded light from the outside. Unlike most other great reredoses, therefore, it was not intended to be a mere dividing wall between the nave and various chapels behind it, but rather would totally define the liturgical east end (geographical west) of the church. It was rather flat in effect, suggestive of the English perpendicular style, but this would complement the more French-Gothic appearance of the arches and columns of the nave. The Saint Thomas reredos was to be one of the largest in the world and larger than any Gothic example known. Standing symbolically at the very Gateway to Heaven, it would forever invite worshipers and communicants at the parish's high altar on earth to lift up their eyes to the heavenly altar above, to join with the whole company of saints in offering the very same Eu-

33. Harris C. and Margaret A. Fahnestock, in whose memory the Great Reredos was given

charistic sacrifice in the worship of eternity. In its carvings of stone (ill. 34), it would offer a vision for mere mortals who would seek, like the living stones in the text of I Peter 2:4-5, to be formed into a spiritual house, to offer spiritual sacrifices acceptable to God, to be united in prayer with the saints upon whose intercessions they rely (pl. V).

On a lighter note, there should be mention of the now-famous "dollar sign" that Goodhue had worked into the ornament to the left of the main front entrance over the small door at the base of the tower now known as "The Bride's Door." It was placed there in conjunction with images of God's hand joining the hands of a bride and groom by means of a stole (all contained inside a ring), of (on the right) both a priest and Christ himself blessing the couple, and (on the left) of the marriage at Cana. When this monetary symbol was discovered in 1921, as Richard Oliver points out in his biography of Goodhue,[27] "there was a minor scandal. Some observers saw in the inclusion of such modern secular images a desecration of a sacred place, but Goodhue was defended in editorials in *The New York Times*." The columnist Truman Talley observed there that "The architect who placed the dollar mark and a hundred or more other indisputable modernisms in Saint Thomas' was following a time-honored precedent . . . [and] what really would have been more startling, in the light of the history of ecclesiastical architecture, would have been the omission by the designers of some sort of accurate twentieth-century symbolism."[28]

The last major work of exterior construction was the building of a new residence for the rector. After the fire of 1905, the plans for the new church involved the use of the land occupied by the old rectory. In its place, a house next door at No. 3 West Fifty-third Street was bought as a new rectory.[29] In the course of time, this house had become unsanitary and otherwise undesirable as a residence. The matter of dealing with it was referred to a committee consisting of Messrs. Robert B. Dodson, William Fahnestock, and William Adams Kissam. In due course, the committee reported that the cost of making the rectory habitable would be about two-thirds the cost of a new building. Common sense therefore dictated that the vestry take the opportunity to build a house which would harmonize architecturally with the church and the parish house and not obscure the three small windows at the

IDENTIFICATION OF FIGURES ON THE GREAT REREDOS

(Numbers in parentheses indicate approximate date of death)

1 St. Polycarp (156)

2 St. Ignatius (107)

3 St. Cyprian (258)

4 St. Stephen, first Christian martyr

5 St. John Chrysostom (407)

6 St. Athanasius (373)

7, 8, 9 Angels holding the Holy Innocents

10, 11 Arms of Diocese and Parish

12 St. Philip the Deacon, 1st Century

13 St. Jerome (420)

14 St. Francis of Assisi (1226)

15 St. Gregory the Great (604)

16 Savonarola (1498)

17 St. Augustine of Hippo (430)

19 Richard Hooker (1600)

20 Bishop Butler (1752)

21 Restitutus, first known Bishop of London (314)

22 St. Columba, Abbot of Iona (597)

23 John Wesley (1791)

24 Canon Liddon, St. Paul's Cathedral, London (1890)

25 Bishop Selwyn, New Zealand (1878)

26 Bishop Patteson, Melanesia (1871)

27 St. Bartholomew, Apostle

28 St. Philip, Apostle

29 St. James the Less, Apostle

30 St. Augustine, Canterbury (604)

31 St. Theodore of Tarsus, Canterbury (690)

32 St. James the Great, Apostle

33 Blessed Virgin Mary

34 Christ the King

35 St. John the Beloved Disciple

36 The Venerable Bede (735)

37 John Wycliffe (1384)

38 St. Andrew, Apostle

39 Thomas Cranmer, Archbishop of Canterbury (1556)

40 William Laud, Archbishop of Canterbury (1645)

41 St. Thomas kneeling before our Lord

42 Samuel Seabury, first Bishop in the United States (1796)

43 William White, first Bishop of Pennsylvania (1836)

44 John Payne, first Missionary Bishop to Africa (1874)

45 Channing Moore Williams, first Missionary Bishop to Japan (1910)

46 George Washington

47 St. Simon, Apostle

48 St. Jude, Apostle

49 St. Matthias, Apostle

50 Phillips Brooks, Bishop of Massachusetts (1893)

51 William E. Gladstone

52 St. John the Baptist

53 St. Matthew, Apostle and Evangelist

54 St. Mark, Evangelist

55 St. Paul. Apostle to the Gentiles

56 St. Peter, Apostle

57 St. Luke, Evangelist

58 St. John the Beloved as Evangelist

59 St. Thomas, Apostle and Patron

60 Daniel Sylvester Tuttle, Presiding Bishop (1923)

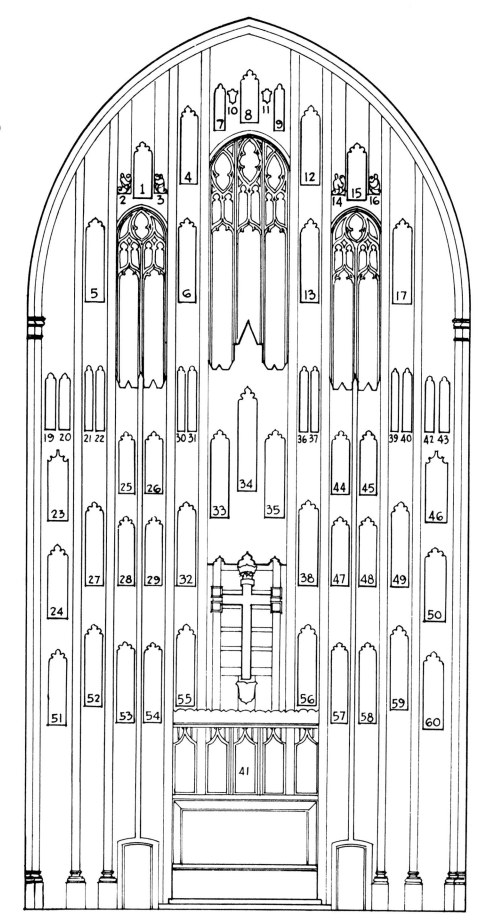

32. Diagram of the Great Reredos, with identification of figures

V. The Great Reredos

Dr. Stires, on The Great Reredos[1]

IN THE CENTRE OF THE REREDOS you observe a cross which, with the surrounding ornamentation, reminds the older parishioners of Saint Thomas of that very beautiful work of art by Augustus St. Gaudens entitled, "The Adoration of the Cross," and which occupied in the old Church which burned, the place of distinction above the altar. Unfortunately, that great work was only in plaster, and the Rector was corresponding with St. Gaudens on the subject of having it cast in bronze when the church burned and that famous composition was destroyed. Perhaps as brilliant a pupil as St. Gaudens ever had, and one who often assisted him with important works, was Lee O. Lawrie, now a distinguished sculptor. It was arranged, therefore, that when Mr. Lawrie was appointed as sculptor of the reredos which had been designed by Bertram Grosvenor Goodhue he should follow as much as possible the work of his master in reproducing in the centre of the reredos a similitude of that work which had been destroyed. Art experts who have made careful study of the original, and of this reproduction, feel that in no respect does this come short of the original, while it possesses many details which make it even more beautiful.

The cross is empty, because we worship not a dead Christ, but a living Christ who is risen, and who is the world's living Saviour and King. Therefore, above the cross you see Him standing as the Ruler of Mankind. Yet you are reminded of the scene at the foot of the cross on Calvary, because on one side, at His feet, you see St. John, and on the other side, His Mother. Across the central part of the cross, and the kneeling adoring angels, you observe texts which, with a good pair of glasses, you will discover are from the central part of the *Te Deum* beginning with "Thou art the King of Glory, O Christ."

Looking a little closer, you will find at the four ends of the cross the symbols of the four Evangelists.[2] You observe the cross surmounted by a Crown, not a crown of thorns, but the Crown of the living King. You see at the foot of the cross the roots of a large grape-vine, with the tendrils climbing up on each side. Among the roots you see sheep feeding. The suggestion of the Shepherd and the sheep; the significance of the grapevine will be clear to you. At the very foot of the cross, underneath the place where the feet would rest, you see a chalice as though to catch the wine of His blood. Around the outer part of this central portion you will see little pictures here and there, the symbols of the Passion – the ladder and the spear, the lantern with which the conspirators entered the Garden of Gethsemane, the whip of cords with which the Master was beaten before Herod and in one of these little pictures you will see the cock crowing. These details should be studied with a good pair of glasses. You will observe that the work everywhere has been done with the greatest care and completeness. The most distant details, those which cannot be closely examined, have been executed with the highest degree of artistic faithfulness. It recalls a remark of Phidias, who spent much time on the hair of a statue of one of the gods. When the sculptor was rebuked for it, and was told that no one would see it because the statue was to be placed high up, and the hair on the back of the head could not be seen at all, he replied, "But the gods will see it." Perfect sincerity is one of the fundamentals of Gothic art, and it is to be found in every detail of the reredos.

Just above the altar and beneath this cross, which we have been describing, you behold the scene in the Upper Room, representing St. Thomas convinced that he is in the presence of the risen Lord. He falls at the Master's feet with his arms outstretched, crying, "My Lord and my God." You note the keen interest of the other apostles who knew that until now he had refused to believe the report that the Master had risen. Obviously, it is the one event in the whole Gospel story most appropriate to appear at this place, and in this Church.

Just above this picture you observe a little frieze. If you were to examine it more closely you would discover the heads of a number of the prophets, and you would notice that in a little circle around the head of each is carved a text. The prophets are those who foretold the coming of Christ, and the texts present some significant words from their prophecies. Around the head of Isaiah you will read "Behold a Virgin shall conceive and bear a child."

It is impossible to recount the story or history chronologically, because, for reasons which will appear, this would necessitate our jumping from place to place in a manner which might bewilder. Therefore, let us begin at the very top. If you were to examine closely with glasses, you would see over the central window three figures of angels each bearing in her arms a little child. These were the first Christian martyrs – the children killed by Herod in his search for the Christ child. On either side of that window are two figures, the one to the left St. Stephen, and the other St. Philip. You recall that St. Stephen is generally spoken of as the first Christian martyr, and you remember that as his enemies were stoning him to death, they laid his garments at the feet of his principal accuser, a certain Saul of Tarsus, who became well-known under another name, as St. Paul.

Over the small window to the left are other figures, three of the early Christian martyrs, Polycarp, Ignatius and Cyprian. Over the window to the right are three other saints. The central figure is Gregory, Bishop of Rome, in the year 590. At that time the papacy was unknown and we find this particular bishop of Rome declaring that if there ever came a time when one bishop claimed supremacy over the other bishops in the Church, he ought to be called Anti-Christ. The love of this bishop for music we recall, for we are familiar with the Gregorian music. It was his keen interest in Britain which caused him to send Augustine to Britain to help to revive and strengthen the Church which had been planted there centuries before. On his left is St. Francis of Assisi, who lived at the end of the tenth and the beginning of the eleventh centuries,[3] and who belongs to all the world. On the right is Savonarola, the noble martyr whom all of us honor.

Looking a little lower you see four majestic figures. Beginning at the left, the first is Chrysostom, Bishop of Constantinople; the second is Athanasius, the hero of the first council of the Church which drew up the Nicene Creed. The third figure is Jerome, who first translated the Bible into the common speech of the people, a version which was therefore called, "The Vulgate." The fourth figure is Augustine, one of the first of the great theologians.

Looking lower still you see four pairs of figures. The first pair are Restitutus who was Bishop of London in 314 A. D., and by his side stands Columba, one of the great British Saints who died in the year 521. These two remind you that the Church was strongly planted in Britain long before Rome took a hand in its development. The next pair are Augustine, whom Gregory sent to England in 597, and who became the first Archbishop of Canterbury. Next to him stands Theodore, also an Archbishop of Canterbury, whose disposition to show his independence of Rome is worth remembering. The next pair are the Venerable Bede, the great historian of Britain, and Wyckliffe, who, two hundred years before the English Reformation, struck a note that echoed throughout all England, and has given him in history the name of "The Morning Star of the Reformation." The last pair were both Archbishops of Canterbury. First you see Cranmer, who, in the reign of Henry VIII, had much to do with the reforming of the Prayer Book. You recall that under Bloody Mary of England he was burned to death. The figure at his side is Archbishop Laud, who also was martyred in 1645.

Coming a little lower, looking to the right of the figure of our Lord, you see a pair of figures, and to the left another pair. The pair on your left are two foreign missionary bishops of the Church of England, Bishop Selwyn and Bishop Patteson, whose stimulating stories you should read. On the other side are two missionary bishops of our American Church, Bishop Payne who went out to Africa in 1851, and Bishop Williams, who went to Japan in 1874, each taking his life in his hands. You will observe the significance of these four missionaries being placed as close as possible to the figure of the risen Lord. They represent the front line of the Church's advance.

Coming down to the lowest line of statues you see that on each side are groups of four. I ask you to look at the two in the middle of each group. On your left the first two are St. Matthew and St. Mark, and the two in the centre of the last group are St. Luke and St. John. St. Luke has an open scroll in his hand, and if you look closely you will see that on it is a representation of the Virgin and her Child, because St. Luke gives us more information concerning the infancy of our Lord, and the life of His Mother, than can be found in any other record. As you look at St. John I ask you to note that there are in the reredos three different representations of him – the one before us, the figure at the foot of the cross, and as he appears in the scene in the Upper Room. You will observe that the sculptor has been careful to carry out the likeness. Having familiarized yourself with the likeness in one case, you could find the other statutes without difficulty.

On either side of these two pairs of figures are others, four in all, in particularly prominent places. The first one on your left is St. John the Baptist. The second figure, with the arm upraised, is St. Paul. His statue is not accompanied by the usual conventional book and sword. Effort has rather been made to present a picture so striking, and so typical of what St. Paul represents, that those who are acquainted with his character and his work might be able to recognize his personality.

On the right you observe another prominent figure. It is that of St. Peter, and there is at least a possibility that this statue has some of the elements of a portrait, for it follows a representation of St. Peter which appears on the now famous chalice of Antioch, which experts have declared was made by a Greek Christian goldsmith in the first century, and these experts have further concluded that in many instances, the artist undoubtedly endeavored to reproduce portraits of Christian leaders, personally known to him.[4] As you carefully observe this statue of St. Peter, you find it very convincing.

The last of these four prominent figures is our own St. Thomas. In accordance with old custom a place of particular honor is given to the Saint whose name is borne by the Parish Church.

We have named some of the apostles; let us lift our eyes to the others. The figure just over that of St. John the Baptist is St. Bartholomew. The next two are St. Philip and St. James the Less. The fourth figure in this more important place is St. James the Greater, almost always represented with his hat on, and a staff in his hand. On the right side in this same line, is the statue of St. Andrew; he holds in his hand a basket in which are five barley loaves and two small fishes. Next are St. Simon and St. Jude; and last is St. Matthias, who was elected to be of the twelve in place of the traitor Judas.

Now turn to the extreme left, next to the wall. Before describing the figures, I ask you to observe a little picture at the very top; it is the Expulsion from the Garden of Eden. If you look closely you will see that Adam is going out of the Garden with his wife, taking her by the hand, and yet standing between her and the angel with the flaming sword.

Over on your right, next to the wall at the top, is a little companion picture, the story of the Annunciation. The significance of these two little pictures we need not explain here.

Returning to this row of figures, at your extreme left on the top, you observe two of the most distinguished scholars of the Church of England, Richard Hooker and Bishop Butler. Beneath them is John Wesley, founder of the Methodists, who besought his brethren to carry on the great revival within the Church and not to leave it or establish an independent Church. Below Wesley is Liddon, the great dean and preacher of St. Paul's, London. And the last of this line is Gladstone, England's great layman.

Leaving the British line, and coming over now to the extreme right, we come to the American line. At the top [are] Bishop Seabury and Bishop White, the first bishops of our American Church. They have in their hands the first American Prayer Book. Just beneath them is a great layman of the American Church, George Washington. Personally, I think this is one of the strongest statues of Washington to be found anywhere. It repays careful study. Below Washington is the figure of the great bishop and preacher Phillips Brooks. This row of figures concludes with one who was living when his statue was placed there – dear beloved Bishop Tuttle, great missionary bishop of the Far West, and Presiding Bishop of the Church for many years.

VI. Large gilt Altar
Cross that was
given in 1891
and survived
the fire of 1905,
still used at the
High Altar
today

VII. The Saint Thomas Bible (1916), designed under
the supervision of Bertram Grosvenor Goodhue

Notes

1 Published in 1927 in [Frank Le G. Gilliss], *A Short Description of the Reredos, Wood Carvings and Other Objects of Interest in Saint Thomas Church New York City* (New York: Gilliss Press, 1927), pp. 12-21.

2 The symbols of the four evangelists are actually placed at the two side-arms of the cross, not at its four ends.

3 He actually lived at the end of the twelfth and the beginning of the thirteenth centuries.

4 Scholars now hold that the Antioch chalice is to be dated a few centuries later than this, and hence that its figures were not personally known to the artist.

VIII. Interior of the present (fourth) Saint Thomas Church, consecrated 1916

IX. Childe Hassam: *Allies Day, May 1917*, oil painting in National Gallery, Washington, D.C.

X. World War I Memorial, dedicated 1927

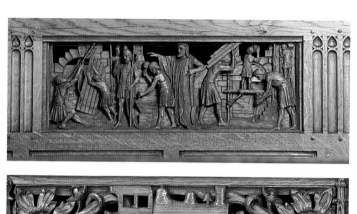

XI. Selected Wood Carvings in the Chancel, given in thanksgiving for the armistice of 1918

XII. Reredos of the Chantry Chapel, 1927

XIII. Baptismal Polyptych, painted by Thomas Watson Ball c.1927

XIV. Chapel of the Resurrection, 1929, with reredos by Tabor Sears

XV. Columbarium in the Chapel of the Resurrection, installed 1990

XVI. World War II Memorial Altar in the Narthex, dedicated 1949

XVII. Brooks Memorial Processional Cross, dedicated 1951

XIX. Our Lady of Fifth Avenue, dedicated 1991

XVIII. High altar with silver in Festal Display

XX. The Loening-Hancock Organ, with rose window above

XXI. Choir School from 1987 at 202 West Fifty-eighth Street. Exterior showing chapel window with cross superimposed

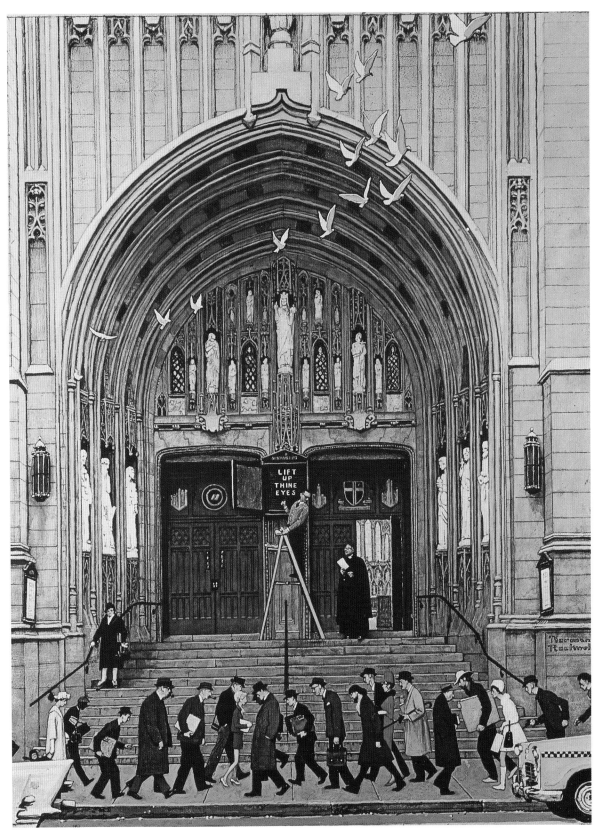

XXII. Norman Rockwell: *Lift Up Thine Eyes*

XXIII. Selected Vessels and Vestments from the Sacristy and Treasury

XXIV. The Eucharist at Saint Thomas on Easter Sunday

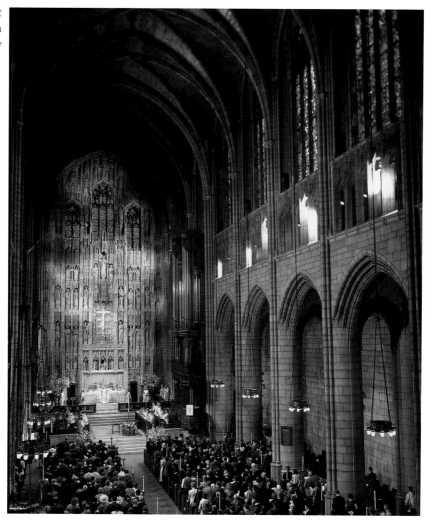

XXV. The Full Choir singing on the gallery stairway at the south end of the narthex

XXVI. Coat of Arms of Saint Thomas Parish since 1975

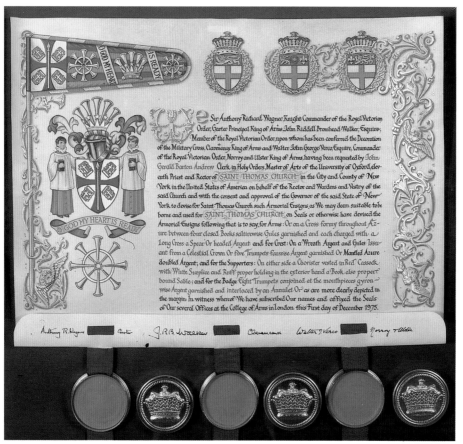

XXVII. Letters Patent from the College of Arms, dated December 1, 1975

summit of the reredos. Such a rectory, the committee gracefully suggested, "would be a fitting tribute to Dr. Stires, in practical recognition of the important and distinguished services which he has rendered to the Church and Parish, among which is the building of our present remarkable church." The rector, however, desired the matter to be considered on its own merits. This it was, and the finance committee was authorized to raise $150,000 for a new rectory. Mr. Goodhue was retained as architect and the building was completed on May 18, 1921, when "the keys were turned over to the Rector and his wife."[30] It was this building that would serve for Dr. Stires and his successor, while subsequent rectors would live at 550 Park Avenue.

In 1921, with the war over, the parish observed the twentieth anniversary of Dr. Stires' rectorship. The Men's Association gave a dinner in honor of Dr. and Mrs. Stires. It was attended by some 340 parishioners, and General Avery D. Andrews, the president of the Association, presided over the commemoration. The main address was given by the Rev. Dr. James B. Wasson, a former assistant minister of the parish and the priest who had been temporarily in charge when the fire broke out back in August of 1905. Dr. Wasson paid due tribute to the rector as the able administrator of a great church and as a pastor ever ready to help the troubled, the needy, the sorrowful, the sick, and the dying. The other featured speaker was the Honorable Chauncey M. Depew, a United States Senator from New York.[31]

The year 1923 marked the centennial of the incorporation of the parish. In the *Year Book* for 1922, Dr. Stires eagerly anticipated the event. "We shall have a week of appropriate services and meetings," he announced, "inviting bishops, clergy and laity of our own and other communions to give us their counsel as we begin our second century; and we shall also ask the foremost experts in sociology and industry to show us how we can better serve humanity." The Men's Association already had reserved the Plaza Hotel for a gala anniversary dinner the following December. In the meantime, the members of the parish were urged to consider the establishment of an adequate endowment fund for the hundredth year. "Our beautiful church must be a strong witness for Christ in the years to come," declared the rector, "in the comfort and stimulation of our services, in our ready participation in all good works, in our sympathy and helpfulness for all sorts and conditions of men."[32] The centennial celebration of what *The New York Times* called "one of the largest, wealthiest, and most benevolent Episcopal congregations in America" began on Sunday morning, December 2, 1923. At this service, Bishop William T. Manning of New York preached, telling the assembled congregation that "the standard of service which you have established, the work which you have accomplished, are the assurance that you will go forward to still greater things as you enter upon the new century of your life."

Before the sermon the bishop dedicated a "Cross of Calvary Stones" (ill. 35) that had been recently embedded in the column nearest the pulpit. Fashioned by Mr. Goodhue and about four feet high, it was made of rather worn stones which had once formed two of the steps leading up to Mount Calvary and which in recent years had rested in the altar of the convent of the Orthodox Church there. The stones were the gift of Mr. and Mrs. Howard S. Rodgers, who had obtained them on a trip to the Holy Land at the request of Dr. Stires. The entire morning service was broadcast by Radio Station WJZ; indeed, for over a year the services had been regularly broadcast every other Sunday by means of equipment installed by the Westinghouse Company.[33]

That afternoon on the second of December, Evensong was sung by the combined choirs of church and chapel. On Monday, a reception was held in the Guild Hall, at which time there was an exhibition of portraits, historical papers, and other objects connected with the history of the parish. On Tuesday evening was the dinner at The Plaza, with the rector as speaker. In the church on the next afternoon, a very thorough lecture was given by him on "The Reredos, Woodcarvings and Plans for Completion of the Interior Decorations."[34]

On Thursday morning, there was a special service to which the clergy of the whole diocese were invited, as well as parishioners. The feature of this service was the historical address on the parish given by the Rev. Dr. E. Clowes Chorley, Historiographer of the Episcopal Church. In this interesting and charming survey, the distinguished historian called attention to four outstanding contributions which, in his estimation, the parish had made to the American Church. The first of these was the honor given to "art" as "the handmaid of religion," as witnessed in architecture and liturgy. Second was the "steadfast witness to the Faith of the Gospel and the teaching of the Church," as evidenced in the preaching of its rectors and the supreme value they had attached to the sacraments. Next, he cited the notable contribution in the field of mission work in the city, where "on the East Side the men and women of Saint Thomas's find and embrace the opportunity for personal Christian Social Service." Lastly, he named what was most important of all – the effort made toward the extension of the Kingdom of God: "Nothing human is foreign to the interest of this parish," Dr. Chorley observed, noting that the congregation's "sense of stewardship is steadily growing." He further declared:

> The glory of this parish is not in its magnificent church with its fretted roof and long drawn aisles; not in the dignity and beauty of its services; not in its social prestige; the supreme distinction of this parish is that it has seen the vision
> > *Of the whole round earth*
> > *Bound by gold chains to the feet of God,*
> and to make that vision real it has given not merely its money, but itself.[35]

Mr. Ernest Peixotto, on The Great Reredos [40]

From the very entrance, the eye is immediately attracted by the exceeding richness of the Chancel, where the great reredos – a gigantic work of art – rears itself aloft, piling its niches, its sculptured figures, and its pinnacles from the Altar to the topmost curve of the main vaults of the church, a height of some eighty feet. This reredos is, I believe, one of the greatest accomplishments in modern ecclesiastical art. The union between architect and sculptor seems quite complete. Its several tiers of niches, peopled with saints and prophets, with great reformers and dignitaries of the Christian Church, rise one upon another, cut in stone of the same warm character as the rest of the church and forming an integral part of it. These niches are shaded by richly carved canopies and separated by slender columns or by delicate buttresses ornamented with exquisite detail. Toward its summit, the reredos is pierced by three openings that reveal windows which, though not intended to be permanent,[41] are glazed in the rich jewel-like tones of the glass at Chartres. Immediately above the High Altar, which in itself is extremely simple, in a deeply recessed porch, stands a group of figures that depict St. Thomas kneeling as he recognizes the Risen Christ. Above this porch towers a great cross, surmounted by a crown of thorns, capped by a diadem, and surrounded by adoring angels enclosed in a flat panel whose frame is embellished with scrolls and foliations, and with shields showing the implements of the Passion. Above the cross again, in a glorified Calvary, appear lifesize figures of Christ, St. Mary, and the Beloved Disciple, while in niches above these and about them appear apostles and saints, missionaries and reformers, divines of the Episcopal Church in England and America. All these figures have been carefully studied in their relationship to each other and to the whole, and produce that wonderful impression of richness combined with order, of dignity combined with grace, that quite overpowers the beholder in the storied retables of Italy and Spain. The work of the sculptor forms no mean part in the success of this accomplishment, for, as in much of the late-Gothic work, the stonecutter's art almost overshadows that of the architect.

Afterward, the clergy present were the rector's guests at a luncheon.

On Friday evening an organ recital by Lynnwood Farnam, the organist at the Church of the Holy Communion in New York City, was given, along with special anthems sung by the Saint Thomas Choir. That Saturday afternoon another service was held on the theme "The Church in the City, in the Nation, and in the World."

The celebration was closed by a service on the following Sunday, at which the rector preached on "The Greater Future." "We are encouraged by the past," Dr. Stires exclaimed, "grateful in the present, hopeful for the future." This hope called for the parish to be "cheered by the certainty that there opens before us the happiest privilege man can know — to give that teaching, that example and that service which the whole world declares today is its most desperate need."

Dr. Stires also emphasized that the mother church of Saint Thomas needed to be made "secure and strong for the years to come and for the greater tasks." This demanded the establishment of an adequate endowment fund. "I shall rejoice," he told the congregation in words that would eventually come to fruition, "when the income from endowment takes the place of pew-rentals, and when, as now, the offerings may go out to help every good work, and not be kept at home to pay for current expenses."

Dr. Stires then reminded the congregation that only one thing was needful as they faced the future: "the certainty of the presence of our Lord, for so surely as God exists He is here." And he concluded with these moving words:

34. Statues for the Reredos, standing in Fifty-third Street before they were installed. L–r: Sts. Bartholomew, Matthias, Andrew, and John the Baptist

Can we not in our spirit almost see Him and hear Him?

I think He gives His approval for much that we have tried to do. I think He is trying to show us how desperate is the need, how vast is our power to help; how pitiful it is that we know so little of the joy of saving lives. I think He is more hopeful of us today; He sees our hands releasing the grasp of things and reaching out to Him in a new impulse of devotion; He hears new stirrings in our hearts as, gathered here before Him at the solemn moment which ends one century and begins another, a simple faith and a true loyalty seem to fill our souls. It may be a moment of high consecration, – let it be so. Then, with His look of approval, of acceptance, treasured in our hearts, let us kneel in the Church and resolve to make the Mother strong; let us go to our homes and make them happy; let us go to our offices and make them holy, yes, holy; let us go to men and make them brothers. Let us do it, really do it, and so begin those greater things to which our Master calls us. In your eyes I see the promise of victories for Him and His people. May that promise be fulfilled!

You and I have had many happy years together in the great work. You know that I love you and thank you. I pray that we may go on together to yet greater service for our Christ.

And this is the end of the sermon, or is it the beginning?[36]

35. Cross of Stones from Mount Calvary, dedicated 1923

Around that time in the centennial year, important gifts were made to the parish church, of which two that survive and are visible today are especially noteworthy. One was "the Bennett tapestry," now hanging on the upper level of the stairs at the south end of the narthex, which was given by Mrs. Louis Bennett in Easter of 1923 in memory of her son who had been confirmed at Saint Thomas Church in 1907 and was killed in action in 1918. This Franco-Flemish tapestry of the seventeenth century, measuring eight feet by fourteen feet and six inches, depicts Moses destroying the tablets of the law when he returned from Mount Sinai and found the Israelites worshiping the golden calf (Exodus 32). The other gift, presented in 1924 and positioned nearby, is a vibrantly colored painting entitled "The Adoration of the Magi" and attributed to Peter Paul Rubens (d. 1640). Measuring eight feet by ten, the canvas was a gift from Mrs. E. F. Hutton, the former Marjorie Merriweather Post and daughter of C. W. Post. She was a pew holder at Saint Thomas, and the family had many connections with the parish. Dated to about the year 1620 and possibly painted by a close associate of Rubens or someone in his school, this painting hangs lower down the same stairwell at the south end of the narthex.[37]

Nearly two years after the centennial, on May 26, 1925, Dr. Stires was elected Bishop Coadjutor of Long Island (ill. 36). He accepted the election, planning to remain in charge of the parish until about the first of December. In the month of September, he attended General Convention as a deputy from the Diocese of New York, and was honored by election as President of the House of Deputies. During the sessions of the convention, Bishop Frederick Burgess of Long Island died. This meant that, when consecrated, Dr.

36. Dr. Stires as Bishop of Long Island, portrait by Frank Salisbury

Stires would be diocesan instead of coadjutor bishop.

On November 24, 1925, Saint Thomas Church was the scene of one more notable and stately service, when Ernest Milmore Stires was consecrated third Bishop of Long Island in the presence of twelve bishops, three hundred clergy, and over a thousand lay people. The chief consecrator was the Rt. Rev. Ethelbert Talbot, the last Presiding Bishop of the Episcopal Church to be so designated by seniority rather than by election; the co-consecrators were Bishop John Gardner Murray of Maryland, who was also the new Presiding Bishop-elect, and Bishop William T. Manning of New York. The preacher on the occasion was Charles Henry Brent, Bishop of Western New York and formerly of the Philippines, and an ecumenical pioneer in the Episcopal Church.[38] Also present was the Most Reverend Alexander, Metropolitan Archbishop of the Greek Orthodox Church in North America. It was a fitting conclusion to a rectorate of nearly twenty-five years that had been as inspirational as it had been monumental. A new city had indeed been set upon a hill, whose stones would connect the earthly to the heavenly. When Bishop Stires left, the number of communicants at Saint Thomas totaled 2,377; there were 1,360 in the parish church and 1,017 in the chapel.[39]

Bishop Stires in his episcopal choir habit and with a mitre above his head, his own coat of arms crossed with that of the Diocese of Long Island, is memorialized outside above the door to the right of the front porch, which is known as "The Bishop's Door" or "The Bishop's Entrance" although seldom used as such. Fittingly, he holds a model of the church in his hand, for in one very real sense, he was its builder. With him, the parish had entered a new church and a new century.

Notes

1 VM 6:135 (26 October 1914).

2 VM 6:155 (12 January 1916), 6:161 (19 April 1916). By comparison, the total cost of St. Bartholomew's on Park Avenue, completed under Goodhue only a few years later, was 1.2 million dollars: Christine Smith, *St. Bartholomew's Church in the City of New York* (New York: Oxford University Press, 1988), pp. 39, 51, 211. The cost of Saint Thomas was $57,587.05 more than the total subscriptions received toward the expense of the new building. The commissions for the architects totaled $58,819.24; see letter from Union Trust Company of New York, dated 13 April 1916: Vestry Minutes, vol. 6, pp. 157-59.

3 E. Clowes Chorley, *Manuscript History of St. Thomas Church* (unpublished manuscript in Saint Thomas Archives, 1943; copy deposited in the St. Mark's Library of the General Theological Seminary, New York City), chapter 14, page 45.

4 The exact year in which these images were created and set in place is uncertain. Of the dates that are given on them, 1824 refers to the laying of the cornerstone of the first church, 1866 to the last service in the second church, and 1905 to the fire that destroyed the third church. The intended references for the dates 1829 and 1910 are less certain.

5 "Saint Thomas's Church, New York," *A Sermon Preached at the Consecration of the New Saint Thomas's Church By the Rt. Rev. David Hummell Greer, D.D., L.L.D., Bishop of the Diocese of New York on Tuesday in Easter Week, April the Twenty-Fifth MCMXVI.* (Published by the Wardens and Vestrymen), pp. 13-14, 16.

6 "The Consecration of a Church," *Year Book* 1916, pp. 20, 24.

7 *Year Book* 1918, p. 13. On Armistice Day, the church was opened from early morning until nearly midnight, "the organ playing from time to time the national airs of the Allies and hymns of praise, while in the quiet moments great numbers of men and women knelt in relief, gratitude and consecration."

8 VM 6:194 (30 April 1918).

9 VM 6:114-15 (3 January 1913).

10 VM 6:119 (13 December 1913).

11 Leonard Ellinwood, *The History of American Church Music* (New York: Morehouse-Gorham Company, 1953), p. 134.

12 *Year Book* 1915, p. 15.

13 VM 6:114-15 (3 January 1913).

14 The history of the Choir School and of music at Saint Thomas Church are too important to be omitted from mention in the general chronological narrative as we follow it along, but they also deserve independent treatment as entities in themselves, and that is given in the first two appendices at the end of this volume.

15 VM 6:192-94 (30 April 1918), 6:201 (19 December 1918), 6:202-3 (29 April 1919).

16 *Year Book* 1919, p. 29; VM 6:202-3 (29 April 1919).

17 *Year Book* 1919, p. 31.

18 VM 6:255 (15 December 1922), 7:3-4 (2 March 1923), 7:11 (19 June 1923), 7:13-15 (4 October 1923), 7:49-50 (7 May 1925). The total expenses for the reconstruction of the Choir House were estimated to be $74,000. The securities donated by Mr. Steele were said at the time to yield an annual income of $18,625 and to have a market value of $288,000.

19 *The Plans and Elevations for St. Thomas' Church made by Cram, Goodhue and Ferguson. . .* (Boston: Merrymount Press, 1908), p. 7.

20 Further see "Mosaic Parapet Rail in St. Thomas' Church, New York City," in *Architectural Record* 47:2 (February 1920): 128-29, 131. Chorley, *Manuscript History*, chapter 14, p. 33, says that Charles Steele was the donor of the Parapet. The word itself comes from the Latin *parare*, meaning to guard, and *pectus*, meaning breast.

21 The inscriptions, from left to right, and their translations are as follows: *navis ecclesiae* ("the ship of the church"), *vos estis lux mundi* ("you are the light of the world"), *ecclesia refugium* ("the church a refuge"), and *adveniat regnum tuum* ("thy kingdom come"). The last is coupled with "League of Nations 1919."

22 These inscriptions, moving from right to left, read as follows: *Sursum Corda* and "Jamestown A.D. MDCVII," *aula municipalis* and "Independence Hall 1776," *e pluribus unum* and "Let us have peace," and *laus Deo* and "Reims 1918."

23 Much later, in 1974, a stone from Canterbury Cathedral was also placed near this spot.

24 Further see Cleota Reed, *Henry Chapman Mercer and the Moravian Pottery and Tile Works* (Philadelphia: University of Pennsylvania Press, 1987), esp. pp. 31, 99.

25 This was some three hundred less than the number of "sittings" that Dr. Brown, the previous rector, had in 1898 estimated for the third church, completed by Upjohn in 1870. Cf. *Year Book* 1898, p. xxvii. Chorley, *Manuscript History*, chapter 14, page 29, offers a figure slightly higher than 1,700 for the Cram (present) church: "The Chantry, seating 257, was on the south side of the church, surmounted by a gallery with seats for 312. The small gallery at the end of the church

had a seating capacity of 128. All in all, the church seated 1,852 persons, not including the chancel and sanctuary." *The Plans and Elevations* published in 1908 by Cram, Goodhue and Ferguson, on the other hand, on page 15 gave the total figure (including nave, chapel, aisles, and galleries) as 1,412. A book published by the parish in 1973 gave the capacity as being 1,700: *Saint Thomas Church: 150th Anniversary Year* (New York: Park Publishing Company, 1973), p. 46. The present total seating capacity, with some pews in recent years removed for re-arrangement of space, is estimated by Addison J. Keim, Verger, at 1,503 (personal interview, 5 December 1999).

26 A prominent family of investment bankers, whose business still lists fourteen entries in the Manhattan telephone directory for the year 2000. Separate portraits of Harris C. and Margaret A. Fahnestock, done in marble relief within bronze frames by Moses Ezekiel in 1894, are still to be seen on the wall of the vestry hallway outside the church and near to the reredos itself (*Insurance Appraisal of Property Belonging to St. Thomas Church*, completed by Christie's of New York and dated 10 June 1996, p. 71, no. 229. Manuscript kept in Saint Thomas Archives). Of the figures included upon the reredos, it may be noted that the only women are Eve, who was Adam's wife, and St. Mary, the mother of Our Lord. Further on the reredos, see below, chapter 12, note 36.

27 Richard Oliver, *Bertram Grosvenor Goodhue* (New York: The Architectural History Foundation; Cambridge, Massachusetts, and London, England: The MIT Press; American Monograph Series; 1983), p. 70. It has not proven convenient for brides to use this entrance.

28 Truman H. Talley, "Satire in Church Decoration," *The New York Times*, 28 August 1921, section 3, p. 18, as quoted in Oliver, *Bertram Grosvenor Goodhue*, p. 70.

29 VM 6:68 (26 May 1910).

30 VM 6:210 (8 December 1919), 6:213, 216, 218-19 (17 April 1920), 6:236 (3 June 1921). The vestry decided that the rector was to be free from any responsibility in raising funds for the new rectory owing to his efforts in the building of the parish church.

31 *Year Book* 1921, p. 83. The vestry and Men's Association made a concentrated effort to raise the remaining funds for the new rectory before the dinner; see VM 6:233 (7 April 1921).

32 *Year Book* 1922, pp. 17-18.

33 *The New York Times*, 25 November 1923, section 2, p.1 ("St. Thomas's Soon Hundred Years Old"); 3 December 1923, p. 9 ("Dedicates Cross of Calvary Stones"); VM 7:16 (22 November 1923), 7:22 (20 December 1923). "The Greater Future," *Sermon Preached by the Rev. Ernest M. Stires, D.D. on Sunday, December 9, 1923, in Commemoration of the 100th Anniversary of the Parish* (privately printed), p. 5. In 1922 the Westinghouse Company had offered to install the necessary equipment to broadcast the services and this was done every other Sunday for the benefit of what Dr. Stires called the "invisible congregation." See VM 6:251 (9 October 1922).

34 Replicated herein following color plate V.

35 E. Clowes Chorley, *The Centennial of St. Thomas's Parish, New York. An Address Delivered at St. Thomas's Church, December 6, 1923* (privately printed), pp. 29-38. Dr. Chorley noted that the *Year Book* of 1922 reported "an expenditure of about $46,000 for the parish church and over $231,000, or five times as much, given to work outside." Almost in corroboration, *The New York Times* of 25 November 1923 (section 2, p. 1) had reported that the parish "for many years put at least $4 on the collection plate for outside benevolences for every dollar it has spent on its own maintenance." See also *The New York Times*, 5 December 1923, p. 8; 7 December 1923, p. 20. As of 1925, the parish's financial records do show that it was spending almost four times as much money outside itself as within, the largest single expenditure of that year being over $400,000 to the Cathedral of St. John the Divine. Chorley himself was a trustee of the Cathedral from 1913 until his death in 1949.

36 "The Greater Future," *Sermon Preached by the Rev. Ernest M. Stires, D.D. on Sunday, December 9, 1923*, pp. 6, 9-12; see also *The New York Times*, 10 December 1923, p. 6.

37 For the Bennett tapestry, see correspondence in the parish archives. For the Saint Thomas Adoration, which was extensively restored in 1968, see a paper written in 1999 by Mr. Joseph

Galvin, also in the parish archives. The painting of the same name by Rubens himself in King's College Chapel, Cambridge, has been dated to 1634. Near the Saint Thomas Adoration, to the right in the southern wall at floor level, is the small but exquisite window of Christ the King.

38 William H. Owen, a former assistant minister, recalls in *I Remember* (privately printed), p. 162, that following Brent's consecration to the episcopate in 1901, Brent was invited to preach at Saint Thomas. That evening there was a dinner at the rectory during which Dr. Stires and the bishop discussed plans for the new cathedral in Manila. Dr. Stires insisted that the style of architecture for the building "should certainly be Gothic as that was the supreme and sublime expression in stone and brick of the religion which we profess." Then Brent, "so quietly and so kindly, and yet with latent force," replied that "that was certainly true of us Nordic peoples, but it is the peculiar genius of Christianity to assume, adopt, and sanctify the characteristic art, etc. of all the peoples of the world." For this reason, Brent cautioned, "it might be well before we decided on the architecture of the Cathedral in Manilla [sic] to discover what style would best express in stone and brick to the Philippinos [sic] their reactions to the Christian faith!"

39 Chorley, *Manuscript History*, p. 543.

40 "Saint Thomas's and its Reredos," *Architecture* 42:1 (July 1920): 193-202, reprinted in [Frank Le G. Gilliss], *A Short Description of the Reredos, Wood Carvings and Other Objects of Interest in Saint Thomas Church New York City* (New York: Gilliss Press, 1927), pp. 6-9.

41 In spite of the original intention, it would seem that these have not yet been replaced. Because of the limited space available at the liturgical east end of the church (geographical west), where the old rectory stood, no great sanctuary window had been possible. Room was preserved for the three smaller lancet windows near the summit of the reredos, "in the heavens" so to speak, when the new rectory was completed in May of 1921, on the same spot behind the church, by building the rectory's top floor just low enough to accommodate the windows above. The totally abstract design of the three lancet windows is striking, with blue predominating over red and green, and it is said that no one piece of glass in them measures more than four inches in any dimension. See [Harold E. Grove], *St. Thomas Church* (New York: n.p., 1965), p. 44.

❧ CHAPTER 11

Simplicity, Financial Stability, & Daily Communion

ROELIF HASBROUCK BROOKS
NINTH RECTOR, 1926-1954

AFTER THE CONSECRATION OF DR. STIRES as Bishop of Long Island, the Rev. Charles K. Gilbert (later Bishop of New York) was in temporary charge of the parish, with Canon Henry Lubeck of Washington Cathedral acting as special Lenten preacher. Once again the vestry set about its most important duty – the calling of a rector. The first choice was the Rev. Dr. Charles Clingman, rector of the Church of the Advent, Birmingham, Alabama, who later became Bishop of Kentucky. He declined the invitation.[1]

On June 10, 1926, the vestry then extended a unanimous call to the Rev. Dr. Roelif Hasbrouck Brooks (ill. 37), rector of St. Paul's Church, Albany, New York, who the previous week had been nominated as Dean of the Cathedral of the Incarnation in Garden City, Long Island. After some hesitation, he accepted the call to Saint Thomas: "I did not want to come – but my predecessor, the Bishop of Long Island and your rector for twenty-five years, and the Vestry placed before me a challenge to preach the Gospel, a challenge such as I could not rightfully decline." He pledged "to maintain the high ideals of Christian service which have made St. Thomas's Church what it is today."[2]

The new rector was fifty-one years old, a native of New York State, and a graduate of Columbia University and the General Theological Seminary. He had been ordained deacon in 1902 and priest the following year by Bishop Burgess of Long Island, and his early years of ordained ministry were spent in that diocese. In 1906, he was elected rector of the Albany parish, and during his administration the communicant list increased from five hundred to over a thousand, an endowment of $200,000 was amassed, and the parish became notable for two things – its missionary outreach and the quality of its musical services. For years, Dr. Brooks was one of the outstanding clergy of the Albany diocese. He was elected deputy to the General Conventions of 1919 and 1922, and, from 1917 to 1926, he was archdeacon of Albany. In 1924 he missed by a narrow margin

37. Roelif Hasbrouck Brooks, Ninth Rector 1926-1954

being elected bishop coadjutor of Albany.

On October 2, 1926, Dr. Brooks conducted his first service as rector of Saint Thomas. In his sermon, which was on "The Simplicity of Christ," he said:

> Jesus did not demand that you look upon Him as a wonder-worker. His deeds were not dramatic. . . . His life was marked by simplicity from the days he earned his own living by his own hands . . . to those three wondrous years when he depended upon the hospitality of his friends. . . . In His teachings He went to the heart of the matter with the same simplicity, using the simplest possible words, leaving little or no doubt in the minds of His hearers, and, using no arguments.[3]

In these words, Dr. Brooks struck, perhaps unconsciously, a dominant theme of his rectorate. Dr. Stires had been a glamorous figure, and his had been the spectacular task of building the great new church. Dr. Brooks was not, and did not want to be, either glamorous or spectacular, although he was certainly a person of old-fashioned dignity.[4] Sound in the faith and not a man of complicated personality, he was regarded as a "central churchman," and therefore held in high regard by the leaders of both Anglo-Catholics and Liberal Evangelicals. He was also a strategist, able to take long views and to pursue his ends with quiet resolution.

But if "simplicity," a trait that he stressed and linked to Jesus in his inaugural sermon, was the word that best describes the character of Dr. Brooks, so then "financial stability," at least to judge from the surviving records, would seem to have been his second over-arching concern. We shall also see, in due course, that "sacramental devotion" would become still another emphasis as his rectorship matured, but that is to get ahead of the story. One of the major tasks that Dr. Brooks saw from the very first was the building up of the endowment fund, a necessity that Dr. Stires had repeatedly urged.[5] A beginning had already been made at this when Dr. Brown was rector, and it was afterwards supplemented, in 1901, when Miss Grace Scoville gave $10,000 to be known as "The John Wesley Brown Memorial Fund." For the parish as a whole, by the time Dr. Brooks became rector, endowments had accumulated amounting to $613,196.54. The larger part of this was specifically designated for non-parochial purposes, such as Saint Thomas Chapel, the Halsey Day Nursery, and other charities. Now the rector and vestry worked intentionally to build up the general endowment fund. Toward this end the vestry in 1927 resolved that the offerings at Christmas and Easter be used to establish a "St. Thomas Endowment Fund." Indeed, Dr. Brooks himself had already started a fund for the same purpose by depositing all the gifts made to him for pastoral services, the first of which was a five-dollar gold piece received in thanksgiving for a baptism.

In the *Year Book* marking the close of his first year as rector, Dr. Brooks pleaded for the people of the parish to give careful and serious consideration to the matter of endowment. What better memorial could one leave behind, he declared, "than a fund, the income of which for all time would be used to enable St. Thomas Church to minister through service and Sacrament to all who may worship here, to care for the poor, the sick and the sorrowing and to insure that right here in the very geographical center of Manhattan the Gospel will for all time be preached!"[6]

The next year Dr. Brooks was pleased to report a splendid beginning. Special offerings had increased and many parishioners were making provision in their wills for this purpose. In the *Year Book* of 1929 the rector informed his parishioners that the annual offerings at Christmas and Easter had raised the endowment by $88,760.59. In the same year, the vestry established group life insurance for all employees of the parish church and chapel, including the choir boys. In 1930, the Men's Association issued a large illustrated brochure to promote the fund and to secure a goal of three million dollars. The rector applauded the effort. In a foreword he wrote: "If Saint Thomas Church is to be a living, breathing, spiritual force fifteen or fifty years into the future, it must be tended now while it enjoys comparative youth."[7]

The endowment fund continued to grow, notwithstanding the hardships of the great depression of the 1930s. At the end of the year 1936, the tenth anniversary of his rectorship, Dr. Brooks was able to announce that the total endowments of the parish amounted to $1,708,906.05. Five years later the amount had increased to over two million dollars, the figure by December of 1941 standing at $2,062,669.59. In 1944, over a million dollars was added, the larger part coming from a bequest in memory of Chauncey M. Depew, former United States Senator from New York. In 1948, the church received its largest single bequest to that time from the estate of Henrietta Porter Lippincott, for the charities and general purposes of the parish; when her estate was finally settled the value of this bequest amounted to $3,541,563.70.[8] On the parish's 125th anniversary in this same year, Dr. Brooks heralded a brighter day. Due to "the generous support of the parishioners and the increase of our Endowment Funds," he declared, "this parish is now financially strong to do its work." The material advancement was also owing, as the vestry had earlier observed, "to a spirit of affectionate understanding and cooperation between the Rector and congregation."[9]

The Episcopal Church's General Convention of 1919 had inaugurated on a national basis the Every Member Canvass, a significant development in financial support and a concept that had already been anticipated by Dr. Neville, the fifth rector, some seventy years earlier during his ministry in New Orleans before he came to Saint Thomas. The old system of pew rents, inherited from the nineteenth century, had provided one limited means of meeting parochial expenses, but such rents were often insufficient and they had certainly perpetuated class distinctions in congregations. In 1926, finding itself in a more egalitarian society, Saint Thomas developed this concept in its own way by inaugurating what it chose to call the "Maintenance Fund," to which communicants of the parish were invited to contribute in proportion to their means, and it was clearly the hope of Dr. Brooks and others that such contributions should increasingly displace pew rents as the chief source of support.[10]

Like the establishment of the endowment fund, the initial response to the Maintenance Fund was promising. The pledges made for the year 1927 met expectations and those the following year were even higher. "It is our hope that every member of the Parish shall share in its financial support and its various activities as a religious obligation," wrote Dr. Brooks in the 1929 *Year Book*. This aspiration was not soon realized, however, and by 1936, although the pledges to the Maintenance Fund were at a record level, nearly half the parish members were said to be giving nothing toward its support. Even so, the income of the parish each year during the depression managed to meet expenses, though certain readjustments were required, and in 1941 the Maintenance Fund amounted to $65,348.48 in comparison to $32,762.67 in pew rents.[11]

As regards the church building itself (illustrations 38, 39, 40), Dr. Brooks initially had to focus his attention upon structural alterations and repairs. In 1925, cracks in the unbuttressed arches of the north aisle were discovered and it became necessary, as was remarked earlier, to place steel beams across every pair of columns above the ceiling – contrary to the principles of Dr. Cram. At about the same time, the city's construction of the Fifty-third Street subway and related blasting necessitated more reinforcements to be made to the frames and bracings of some clerestory windows on the south side and to the roof and other exterior parts of the church, together with repairs to the nave vaulting.[12]

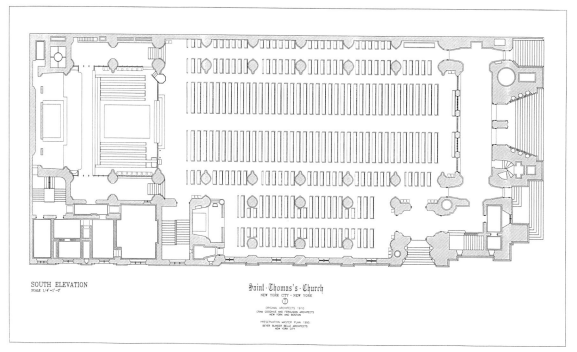

38. Floor plan of the church

39. Lateral section
plan of the church

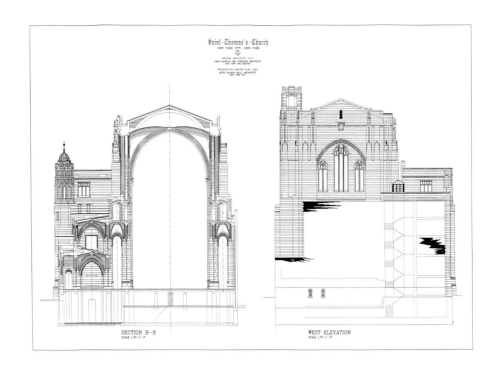

40. Front elevation
plan of the church

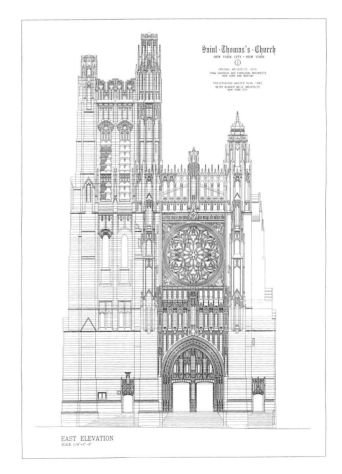

SIMPLICITY, FINANCIAL STABILITY, & DAILY COMMUNION

The memory of the First World War was still strong and painful (pl. IX), even though the armistice of 1918 was already nine years past, and in 1927 a memorial was dedicated to those who had served (pl. X). Placed around and above the carved oak door at the southeast corner of the nave, it was designed in art-deco style by Lee Lawrie, the same sculptor who had designed the figures on the Great Reredos. At the top the winged Archangel Michael drives his lance into the dragon (representing Satan, evil, and the war). The inscription *Quis ut Deus* ("Who is like to God?," the English meaning of the Hebrew word "Michael") implies that none of the demonic forces is God's equal, for Michael puts all God's enemies under question and judgment. The various words of Scripture relate the war to the conviction that it was fought for God's sake. Below, a bas-relief of carved stone in the lintel depicts American soldiers going forth from Saint Thomas Church to fight in France, represented by Rheims Cathedral, so badly damaged in the war and located near the area where Dr. Stires himself had served. The names cut into the wall below are of parishioners who served, the names in gold being the twenty men of Saint Thomas who lost their lives. Included in the 335 names are Dr. Stires himself, as well as "Major Paul Moore," the father of the future (thirteenth) Bishop of New York. The colored shields on the stone wall represent the branches of the armed services; those in the wooden panels of the door the sixteen Allied Nations (including the double eagle of Russia and the rising sun of Japan). This door, its lock handwrought in iron by Goodhue, has remained closed ever since, out of respect. In addition, the extensive wood carvings throughout the chancel, designed by Goodhue and executed by Irving and Casson of Boston, were given by Charles Steele as a thank offering for the signing in 1918 of the same armistice (pl. XI).[13]

Also by 1927, the reredos, altar, and fittings of the Chantry in the south aisle, the gifts of Mrs. Hamilton McKown Twombly and her daughters, were in place, as was the Baptismal Font nearby. The most common uses of the Chantry are indicated, in fact, by the subject matter of the reredos above its altar (pl. XII), for here in this smaller chapel are held Baptisms, weddings, funerals, and other services whose attendance would not require the use of the whole church, and upon this reredos are depicted, from left to right, the baptism of Jesus, the marriage banquet at Cana, and the raising of Lazarus from the dead. The inscriptions beneath these panels relate to the same three themes: "One Lord, one Faith, one Baptism"; "Whatsoever He saith unto you, do it"; and "I am the Resurrection and the Life."[14] Also in this chapel the regular daily celebrations of the Holy Communion are held, and here the monthly Requiem Mass for departed members of the parish is celebrated. At the top of the reredos, which is said to be a copy of one in Florence, is the Annunciation, Gabriel on the left and Mary at the right, with adoring angels at either side. On the front of the marble altar, which has five brass crosses inserted into its face, are two panels with inscriptions that relate, appropriate-

The Wood Carvings in the Chancel[52]

The oak carving in the chancel was donated by Mr. Charles Steele as a thank offering for the armistice signed in 1918. Its detail is worthy of careful inspection. The carving was done by the woodworking firm of Irving and Casson of Boston according to designs by Mr. Bertram Goodhue. Typical of the custom in Gothic buildings, some carvings of contemporary scenes, themes, and figures are included.

On the kneeling rails in the front rows of the choir stalls are small carved panels representing various professions, occupations, and industries of human society as well as historic events and persons. On the north side from nave to altar are: (1) Christopher Columbus' shield and his ship, the Santa Maria; (2) Theodore Roosevelt; (3) a steamship; (4) Lee Lawrie, the sculptor; (5) a telephone; (6) a blacksmith; (7) a railway; (8) a radio; (9) music; (10) architecture; (11) literature; (12) finance, with the initials of J. P. Morgan and three money bags; (13) engineering; and (14) medicine. At the altar end of these kneelers on the north side Our Lady's Juggler performs, and on the nave end is a beehive, symbol of "sweet speech" or of St. Ambrose.

On the south side, again from nave to altar, we see: (1) Henry Hudson's ship, the "Half Moon"; (2) Abraham Lincoln; (3) an airplane; (4) painting; (5) an automobile; (6) Fulton's steamship, the "Clermont"; (7) telegraphy; (8) wood carving; (9) a dirigible; (10) agriculture; (11) electricity; (12) iron and steel; (13) teaching; and (14) law. At the altar end on the south side is a carved cock and on the nave end the notes of the Sursum Corda ("Lift up your hearts").

Carved at the top of the back row of choir stalls are small panels, although in some places the wood has been carved away entirely. Those carvings on the north side depict Old Testament scenes. For the sake of chronology they should be viewed from altar to nave: (1) Adam and Eve expelled from the Garden of Eden; (2) Abraham's near-sacrifice of Isaac; (3) Jacob's dream; (4) the crossing of the Red Sea; (5) David and Goliath; (6) Solomon building the temple of Jerusalem; (7) Elijah rebuking King Ahab and Jezebel; (8) Belshazzar's feast; and (9) Nehemiah rebuilding the Temple. Across the chancel, again in order from the altar to nave, are scenes from the New Testament and later history: (1) the Church in America; (2) the Nativity; (3) the Magi and shepherds; (4) feeding the multitude; (5) the descent of the Holy Spirit at Pentecost; (6) St. Paul preaching from Mars Hill; (7) the martyrdom of Bishops Cranmer, Latimer, and Ridley; (8) missionaries speaking to peoples of many races and tongues; and (9) General Allenby entering Jerusalem after World War I.

Carvings of four famous organists appear on the altar ends of the choir seats: James Nares, Samuel Sebastian Henry, William Croft, and William Boyce. On the nave ends appear four more: John Merbecke, Richard Farrant, Orlando Gibbons, and Henry Purcell. All are shown seated at the organ console.

At Saint Thomas there are *misericords* (hinged ledges on the seats to give "merciful" relief from standing too long) in the back row of the choir stalls on either side, each individually designed and carved underneath. The north row depicts, from altar to nave: (1) a lion eating straw like the ass; (2) the dove and the ark; (3) the cow and the bear feeding together; (4) "The swallow [hath found] a nest for herself, even thine altars, O Lord" (Psalm 84:3); (5) the wolf and the lamb; (6) the phoenix; (7) young lions seeking their prey; (8) "The foxes have holes and the birds of the air have nests" (Matthew 8:20); (9) the Russian bear being doped; (10) the Gallic cock; and (11) the vine (at the seat behind the pulpit, with the figures of Dr. Morgan and Dr. Brown carved above it). On the south row, from altar to nave, are: (1) Philip baptizing the Ethiopian eunuch; (2) St. Christopher carrying the Christchild on his back; (3) St. George and the dragon; (4) Prohibition overcoming Bacchus; (5) the American Eagle plucking the Imperial Eagle; (6) Labor and Capital binding Industry; (7) a dead lion − "out of the strong cometh sweetness"; and (8) a Salvation Army lass with doughnuts.

The seats now designated for the rector and the senior curate are at the left of the chancel, opposite the pulpit. On the front of the rector's kneeler is a carved panel of the conversion of St. Paul. The front kneeler, for the senior curate, depicts the Council of Nicaea at its back and on its front John Milton and John Bunyan. On the ends toward the altar are the Lamb and the Cross, the Chalice and the Host, and an open Bible, and on the side towards the congregation are E. B. Pusey, Shakespear (spelled without a final "e") and Chaucer. On the other side

at the right immediately inside the parapet, on the back of the seat now designated for a curate, is carved the Ascension. The kneeler depicts, at the altar end, three crosses and the symbol INRI (for "Jesus of Nazareth, King of the Jews") resting on a skull and rocks, and, on the congregation side, Jeremy Taylor and Dante. On the front of this kneeler are Saints Augustine of Hippo and Thomas à Kempis.

From the tops of the slim carved columns behind the choir stalls, small carved heads of contemporary personages and representative figures peer down almost as gargoyles. On the south side, from altar to nave, are: (1) Robert G. Lansing, Wilson's Secretary of State; (2) President Woodrow Wilson; (3) Premier Paderewski of Poland; (4) King Victor Emmanuel of Italy; (5) Admiral Henry T. Mayo; (6) General John J. Pershing; (7) Marshal Ferdinand Foch; (8) a French admiral; (9) General Peyton C. March; (10) Herbert Hoover, then Food Administrator; (11) General E. H. H. Allenby; (12) a soldier; (13) the Red Cross; (14) an artilleryman; (15) Bishop Charles Sumner Burch of New York; (16) Bishop Charles H. Brent of the Philippines and later of Western New York; (17) Burgomeister Adolphe Max of Brussels; (18) Cardinal D. J. Mercier of Belgium, who advocated Roman Catholic unity with Anglicans; and (19) Mr. Irving, the wood carver. On the north side, approaching the pulpit as one moves from altar towards nave, we see: (1) King George V of England; (2) King Albert of Belgium; (3) Prime Minister Georges Clemenceau; (4) Prime Minister Raymond Poincaré; (5) Prime Minister David Lloyd-George; (6) Marshal David Haig; (7) Admiral David B. Beatty; (8) Marshal J. J. C. Joffre; (9) a naval aviator; (10) a sailor; (11) the service supply; (12) a Red Cross nurse; (13) Dr. T. Tertius Noble, the organist; (14) Charles H. Steele, donor of the chancel wood carvings; (15) Bertram G. Goodhue, the architect; (16) Dr. Ernest M. Stires, then Rector; and (17) Mr. Casson, the wood carver. In the recesses behind the small heads are carvings of the arms of some of the dioceses of the Episcopal Church in the U. S. A.

On the doors of the aumbry, the recess to hold the Blessed Sacrament and sacramental vessels near the passage into the Chapel of the Resurrection, are four beautifully carved figures: Aaron, Bishop Greer of New York (who consecrated the present church), Miriam (sister of Moses and Aaron), and the Virgin and Child.

Against the wall at the left of the altar is the bishop's chair with clergy seats on either side. On the arms of these are to be found carvings of the heads of Moses, Aaron, Timothy, Titus, and Saints Ignatius and Polycarp. At the tops of the seat-backs are carved angels and fruits. Two carved figures of bishops with mitres above them form the risers for the canopy over the bishop's chair. The front of the left kneeler shows the Apostles being sent out to preach, the inscription reading "Go your ways − behold, I send you forth." The front of the right kneeler shows Christ's admonition to Peter: "Feed my sheep, feed my lambs." The large center panel represents St. Paul in the laying on of hands, with four smaller scenes around it; the consecration of Bishop William White; the consecration of Bishop Samuel Seabury; Bishop Greer of New York laying the cornerstone of Saint Thomas Church; and Bishop Greer consecrating the church. At the tops of the seat-backs are carved angels, fruits, and mitres.

On the other side of the sanctuary from the bishop's chair are the sedilia for the assistant clergy. Along the top are symbols of the four Evangelists: for St. Matthew, the winged man or angel; for St. Mark, the lion; for St. Luke, the ox; and for St. John, the eagle. Just below these are four deacons, from left to right: Saints Stephen, Philip, Lawrence, and Francis of Assisi. The seats also contain three panels honoring some clergy of Saint Thomas who later became bishops, with the arms of the dioceses where they served. These are Frederick Courtney, an assistant, who became Bishop of Nova Scotia in 1888; Henry John Whitehouse, rector from 1844-1851, who was Bishop of Illinois from 1852 to 1874; and Alexander Mackay-Smith, an assistant, who left Saint Thomas in 1886 and became Bishop of Pennsylvania in 1911.

The altar rail itself is made of oak with four carved angels bowing their heads toward the altar in adoration, its bronze grille depicting various symbols of the Eucharist in eight panels that are repeated in succession from left to right on both sides of the opening. These symbols are the Chalice and Host, the pelican feeding her young from the blood of her breast, the fish, the pomegranate (symbol of endless life because of its abundant seed), wheat (indicative of the Bread of Life), a Canterbury cross surmounted by a crown, grapes, and the initials symbolic of "Jesus who conquers" (INRI: NIKA).

ly, to the eucharistic banquet that is celebrated thereupon. The presence on the reredos of the shields inscribed with "MR" (*Maria Regina*, for Mary the Queen of the Saints, or Queen of Heaven) and with the flower of the incarnation remind the viewer that this chapel also serves as the nearest thing in Saint Thomas Church to a traditional "Lady Chapel" with St. Mary as its patron. This theme would receive greater prominence with the dedication of "Our Lady of Fifth Avenue" during the tenure of a later rector.[15]

Closely related to the Chantry Chapel and of about the same date is the nearby Baptismal Font with its oaken cupboard above, the gift of John and Alexander Hadden and other descendants of David Hadden, one of the first wardens of the parish, who had given the original stationary marble font back in 1831. That font had survived the fire of 1851, but only fragments of it remained after the fire of 1905, and these pieces were now cut into small medallions and set within the eight sides of the new font. Just as Holy Baptism is full initiation by water and the Holy Spirit into Christ's Body the Church, so the number eight associated with it has been taken ever since the time of St. Augustine of Hippo in the early fifth century as symbolizing "the new day" beyond the seven-day week of the old creation, when humanity gets a fresh start, so to speak.[16]

The oaken cupboard polyptych above the font (pl. XIII), painted by the artist Thomas Watson Ball and really an enclosure of hinged, folding panels, depicts eight "virtues," the last seven of which (Temperance, Faith, Love, Hope, Prudence, Justice, and Fortitude) have been associated with Baptism, and the first of which, Chastity, added on the far left, is associated especially with St. Mary the Virgin, the patron of the nearby Chantry Chapel.[17] Each virtue is represented in gold lettering on the polyptych by a feminine figure holding in her hand a symbol appropriate to that virtue (a lily for Chastity, a horse's bit for Temperance, a cross for Faith, a heart for Love, an anchor for Hope, a lock for Prudence, scales for Justice, and a sword for Fortitude). Beneath each figure, spelled backward (in Latin), in black color and without the dignity of a capital letter, is the name of the corresponding vice that has been overcome and trampled upon by each virtue (*libido* overcome by Chastity, *luxuria* by Temperance, and so on). Painted above the font is a dove, symbol of the Holy Spirit. At the base of the polyptych is an unpunctuated inscription linking the entire baptismal ensemble to one of the earliest and most venerable families of the parish: "In memory David Hadden and Anne Aspinwall their sons William David John daughters Isabella Mary Margaret Sara Anna Eleanor Laura Elizabeth."

The initial flurry of construction was largely completed by the year 1929, freeing the rector's energy for completion of the interior and exterior of the building itself, to "make it the complete thing of beauty it was destined to be." Accordingly, Dr. Brooks, with the aid of Goodhue Associates, prepared a booklet for the parishioners describing what was necessary and inviting gifts toward this end as memorials and thank offerings. On Easter Day of 1929 a mortuary chapel bearing the name of the Chapel of the Resurrection, located in the north ambulatory aisle to the right of the chancel, was dedicated (pl. XIV). The gift of Miss Margaret Crane Hurlbut in memory of her mother, Margaret Havens Hurlbut, its reredos features a triptych of the Resurrection by the artist Tabor Sears and depicts the risen Christ in the center with two sleeping soldiers, an angel on the left, and on the right the three women at the tomb. Inside the right wall to the front a panel can be removed giving access to a hidden staircase that leads up to the organ pipes, its outline visible on the wall in the pattern of the incised blocks. Nearby some ancient panels of ecclesiastical embroidery are displayed. Eventually some funerary urns would be embedded within the walls of this chapel, and they would serve as precursors of the columbarium installed in the north wall here in 1990 (pl. XV). This chapel today is used for small services, meditation, hearing of confessions, interments, and memorials of the faithful departed, although it originated back in a period when coffins might lie in state here before the proliferation of commercial funerary parlors.

On All Saints' Day of 1929 a chime of twenty-one bells in the tower was dedicated (each to be played by hand), the gift of Mrs. George Arents, George Arents Jr., and Mrs. Dorothy Arents Brooks, in memory of the senior George Arents.[18] The largest bell weighs 5,600 pounds, and in addition to the memorial inscription bears the words: "O praise the Lord for His goodness and declare the wonders that He doeth for the children of men" (Psalm 107: 8, 15, 21, 31). The inscription upon the second largest records that metal from the original set of bells, given in 1873 and destroyed in the fire of 1905, was used in its casting. The smallest bell weighs 252 pounds. They are played by a clavier located in the same tower on the floor below, the degree of loudness or softness regulated by the amount of force applied.

Over the next several years the work of finishing the church went forward. At Christmas time in 1929 the first of a series of windows given by Mrs. Hamilton McKown Twombly and her daughters had been dedicated for the Chantry.[19] Finally, in 1936, the rector reported that all the permanent windows in the Chantry and its gallery above, those over the Great Reredos, the Rose Window (of flamboyant Gothic tracery similar to the one at Amiens and some twenty-five feet in diameter), and half of the windows for the clerestory (each eighteen feet wide and thirty-two feet high, the sills rising sixty-eight feet above the pavement) were now in place, all representing an expenditure of $160,000 and funded by memorials and gifts from parishioners.[20] The glass in the rose, of abstract blue and red like that in the reredos, was designed to be best viewed halfway down the center aisle in the early morning. The first window in the clerestory to be dedicated, the third from the altar on the south side, already complete by 1927 and the gift of Mrs. William A.M. Burden and her sons, features Saint Thomas the Apostle in the central lancet. It would be impracticable to describe all the clerestory windows in detail,[21] difficult as they are to see from the floor of the nave, but in a general way it may be said that each is devoted to a specific theme with a large central figure and several smaller subsidiary ones. The overall scheme involves nine windows on the north side from the street to the altar representing the fruits of the Spirit (Galatians 5:22-23) – Faith, Meekness, Goodness, Temperance, Gentleness, Joy, Love, Music (over the organ pipes, instead of Longsuffering), and Peace – and eight on the south side from street to altar depicting four of the Sacraments (Ordination, the Eucharist, Confirmation, and Baptism) as well as the Incarnation, Saint Thomas, Preachers, and Builders. All but the last two clerestory windows were created by Whitefriars of London, their logo of a monk in white habit usually appearing in the lower right corner of each.

Still other "tokens of love and affection" (as Dr. Brooks was wont to call them) included the Book of Remembrance (illuminated by hand on vellum and still in use today) and its Shrine, located at that time on the right-hand wall of the ambulatory of the Chapel of the Resurrection; the great figure of Christ the Teacher in the niche between the two main Fifth Avenue entrance doors (replaced in 1962); and gifts of communion silver, altar hangings, and other exquisite fabrics. By 1943 the narthex was completed, made possible by a bequest from Mrs. Robert B. Dodson in memory of her husband and herself. All that was now needed for the completion of the interior, according to Dr. Brooks, was the remaining windows for the clerestory.[22]

During the hard times of the depression the Saint Thomas Chapel, since 1872 located at 230 East Sixtieth Street between Second and Third Avenues, carried on a useful mission on the East Side. The neighborhood around the chapel had changed considerably, with some members of the congregation having moved away and the houses nearby occupied for the most part by transients. Those who attended the chapel found ready assistance, though the relief work was demanding and worrisome, as the vicar related in 1934. There was rent to be paid, gas bills to be settled, medical and dental care to be provided, and food and clothing to be collected and distributed. All this was undertaken mainly by the chapel staff, which included two social service workers, Misses Margaret Mitchell and Elizabeth L. Linsley. People not belonging to the chapel who applied for assistance were directed to the organization set up to care for their particular needs.[23]

The gifts of parishioners of the mother church to a Parish Unemployment Fund helped to support the work of the chapel where, in the words of Dr. Brooks, "the Vicar and his Staff have held up the morale and stabilized the courage of those who were in great distress through their inability to secure work." In addition, parish contributions to the Camp Fund allowed numerous underprivileged children to enjoy life in the open air during the summer at the Saint Thomas Camp on Lake Kanawauke, near Tuxedo, New

York. This camp was opened in 1929 after the closing of the old summer home on Long Island four years earlier. Parish giving also sustained a Milk Fund which furnished milk to many undernourished children.[24]

Dr. Brooks and his own staff offered aid to those who came to the doors of the church. "The conferences with persons in distress, bewildered souls, men and women seeking employment," he reported in 1934, "have increased tremendously." To help such individuals, work rooms had been organized by the parish "where hundreds of persons have been employed." It was far "better to furnish work of a necessary character for which payment is made," the rector believed, "than to support the unemployed by granting them a dole." Mental health was another area that received attention. The senior assistant, the Rev. Otis R. Rice, was trained in the field of psychiatric care and devoted his services to those in need. This special ministry had received "commendation on all sides," according to Dr. Brooks, and was "a contribution through practical Christianity in dealing with human problems of which the Parish has every right to be proud." For many other people the open doors of the church afforded a welcome of spiritual comfort, providing sanctuary in which to rest, to find a quiet space away from the noise and turmoil of the streets, and to pray.[25]

Saint Thomas Church was often characterized in newspaper articles as an "aristocratic Church," "a wealthy congregation," or a "rich parish," and from time to time Dr. Brooks would take the occasion to correct or modify that impression. The use of such terms, he would reply, fostered a class distinction and was untrue. "We minister to persons of every walk in life," he reminded his parishioners. "If we be aristocratic, wealthy or rich, it is by reason of the service we would perform." In the depression years the parish strove mightily to live up to the calling to serve. "When the faith of men in the stability of material things, in governments and in the plighted word has been shattered," Dr. Brooks exhorted, "the Church must keep abreast of the times with a message of spiritual hope and encouragement." It cannot know a season of ease, nor enjoy contentment. "Its missionary zeal must be greater than ever before." Saint Thomas, he never tired of saying, "does not live unto itself alone."[26]

Upon assuming the rectorship of Saint Thomas, Dr. Brooks had soon discovered that the neighborhood around the church was changing and changing rapidly. Fifth Avenue below Fifty-ninth Street was now a business thoroughfare and the side streets were fast losing their residential status. Saint Thomas was no longer an uptown church, and many parishioners lived a considerable distance away. To meet this new order of life Dr. Brooks determined to reach out and minister to the throngs of people who passed by the church each weekday. In 1927, he inaugurated a noon-day Lenten pulpit series, inviting notable preachers of the Episcopal Church. The following year he proposed the institution of a daily service of Holy Communion. This was done in 1929, along with a daily noonday service and address. It is believed that Saint Thomas was the first Episcopal church in New York not bearing a specific Anglo-Catholic label to have a daily Eucharist.[27]

The response to the daily services was most encouraging and indicated a spiritual hunger that was now being met. Over the years attendance continued to grow. In 1936 the rector reported that the congregations that year totaled nearly seventy thousand, or an average of thirteen hundred persons per week. A handsome sign was installed on the front steps in 1938 inviting passers-by to come inside, and the building was now kept open two additional hours, until eight o'clock in the evening. That year in the months from May to October, over five thousand persons visited the church during these hours alone. Fifteen years later, in 1951, there was an average attendance of a thousand persons during the week and a thousand communions a month. The next year the attendance on Good Friday was recorded at 5,239 and on Easter Sunday there were 1,162 communicants for the three services.[28]

In this developing emphasis upon daily services and a church whose doors were open to all, the rector, who had begun his ministry at Saint Thomas with an emphasis upon simplicity and financial stability, now gave clear evidence that he saw such virtues as serving a higher end, a return to the deeper spiritual life that had been a noted focus as early as the years of Dr. Brown. Dr. Brooks firmly maintained that Holy Communion was at the heart of parish life. "Believing as we do that the Christian religion has its center in the Sacrament of the Holy Communion," he told his parishioners, "we have endeavored to lead you to an appreciation of the spiritual help which comes from a faithful and regular participation in the same." In this way, and in steadily holding fast to the fundamental principles of the Christian faith, he asserted, Saint Thomas exercised its ministry. "We attempt nothing that is spectacular," Dr. Brooks once elaborated; "the Prayer Book is our rule and guide for services; good music is our aim; and leading men to God and His Christ through the exercise of religion and the use of the Sacrament sums up what we try to do."[29]

The rectorate of Dr. Brooks saw a steady growth in the work of the Choir School. Mr. Charles Steele, who had done so much to make it possible to start the school, continued his benefactions, giving it over half a million dollars between 1934 and 1939. When Mr. Steele died in 1939, the vestry passed the following memorial minute:

> As patron of music, he gave in 1922 the buildings which house the Choir School, and endowed the school; he caused another building to be erected in 1939 and increased the endowment, and in his will he made a further addition to its endowment, making his gifts to this object over a million dollars. More than once did he refer to the school as the best investment he had ever made. He called the choir boys his dividends.[30]

Reference was made here to "another building." By 1937, the quarters used by the school were found to be inadequate to its growing needs. Therefore, in that year, Mr. Steele bought a lot in the rear, facing on West Fifty-sixth Street. On this was erected a two-story building to provide three classrooms, a study hall, and a fully equipped gymnasium. The new facilities allowed for the enlargement of the dormitory rooms in the old building, providing for the residence of ten additional boys, or forty in all.

In 1932, the Music window in the north clerestory above the organ screen had been dedicated in gratitude for the life and work of Dr. Noble, and in the same year the honorary Lambeth degree of Doctor of Music was conferred upon him by Bishop Manning, acting for the Archbishop of Canterbury, Cosmo Gordon Lang.[31] On April 26, 1938, Dr. Noble celebrated his twenty-fifth anniversary as organist and choirmaster at Saint Thomas, and a dinner was given at the Union Club by the rector and vestry to mark the occasion.

Almost as a verbal signature to his musical accomplishments at Saint Thomas, Dr. Noble in 1943, the year that marked the twenty-fifth anniversary of the founding of the Choir School, published a pithy little twenty-four page tractate entitled *The Training of the Boy Chorister*, which was "dedicated to the choristers of St. Thomas Church." In addition to his technical comments on the music, Dr. Noble set forth three general principles: 1) "The Anglican Chant is frequently sung very badly because too much accent is given to the first beats of each bar." 2) "The hymn must never be treated as a part-song, just sung by the choir to entertain the congregation!" And 3) "Let us strive to sing in a devotional manner, doing our utmost to interpret the sung words with due thought to their meaning."[32] In that same summer of 1943, after thirty years of service, Dr. Noble retired from his post as Organist and Master of the Choir. "Too much credit cannot be given to Dr. Noble for the fine work he accomplished at St Thomas," Dr. Brooks wrote in the *Year Book*, "a work which has given the Parish a world-wide reputation for good church music." The vestry, in appreciation, appointed him "Organist emeritus" and voted him a pension.[33] In February of 1947, at almost the age of eighty, he gave one final organ recital in Saint Thomas before an audience of over eight hundred.[34] He died on May 4, 1953, and the parish would later celebrate on Sunday, May 7, 1967, the one hundredth anniversary of his birth.[35]

Dr. Noble was succeeded, most appropriately, by his friend and fellow Englishman, Dr. T. Frederick H. Candlyn. Dr. Candlyn had been organist at St. Paul's Church in Albany while Dr. Brooks was rector there. During his term of office in Albany, he had built up a nationwide reputation as organist, choirmaster and composer; he went on to become head of the music department of the State College for Teachers in the capital city. There could have been no more fitting person to step into the place left by the retirement of Dr. Noble, and no better assurance that the music of Saint Thomas would continue at its accustomed level.[36]

Dr. Candlyn served for ten years. Because of increasing infirmity and ill health, he retired with a pension from the parish in 1953. In 1954, Mr. William Self was called as organist and choirmaster from All Saints Church in Worcester, Massachusetts, where he had served for twenty years. There he had established a well-merited reputation as one of the nation's outstanding experts in the training of boys' voices.[37] His appointment to Saint Thomas, on July 1, 1954, at the age of forty-eight, came at the same time as the completion of a new building for the Choir School. His intriguing autobiography details his rich career of musical service at the parish up to the point of his retirement in 1971, by which time the acoustics of the church had also finally been improved.[38]

In 1949, while Dr. Candlyn was still organist and choirmaster, a vestry committee was established to consider plans for the future development of the Choir School. This committee recommended the purchase of adjoining property on the east at 117 and 119 West Fifty-fifth Street, and the erection of a new building on the old choir school site. The vestry approved the plan, but it was another three years before full possession of the additional property was obtained and construction could begin. In the end, a new fireproof structure was built, occupying the property from 117 to 123 West Fifty-fifth Street and connected to the gymnasium and classroom building to the north on West Fifty-sixth Street. The facilities, which cost over half a million dollars, provided dormitories and a refectory for forty boys, as well as rooms for the school masters, housemother, and other staff and a modern kitchen and storerooms. The Choir School was dedicated by Dr. Brooks on May 26, 1954.[39]

One death during this period should be noted. In 1942, Alexander Hadden, grandson of that David Hadden who had been for decades the leading layman of the parish, died at the age of eighty. And thus, for the first time since 1823, the name Hadden disappeared from the list of wardens and vestrymen.

The outbreak of World War II found Saint Thomas responding to the national effort in the same spirit that the church had shown over twenty-five years earlier. The various parochial societies busied themselves with the cause, and the parish house was used for such volunteer activities as Bundles for Britain and the Red Cross. Hundreds of men and women in uniform received a warm welcome, being invited as they entered the church to sign a card giving their name and the name and address of their home folks. During the week, Dr. Brooks sent a letter to each and every such family, letting them know that their relative had worshiped at Saint Thomas. Following the Sunday services those in the armed forces were entertained for luncheon at the Hotel Gotham where they mingled with parishioners and military officers. "At one of our bases in the Pacific," Dr. Brooks related in the 1944 *Year Book*, "a Navy nurse, a soldier and a sailor recently met, and what was it they talked about? – the pleasure of worshiping in St. Thomas and the good time they had as guests of the Parish at luncheon."[40]

Like so many other parishes across the country during the war years, the Fifth Avenue congregation was bereft of all its own young men and a number of women who were in the service. Many of the men in the choir were gone and the sexton's staff was depleted. At various times Dr. Brooks himself was away on tour of duty, serving as chaplain to the "Old Seventh [Regiment] of New York." The Roll of Honor of those in uniform eventually reached 449, with 34 of them making the supreme sacrifice for their country.

Before the war's end, plans were already underway for the erection of a World War II Memorial in the narthex as a thank offering for peace (pl. XVI). Designed by Francis L. S. Mayers, an associate of Goodhue, and dedicated on June 5, 1949, it features a floor of rare marbles with mosaic inlays on the theme of "One World," a globe with the continents in white, the seas in blue, a cross in the center, and the quotation "Peace on Earth to Men of Good Will" (Luke 2:14). Around this design are symbols of the Allied Nations, the four large shields representing (clockwise) the United States, Great Britain, France, and Soviet Russia, and the smaller ones (clockwise from the top) representing China, Greece, Belgium, South Africa, Australia, Canada, the Netherlands, and Poland.[41] A shrine was placed at the north end, its small altar of mottled marble incised with five crosses, and above it an illuminated prayer, flanked by the archangels Michael and Gabriel, for those who died and for peace . In their honor and memory, the Eucharistic sacrifice is still offered at this altar twice a year, on Veterans' Day and Memorial Day. There is a glass case for the parish's roll of honor, illuminated with the names of those who served in the war, with the names of those who gave their lives colored in red; the pages are turned throughout the year. Above are symbols of the various branches of the armed forces, and at the top are carved busts of the chiefs of staff of the Army, Navy, Air Force, and Marines. In the corners of the ceiling of the original narthex planned by Goodhue one can still see the carved stone corbels representing the four elements (earth, air, fire, and water), and in the ceiling over the central doors the four seasons of the year as well as four angelic beings. All of these silent stones look down, hopefully with approval, upon those who enter and leave.

A few months before the dedication of the World War II Memorial, Dr. Brooks was awarded "The King's Medal for Service in the Cause of Freedom" by His Majesty King George VI. The award was presented by Sir Francis Evans, the British Consul General, during a military review held at the Seventh Regiment Armory. The citation commended the New York rector for his "warm and courageous friendship" toward the United Kingdom and for the pastoral ministry shown toward British organizations even before America had entered the war as well as in the years afterward. It went on to say:

> He made helpful broadcasts during the War, and has repeatedly opened his pulpit to British clerical and lay speakers. During the war, he and his congregation entertained visiting British service-men by hundreds, and devoted much time to personal correspondence with the families of men who attended his services.[42]

The war years brought many changes. This was especially the case for Saint Thomas Chapel on East Sixtieth Street, where the surrounding neighborhood again underwent change as tenements were torn down and replaced by large apartment buildings inhabited by a more affluent population. In 1946, the Halsey Day Nursery was closed owing to the mounting cost of maintenance and the lack of children from the chapel requiring its services. In 1953 the Association for the Employment of the Industrious Poor, founded in the last century, quietly disbanded.[43]

Saint Thomas Chapel was becoming more a conventional parish and less a mission. And with each passing year the congregation became more self-supporting. In 1949, it raised for its own maintenance the sum of $15,000. The following year the chapel committee of the vestry was reorganized to include representatives of the East Side congregation itself; it was to act as an advisory body to the vicar. This was a first step toward making the chapel an independent parish. In the meantime, its activities continued to receive the attention and support of the mother church. Indeed, in 1952 the chapel buildings were completely renovated with funds from the Lippincott endowment.[44]

In the postwar period, Dr. Brooks took care not to let Saint Thomas forget its vocation to be an agent for good works in the service of the Gospel. In his annual appeal for the Maintenance Fund at the end of 1945, he strongly reminded his people of their obligation to support not only the chapel but also diocesan and national church missions and activities. "We have, as a Parish, been at the top of the list of churches the past year," he pointed out, "in the amount of money given to the Episcopal City Mission Society, the United Hospitals Fund, the Red Cross, missions and other charitable and educational objects." Beyond such financial contributions, moreover, Saint Thomas could also lend its strategic location to lectures that raised consciousness and stimulated thought about the Christian obligation to the creation of a better society. One such event was a series of "St. Bede lectures" given at Saint Thomas in February of 1948 by the Honorable Frances Perkins, who had been the Secretary of Labor under President Franklin D. Roosevelt and the first woman to serve in a presidential cabinet. It was there that this devout Episcopalian and political thinker of the New Deal articulated to a fascinated audience the religious rationale that had been central to the development of the Social Security Act of 1935.[45] That such an address could be given at Saint Thomas can certainly be taken as testimony to the seriousness with which the rector's appeals for good works were being heard. Dr. Brooks was a member of the committee that had planned the lectures.

As earlier in 1936, so still in 1945 less than half of the enrolled members of the parish made any contribution to the Maintenance Fund. "Any Parish which depends upon the gifts of the dead instead of the contributions of the living for its support," Dr. Brooks bluntly warned, "is bound sooner or later to die of dry rot." Late in 1953, in the last appeal of his rectorship, Dr. Brooks could report that, due to the action of the vestry in reducing pew rentals, only $15,000 a year was now realized from this source, and he hoped the day was not far distant when Saint Thomas would become a "Free Pew Church."[46] "I trust you will do your best for your church," he concluded, "that it may meet its obligations to the Church at home and abroad, to the Diocese and to ourselves."[47]

In 1951, Dr. Brooks was seventy-six years old, but still vigorous and active. He had been rector of Saint Thomas for twenty-five years. The anniversary was celebrated by a great service on October 7, one feature of which was the presentation and dedication of a magnificent processional cross, given in memory of his quarter century of service to the parish (pl. XVII). The cross was fashioned from gold and silver, and encrusted with precious and semi-precious jewels contributed personally by over one hundred parishioners from their own possessions.[48]

The preacher on the occasion was Horace W. B. Donegan, the twelfth Bishop of New York, who had become the diocesan bishop in the previous year and was the former rector of St. James' on Madison Avenue. In his sermon, Bishop Donegan properly noted the achievements which had marked the rectorship of Dr. Brooks. More importantly, though, he called attention to the pastoral ministry he had exercised. It would have been easy for Dr. Brooks to allow himself to become merely an administrator and to delegate the pastoral care to others. But this he had refused to do. "Your Rector has maintained a pastoral, personal ministry to the people of this church and to people of no church," the bishop told the congregation. "He has been ready to respond whenever appealed to for help, and to give not only his counsel but also his friendship."[49]

Dr. Brooks had begun to look forward to his inevitable retirement. By formal resolution of the vestry, he was to be granted at that time a very liberal pension, a residence, and the title of Rector Emeritus, with his agreement to perform such duties as the vestry might request. On October 26, 1953, Dr. Brooks requested that the vestry appoint a search committee for a new rector who would assume his duties the following autumn. He did not intend to resign officially until his successor was duly elected, however, fearing that any announcement of his retirement would adversely affect the raising of funds for the church.[50]

On September 23, 1954, Dr. Brooks presided over his last vestry meeting as rector of Saint Thomas. The vestry took the occasion to record its gratitude and affection for him in the minutes. "Under Dr. Brooks' administration, St. Thomas Church has increased its prestige in the Diocese of New York and effectiveness in the religious life of the City," the tribute read in part. It went on to cite the departing rector's many accomplishments, among them an endowment fund that now amounted to nearly nine million dollars. The Rector's Fund that began in 1926 with a five-dollar gold piece given in thanksgiving for the baptism of a child had grown to over $240,000. This fund was to be added to the endowments of the Choir School in the name of

Dr. Brooks. "But it is as pastor and counsellor in the life of this Parish that best establishes him as a friend of countless parishioners including every member of this Vestry," the tribute ended.[51]

At the time of his retirement on September 30, 1954, Dr. Brooks was eighty years old, and had served as rector for twenty-eight years. It was a tenure at Saint Thomas second in length only to that of Dr. Morgan. Inheriting a church building that still needed completion, he had not only supervised that but had also overseen the accession of a great number of complicated and permanent memorials, the designs, inter-relationships, and placement of which all needed some sophisticated knowledge of ecclesiastical art and classical theology. Moreover, more than half of his rectorate was passed in the difficult years of the great depression and the Second World War. He had wisely realized that, although Saint Thomas because of its location and beauty would always have a congregation, the parish would also require a substantial endowment fund because the occasional contributions of transient or passing worshipers alone would not support it. To Saint Thomas Dr. Brooks had brought simplicity and financial stability, almost complete freedom from pew rents, a church open every day and equally accessible to all, and, in addition, a deepening of sacramental devotion in the weekday services and the daily offering of the Eucharist. "We attempt nothing that is spectacular," he had explained, but in the very same breath he had added: "the Christian religion has its center in the Sacrament of the Holy Communion." Who could disagree?

Notes

1 VM 7:102 (3 May 1926), 7:106 (10 June 1926).

2 VM 7:106 (10 June 1926), 7:111-12 (25 June 1926); *Year Book* 1927, p. 9. The call to Dr. Brooks was issued at the same vestry meeting that learned of Dr. Clingman's refusal.

3 E. Clowes Chorley, *Manuscript History of St. Thomas Church* (unpublished manuscript in Saint Thomas Archives, 1943; copy deposited in the St. Mark's Library of the General Theological Seminary, New York City), p. 551.

4 Personal interview 6 September 1999 with Miss Claire Virginia Rouse, parishioner.

5 VM 5:87-89 (25 April 1901). Dr. Stires, in his centennial sermon, had exhorted parishioners to "count over your treasures, and give at least a child's share to the Mother [the parish church], that she may be strong to care for many children in the coming years." See "The Greater Future," *Sermon Preached by the Rev. Ernest M. Stires, D.D. on Sunday, December 9, 1923, in Commemoration of the 100th Anniversary of the Parish* (privately printed), p. 11.

6 VM 7:132-33 (24 March 1927), *Year Book* 1927, pp. 11-13. Upon legal advice and as a result of misuse of the corporate title of the parish, the vestry acted in 1926 "to vest record title to this corporation's real property in its correct name, viz., 'St. Thomas Church in the City and County of New York'." See VM 7:114 (25 June 1926), 7:120 (22 November 1926). Beginning with the second Sunday after Easter, 1 May 1927, the service bulletins were headed "Saint Thomas Church."

7 *Year Book* 1928, pp. 10-11; *Year Book* 1929, p. 11. *Endowment: That Saint Thomas Church May Stand Unmoved by the Concussions of Change* (Published by the Men's Association of Saint Thomas Church in New York: Redfield-Downey-Odell Co., Inc., 1930).

8 *Year Book* 1936, p. 13; *Year Book* 1941, p. 168; *Year Book* 1944, p. 11; VM 11:2 (18 November 1948) [in volume 11, the minutes of each separate vestry meeting are paginated separately]; see also *Legacies and Gifts which constitute the Endowment of St. Thomas Parish* (manuscript in Saint Thomas Archives). The Lippincott Fund was established in 1950 and in 1952 was valued at approximately $3,800,000, producing then an annual income of about $125,000; see VM 11:1 (28 February 1952).

9 *Year Book* 1948, p. 9; *Year Book* 1946, pp. 12-13.

10 By name, the Every Member Canvass did not come to Saint Thomas until 1957, all pew rentals being terminated four years later.

11 *Year Book* 1927, pp. 10-11; *Year Book* 1928, p.10; *Year Book* 1929, pp.10-11; *Year Book* 1936, p.12; VM 8:3-4 (15 October 1942).

12 VM 7:62-63 (15 October 1925), 7:66 (5 November 1925), 7:79-80 (18 December 1925), 7:126 (30 December 1926), 7:128 (11 February 1927), 7:143 (13 October 1927), 7:155 (10 January 1928), 7:183 (14 February 1929), 7:186-87 (14 March 1929), 7:205-6 (9 January 1930), 7:255 (12 November 1931). See above, chapter 9, note 57. The church filed a claim in 1930 in the amount of $51,000 against the city for damage caused by construction of the subway.

13 For the details, see page 161.

14 Perhaps the middle inscription, from John 2:5, would be an unlikely choice for a wedding text today!

15 See below, pages 217-18.

16 For the symbolism of Baptism as the eighth or new day of God's new creation, see *The City of God*, book 22. For the earlier history of the font at Saint Thomas, see Chorley, *Manuscript History*, chapter 14, p. 34; and above, sidebar on p. 70.

17 The seven gifts of the Holy Spirit traditionally understood to be given in Confirmation (Wisdom, Understanding, Counsel, Ghostly Strength, Knowledge, True Godliness, Holy Fear) are depicted in a window of the southern clerestory.

18 The name of Arents is associated with invention of machines that roll cigarettes and package them. Further on the Arents family, see below, chapter 12, note 81.

19 VM 7:175 (28 December 1928), 7:192 (11 April 1929); *Year Book* 1929, p. 12.

20 *Year Book* 1936, pp. 12-13.

21 Fairly full descriptions of most of them are given in [Harold E. Grove], *St. Thomas Church* (New York: n.p., 1965), pp. 22-28. As regards the last three: on Music (1932), see p. 167, and on Ordination (1970) and Temperance (1973), which were not made by Whitefriars, see pp. 200, 219. The themes of the windows in the north clerestory are remarkably paralleled in the inscriptions on the windows of the Chantry Chapel; see below, chapter 13, note 26.

22 *Year Book* 1936, pp. 12-13; *Year Book* 1943, p. 12.

23 *Year Book* 1934, pp. 123-27, 141-42, 144. The two social service workers reported making over 400 hospital visits and sick calls in 1934, and 131 patients were cared for at home. The director of women's activities for Saint Thomas Chapel reported that same year that "the list of those in the Chapel congregation seeking employment has increased so rapidly that it has not been possible to find work for all." However, in 1934 the vicar was able to say that "so far none of our people have been evicted or suffered privation."

24 *Year Book* 1934, p. 11; *Year Book* 1935, p. 12. In 1936, individual parishioners gave a total of $10,678.02 to aid the relief work of the chapel. This sum is exclusive of giving for other charitable, educational, and missionary purposes; see note in *Sermon Preached in St. Thomas Church, December 5, 1937 By the Rector, Rev. Roelif H. Brooks, D. D., D.C.L.* (privately printed), p. 15. The proceeds from the sale of the Long Island property amounted to $36,071.15 and were designated "The John Wesley Brown Fund," the income to be used for Fresh Air Work; see VM 7:209 (13 February 1930). The camp at Lake Kanawauke was closed in 1943 and a new camp in Ivoryton, Connecticut, was used in cooperation with the Chapel of the Incarnation.

25 *Year Book* 1932, p. 12; *Year Book* 1934, pp. 11-12; *Year Book* 1935, pp. 11-12.

26 *Year Book* 1932, p. 12; *Year Book* 1937, p. 11; *Sermon Preached in . . . 1937*, p. 15.

27 *Year Book* 1927, pp. 9-10; *Year Book* 1929, pp. 9-10; VM 7:121 (22 November 1926), 7:146 (13 October 1927), 7:192 (11 April 1929), 7:201 (24 November 1929).

28 *Year Book* 1936, pp. 11-12; *Year Book* 1938, p. 13; *Year Book* 1951, p. 12; VM 11:3 (24 April 1952).

29 *Year Book* 1932, p. 11; *Year Book* 1936, p. 11; *Year Book* 1938, p. 11.

30 *Year Book* 1939, p. 15.

31 *Year Book* 1937, p. 12; *Year Book* 1938, p. 12; VM 7:239 (12 March 1931), 7:264 (11 February 1932). In 1938, the "Angel Choir" window was dedicated at Easter. It was located on the stair landing at the back end of the Chantry aisle, outside the vestry room (now clergy sacristy), where the choir formed in procession. The window was the gift of Henry E. Felton in memory of Anna M. Stiles.

32 T. Tertius Noble, *The Training of the Boy Chorister* (New York: G. Schirmer, Inc., 1943), pp. 9, 11.

33 *Year Book* 1943, pp. 10-11. "Thirty seems to be a mystical number," Dr. Brooks observed, "for Dr. Warren likewise served for thirty years in the same capacity."

34 VM 11:4 (27 February 1947).

35 William Self, organist and choirmaster at Saint Thomas from 1954 to 1971, records this event in his autobiography, *Mine Eyes Have Seen the Glory* (Worcester, MA: Worcester Chapter of the American Guild of Organists, 1990), p. 200.

36 Dr. Warren also had been organist at St. Paul's in Albany.

37 VM 11:2-3 (22 April 1954), 11:1-3 (29 April 1954). Mr. Self came to the attention of the music committee when he gave a special concert at Saint Thomas Chapel, featuring the boy choir from Worcester.

38 William Self, *Mine Eyes Have Seen the Glory*, pp. 177-78. Problems with the church's acoustics began with the Guastavino tiles installed in the ceiling when the edifice was built, and they were exacerbated by the hanging of several tapestries on the north wall of the nave.

39 VM 11:3 (28 April 1949), 11:3 (26 May 1949), 11:2-3 (27 October 1949); *Year Book* 1951, p. 12; VM 11:3-5 (24 May 1951), 11:2-3 (22 September 1952), 11:2 (16 December 1952), 11:4 (22 April 1954) [in volume 11, the minutes of each separate vestry meeting are paginated separately]. The delay in constructing the building was due to legal difficulties in evicting the existing tenants from the newly acquired property.

40 *Year Book* 1942, p. 11; *Year Book* 1943, pp. 11-12; *Year Book* 1944, p. 10. During the war years, the church was not decorated with the customary greens and trees.

41 Curiously, New Zealand is omitted. Soviet Russia is here represented by the hammer and sickle, whereas the earlier World War I memorial on the wall at the southeast corner of the nave employed the double eagle to represent Tsarist Russia.

42 VM 11:2 (24 March 1949); *Year Book* 1951, p. 11. Dr. Brooks served for fifteen years as chaplain to the Seventh Regiment of the National Guard and came to hold the rank of Brigadier General, retired.

43 See *Year Book* 1943, p. 115; *Year Book* 1946, p. 10; VM 11:6 (24 October 1946); *Year Book* 1948, p. 13. The Halsey building was leased for one dollar annually to the Jewish Board of Guardians for a child development center. The income from the Halsey endowment was given to assist St. Luke's Hospital in the care of sick children.

44 *Year Book* 1949, p. 104; VM 11:2 (26 January 1950), 11:2-3 (24 April 1952). From 1937 onward, Dr. Brooks contested diocesan efforts to assess the chapel, arguing that it had no corporate existence and was a mission of the church. The diocese maintained that the assessments were based on the operating expenses of both the mother church and chapel; see the correspondence in the Parish

File Box for Saint Thomas Church, 1885-1964, in the Archives of the Diocese of New York.

45 Columbia University, Rare Book and Manuscript Library. Frances Perkins Papers: Cogge-shall Collection, Box 124. I owe this information to the research of Mr. Donn Mitchell.

46 Indeed that day was only some eight years off; it would come during the next rectorate, on 5 November 1961.

47 *Sermon Preached in St. Thomas Church, New York City, Sunday, December 9, 1945, By the Rector* (privately printed), pp. 7-9; *Sermon Preached in St. Thomas Church, New York City, Sunday, December 9, 1951, By the Rector* (privately printed), pp. 8-11; *Sermon Preached in St. Thomas Church, New York City, Sunday, December 13, 1953, By the Rector* (privately printed), p. 8. Dr. Brooks noted that the total expenditures for the support of the parish and the payment of diocesan assessments and the quota for the work of the National Council of the Episcopal Church (now the Executive Council) amounted to $208,168.77. He urged the parishioners to use weekly or monthly envelopes supplied by the parish office for giving.

48 A list of the donors and of the jewels and precious stones for the processional cross is preserved in the Saint Thomas Archives. Among the stones is a 53-carat Siberian amethyst. The cross was designed by Lewis F. Glasier. Its staff is made of olive wood, cut from a tree in Bethany, the home of Mary and Martha and Lazarus. The inscription reads: "To the Rev. Roelif H. Brooks, D.D., on the occasion of his 25th anniversary as rector of St. Thomas Church, an expression of esteem and affection from his parishioners." See newspaper article entitled "St. Thomas to Honor Pastor of 25 Years" from *The New York World-Telegram and Sun*, 6 October 1951, in Book no. 8 of Leaflets 1947-1953, in the Saint Thomas Archives.

49 *Sermon Preached in St. Thomas Church, New York City, The Twentieth Sunday after Trinity, October 7, 1951, By the Rt. Rev. Horace W. B. Donegan, D.D., Bishop of New York, On the Occasion of the Twenty-Fifth Anniversary of the Rev. Roelif H. Brooks, D. D. As Rector* (privately printed), pp. 3-7. Present at the anniversary celebration were the bishops of Albany, Delaware, and Western New York, and the retired bishop of New Hampshire. The master of ceremonies was Edward N. West, canon sacrist of the Cathedral of St. John the Divine.

50 VM 11:3-7 (25 May 1950), 11:5 (29 October 1953). A special committee of the vestry had been appointed as early as 1950 to consider the future retirement of the rector and to recommend the provisions for it. In a confidential communication to the vestry dated 21 October 1953, Dr. Brooks stated his intention not to resign until his successor had been selected; he believed no notice of his resignation should be made until after the Maintenance Fund was well in hand for the next year. Some individuals had indicated to the rector their intention to leave the parish upon his retirement.

51 VM 11:11-13 (23 September 1954). The rectorship of Dr. Brooks is also noteworthy for the first televised services. On 19 December 1948, a candle-light service at Saint Thomas was, according to Dr. Brooks, "for the first time in history . . . successfully televised with favorable reports on the reception being received from many sections of the country." The midnight service on Christmas Eve was televised in 1950; see VM 11:7 (23 December 1948), 11:6 (28 December 1950).

52 This survey is taken from: [Harold E. Grove], *St. Thomas Church*, pp. 34-43 (with many corrections). It would be impracticable to list in detail all the carvings of the pulpit, lectern, and organ case, which are given in Grove, *St. Thomas Church*, pp. 30, 31, and 41. For Charles Steele as their donor, see Grove, *St. Thomas Church*, p. 39, and [Frank Le G. Gilliss], *A Short Description of the Reredos, Wood Carvings and Other Objects of Interest in Saint Thomas Church New York City* (New York: Gilliss Press, 1927), p. 37. On the pulpit (to the right), which was given in memory of Samuel Hempstead Valentine (d. 1916) by his wife, are represented nineteen distinguished preachers carved in elongated Gothic figures. Above, the dove of the Holy Spirit and the seven Old Testament prophets on the sounding board remind the preachers that it is God's Word, not their own, that is to be preached. The lectern (to the left) depicts, in its lower tier from the Old Testament, Moses (with horns), Elijah, Job, and Isaiah, and on its upper tier the four evangelists. Above, on the side of its desk facing outwards, is the inscription "My Word shall not pass away" (Matthew 24:35, Mark 13:31, Luke 21:33).

CHAPTER 12

Responsible Discipleship

FREDERICK MYERS MORRIS
TENTH RECTOR, 1954-1972

41. Frederick Myers Morris, Tenth Rector 1954-1972

AFTER CONSIDERING SOME eighteen possibilities, the vestry on May 27, 1954, decided upon and called unanimously the Very Reverend Frederick Myers Morris, D.D., Dean of St. Mark's Cathedral, Minneapolis, to be the tenth rector of Saint Thomas Church in the City of New York (ill. 41). A direct descendant of Lewis Morris, one of the signatories of the Declaration of Independence, Dr. Morris was a graduate of Hobart College and the Virginia Theological Seminary. The son of a priest, Dr. Morris at the age of forty-eight brought to the parish a varied experience as missionary to the Arapahoe Indians in Wyoming, rector of parishes in Maryland and Massachusetts as well as Minnesota, and lecturer in homiletics, first at the Episcopal Theological School in Cambridge, Massachusetts, and later at Seabury-Western Theological Seminary in Evanston, Illinois. His wife, the former Dorothy Quincy Hastings, was the daughter of the priest under whom Dr. Morris had first served in Wyoming, and two of her brothers also became priests; one of them, Bradford Hastings, would become the Suffragan Bishop of Connecticut.

The service in which Dr. Morris was instituted as rector, held on October 10, 1954, brought together the talents of three masters: William Self (who had been in charge of the parish's music for only three months), Canon Edward West of the Cathedral of St. John the Divine as master of ceremonies, and the Bishop of New York, the Rt. Rev. Horace Donegan, as the officiant. It was a stellar cast, both for planning and performance, especially with the newly reorganized choir, and the service closed with a musical flourish that was spectacular but unexpected. After the members of the vestry were called forward to the altar rail one by one, Stanford's *Te Deum Laudamus* in B-flat was begun. At an appropriate point on a given signal, the choir and organ both came to a complete stop, and from a recessed area above the rear balcony a stunning fanfare was played by the brass from the New York Philharmonic. Then after a brief pause the organ came back to life and the choir joyously sang the last section of the *Te Deum*.[1]

By the end of his first year as rector, Dr. Morris had established as the norm for Sunday worship at Saint Thomas the service of Morning Prayer, reducing the frequency of Holy Communion as the principal Sunday service from twice a month, the standard set long ago by Dr. Stires, to the first Sunday of each month only. He accomplished this by first listing the change in the weekly service leaflet and in the monthly bulletin at the beginning of the summer of 1955 as being merely "The Summer Schedule"; but then when fall arrived the same schedule continued to be listed, the word "summer" being removed but no pastoral explanation given. No reason was given in his message in the *Year Book* for 1955 either, nor was any notice of the change recorded in the Vestry Minutes for the summer or fall of that year. Some years later, however, a rationale was offered. Morning Prayer, according to Dr. Morris, was a more evangelical and missionary service, providing the means for those unfamiliar with the Episcopal tradition to learn its ways and then to be led to the advanced step of receiving communion. Morning Prayer Sundays, in his view, were properly understood as a preparation for the monthly celebration of the Holy Communion. Dr. Morris strongly believed that this "rhythmic" pattern of worship contributed to "a higher appreciation of Holy Communion and is helpful in avoiding the inattention which so easily follows upon a too constant and too entirely unvaried sameness or uniformity of procedure." Thus he did not agree with the growing liturgical belief in much of the Episcopal Church – with which an increasing number of Low Church Evangelicals concurred – that the Holy Communion should be the main service every Sunday. Indeed, it was incumbent upon Saint Thomas and other parishes, he urged, to champion the Morning Prayer tradition in order to maintain the true character of the Episcopal Church as both catholic and evangelical.[2]

The Saint Thomas Church to which Dr. Morris came in the autumn of 1954 was widely regarded as a wealthy, fashionable, and somewhat exclusive parish. This was certainly an image that the new rector strongly wished to dispel. He wanted to see Saint Thomas fulfill its unique potential as a church located in the heart of a great city by reaching out to "all sorts and conditions" of humanity. The principal means toward accomplishing this great commission would be good worship and sound preaching. Faithful attendance on Sundays, then, was to be a major concern.

"I come to you in the name of the Lord as your leader in worship," Dr. Morris announced in his first sermon. Worship, he told his new congregation, is "an exciting and glorious activity," and should be entered upon with "a spirit of eager expectancy and receptiveness." He continued:

I know there are hosts of people who find churchgoing to be disappointing business. But I am convinced it is to a large extent because they expect too little, because their convictions are too small and because they are not willing to pay a fair price for it in faithful regularity and in the sacrifice of ease and convenience. Given the right attitude and the right degree of disciplined obedience and we shall soon begin to see measurable development in our perceptions, in our sense of life's true meaning, in our relationship with one another.[3]

Attendance at worship and growth in discipleship went hand in hand for Dr. Morris, and so he remarked in an early issue of the Sunday bulletin: "Every once in a while we hear it said of some clergyman, 'He fills his church every Sunday.' I do not like the philosophy behind such a remark. As your clergyman I repudiate the responsibility for filling this church. It is YOUR responsibility just as it is YOUR church quite as much as it is mine." Christian growth thus required self-discipline. This was the very meaning of discipleship, and through obedient and faithful attendance at the services of the church the individual would come to know the spiritual power of God. "You are to come with this question foremost in your minds," Dr. Morris urged: "What does the Lord want to say to me and do with me in this service through my participation in prayer and praise and devotion in the company of my fellows?"[4] Such obligations rested upon his parishioners, he seemed to feel, regardless of the changes he might make in the services and schedules of worship.

The members of the vestry used the occasion of Dr. Morris's initial meeting with them to express their confidence in his selection as rector. "In your sermons and at the meetings of the Men's Association you have told us of the plans you hope to carry out," noted the senior warden. They were plans, the vestry was confident, that "will strengthen the congregation's belief in God and the hereafter – beliefs which are sorely needed today to bring hope and peace to a troubled world."[5] With good reason, however, Dr. Morris understood that fresh leadership was not always welcomed. "I am aware of and sympathize with the distress which some people experience whenever changes are encountered in their church," he wrote in the parish bulletin of January 1955. He realized that a change in rectors would inevitably bring changes in concerns and styles, since no two persons are alike and each has a unique contribution to offer. However, growth could not take place without change. The parishioners of Saint Thomas, said Dr. Morris, were inheritors of "a great obligation, which is also a glorious opportunity, commensurate with the size and beauty of our magnificent church building and also with the conspicuous place it occupies in the life of the whole Episcopal Church." The discharge of this obligation and the realization of the opportunity required "renewed zeal and devotion" which would promise "blessings and joy and satisfaction of the deepest sort." He continued:

With increase of attendance at church services comes a new esprit de corps and an increase of that mysterious yet powerful force known as morale. These values are extremely contagious and everyone involved gets from that an inspiration and a spiritual stimulus which are real and precious. Yes, it is indeed an opportunity for an exciting new adventure in the progress of our Christian discipleship from strength to strength.[6]

The establishment of a personal relationship with each parishioner was an important pastoral priority for Dr. Morris. Toward this end he stated in the February 1955 issue of *The Saint Thomas Church Bulletin* his intention to call at the home of each member. "For us all to be united in mutual friendship, as well as in our mutual love of Christ and in our common concern for promoting the strength and influence of His Cause through His Holy Church," he wrote, "will result in an outpouring of the Spirit upon our parish and in our personal lives."[7]

In the first eight months of his rectorship, Dr. Morris reported having called at over six hundred addresses. In only two hundred instances did he find anyone at home. This was a smaller average than in other cities according to his past experience. Life in the New York metropolis, however, did not compare with that in most cities, as Dr. Morris was discovering. Still, several of the calls where no personal contact was made did result in telephone conversations and exchange of correspondence as a consequence of the rector's card found at the door. A year later, in 1956, Dr. Morris had managed to register an additional 350 calls and to converse in person with about 210 parishioners. He pledged to continue every effort to know all his people and in this endeavor urged them also to take whatever initiative might be possible.[8]

This program of home visits led Dr. Morris to conclude that the parish membership rolls were inflated. He found over five hundred names on the "active" list who had never made a pledge or a gift to the support of Saint Thomas, and many of these same people were seldom in attendance at worship. "We cannot allow anyone to suppose that by having his name on the rolls he is doing a favor to God or to the Church," declared the rector. Therefore, Dr. Morris continued, "We shall keep in the inactive file all who, by virtue of baptism or confirmation, are technically members. But we shall count for practical purposes and for official reports only those who give visible evidence of understanding and appreciation of this blessed privilege. One may change his status from inactive to active at any time by his own decision."[9]

To Dr. Morris, his duty as a priest of the Church and rector of a premier parish was absolutely clear. And he was not shy in expressing that duty boldly. "My task is to proclaim the Gospel," he exclaimed, "and to seek in every way to persuade listeners to commit themselves to it." It was not his task to court "admirers" or to win "a popularity contest." If respect and friendship were attained, it could not be from trying to be "all things to all men" or by compromising any of the integrity of his position as a priest and preacher. His hope for Saint Thomas was that the day would come when the parish was not only known for its architectural splendor, but also for "the devotion and loyalty of its people." What did he mean by this? "The only people who really love and value and understand the meaning of Christian discipleship," he explained, "are those who are faithful, in season and out, at worship, who give honestly and generously to the support of the Church and who seek a deepening sense of relationship with their fellow worshippers and fellow disciples." [10]

Responsible stewardship was the second aspect of Christian discipleship that Dr. Morris stressed upon assuming the Fifth Avenue rectorship. In a sermon entitled "The Spiritual and the Practical," delivered in December of 1954, Dr. Morris described the giving of money for the work of the church as "a positive practical opportunity for the expression of spiritual vitality and earnestness." "A financial offering," he said, "is a means of self-giving and if it is a generous and gladly given offering, it is as much a part of true worship as singing praises and saying prayers." There is a constant need to remember that it costs something to be a Christian. "That which is cheap and easy touches a man only on the surface and calls forth only a superficial response, if indeed any response at all. The more an ideal or a cause demands of a man, the more it reaches down into the finest and noblest responses of which he is capable."

Dr. Morris was appalled at the level of giving to Saint Thomas indicated by the early return of pledge cards in the weeks following his arrival. "In all the 25 years of my ministry," he bluntly informed the congregation, "I have never seen a situation comparable and I thought I had seen some pretty reprehensible ones." To those who believed Saint Thomas to be so well endowed that they need not make a pledge, he offered three facts to consider. First, the endowment income was not sufficient to pay the way of the parish "by a very wide margin." Second, even if it were sufficient, this would not condone committing "spiritual suicide by taking a free ride on what someone else has done." Third, Saint Thomas was only minimally supporting the mission work of the larger church and it should be doing more than the minimum. [11]

The Maintenance Fund had been established at Saint Thomas back in 1926 under the rectorship of Dr. Brooks, and for it in 1955 the vestry had set a goal to raise $100,000. This was an increase from the $60,000 for 1954. A letter from the chairmen of the Maintenance Fund and the Finance Committee to members of the parish, dated December 8, 1954, outlined the heavy financial obligations the parish faced. A new apartment at 550 Park Avenue had been purchased during the year for Dr. Morris and his family, as well as an apartment for Dr. Brooks, the rector emeritus. A reconditioned and refurnished study had been provided in the church for the new rector, while the former rectory next door to the church was being opened for general parish purposes. In addition, the parish house stood badly in need of renovation, particularly the choir's vesting and rehearsal rooms. General reserves would meet many of the improvements and renovations, but part of the expense must come from the Maintenance Fund. This fund furthermore was required to support the salaries of the clergy, the diocesan assessments for the work of the church at large, and parish aid to Saint Thomas Chapel on the East Side. These last items alone totaled nearly $100,000. The full budget of the parish was $370,000, and any difference would have to be met by endowment income.

Parishioners were informed that offerings to the Maintenance Fund had dwindled in recent years. Consequently, an increase in pledges and a much larger percentage of individuals pledging were needed. "We are confident that as we move ahead in this area of increased financial responsibility," concluded the letter, "there will be an upsurge of new enthusiasm and new spirit throughout the life of the parish."[12] A direct mail campaign for the Maintenance Fund met with some success, and recourse was then had to a canvass of parishioners. Even so, giving to the Maintenance Fund at the end of 1955 had barely exceeded $70,000.[13]

Dr. Morris was not one to relax his hand once it was set to the plow. To promote systematic giving he advocated weekly pledges to the Maintenance Fund and asked the vestry to lead the way in making their annual pledges on a weekly basis, with allowance for it to be paid annually, semi-annually, or quarterly. It was important, he said, to pledge a designated amount each week, and "to see that our pledge has some relationship to our income and to what we spend on matters of pleasure and travel and recreation generally." The amount given should be based on what one needs to give for his or her "spiritual well-being" and not on what the needs of the church are thought or supposed to be. In his efforts to institute the weekly pledge system Dr. Morris received the hearty support of Bishop Donegan. "For more than 35 years our Church generally has been using this system," the bishop wrote, "and it has proven to be a great boon spiritually as well as financially."[14]

Dr. Morris was encouraged by the early response of parishioners to the 1956 Maintenance Fund. The downward trend of recent years seemed to be reversed. The rector recommended that the vestry consider a new name for the Maintenance Fund Committee that would better reflect its purposes and functions. As he explained to the parish in the *Bulletin*, the term 'Maintenance" had been a source of much confusion, especially for newer members, and suggested some special or extra fund, rather than the principal means of support for the work and mission of the parish. It was the considered opinion of the vestry that the name "Contributions Committee" would be more appropriate.[15]

By February of 1956 a twenty percent increase in the giving of those who had pledged the year before and a thirty percent increase in money received was recorded, with the number of pledges having grown from 386 to 426. By the end of April the pledges exceeded the giving for the last year. In June, Dr. Morris reported that the financial support of parishioners had risen over fifty percent since 1954. "For the first time in years," he noted, "there are now more people on the membership list who contribute than those who do not." Disappointingly, however, the 1956 Maintenance Fund failed to reach its goal, with receipts amounting to $89,505.71, although the number of contributors had climbed to 577.[16]

A proposal to form a Men's Council to marshal the leadership of the parish was adopted by the vestry in March of 1957. This Council was to be composed of twenty to thirty-five men who would assume certain tasks to assist the vestry in their duties and to pursue other projects. It was anticipated that this body would also oversee canvassing, ushering, and social activities. By the following autumn the Men's Council was functioning under the presidency of Mr. Frank Simon, and its Every Member Canvass Committee was in full operation, sending letters and literature to parishioners urging them to make a pledge and calling on those who had not responded. The weekly pledge was commended as "the proper Christian method" of giving, providing "one way of 'keeping holy' the Lord's Day and one aspect of our weekly worship."[17]

The work of the Every Member Canvass Committee soon bore fruit. The number of pledges in 1958 that were on a weekly or continuing basis had reached 507 as compared to 441 in 1957, while those on an annual or non-continuing basis had decreased from 141 to 108. The following year, in 1959, pledges achieved a record high of $105,906. At the same time the number of weekly pledges had grown to 582 and the non-continuing to 163, making a total of 745 contributors. Dr. Morris always insisted that he was not interested merely in collecting dollars or in financial figures for their own sake, but in the spiritual values these represented. He firmly believed in "the power of proper giving to stimulate renewed zeal and devotion."[18]

After attendance and stewardship, the third priority of Dr. Morris as rector of Saint Thomas was to expand "the mutual acquaintance and sense of community" within the parish. In the Sunday service bulletin, Dr. Morris asked parishioners to take a friendly interest in one another. "We want St. Thomas Church to be known as a 'warm church' where strangers and newcomers are made to feel that we are glad to have them." He urged members therefore to make it a habit to speak to people whom they did not know after service and to inform him of the names and addresses of those expressing an interest in the parish.[19] He also urged the congregation to stay on for a brief hymn rehearsal after the benediction on the second and fourth Sundays of each month.[20] Still another feature of the new emphasis upon community was the Service of Christmas Lessons and Carols held for the first time at Saint Thomas on Sunday afternoon, January 2, 1955, under the direction of the equally new organist and choirmaster, William Self.[21]

To encourage the creation of an enhanced sense of community, Dr. Morris undertook to revive and restructure parish organizations, as well as to provide new opportunities for fellowship. Among the first organizations to be revived was the Sunday School. In 1939 Dr. Brooks had found it nearly impossible to maintain such a school given the location of Saint Thomas outside a residential neighborhood. The post-war years, however, saw a resurgence of interest in Christian education throughout the Episcopal Church, and Dr. Morris, like others, recognized the importance of a good Sunday School for drawing young families into the life of the church and fostering Christian discipleship. At his request, the vestry established a Sunday School Committee in January 1955 to oversee this field of parish work. Within a few weeks the chairman of this committee, Mr. Walter Wilds, reported that enrollment in the Sunday School had grown to 45 children as compared with an average of 31 children a few months earlier. The committee also found upon investigation that there was a potential of 175 children for it. New equipment was purchased for the program, now housed in the renovated rectory.

In June of 1955 Dr. Morris announced that an arrangement had been made for Windham House, the Episcopal Church training school for graduate women churchworkers in New York City, to use the parish Sunday School at Saint Thomas as a field laboratory. The plan was for women students from Windham House, under the supervision of the faculty from that institution, to work in association with one of the clergy assistants at Saint Thomas and one or two seminarians from the General Seminary "to build up an effective school and to integrate it into the life of the whole parish." Dr. Morris saw this initiative as "a very significant step forward in the development of a progressive parish program."[22] He also approved of a program to have seminarian assistants working part-time, especially on Sundays, so that, for example, in the year 1962 the parish benefited from the services of Thomas L. Dixon from General Seminary and Marshall Braxton from Union, both of whom were students in divinity.

In the autumn of 1955, the chairman of the Sunday School Committee reported that the new educational program under preparation would provide for family participation and that the teaching staff intended to develop a team approach and to foster closer ties with the parents. It was also noted that parish calls were to be made on families with children of Sunday School age.

RESPONSIBLE DISCIPLESHIP

Progress in building up the Sunday School steadily continued; within three years there was a total of 65 pupils, ranging in age from six months to fourteen years, and by the following year, 1959, the number grew to 122. The nursery program was one of the most exciting areas of parish life and was credited with the increase in the numbers of young parents attending Saint Thomas. The nursery even merited special attention in an article in *The New York Times* at the end of December 1959. "The Sunday School, especially the nursery and kindergarten," Dr. Morris wrote in the *Year Book* for 1959, "threatens to burst the walls of the 'old rectory'." The parish now faced the happy problem of "developing our facilities or turning people away from our doors."[23]

The Woman's Auxiliary, which had been so-named under Dr. Stires back in 1901, was another parish organization revitalized under Dr. Morris. The activities of the Auxiliary were expanded, with new educational and devotional programs as well as fund-raising activities. In 1956, the Auxiliary and other women's groups, such as the Altar Guild, the Service Club, the United Thank Offering, and the Church Periodical Club, were all centralized under the new name of "The Women of St. Thomas Church," with Mrs. Herbert E. Twyeffort serving as president. This step was taken, in the words of Dr. Morris, "to mobilize the woman power of St. Thomas Church." For a number of years, only very few women had been active in church work. The new organization was intended, said the rector, to better employ the "great resources in ability and talent and leadership among our membership," and to restore Saint Thomas "among the strong parishes of the Diocese" in the ministry of women. In the first season of work together, the Women of Saint Thomas proved most effective in a variety of undertakings and in attracting more members, and continued success was promised with the engagement of a recent graduate of Windham House, Mrs. Kenyon Young, as a full time Executive Secretary in the summer of 1957.[24]

When Dr. Morris arrived at Saint Thomas he also discovered that the Altar Guild had "evaporated." He asked Katharine S. Fales to reorganize it, and its membership soon came to number thirty-five. Services on Sundays and weekdays once more were being vigilantly cared for by this guild and a tradition of devotion and high standards was established. The Altar Guild also supervised a "needlework project" among members of the parish, to adorn the sanctuary and chapels of the church.[25]

The former Men's Association was incorporated into the new Men's Council in 1957. This organization sponsored several social events to foster fellowship among the men of the parish, as well as benefit performances to aid the Choir School Scholarship Fund. In addition to being responsible for the Every Member Canvass and the Board of Ushers, members of the Men's Council conducted tours of the church, served as acolytes at celebrations of the Holy Communion during the week and at eight o'clock on Sunday mornings, and arranged adult education programs.[26]

Among the new opportunities for fellowship instituted by Dr. Morris was the "coffee hour" following the eleven o'clock Sunday morning service. This proved a popular project, although some people were resistant to it on the grounds that one should go home from church quietly meditating upon the blessings of worship. Dr. Morris, however, argued that "the unity of Christian people gathered at the Lord's Table must be carried away in their hearts to find added expression in the everyday, prosaic and humanly simple associations with one another in the commonplace activities of ordinary life." "God the Holy Spirit," he said, "can be made welcome in the parish house as well as in the sanctuary of the church."[27]

A Choral Society was organized to bring together those interested in music who wished to assist in the services of the church. The society made its debut at the Service of Lessons and Carols in Christmastide of 1955. A Wednesday evening Young Adult Group was formed to provide the single urban dweller both a time for Christian formation and a time for social recreation. The After Five Club offered business and professional women a monthly dinner and program on a wide variety of subjects, religious and cultural.[28]

Parish dinners were held in 1958 and 1963 to commemorate the 135th and 140th anniversaries of the founding of the church. That in 1958 was held at the Pierre Hotel on December 11. The featured speaker was former New York Governor and Presidential candidate Thomas E. Dewey, and those present were given a copy of the newly published parish history by the Rev. Canon George E. DeMille.[29] This dinner occurred not long after Dr. Morris entered upon his fourth year as rector. In the *Saint Thomas Church Bulletin*, he reflected on how much had been accomplished in such a short, swift time. The Sunday attendance had more than doubled and significant steps had been taken toward responsible stewardship on the part of congregation members. One must not suppose, he warned, that little remained to be done. "Our only justification for maintaining so large a church building is to have it filled regularly," observed Dr. Morris. As for financial support of the parish, there were still those who had not learned the value of systematic giving and whose pledges were "woefully inadequate as compared to their resources." This obligation was something the rector considered himself conscientiously bound to keep before his people.[30]

This tenth rector of Saint Thomas, like his predecessor Dr. Stires, was a graduate of the Virginia Theological Seminary. He had graduated from that institution in the class of 1930, and in 1959 he was invited by *The Seminary Journal* there to write about his ministry of the past five years in the Fifth Avenue parish. Dr. Morris related therein that in the years before his arrival

Saint Thomas had for the most part continued to live out the role of "a wealthy, fashionable and exclusive" church, relying upon its endowment to maintain "dwindling congregations" that were bereft of "any vestige of community." In recent years, under the inspiration of the Bishop of New York, the parish had endeavored, he said, to reach out to "all sorts and conditions" of people. This had been done "by indefatigable pastoral calling, by reviving organizations and groups and study classes, by a program of Sunday afternoon and weeknight musical services, with a repertoire quite different from the conventional." As a consequence, he wrote, "the influx of people has accelerated and the parish rolls have increased dramatically" and there has been "a resurgence of general vitality and a warmth of personal association." Dr. Morris further remarked:

> "The clergy admit freely among themselves and to the people that they do not know for sure or in any complete sense what is the peculiar ministry of a church so conspicuously located. But they conscientiously seek for a definition and persistently bespeak the help of the members of the congregation in the search. Experiments are constantly attempted in the field of weekday services at various hours, in the use of the boy choir for television and radio programs, in fund raising activities for the benefit of charitable enterprises in the community and in a variety of advertising methods."

Above all, the unique ministry of the parish was to maintain a high standard of worship and preaching, and to make it relevant to the contemporary situation. There was also the responsibility of providing sound programs in Christian formation and discipleship. Dr. Morris then set forth the program he had been following as the rector of Saint Thomas:

> We believe that the Episcopal Church has a very special contribution to non-Roman Christendom in the dignity and formality of her worship. . . . In these days, when that tradition of worship is in danger of serious dilution, if not actual loss, in the growth of "family services" with their inevitable sacrifice of dignity and beauty, we seek to maintain and to exemplify the highest possible standard of "Episcopal worship" at its best.[31]

One obstacle to opening the doors of Saint Thomas fully to the city was the archaic system of pew rentals which Dr. Stires had questioned and Dr. Brooks had sought to eliminate but which had been with the parish since its beginning. In January of 1956, Dr. Morris urged the Pew Committee of the vestry to consider the long range policy respecting pew rentals and the possibility of doing away with them at some point in the future. A preliminary report of the committee indicated that the number of rented pews stood at 101 and the number of rented sittings at 213. All the rentals had already been reduced by nearly one-half and now ranged in price from $75.00 down to $10.00, depending on location. The chairman of the Pew Committee also reported that a recent survey indicated that St. Bartholomew's, St. James', and

Heavenly Rest, the other neighboring churches with rented pews, had no current intention of ending the system and, like Saint Thomas, were dependent upon the income to a significant degree. The committee subsequently recommended that the policy of renting pews be maintained. There were sufficient free pews, it was considered, to accommodate occasional Sunday attendance properly.[32]

In late February of 1957, however, Dr. Morris informed the vestry that the rector of St. James' had announced that next fall pew rentals would be discontinued in the Madison Avenue parish. Four years later the vestry was notified that Grace Church on lower Broadway had ended the practice of renting pews. Finally, in May of 1961, the vestry of Saint Thomas unanimously approved a motion to make the Fifth Avenue parish a "Free Pew Church." A letter was sent to all pew holders the next autumn informing them of the decision, which was to become effective on November 5, 1961.[33]

In *The Saint Thomas Church Bulletin*, Dr. Morris described the vestry action as a "historic turning point" in the life of the parish, "the symbol of a new era and, in the eyes of the public, almost an about-face in the policy and attitude of the parish." The idea of rented pews had suggested to many an "exclusiveness and special privilege and even deference to wealth," and Saint Thomas had long suffered from such a reputation, whether justified or not. No one, of course, expected a sudden surge of new members or dramatic increase of worshipers, but over the course of time the freeing of the pews would help to sustain and possibly augment the rate of growth already enjoyed both in membership and in Sunday attendance. The parish could rejoice, Dr. Morris observed, that this development had been achieved without serious disagreement or discord, adding that the attention shown by the newspapers and television reporters "indicates the importance of this move in the eyes of the public."[34]

Maintaining a church structure as extensive as that of Saint Thomas demanded constant attention and in this matter Dr. Morris relied heavily on the vestry's Buildings Committee. In just the first year after the arrival of the new rector, the church saw the installation of new lighting, the cleaning of all woodwork and the Great Reredos (to which certain missing pieces were restored), repairs to several of the windows, and the modernization of the heating and ventilation systems. In addition, there were renovations, including the introduction of an automatic elevator, made to the old rectory and parish house to accommodate staff, organizations, and the Sunday School.[35]

New construction on Fifth Avenue in the late 1950s, both to the north and the south of the church, compelled the rector and vestry to take proper steps to safeguard and protect the church building. Insurance policies were reviewed and the same engineer who oversaw repairs to the church many

42. Selected statuary from the Scott Memorial (Fifth Avenue façade, 1962-63): Sts. Bartholomew and Matthew, Christ the King, Sts. James the Less and Jude

years earlier in the aftermath of the building of the Fifty-third Street subway station was once more retained. In the end, the church suffered minor damage from blasting operations estimated at $10,000. Still, the continued development around Saint Thomas called for the utmost vigilance. There was, for instance, a proposed enlargement of the same nearby subway station in 1959. Three years later concerns were aroused by the construction of an addition to the Museum of Modern Art to the west of the church and parish house. This resulted in a claim against the Museum for damage of approximately $13,000, chiefly related to the reredos.[36]

Completion of the Fifth Avenue façade of the church was now a primary interest of Dr. Morris (ill. 42). In 1957 the rector, together with two members of the vestry's Standing Committee, undertook a review of the original plan for the exterior proposed by Bertram Goodhue. This plan had called for the placement of nearly fifty statues and extensive carving, including over two hundred shields, panels, and bosses. In consultation with Canon Edward N. West of the Cathedral of St. John the Divine, an authority on ecclesiastical art and symbolism, the Goodhue design was partially revised and rearranged. Approval to proceed with the project was granted by the vestry in the autumn of 1958. It was also agreed to make legal application to draw upon the legacy of George S. Scott, a parishioner, to fund the work, which would be known as "The Scott Memorial."[37]

At length in 1961 the Surrogate's Court of New York entered an order to allow use of certain funds from the Scott legacy to provide "a visible memorial" on the Fifth Avenue exterior of the church.[38] Mr. Theodore Barbarossa was chosen to design the sculpture, and the stone carving was executed by the firm of Rochette and Parzini of New York. Canon West was retained as a consul-

Description of the Scott Memorial (Fifth Avenue Façade), completed 1962-1963[94]

At the sides of the doorways are figures, three on each side. Left to right, they represent St. Peter with the keys of heaven, St. Andrew with an X-shaped cross, St. James the Great with scroll in his right hand, St. John the Evangelist with chalice and serpent, St. Philip with scroll and long cross staff and St. Paul with sword. In the center of the pointed arch above the doors is Christ the King in imperial robes, His right hand raised in blessing, His left hand holding the orb of power, symbolizing His kingship of this world. At the left is the Virgin Mary with her symbol, the pierced heart, and at the right, John the Baptist with a Maltese Cross. A row of six smaller figures toward the bottom of the arch shows Saints Simon, Bartholomew, Matthew, James the Less, Jude and Matthias. Above are Saints Mary Magdalene and Martha. At the bottom of the arch are four panels of bas-relief figures representing various aspects of St. Thomas' career – from left to right, his despair, doubt, confession of faith and ministry in India.

In the three parallel bands of the main portal arch are blocks of carved stone. Foliated blocks alternate with other carved symbols. In the outer row appear symbols of the gifts of grace which the Holy Spirit bestows at Confirmation: wisdom and understanding, counsel and ghostly strength, the Holy Spirit Himself, knowledge and true godliness, and holy fear. In the middle row are symbolized various branches of learning: medicine, science, theology, letters, philosophy and law. In the inner arch are depicted labor, management, social service, education, art and music....

On the buttresses just outside the portal are four large figures. The two at the left are famous figures of the Western Church. High up is St. Ambrose (died 397), Bishop of Milan, remembered especially for his scholarship and interest in liturgy and church music; below is St. Augustine of Hippo (354-430), theologian and author of *The City of God* and the *Confessions*. Those on the right buttress are two noted fathers of the Eastern Church: above, St. Athanasius (c. 296-373), Bishop of Alexandria, who helped formulate the Nicene Creed; and below, St. John Chrysostom (c. 347-407), called the "goldenmouthed" because of his eloquence (his prayer on common supplications is used in the service of Morning Prayer). Below St. Augustine is the Latin cross of the Western Church. Below St. John Chrysostom is the Greek cross of the Eastern Church.

Just above the main portal and below the rose window are seven figures. A large statue of St. Alban, the first martyr in England, who died about 209 A.D., is the central one. Just below him two angels hold a shield bearing an X-shaped cross. Flanking St. Alban in the usual order are St. Augustine, first Archbishop of Canterbury, "Apostle of the English," who died c. 604-9; St. Andrew, Apostle, patron of Scotland, shown with the boy who furnished the loaves and fishes with which Christ fed the multitude; St. George (died about 303), patron saint of England, shown driving his lance into the dragon's mouth; St. Patrick (c. 389-461), patron saint of Ireland; St. David (c. 500-600), patron saint of Wales; and St. Columba (521-597), evangelizer of Scotland. The shields of these saints are placed below the figures.

Around the rose window are the symbols of the four Evangelists. At the upper left is the winged man or angel, symbol of St. Matthew, and at the upper right is the lion of St. Mark. The lower left shows the ox of St. Luke and the lower right the eagle of St. John. Inscribed above the rose window is a line from the Te Deum: "Thou art the King of Glory, O Christ." At the center of the quotation is a large winged crown.

Still higher up is a row of nine figures. The central one is St. Edward the Confessor, last Saxon king of England, who died in 1066. At the left in the open spaces are: William Temple, ninety-eighth Archbishop of Canterbury, scholar and social reformer who died in 1944; John Mason Neale (1818-1866), remembered as a writer and translator of hymns; Lancelot Andrewes (1555-1626), Bishop of Winchester and one of the translators of the Authorized Version of the Bible; and Thomas Cranmer (1489-1556), sixty-ninth Archbishop of Canterbury, responsible for a uniform liturgy in the Church of England and compiler of the Book of Common Prayer. At the right of St. Edward are four corresponding figures: Samuel Provoost (1742-1815), American patriot and first Bishop of New York; John Henry Hobart (1775-1830), third Bishop of New York and a great missionary genius; Henry Codman Potter (1834-1908), seventh Bishop of New York and an outstanding social reformer; and William Reed Huntington (1838-1909), Rector of Grace Church, New York City, liturgical scholar, and reviser of the Book of Common Prayer. The arms of all these men appear below their statues. It is interesting to note that the four figures to the left of St. Edward are prominent English churchmen, the four to his right, American churchmen.

At the very top center is the Rood group. The Crucified Christ looks down toward man below, between the Virgin Mary and John, the Beloved Disciple.

---

tant, with general responsibility to supervise and guide the work. Installation began in 1962. "The decorative and intricate stone carving combined with the statuary suggests the glory of the reredos on the inside of the church," readers of the *Saint Thomas Church Bulletin* were told, "and will convey to the passing public something of the message of the Gospel as exemplified by the saints and martyrs of Christian history." The central feature of the Scott Memorial, replacing the former Lawrie statue known as Christ the Teacher in the niche between the two main Fifth Avenue entrance doors, was a striking statue of Saint Thomas with downcast eyes and outspread palms at the moment of declaring his faith in the risen Christ.[39] In effect, he invites the passers-by to enter the Gate of Heaven and with him to confess Christ as "Lord and God"

(John 20:28). On Sunday, November 3, 1963, the finished façade was dedicated, displaying "a unified plan of superlative magnificence."[40]

The following year, the side entrance on Fifty-third Street was adorned by five more splendid statues, dedicated on October 25, 1964. A gift from the legacy of Mary T. Kenny, they were designated "The Lyon Memorial" in memory of Leonie de Bary Lyon Brewster and Adolph de Bary Lyon.[41] They comprise the Archangel Gabriel at the center of the door, flanked by four famous women who were mothers: Sarah and Hannah on our left, and Saints Elizabeth and Monica on our right. The subject matter was entirely appropriate, given the maternal and Marian themes that are featured in the chapel just the other side of this doorway.

To make the church even more inviting to the passersby on Fifth Avenue, thought was given to opening up the view of the church interior by the installation of glass doors. After some controversy, the vestry in 1962 approved replacing the carved oak inner doors of the main portal and the oaken screen between the nave and the narthex with clear plate glass. In this alteration, professional assistance was sought from Mr. Theodore F. Young, architect of the firm of Eggers and Higgins, and also, of course, from Canon West of the Cathedral.[42]

In the autumn of 1961 arrangements were made to keep the church open every evening until midnight. The new hours immediately met with a ready response. Indeed, one evening as many as six hundred people passed through the welcoming doors on Fifth Avenue. Three years later over a thousand people were counted as visiting the church on summer evenings, and during the Christmas season the number ranged from six hundred to sixteen hundred.[43] At the time of President John F. Kennedy's funeral, on November 25, 1963, the entire church was packed, including both balconies, and even standing room was at a premium.[44]

The ministry of Saint Thomas Chapel naturally received much attention from Dr. Morris. From the beginning he looked toward the future independence of the chapel and set about to achieve this goal. He expressed the strong desire to see the vicar and his assistant, together with a Chapel Council, assume more responsibility in the formulation of policies and their implementation as related to the work on the East Side. This included such matters as drafting a budget for the chapel, the oversight of financial affairs, and the maintenance of the physical facilities. A forward step in this direction was taken in the autumn of 1955 when the vicar and Council were invited to submit a proposed budget for the upcoming year to the Saint Thomas vestry, along with a list of any additional capital expenditures deemed necessary to put the chapel properties in good repair. This proposed budget and

43. All Saints Church, independent since 1965

list was then to be reviewed by Dr. Morris, the church treasurer, and the
vestry's Chapel Committee, who would determine the amount of quarterly
grants to be made to the chapel for the ensuing calendar year. In a further effort to advance the self-support of the chapel the first Every Member Canvass of the East Side congregation was undertaken.[45]

Over the next several months the chapel showed increasing attendance at
services and progress in its fund raising. But late in 1957 it was revealed that
the City Traffic Commissioner had recommended the condemnation of the
entire block in which the chapel was located for the purpose of building a
parking garage and improving the approaches to the Queensboro Bridge. If
the chapel property were condemned, the Saint Thomas vestry decided not to
contest the decision, and in the meantime it approved plans for a new façade
for the chapel, pending a final ruling. In February of 1959, the condemnation
proceedings were dismissed by the Board of Estimate, and so work on the
façade of the chapel commenced, reaching completion that November.[46]

The period of uncertainty as to the fate of the chapel strained relations
with the mother church, especially those between the vicar, on the one hand,
and the rector and vestry on the other. The vicar had strongly resisted the
stance taken by the vestry concerning the prospective obviation of the
chapel, and in the interim members of the East Side congregation had become indifferent as to whether they should be self-supporting. Dr. Morris
believed that the vicar had failed to exercise responsible leadership and was

RESPONSIBLE DISCIPLESHIP

"convinced that the Chapel must either prove itself able to be self-support-ing in a few years or else should be sold and the money used for a new mis-sionary venture in an honestly ill-favored part of the city or for the founding of a new chapel in an area which has promise of ability to become self-sup-porting within a few years." For too many years, he believed, the present chapel had been treated almost blindly as an "object of charity" and had been "encouraged to function on a scale far more luxurious than could be justified in comparison to other New York City parishes of similar size and location." The time had come, said Dr. Morris, for a change of leadership, and in the autumn of 1959 the vicar was requested to secure another position. And so at the close of the centennial of the chapel's founding at Prince and Thompson Streets in lower Manhattan, the epilogue to the East Side work of Saint Thomas Church was about to be written.[47]

On May 1, 1960, the Rev. R. DeWitt Mallary Jr. was formally instituted as vicar of Saint Thomas Chapel. The new vicar and the rector of Saint Thomas harmoniously and enthusiastically pursued the goal of parochial status for the chapel. Plans for independence and the establishment of an en-dowment fund were warmly approved in principle by the vestry in 1962.[48] The following year, on Easter Day, the name of the chapel was changed to All Saints Church (ill. 43). This was another important step on the way to in-dependence, now scheduled for January 1, 1965. The next months were busi-ly occupied in settling the terms of separation and obtaining the consent of the Bishop and Standing Committee of New York, as well as the necessary New York County Supreme Court approval. At long last the anticipated day arrived and on May 11, 1965, All Saints Church was admitted as a parish into union with the Diocese of New York. Under the portrait of Dr. Morgan, dur-ing whose rectorship the former chapel was founded, the final papers ac-knowledging the mother church's official parting with her offspring were handed by Dr. Morris to the new rector of All Saints.[49]

The year 1964 proved to be another milestone in the life of Saint Thomas. First, the vestry sanctioned a plan for instituting a "rotating system" for the election of its membership. This had long been a hope of Dr. Morris, who saw the practice as a means of introducing the talents and gifts of an in-creasing number of church members into the government of the parish. The proposal required that each member of the vestry take at least a year off from service at regular intervals.[50] "I am convinced," said Dr. Morris, "that it strengthens the lay sense of responsibility and increases the general effec-tiveness of the lay 'apostolate'." The other benefit of a rotating system was that it would make the annual parish election "a real event rather than just a 'gesture,' as it has been heretofore."[51] Toward this end the vestry was also rec-ommending that women be given the right to vote in the annual meeting.

This recommendation was formally submitted to the annual meeting on November 30, 1965, and unanimously adopted.[52] Dr. Morris warmly greeted this change, reporting in the 1965 *Year Book*:

> I suppose there are a few areas in which the "equality of the sexes" has not yet become a fact. It is strange that the Christian Church has been as reluctant as any other institution or area of society to move ahead firmly in this respect. For the emancipation of women and the upgrading of their status in a male dominated society was one of the great causes and accomplishments of the early days of the Church's existence. It was not until the Annual Election of the parish on November 30, 1965 that women were enfranchised in St. Thomas Church.[53]

44. Miss Ann Exline, first woman member of the Vestry 1973-78, Warden 1981-90

Another four years would pass before women were at last allowed to serve as wardens and vestry members. This turning point took place at the annual meeting on December 2, 1969, when a resolution to this effect was adopted by a two-thirds vote. The first woman to be elected to the vestry under the provision was Miss Anne J. Exline (ill. 44), elected in December of 1972 for a term beginning in 1973.[54] A year earlier Miss Julia P. Sibley, a member of the parish and also a chaplain in the East Midtown Hospitals, was one of the first two women to be ordained deacon in the Diocese of New York.[55]

The 1960s was a decade of challenge and turmoil for the national church. One of the exciting prospects of the time was the ecumenical movement and the birth of the Consultation on Church Union, known as "COCU." A fresh spirit of cooperation and fellowship was sweeping across the denominational landscape and Dr. Morris was among those who enthusiastically greeted it, dreaming of a reunited church "truly reformed, truly catholic, and truly evangelical." He was especially keen to have Saint Thomas Church be a leader in this adventure. In 1961 the rector, with the support of the vestry, initiated a summer ecumenical preaching series, inviting distinguished preachers from other denominations to grace the Saint Thomas pulpit on Sundays at the eleven o'clock morning service. "The Vestry believes," wrote the rector in *The Saint Thomas Church Bulletin*, "that Saint Thomas Church, located in so conspicuous a place and surrounded as it is, especially in the summer, with visitors from all over the country and from many branches of the Christian Church, should demonstrate a spirit of cooperation and of fellowship with Christian bodies and that from this pulpit should be heard the most eloquent voices possible in the proclaiming of the saving Gospel of Jesus Christ." This endeavor was in keeping with "our Catholic as well as our Evangelical tradition."[56]

The first summer program featured such figures as Elton Trueblood of the Society of Friends, Mark Depp of the Methodist Church, Samuel H. Miller of the Baptist Church, and Lutherans Paul Scherer, Joseph Sittler Jr., and Edmund A. Steimle. The series remained popular throughout the 1960s and made a worthy contribution in advancing the ecumenical cause. So too did the United Lenten Services between Saint Thomas and nearby Fifth Avenue Presbyterian Church, launched in 1964.[57]

The summoning of Vatican Council II by Pope John XXIII promised to provide further impetus to the ecumenical movement. "A wonderful new spirit of warmth and friendliness has flowed from the attitude and leadership of the present Pope, both within and without the Roman Church," rejoiced Dr. Morris in 1963. "And it behooves us to be glad and supportive in our response and in our outlook toward all other Christians."[58]

At the same time, there was, warned Dr. Morris, an element within the Episcopal Church that would prefer to keep it isolated, and this was the so-called "catholic party," for whom the Saint Thomas rector had little patience or use. The "narrow, fearful 'scrupulosity'" of this party was "crippling and suffocating to the life of the Church," declared Dr. Morris, and it was vital for "parishes of strong, evangelical as well as catholic zeal" to mount a resistance.[59] The failure of the General Convention House of Deputies in 1964, he believed, to open communion to those of other denominations was the work of this faction "who wish to maintain high and impregnable fences against all the rest of Protestant Christendom, thus taking over the position of intransigence currently being forsaken by Rome."[60] These same forces had already succeeded in undoing earlier efforts toward union, all "because the liberal and broad-minded elements have remained silent."[61]

Dr. Morris desired to see Saint Thomas play a constructive role in supporting the Consultation on Church Union, an ecumenical effort that the Episcopal Church joined with eight Protestant denominations around this time. In a public demonstration of support, the rector in 1966 invited the Rev. Dr. James I. McCord, president of the Princeton Theological Seminary, to preach on the occasion of the fiftieth anniversary of the consecration of the present Saint Thomas Church, which coincided with a day that had been designated as a time of intentional prayer for the Consultation on Church Union.[62] Some months afterward, the president of the American Church Union, an organization which Dr. Morris described as a High Church lobby and pressure group, was quoted in *The New York Times* as calling the Consultation "a Protestant plot to destroy the Episcopal Church." To this charge the Saint Thomas rector fired back "that the Episcopal Church needs no plot to destroy it. It will die of malnutrition on its own just by drawing to the side of the road and allowing the rest of the world to go by."[63]

The defeat of a proposed plan of unity between the Church of England and the Methodists in 1969 aroused consternation on the part of Dr. Morris. He viewed the Anglican rejection of that scheme as a deadly blow and declared that the Episcopal Church was "in equal danger of suicide":

Its strongly organized minority of high churchmen has succeeded more than once in intimidating the majority with threats of secession when unity proposals have been under consideration. There is powerful vocal opposition expressed these days by this same minority to the Consultation on Church Union in which the Episcopal Church has been officially engaged for a decade and a half. Only the determination of laymen can prevent a tragic resurgence of ecclesiastical isolationism which has thwarted the Church for so long. The Christian Church cannot survive the 21st century in the divided, competitive state of a past era.[64]

An entirely congruent approach can be seen in the rector's support of Bishop James A. Pike of California. The former dean of the Cathedral of St. John the Divine in New York was no stranger to Saint Thomas and on several occasions occupied its pulpit at the rector's invitation. In 1964, the publication of *A Time for Christian Candor* by Pike had caused considerable stir in this country not unlike that of Bishop J. A. T. Robinson's *Honest to God* in England a year earlier. In this work Pike seemed to many within the Episcopal Church to have gone too far in his quest to restate the Christian faith in contemporary terms and repudiate its traditional doctrine. Dr. Morris, however, stoutly defended the maverick bishop, observing:

> The fact that the writings of Bishop Pike and Bishop Robinson are so avidly read indicates two ideas. One is that people welcome a less conventional attempt to state the Faith and the other is that the central content of the Christian Religion is still regarded as of greatest importance and urgently worth investigating and listening to. This is encouraging.[65]

Dr. Morris told his people: "If you disagree with him, be sure you know why. Even more important, if you do agree with him be sure you know what he is saying." Dr. Morris made it clear that even he did not agree with all the bishop said or the manner in which he said it, adding that he wished the bishop "could be more consistently thoughtful and moderate in his speech, . . . avoiding what appears too much like demagoguery and catering to the religious illiteracy of 'the crowd'." Nonetheless, the rector continued to regard the bishop as a figure "of courage in the face of prelacy and authority."[66]

In the autumn of 1966, the Bishop of South Florida, the Rt. Rev. Henry Louttit, brought a formal presentment against Bishop Pike accusing him of heresy. The presentment was taken up by the House of Bishops and a majority of them decided against proceeding with a heresy trial. Nevertheless, the bishops did feel compelled to censure Pike. In the wake of this action, Dr. Morris proceeded to invite the reprimanded bishop to preach at Saint Thomas yet again during the forthcoming Lenten season. As usual, Pike drew large crowds, and this time his appearance at the church even prompted the William B. Eerdmans Publishing Company to produce a small volume entitled *Bishop Pike: Ham, Heretic or Hero?* based on a sermon by Dr. Morris. It sold very well. The bishop's visit in 1967 proved his last, however, for in the days that followed, Pike ventured far afield into the pursuit of spiritualism, and the rector felt compelled to divorce himself from an enterprise that was, as he put it, "definitely not congenial to my convictions and views."[67]

The election in 1964 of the Rt. Rev. John Hines as Presiding Bishop of the Episcopal Church had been similarly hailed with enthusiasm by Dr. Morris, at least at first. The choir boys of Saint Thomas sang for his installation, and Bishop Hines' election, Dr. Morris said, was a source of deep personal satisfaction and an occasion for profound gratitude. Hines, the Bishop of Texas at the time of his election, was, like Morris, a graduate of the Virginia Theological Seminary, and Dr. Morris considered Hines a champion of his own "low church" tradition. The new chief pastor, he declared, "is a most competent and forthright leader of strong evangelical zeal with the courage of his convictions under fire."[68]

Under the leadership of Presiding Bishop Hines the Episcopal Church became deeply involved in the social issues of the day. Dr. Morris shared this concern, supporting the Church's engagement in the Civil Rights movement. When the Bishop Coadjutor of Alabama defended the conduct of the police in handling demonstrations in 1963, Dr. Morris expressed outrage, suggesting a lack of "courageous leadership in behalf of justice and the law of the land and in defense of the Constitution."[69] Next, at the 1967 General Convention in Seattle, the Presiding Bishop issued a resounding call for action to aid the disenfranchised in society and asked the church to appropriate three million dollars a year over the next triennium to "empower" minority groups and community development programs in urban and rural areas. This was voted, and the General Convention Special Program was born. Dr. Morris hailed this as a bold initiative at first, an encouraging sign of "the earnestness, vitality and idealism" in the Episcopal Church.[70]

Like many, though, Dr. Morris became disgruntled with the social program that the national church leadership was pursuing. The church was not, in his view, intended to be merely "a sanctified social agency." A preoccupation with urban work to the neglect of other missionary endeavors deeply distressed him, as did the excess of attention being given to black militant voices while others equally engaged in the crusade for racial justice were disregarded. He watched the growth of the national church bureaucracy and questioned its value and use of resources.[71] That the Presiding Bishop would dismiss as "pious clap-trap" the misgivings expressed by so many over this official obsession with social issues deeply distressed Dr. Morris. He believed the Presiding Bishop had undervalued the spiritual motivations of his opposition in a way they did not deserve. "From all over the nation we hear reports of a decline in the number of worshippers," asserted Dr. Morris, "and I believe one reason is the loss of balance and perspective on the part of all too many clerical leaders."[72]

Dr. Morris was not alone in considering the General Convention of 1970 in Houston a critical moment in the life of the Episcopal Church. Under his leadership, Saint Thomas Church, in the growing company of other parishes and dioceses across the country, had even begun to withhold some of its giving to the national church and instead to direct it toward diocesan needs and other missionary purposes.[73] The overall decline in giving to the national program led to a severe reduction in the staff at the Episcopal Church Center in New York, a move Dr. Morris had long advocated.[74] Never before, it seemed, had there been such serious questioning of national leadership, whether in church or government. There were major cultural and political changes under way: the war in Vietnam, the struggle for racial justice, the emergence of feminism, changes in sexual mores, increasing secularism, a falling-off of church attendance, the decline of the national church ideal. Saint Thomas parish, even its rector, was not immune from the uncertainties of the time. Church leadership can "inspire great movements," Dr. Morris approvingly observed, but it cannot "force them, nor manipulate them," he added realistically.[75]

Prayer Book revision was another issue that troubled many Episcopalians. In 1964 the General Convention had directed the Standing Liturgical Commission to begin the process of revising the Prayer Book and over the next several years a series of rites for trial use were authorized. Dr. Morris was not opposed to revision, but he found some of the proposed changes excessive and unjustified. Nothing appeared immune to the meddling of the liturgical scholars. "Beautiful, euphonious phrases," he said, "are being discarded in favor of clumsy and awkward language. Evangelical theology is being crowded out by uncouth, anachronistic revivals of archaic and Romish concepts."[76] The revisionists seemed, in his view, to believe that "the vitality of the Church is to be measured by the number of celebrations of Holy Communion that can be crowded into one year."[77] Dr. Morris, as we have seen, had never agreed with such a view, at least not since the time of his arrival at Saint Thomas.

As is often the case with rectors of major parishes, Dr. Morris was much in demand as a guest preacher. In his years as rector of Saint Thomas he was invited to preach in more than a hundred churches in the United States and Canada, and on other occasions graced pulpits in England and the American Cathedral in Paris. In the year prior to his election as rector of Saint Thomas, he had given a series of lectures on preaching at Seabury-Western Theological Seminary in Evanston, Illinois, that were later published by

Morehouse-Gorham Company under the title *Preach the Word of God*.[78] On May 25, 1967, Dr. Morris was the recipient of an honorary doctorate from Virginia Theological Seminary, marking the fourth such honor for him; he had already been so honored by Hobart College, Seabury-Western Seminary, and the Episcopal Theological Seminary in Kentucky. In the citation from Virginia, his alma mater described him as an "oracle in the coracle" whose ministry had brought a return of "authentic prophecy to the Church":

> At a time when the frail craft, the coracle of the Church, is regarded by many as expendable, you have staunchly insisted on its relevance, and with candor and boldness defended its essential soundness from attack, within as well as from without, from the perils of sham, hypocrisy, arrogance and ignorance. With the courage of informed conviction, and in an exemplary way, you have intelligently preached the faith, explained the holy mysteries and ministered to the whole people of God.[79]

In the meantime, the Saint Thomas rector was busy on another front. There is no question that Dr. Morris drew the attention of many not only to his preaching but also to the church of which he was the rector, and the only surprising fact about the public conferral of an official "Landmark" status upon Saint Thomas was that it had not come earlier than October 19, 1966, the day that it was granted. Whether he himself was actually the cause of this will probably never be known; what is known is that he opposed the conferral of this status upon the former rectory located next door on West Fifty-third Street, and the New York City Landmarks Preservation Commission lifted it about a year later at his request.[80]

Dr. Morris was determined that Saint Thomas provide music of the highest quality. Soon after the rector's arrival, a splendid new Aeolian-Skinner organ was given by senior warden Mr. George Arents (ill. 45) in memory of his wife at a total cost of $200,000 and dedicated in the chancel on November 19, 1956.[81] Then, by way of supplement or complement to the Arents Memorial Organ less than fifteen years later, the Loening Memorial Organ was given and dedicated in the east gallery beneath the Rose Window on November 23, 1969.[82] Throughout these years Saint Thomas offered the New York community a series of organ recitals featuring such talents as Pierre Cochereau, Fernando Germani, Marcel Dupré, and E. Power Biggs. Already in 1962 Evensong with full choir had been introduced at four o'clock on Sunday afternoons. At this service, Saint Thomas regularly hosted visiting choirs from across the country and from abroad. Several musical organizations also gave programs in the church on other occasions. For the Saint Thomas Boys' Choir there were also many concert tours and special appearances on television.[83]

45. George Arents, Vestryman 1934-60 and Warden 1950-60, donor of the Arents Memorial Organ 1956

Throughout the rectorship of Dr. Morris the Choir School continued to grow and expand. In 1960, the vestry authorized the addition of a fourth floor to the Choir School building and the renovation of much of the building's interior.[84] Improvements continued on a yearly basis. In 1964 the school realized its largest enrollment ever, fifty students. This growth and the expanding needs of the school program prompted Dr. Morris and the vestry to establish in 1971 a Choir School Advisory Committee to assist and support the headmaster. Plans for the construction of a new building were already being discussed.[85]

In 1969 the Saint Thomas Choir School celebrated its fiftieth anniversary. On the Second Sunday in Lent the anniversary was observed. Randall Thompson, an eminent American composer, was commissioned to write a composition, "The Place of the Blest," which was first sung at Evensong that day. The ministry of the Choir School was also commemorated at a parish dinner held in the Pierre Hotel the following October.[86] In conjunction with the Choir School anniversary, Dr. Morris observed his fifteenth anniversary as rector. At the same dinner in October of 1969, Dr. and Mrs. Morris were presented a trip around the world by the vestry, on behalf of the people of Saint Thomas. It was an appropriate tribute for a rectorship that had recorded so many historic milestones.

Mr. William Self retired as Organist and Master of the Choir in 1971, after seventeen years of exemplary service. "No one could have been more diligent or more devoted to the interests of the whole parish as well as to its music," declared Dr. Morris.[87] That September the parish welcomed Mr. Gerre Hancock as the new Organist and Master of Choristers, and his wife Judith as assistant organist.[88]

In 1971, Dr. Morris informed the vestry of his intention to retire as rector in October of 1972, at the completion of eighteen years of service. The time had arrived, as he later informed the parish, for a "new surge of vitality and effectiveness in the life of the parish" that a younger rector would provide. Another reason for his decision, which he also acknowledged, was that he found himself "at odds with many of the trends in national and diocesan leadership."[89]

In the last years of his rectorship, there were some notable additions to the adornment of the church in the completion of the statuary on the tower. It was decided to honor in these statues the ideal of "Liberation," and for this reason the figures selected were William Wilberforce, the British emancipator; Abraham Lincoln, the American emancipator; Martin Luther King Jr., the Civil Rights leader; and Mary McLeod Bethune, the African-American educator. "It is far more interesting and significant to have this sort of emphasis in modern church adornment than to represent only ancient and traditional saints," Dr. Morris approvingly observed. The other major adornment was the "Ordination" window in the clerestory on the south side, put there in 1970. One feature of this window was the depiction, in the upper right hand panel, of the ordination of Dr. Morris to the priesthood in 1930 in the chapel of St. Michael's Mission School for Arapahoe Indian Children at Ethete, Wyoming. During his years as rector of Saint Thomas, the parish had taken a special interest in the work of the church among Native Americans, and this had been a source of immeasurable pleasure to Dr. Morris.[90] The central figure in the depiction is Melchizedek ("Priest of the Most High God" in Genesis 14:18), and one also sees Aaron, Philip the first deacon, Bishop Donegan ordaining in the Cathedral of St. John the Divine, a deaconess, a black bishop in Africa, a newly ordained priest, and others.

To the end, Dr. Morris did not relent in his insistence upon attendance at worship as the mark of true discipleship. "The most significant contribution you can make to the effectiveness of St. Thomas Church in its ministry to you and to the community," he exhorted even while announcing his retirement, "is in faithful attendance at public worship."[91] Responsible stewardship also remained a constant emphasis. Too many people were still "tipping God," as he put it. The last full year of Dr. Morris's tenure saw the total voluntary giving of the parish move modestly ahead of the preceding year for the first time since 1965. The endowment of the parish, though, had increased by nearly three million dollars during his rectorship. Toward assuring its continued growth, Dr. Morris in a final act as rector contributed from his own resources the sum of $414,319 to establish a fund for the corporate purposes of the parish.[92] He died on March 27, 1998, at the age of 92, survived by three daughters and fifteen grandchildren.

In its tribute to Dr. Morris at his retirement, the vestry expressed appreciation first for his consistent emphasis upon the centrality of worship; second, for his teaching of the historic faith; third, for his awakening of a greater social conscience of service to the community; and, finally, for his support for a strong lay ministry. Dr. Morris had been a man of contradictions in some ways, but he had created a congregation out of the eclectic crowd of churchgoers he found when he arrived, he had led them to abolish the pew rentals, and he had enabled the parish of Saint Thomas to weather the turbulent 1960s. He had revived the Sunday School and other organizations, established a method for systematic giving, achieved independence for the chapel on the East Side, made the entrance of the mother church open and visible, begun the tradition of Sunday Evensong with full choir, introduced new talent to the vestry on a rotating basis, secured the right to vote for women, and introduced a dialectic with the theological, political, ecumenical, and liturgical concerns of the day. He also had the sense to pull back when he thought things went too far. He was remembered as being rather strict and somewhat authoritarian, but he was also admired for those very same qualities.[93] "Responsible discipleship" is the phrase that seems most apt to summarize his tenure, for it was this sort of discipleship he had asked his people to show in their attendance, their stewardship, and their community engagement. It was a discipleship that he had also tried to preach and live.

Notes

1 William Self, *Mine Eyes Have Seen the Glory* (Worcester, MA: Worcester Chapter of the American Guild of Organists, 1990), pp. 154-55.

2 *The Saint Thomas Church Bulletin*, November 1960, p. 1, and May 1964, pp. 2, 3. Dr. Morris also discontinued the celebration of Communion as the regular noonday service on saints' days and other holy days. Instead, on those days a celebration of Communion was to follow the regular, non-eucharistic noonday service. He also actively encouraged that the Blood of Christ be received from the chalice by means of intinction; this was "emphatically requested" of anyone wearing lipstick, and advised but not compulsory for others: Sunday service leaflet, 17 October 1954, p. 2.

3 The first sermon of Dr. Morris is not found among his collected sermons in the Saint Thomas Archives. This excerpt is found in *The Saint Thomas Church Bulletin*, April 1965, p. 6. He had also made the same emphasis in *The Saint Thomas Church Bulletin* for May of 1955 (p. 1).

4 Sunday service leaflet, 31 October 1954, p. 3; *The Saint Thomas Church Bulletin*, April 1965, p. 6.

5 VM 12:1 (28 October 1954).

6 *The Saint Thomas Church Bulletin*, January 1955, pp. 1-2.

7 *The Saint Thomas Church Bulletin*, February 1955, p. 1.

8 *The Saint Thomas Church Bulletin*, June 1955, pp. 1-2; June 1956, p. 2.

9 *The Saint Thomas Church Bulletin*, October 1955, pp. 1-2; September 1956, p. 1; *Year Book* 1955, pp. 12-13.

10 *The Saint Thomas Church Bulletin*, September 1956, pp. 1-2.

11 "The Spiritual and the Practical," 5 December 1954, in *Sermons by Dr. Morris, 1954-1960* (Saint Thomas Archives).

12 Letter of William DeForest Manice and Walter C. Baker to Members of Saint Thomas Church, 8 December 1954, in Saint Thomas Archives.

13 VM 12:4 (24 March 1955), 12:2 (26 May 1955), 12:2 (1 January 1956).

14 VM 12:4 (22 September 1955); *The Saint Thomas Church Bulletin*, April 1955, p. 2; letter of Bishop Horace Donegan to Dr. Morris, 19 May 1955, in the Saint Thomas Parish File, Archives of the Diocese of New York. Bishop Donegan would also echo the same theme in his address to the 1956 diocesan convention.

15 VM 12:5 (15 December 1955), 12:3 (19 January 1956); *The Saint Thomas Church Bulletin*, January 1956, p. 2; VM 12:4 (16 February 1956).

16 VM 12:3 (16 February 1956), 12:2 (26 April 1956); *The Saint Thomas Church Bulletin*, June 1956, p. 2; VM 12:2 (24 January 1957), 12:2 (23 January 1958).

17 VM 12:5 (28 March 1957), 12:3 (25 April 1957), 12:2 (21 November 1957). A paper describing the purpose, methods, and principles of the Every Member Canvass Committee at this time is in the Saint Thomas Archives.

18 VM 12:2 (18 December 1958), 13:1 (21 January 1961); *The Saint Thomas Church Bulletin*, January 1956, p. 2. In 1959 the parish contributed $194,144.27 to the 175th Anniversary Campaign of the

Diocese of New York; see VM 13:2 (20 February 1959).

19 "A Message from Your Rector," in the Sunday service leaflet, 24 October 1954.

20 Service leaflet for 13 March 1955, p. 3.

21 William Self, *Mine Eyes Have Seen the Glory*, p. 163.

22 *Year Book* 1939, p. 11; VM 12:5 (24 February 1955), 12:3 (24 March 1955), 12:1 (26 May 1955); *The Saint Thomas Church Bulletin*, June 1955, p. 1.

23 VM 12:2 (22 September 1955), 13:3 (26 October 1960); *Year Book* 1959, pp. 13, 35-37.

24 *Year Book* 1955, pp. 47-48; *The Saint Thomas Church Bulletin*, June 1956, p. 1, and June 1957, p. 1. Before 1901, the Woman's Auxiliary (its name then was spelled "Woman" and not "Women") had been known as the "Woman's Missionary Association" and before that as the "Ladies Missionary Society," which was founded in 1875 as an outgrowth of still earlier collective activities of the women of the parish.

25 *Year Book* 1955, pp. 41-42; *Year Book* 1959, pp. 13-14, 50.

26 VM 12:5,6 (25 September 1958), 13:2 (22 October 1959); *Year Book* 1959, pp. 44-47. An Acolytes' Guild for men and boys was founded by Dr. Morris soon after his arrival.

27 *Year Book* 1955, p. 12; "The Holy Communion and the Coffee Hour," *Sermons by Dr. Morris, 1954-1960* (Saint Thomas Archives).

28 *Year Book* 1955, pp. 12, 40, 59; *Year Book* 1959, pp. 61, 63. On Dr. Morris's support for the Choral Society, see William Self, *Mine Eyes Have Seen the Glory*, p. 169.

29 VM 12:3 (24 April 1958); George E. DeMille, *Saint Thomas Church in the City and County of New York 1823-1954* (Austin TX: Church Historical Society, 1958; Publication no. 47).

30 *The Saint Thomas Church Bulletin*, September 1958, p. 2.

31 "St. Thomas Church, New York, The Rev. Frederick M. Morris, V.T.S. '30," reprinted from the March 1959 issue of *The* [Virginia] *Seminary Journal* and distributed with *The Saint Thomas Church Bulletin*, April 1959, n.p.

32 VM 12:4 (19 January 1956), 12:4 (16 February 1956), 12:2 (22 March 1956) ; see also VM 12:4 (28 April 1955). The Pew Committee noted that there were 990 sittings in the main body of the church and only 211 sittings rented to pew holders. It recommended that applicants for pews henceforth be approved by the vestry.

33 VM 12:4 (28 February 1957), 13:3 (26 January 1961), 13:1,2 (25 May 1961), 13:4 (28 September 1961).

34 *The Saint Thomas Church Bulletin*, October 1961, p. 1, and November 1961, p.1.

35 VM 12:5 (28 October 1954), 12:5 (28 April 1955); *The Saint Thomas Church Bulletin*, October 1954, pp. 4, 5, and September 1955, p. 2.

36 VM 12:3 (17 November 1955), 12:6 (15 December 1955), 12:3 (19 January 1956), 12:2, 3 (24 January 1957), 12:2,3 (28 February 1957), 12:3,4 (28 March 1957), 13:2 (28 May 1959), 13:2 (24 January 1959), 13:2 (27 December 1962), 13:2, (24 January 1963), 13:2 (23 April 1964). The stone for the reredos was earlier believed to have come from Danville, Ohio, but in 1971 it was learned that the stone came from a quarry in Downsville, Wisconsin. The source of this discovery was the former manager of the Wisconsin quarry, Mr. Stanley Borm, who paid his first visit to New York and Saint Thomas in April of 1971. Mr. Borm remarked that the original intention had been to use stone from Caen, France, but that World War I prevented this; stone of equal quality was found in Wisconsin and shipped to New York early in 1918. The figures were carved elsewhere but the tracery was carved in place, the time of assembly being some ten months but the total execution of the work apparently taking "about three years" (according to the report of Dr. Morris in *The Saint Thomas Church Bulletin*, May 1971, p. 1).

37 VM 12:6-9 (25 September 1958). George S. Scott had died in 1912 and his will had provided a bequest to Saint Thomas for the purpose of erecting a building or buildings for the care of tu-

berculosis patients. The bequest was to be received upon termination of the residuary trusts established for his lineal descendants. The last surviving descendant, Jeanne Marie Scott, died in late December 1957. The lack of necessity for new tuberculosis treatment facilities prompted the vestry to seek other use of the funds.

38 VM 13:3 (25 May 1961). The Court ruled that $350,000 from the Scott legacy be set aside for the façade and the balance, estimated in excess of $1,000,000, be held by the parish in an endowment account to be called the "Scott Memorial Fund," the income from which was to be paid to St. Luke's Hospital to provide a program of convalescent care and rehabilitation at St. Luke's Convalescent Home. This latter facility was discovered to have closed and it was subsequently agreed that the funds be used to develop the cardio-pulmonary program of the hospital; see VM 13:2 (21 January 1965).

39 The Lawrie statue of Christ the Teacher, his book inscribed with the alpha and omega, is now placed against the wall at the west end of the ambulatory or choir aisle, near the organ console and the sacristies.

40 VM 13:3,4 (25 May 1961); *The Saint Thomas Church Bulletin*, September 1962, p. 3, and January 1963, p. 4. The total cost of the new façade, including installation and consultant fee, was $363,490. In a resolution, the vestry expressed appreciation to Mr. George A. Wilson, warden and counsel, for his services in the accomplishment of the Scott Memorial. Mr. Wilson was senior partner in the firm of Breed, Abbott, and Morgan that had represented Saint Thomas. See VM 13:1,2 (21 November 1963). Further on the details of the Scott Memorial, see page 189.

41 VM 13:1, 2 (23 April 1964). The Lyon Memorial cost approximately $27,000 and was dedicated on Sunday, 25 October 1964. In 1965 a handsome and informative historical guide to the parish, featuring black and white photographs of the architecture, statuary, carvings, and furnishings was published, and it included both the Scott and Lyon Memorials. Published anonymously but largely the labor of Mr. Harold E. Grove, the work was simply entitled *St. Thomas Church*. It gives detailed descriptions of still other of the church's memorials that have not been included in the present volume because their historical dates of origin could not be ascertained.

42 VM 13:4 (28 September 1961), 13:2 (25 January 1962), 13:2,3 (26 April 1962), 13:2 (31 May 1962). The old wooden entrance doors and the doors between vestibule and chantry were moved from the Fifth Avenue entrance to a location behind the closed doors of the World War I Memorial in 1962. The vestry also authorized the installation of air conditioning in the church in April of 1962, and Dr. Morris was careful to emphasize that this action was not to attract people to church or to make things easier, but "to eliminate unnecessary discomfort for those who would have been in church anyway." See *The Saint Thomas Church Bulletin*, May 1962, p. 2.

43 As recently as 1955 the church had been open daily from 8 a.m. to 8 p.m. (*Year Book* 1955, p. 15). Further see *The Saint Thomas Church Bulletin*, September 1961, p. 3, and February 1965, p. 3. In 1982 its hours of opening were stated to be from 7:30 a.m. to 6 p.m. (*Year Book* 1982, p. 37). As of the time of the present writing in 2000, the church is generally open from 7 a.m. to 7 p.m.

44 *The Saint Thomas Church Bulletin*, December 1963, p. 2.

45 VM 12:2-4 (24 February 1955), 12:3,4 (22 September 1955), 12:2 (17 November 1955). In 1955, the vestry decided to remodel Dortic House, the former Deaconess House on East Sixtieth Street adjoining the chapel, for the purpose of housing a chapel assistant and other staff, as well as a curate of the church. On 30 October 1955, the newly renovated Dortic House was dedicated.

46 VM 12:1,2 (26 December 1957), 12:1 (22 May 1958), 13:4 (22 January 1959), 13:2 (20 February 1959), 13:2 (26 March 1959).

47 Dr. Morris reviewed the situation between the chapel and the parish itself in a letter to Walter C. Baker and George A. Wilson of the Standing Committee of the vestry, dated 18 February 1959 (copy in Saint Thomas Archives); see also VM 13:3 (24 September 1959), 13:2 (17 December 1959); *Year Book* 1959, pp. 122-23. The Rev. Paul Curry Armstrong resigned as vicar of the chapel in 1959 after nearly fifteen years in that office.

48 VM 13:2 (26 May 1960), 13:2,3 (27 September 1962).

49 VM 13:2 (26 May 1960), 13:2, 3 (27 September 1962), 13:2 (28 March 1963), 13:1 (26 March 1964), 13:2 (22 October 1964), 13:3 (21 January 1965), 13:2 (18 March 1965), 13:3 (22 April 1965); *Year Book* 1965, p.11. The preliminary agreement between Saint Thomas and All Saints Church was unanimously approved by the Standing Committee of the Diocese of New York on 3 December 1964; see the Standing Committee Memo, 3 December 1964, in the Saint Thomas Parish File, Archives of the Diocese of New York. In December of 1969 Saint Thomas completed its agreed program of financial assistance to All Saints as part of the settlement; see VM 15:5 (28 January 1970).

50 VM 13:3 (26 December 1963), 13:2 (26 March 1964), 13:2 (23 April 1964).

51 *The Saint Thomas Church Bulletin*, January 1963, p. 3, and May 1964, p. 2. Dr. Morris reported in the January 1963 *Bulletin* that a rotating vestry system had proven successful at St. James' Church in the city, and recently had been instituted at Grace Church and Heavenly Rest.

52 VM 13:3 (28 October 1965); Minutes of the Annual Election in VM 13:2 (30 November 1965).

53 *Year Book* 1959, p. 11.

54 VM 14:4 (20 November 1968); Minutes of the Annual Meeting in VM 14:2 (3 December 1968); Minutes of the Annual Meeting in VM 14:1,2 (2 December 1969); *The Saint Thomas Church Bulletin*, December 1972, p. 3.

55 *The Saint Thomas Church Bulletin*, October 1971, p. 2. Miss Sibley was ordained Deacon on 13 November 1971. A graduate of Union Theological Seminary, she began her chaplaincy work under the sponsorship of Saint Thomas in the summer of 1963; see *The Saint Thomas Church Bulletin*, April 1963, p. 5.

56 *The Saint Thomas Church Bulletin*, April 1961, p. 1.

57 *The Saint Thomas Church Bulletin*, October 1964, p. 2. The United Lenten Services were announced late in 1964 and initiated the following Lent. In previous years the neighboring Presbyterians co-sponsored a Lenten noonday service at Saint Thomas, but declining attendance led to services being scheduled alternately between the two churches at various times.

58 *The Saint Thomas Church Bulletin*, October 1964, p. 8.

59 *The Saint Thomas Church Bulletin*, April 1963, p.8.

60 *The Saint Thomas Church Bulletin*, November 1964, p. 2.

61 *The Saint Thomas Church Bulletin*, February 1966, p. 3. Presumably speaking on behalf of such "liberal and broadminded elements," Dr. Morris made it clear that he did not abide the "haberdashery" of Anglo-Catholics, considering chasubles, copes, and mitres to be "anachronistic hangovers" from the medieval age. "I dislike intensely seeing men (be they bishops or anything else) dress up in fancy, expensive and elaborate garb," he said. See *The Saint Thomas Church Bulletin*, April 1966, p. 3, and September 1968, p. 9.

62 *The Saint Thomas Church Bulletin*, April 1966, pp. 2, 3.

63 *The Saint Thomas Church Bulletin*, March 1967, p. 7.

64 *The Saint Thomas Church Bulletin*, September 1969, p. 3.

65 "Will the Church Survive?" *Sermons by Dr. F. M. Morris 1965-1968*, p.2 (Saint Thomas Archives).

66 *The Saint Thomas Church Bulletin*, October 1966, p. 2, and December 1966, pp. 2, 3; "Pike's Pique," *Sermons by Dr. F. M. Morris 1965-1968*, pp. 2, 3 (Saint Thomas Archives); *Year Book* 1966, pp. 12-13.

67 *Year Book* 1967, p. 15. Further see William Stringfellow and Anthony Towne, *The Death and Life of Bishop Pike* (New York: Doubleday & Company, 1976); see pp. 437-43 for the text of the heresy charges, which alleged denials of the Trinity, the person of the Holy Spirit, the Incarnation, the plain meaning of Holy Scripture, and other matters.

68 *The Saint Thomas Church Bulletin*, November 1964, p. 2.

69 *The Saint Thomas Church Bulletin*, June 1963, pp. 2, 3.

70 "What Happened in Seattle?," *Sermons by Dr. F. M. Morris, 1965-1968*, pp. 1-4 (Saint Thomas Archives).

71 *The St. Thomas Church Bulletin*, January 1965, p. 2, and January 1970, p. 4.

72 *The Saint Thomas Church Bulletin*, October 1969, p. 1.

73 The vestry first directed this withdrawal of support to the national church in 1969, but the diocesan staff had refused to acknowledge the vestry's right to determine where the parish's money should go. The following year the parish withheld from its diocesan quota a portion of the amount designated for the national church. This policy remained in effect during the last years of Dr. Morris's rectorship. VM 14:4 (26 March 1969), 15:7 (25 March 1970), 15:4 (25 February 1971), 15:4 (26 October 1972).

74 VM 14:6 (29 November 1967).

75 *The Saint Thomas Church Bulletin*, January 1971, p. 2.

76 *The Saint Thomas Church Bulletin*, April 1972, p. 3.

77 *The Saint Thomas Church Bulletin*, March 1965, p. 5. Dr. Morris was not in favor of the addition of minor holy days or more commemorations in the church calendar. He saw this as a change in the Church's teaching from an emphasis upon the Bible to an emphasis upon history or tradition.

78 Frederick M. Morris, *Preach the Word of God* (New York: Morehouse-Gorham Company, 1954), pp. 109, 115.

79 *The Saint Thomas Church Bulletin*, June 1967, p. 4.

80 VM 14:5 (28 Dec. 1966), 14:6 (27 September 1967).

81 For the grant and endowment of this organ and its full specifications, see William Self, *Mine Eyes Have Seen the Glory*, pp. 166, 173, 205-13. It was also the Arents family that had given the 21-bell chime in the tower back in 1929; see above, page, p. 163. The Arents family business and interests are summarized in the Arents Tobacco Collection, the world's largest and most comprehensive library on the history, literature, and lore of tobacco, now housed and displayed in rooms on the third floor of the New York Public Library. Further see Jerome E. Brooks, *Tobacco: Its History Illustrated by the Books, Manuscripts and Engravings in the Library of George Arents, Jr.*, 4 vols. (New York: The Rosenbach Company, 1937-1943); an index and supplements have been issued. For a summary, see Sam P. Williams, *Guide to the Research Collections of the New York Public Library* (Chicago: American Library Association, 1975), pp. 293-96. For assistance with this information, I am indebted to the Rev. Dr. Warren Platt. The Arents family were also the donors to Saint Thomas Church of an English Bible of 1611 and a leaf from a Gutenberg Bible (*Insurance Appraisal of Property Belonging to St. Thomas Church*, completed by Christie's of New York and dated 10 June 1996, p. 58, nos. 208 and 210. Manuscript kept in Saint Thomas Archives).

82 For the generosity of the original donors, the full specifications of the original instrument, and its first recital, see William Self, *Mine Eyes Have Seen the Glory*, pp. 214-23. This organ was entirely replaced and partly re-named in March of 1996; see Appendix 1 at the end of this volume.

83 VM 12:5 (24 February 1955), 14:4 (29 November 1967); *The Saint Thomas Church Bulletin*, September 1962, p. 2, and November 1969, p. 6.

84 VM 13:2,3 (28 April 1960).

85 VM 14:2,4 (24 September 1969); *Year Book* 1971, p. 43.

86 *The Order of Service for the Fiftieth Anniversary of the Founding of St. Thomas Choir School, New York City, Sunday, March Second, A.D. Nineteen Hundred Sixty-Nine, Second Sunday in Lent At Eleven O'Clock in the Morning and At Four-Thirty in the Afternoon,* in the Saint Thomas Archives; *The Saint Thomas Church Bulletin*, September 1969, p. 2. Further on the fiftieth an-

niversary, see William Self, *Mine Eyes Have Seen the Glory*, p. 201.

87 Mr. Self in his autobiography tells of the laughter of the choirboys occasioned during an eloquent sermon that Dr. Morris preached around the year 1966 against a group of "human frailties all beginning with the word 'self' – selfishness, self-righteousness, self-gratification." The sermon's climax forcefully asserted that "sin and self are one," the rector apparently oblivious to the linkage of the "sinful self" to the last name of the organist and choirmaster! William Self, *Mine Eyes Have Seen the Glory*, p.203.

88 *Year Book* 1971, p. 14.

89 *Year Book* 1971, p. 13.

90 *The Saint Thomas Church Bulletin*, January 1972, p. 3; Harold Grove, ed. *Saint Thomas Church.* (New York: Park Publishing, n.d. [1973]), p. 52. In 1965 the parish adopted St. Elizabeth's Mission in Wakapala, South Dakota, where it built Saint Thomas Hall and supported the ministry there. Dr. and Mrs. Morris visited the mission annually, usually in attendance at the Annual Niobrara Convocation of Episcopal Native Americans.

91 *The Saint Thomas Church Bulletin,* March 1972, p. 2.

92 Letter of William B. Banks, Stewardship Chairman, to Dr. and Mrs. Frederick M. Morris, 6 December 1971, in the Saint Thomas Archives; *Year Book* 1971, p. 15; VM 15:2 (28 September 1972). The list of charitable grants in the last years of Dr. Morris's rectorship shows support, among other organizations, of the NAACP, the Urban League, the Council of Churches, East Harlem Protestant Parish, Emmaus Community, and St. Augustine College.

93 Personal interview of the author with Mrs. Joan E. Hoffman, 19 December 1999.

94 [Harold E. Grove], *St. Thomas Church* (New York: n.p., 1965), pp. 7-11. The material omitted following the second paragraph of this description pertained to the Bride's Door and the Bishop's Door, which are not part of the Scott Memorial and are discussed elsewhere in the present volume. Dates in the subsequent paragraphs have been corrected. See ill. 42.

CHAPTER 13

To Make the Worship Beautiful

JOHN GERALD BARTON ANDREW
ELEVENTH RECTOR, 1972-1996

WITH THE TENURE OF THE ELEVENTH rector, the story of the parish of Saint Thomas enters the period of recent events and becomes a story that can, and must, be told as much from living memory as from written records. A few lines written in the vestry minutes for March 23, 1972, indicate the decision that was to make all the difference to the history of Saint Thomas Church for the greater part of the late twentieth century:

> Dr. Pierson, Warden and Chairman of the Search Committee to recommend a successor to the Rector [Dr. Morris], reported on the efforts made by that committee as a body and by individual members to find the candidate most worthy to be the next Rector of St. Thomas Church.
> Dr. Pierson reported that the Search Committee unanimously recommended: The Reverend John G. B. Andrew.[1]

As in previous searches, this one too had been careful and serious, starting with a field of fifty-five. Prospects were invited to preach during the preceding autumn's Advent Preaching Series, and several were asked for return visits. With the list narrowed to six, the search committee members themselves took trips to the candidates' home parishes, even to England, where they observed them in their own milieux. On the very first vote, the unanimous choice fell on John Andrew (ill. 46).

Born in Yorkshire on January 10, 1931, to Thomas B. Andrew and the former Ena Maud Friend, John Andrew was educated at Beverley School in the north country. From the age of seven, he was a boy chorister at Anlaby parish church in East Yorkshire. After serving two years as an officer in the Royal Air Force, he earned his B.A. in theology at Keble College, Oxford, later proceeded to the M.A., and then went to prepare for ordination at Cuddesdon College, Oxford. Already a devotee of classical music, he sang in the choirs at Keble College and at Pusey House in Oxford, serving also

46. John Gerald Barton Andrew,
Eleventh Rector 1972-1996

as cantor at Cuddesdon, experiences that would prepare him well for eventual service in a parish with a strong musical tradition. Ordained in York Minster by Archbishop Arthur Michael Ramsey to the diaconate in 1956 and then to the priesthood in 1957, Father Andrew's first pastoral work took him to Redcar Parish Church, on the northeast coast of his own Yorkshire. In this industrial area, he ministered among steel workers for some three years, earning valuable parochial experience.

The fledgling and adventuresome Father Andrew next found himself crossing the Atlantic in 1959, at the age of twenty-eight, to serve as curate at St. George's-by-the-River in Rumson, New Jersey. Not for long would he remain there, however. On October 1, 1960, the Most Rev. Arthur Michael Ramsey, Archbishop of York, recalled him after just nineteen months in Rumson to become his chaplain. But again not for long, for on January 17, 1961, Ramsey was appointed the one-hundredth Archbishop of Canterbury and took John Andrew to Lambeth Palace as his Domestic Chaplain.[2] Contributing his own young lustre to the most illustrious career of any Primate of All England in recent memory, Father Andrew succeeded as Senior Chaplain at the end of 1965. Among his many duties he found time to preach before Her Majesty the Queen and her family by express invitation on several occasions.

After some eight years at Lambeth, Father Andrew in 1969 received a major parochial appointment as the Vicar of Preston in Lancashire. This unassuming title put him in charge of a team of seven clergy and six downtown churches, as well as making him the rural dean of Preston, a jurisdiction that included some thirty-nine priests. In addition to this work he gave ordination retreats to young men – in both England and in the Church of Ireland – sharing with them especially his spiritual insights on the nature and duties of the Christian priesthood. It was from Preston that John Andrew would be called to New York, taking with him the example and memories of his patron and model Archbishop Michael Ramsey, to whom, he later recalled, "I owe everything in my priesthood."[3]

Father Andrew had first seen Saint Thomas Church, and had fallen in love with it, on May 8, 1959, his third day in the United States as a curate in New Jersey.[4] In the same year he had already made important American friendships in the persons of Horace Donegan, then Bishop of New York, and Edward West, the canon sacrist of the Cathedral of St. John the Divine. By invitation of Dr. Morris and with the encouragement of the warden Dr. John Pierson, he had preached several times at Saint Thomas throughout the 1960s, the latest being the summer of 1971 when he and Dr. Morris had exchanged parishes. At his institution and induction as eleventh rector of Saint Thomas by Bishop Paul Moore on December 3, 1972, the new rector wrote to his new parish: "I come to you to serve you and to love you as best I can. . . . Never has there been an occasion when, upon entering St. Thomas', I have not felt awed and humbled at the faith of those who loved God enough to give so superb a house as this for His glory and praise."[5] Father Andrew, who possessed a deep affection for the music of the Anglican cathedral tradition, had come to Saint Thomas shortly after the Hancocks, and together they formed a dynamic music team. He no doubt appreciated the emphasis on "responsible discipleship" that he had inherited from the era of Dr. Morris, and, with the ready assistance of the choir, he was soon to transform and complement that by a renewal of beauty and holiness in eucharistic worship.[6]

On the following Sunday, December 10, 1972, the principal service was still Morning Prayer. On that day, Father Andrew's first sermon as rector made clear his own priorities, aims, and responsibilities for the parish. Preaching on the text "Give thy servant therefore an understanding heart" from I Kings 3:9, he said:

> I come as your eleventh priest and rector, your servant, your minister, your friend. . . . My prayer is to be given an understanding heart as I face the years ahead with you. "Priest and rector," the service described me. Priest first. My duties in these two words are clear. Loyalty in worship to God takes first place in my life. God first: God first, as Michael Archbishop of Canterbury used to say to himself getting out of his seat in a great cathedral when the Queen was there. It was to the altar that he gave his first bow. . . . God first then, in worship, in the daily prayers I shall offer for you and all your loved ones to whom my attention has been called; for sickness, for grief, for despair, for thanksgiving, in joy, in bereavement, for your dead, for your children yet unborn. You will find me at the altar most mornings, for that is how I run my life. At it, offering the Eucharist for you. . . . *That* is the first duty of a priest.[7]

This assertion of the priority of worship came as no surprise to those who knew the earlier past of Saint Thomas Church or to those who knew Father Andrew's own background. The search committee knew the churchmanship of the man they nominated, and Archbishop Michael Ramsey, his mentor, was already well-known as the greatest modern product and exponent of Catholic Anglicanism. Now at the age of forty-two, John Andrew would henceforth be living in New York, in the middle of a city plagued with social ills, in response to which he would have ample opportunity at a place like Saint Thomas to incarnate the traditional Anglo-Catholic axiom that Christ lives both in the Blessed Sacrament of the Eucharist and also in the poor of this world. Reflecting later upon his twenty-four years at Saint Thomas, John Andrew summarized the opportunity that had been given him: "I inherited a great and glorious history of music at Saint Thomas, the only residential choir school left in America, a strategic location in the center of New York City, the busiest place in the world, and, above all, a superb building designed by a Catholic Anglican for Catholic worship in the Anglican tradition. The challenge was to make the worship as beautiful as we could, with God's grace, and to combine it with a Gospel preached as intelligently, cogently, and courteously as possible. This done, the people just might respond. And they did"[8] (pl. XVIII).

Almost directly following his installation as rector, Father Andrew found himself in the midst of preparations for the sesquicentennial of the incorporation of the parish. In the 150 years since the first services in that primitive room on Broome Street, the changes had been much more frequent than the constants. If the city itself was unrecognizable to residents of fifty years before, so too the Episcopal Church had changed. Underneath the fleeting temporalities of life, however, was to be found a constancy in the same Lord confessed and encountered by the people gathered at Fifth and Fifty-third under the patronage of the great Apostle Thomas. The rector set these changes in their proper context as he registered a decidedly forward-looking and hopeful note at the anniversary celebration in 1973:

> We look to the future. It is to a life very different from the lives of those who built this noble place. The needs of people have not in fact changed so much as has the complexion of needs been altered. A sensitive awareness to opportunities to serve the Lord joyfully and intelligently in worship, in self-giving to those who need our help, is the challenge of our next centuries. God raises up men in every generation who by seeking to do his will in fact do it, and my prayer as the pastor and servant of this great family is that we may have the courage to seek to find his will and in seeking it, the strength and perseverance to perform it.[9]

The 150th anniversary dinner, commemorating the parish's founding in 1823, was held at the Plaza Hotel on October 17, 1973. More than five hundred guests attended, Bishop Paul Moore and Doctor Morris delivered talks, and the new rector observed that this anniversary gathering was sure testimony of the family feeling that produced so remarkable an atmosphere.

In the mid-1970s Father Andrew invited the Rev. Gary Fertig, then serving as Assistant to the Dean at Nashotah House Seminary in Wisconsin, to become his senior curate and primary associate, later vicar, a relationship that lasted for most of Father Andrew's time at Saint Thomas. Coming there in 1977, Father Fertig was valued by Father Andrew for his efficiency and decisiveness, and the rector would soon entrust to his vicar a great measure of leeway and initiative to do the actual running of the parish, rightly sensing him to be absolutely loyal, single-minded, highly motivated, matter-of-fact, and without hidden agenda. Father Andrew came to be known as something of an expert in the choice of curates, considering his own rectorial skill to be that of a "prime delegator" and, in his own words, "always looking for somebody better at doing something than I was, for the sake of complementari-

Principles for Preaching at Saint Thomas[51]

Preaching is treated with respect here by those of us who do it and those who share in it. Frankly, I have to *slave* at sermons. You would think that after thirty-eight years in the priesthood certain things would come more easily, like preaching. I do not find this so. I am haunted by the fear of sounding stale. Notice that I did not say *repetitive*. A preacher must be repetitive, in order to bang nails firmly home. I make no apology for that. The art is to represent the thrill of the gospel imaginatively, cogently, and accurately. It takes all I have to try to maintain this ideal.

People help: their experiences, their fears, their frustrations, their fulfillments, and their triumphs of grace in their lives are a wellspring of inspiration. "All my fresh springs shall be in thee" is a phrase from the psalms that I know to be true in my life as a priest and friend and teacher and preacher. Seeing Christ living in my beloved family members here at Saint Thomas is a great corrective for dullness and self-concern. Books help, too. I always have several going at once, all different: theology, biography, poetry, art, mystery novels, history.

But you have to be on the look-out for parables too, and they sprout everywhere: in shop-window displays; on the sides of buses; in street exchanges between myriad kinds of humanity; in situations where there is humor to be found; on the television; around the supper table; in museum exhibitions or in the theater. I think you get into the habit of picking up on things; certainly my friends will observe that I might pocket such and such an incident or remark for a sermon. "Take care!" they warn. "He'll use it in the pulpit!" Often, true.

You can gather that though I regard sermon preparation as a burden, it is never a *chore*. It is, I suppose, a costly delight; I love it but it takes its toll. And it is an honor. One good word is not as good as another, and every word has to be written and balanced and assimilated. There is a curious accolade of honor bestowed on the person who can "preach without notes," as if somehow the message is worth more for its invisible source of delivery. . . . I can see why, but I can't do it myself.

Not least am I helped by my colleagues, often much younger than myself. The presence among us at Saint Thomas of a lively and very amusing young priest with real homiletic *punch* has earned my gratitude increasingly in the two years he has served here. I look forward to hearing him every time he preaches.

I also need to pay tribute to the Sunday congregations who have challenged us preachers with their keen attention and critical support, their intelligence and their encouragement. We have a great deal for which to thank God.

ty."[10] That he chose so well is attested, in part, by the significant parochial appointments to which so many of them were eventually called as rectors. Gary Fertig after eighteen years became the rector of the Church of the Ascension in Chicago; Stuart Kenworthy went on to become the rector of Christ Church, Georgetown; Douglas Ousley was later canon at the American Cathedral in Paris and then rector of the Incarnation on Madison Avenue; Dorsey McConnell moved on to the chaplaincy at Yale and then to the Church of the Epiphany in New York City; Richard Alton went to St. Mark's in Philadelphia; and there were still others.

John Andrew was already known to be a good preacher before he went to Saint Thomas, and the high quality of the sermons during his time was remarkable. Three volumes of them were published and were widely distributed as selections of the Episcopal Book Club as well as for general sale.[11] It is sometimes erroneously thought that "good preachers are born, not made," but John Andrew put much thought and care into sermon preparation. The advice he often passed on to his assistant clergy began with the admonition that they should spend at least a half-hour in preparation for every minute that they planned to preach. He urged them to read the sermons of the great preachers, to study every book about "how to preach" they could find, to keep their eyes open to the world around, and to start their preparation on the Monday before the Sunday. Above all, as their aim in preaching, he urged them to reflect upon the summary of purposes attributed to St. Augustine of Hippo: *Placere, Docere, Movere*: "To please, to teach, to move." Interestingly, Father Andrew always gave titles to his sermons, but only after they were written and preached.[12]

One of Father Andrew's earliest actions as rector drew attention to the spiritual patron of the parish, to the wider communion of saints, and to the church's linkage within the wider Anglican Communion. A concrete link with a holy Thomas other than the Apostle was established on December 29, 1974, with the dedication of a stone from the Canterbury site of the martyrdom of St. Thomas Becket on that same date in the year 1170. When the original site was being done over to accommodate the new "Altar of the Sword's Point" at Canterbury, an Elizabethan funerary plaque had to be removed and some of the original stone with it, of which a piece was secured for Saint Thomas Church in return for a significant contribution from the rector's discretionary fund. The stone, Father Andrew explained, "was placed in the chancel floor and hallowed, linking us forever with that brave and saintly man who gave his life for his faith . . . and was proud to share the name of our own patron saint."[13] It remains embedded within the pavement at the head of the chancel steps, a silent stone that witnessed the martyrdom of the most famous Archbishop of Canterbury, now located in a spot at Saint Thomas where every modern pilgrim who passes by on the way to communion may feel some sense of spiritual fellowship with those who have gone before.

In still other ways as well, Father Andrew led the parish to celebrate and appropriate its Anglican heritage. On Sunday, February 3, 1974, the Most Rev. and Rt. Hon. Arthur Michael Ramsey had become the first Archbishop of Canterbury to visit and preach at Saint Thomas, now the church of his protégé and former chaplain. And in September of 1976 his successor Frederick Donald Coggan visited to preach on a Monday at noon to a crowded church. In fact, every Archbishop of both Canterbury and York during Father Andrew's twenty-four years at Saint Thomas preached and dined there, as well as the Bishops of London, Liverpool, Chichester, and Rochester, the Deans of Westminster Abbey and of Canterbury and St. Paul's Cathedrals, and other notable British churchmen. Nor was the Royal Family absent from the notice of Saint Thomas Church's liturgical observances, for the fourth of August in 1980 saw a service of "Thanksgiving and Celebration for Eighty Years in the Life of Her Majesty Queen Elizabeth The Queen Mother." The British Consul General was in attendance and read the second lesson; also attending were clergy from local Roman Catholic and Presbyterian churches. Wednesday, August 1, 1990, saw a similar celebration for the same woman's ninetieth birthday, as Father Andrew bade the congregation to give thanks for a woman whose "renowned commonsense is a reflection of her robust faith," who "moves with serenity and trust, and walks humbly with her God."[14]

The *Year Book* for 1976 – a very American year indeed by virtue of the bicentenary of the Declaration of Independence – records one more contact with England: "A colorful intrusion into our lives occurred in early May when Mr. John Brooke-Little, Richmond Herald of Arms, came complete with Herald's Tabard to deliver to us the church's new coat of arms (pl. XXVI), the first church in 800 years to be granted arms and with the unique distinction of supporters – figures standing on either side of the shield."[15] The certificate of this grant from the College of Arms, consisting of Letters Patent dated December 1, 1975, now hangs proudly in the parish house (pl. XXVII), and the arms themselves now grace many objects and items associated with the life of the church.[16] Needless to say, this armorial device had been largely designed by Father Andrew, as he likewise in 1976 created the parish's motto: "O God, my heart is ready." Taken from Psalm 108 in the classical translation of Coverdale, this verse had been the favorite scripture text of Archbishop Ramsey, suggesting his own eager and affective piety as a model for emulation. Because the rest of the verse ended with the musical promise of the psalmist "I will sing and give praise with the best member that I have," it was also a text appropriate both to the parish and to the Choir School, which were already linked by the presence of the choristers on the arms they now shared in common. This psalm would also happen to be the one sung by the choir on June 9, 1996, Father Andrew's very last Sunday as rector.

One other feature that appeared on the landscape around this time related to Father Andrew's appointment in 1975, under the influence of Canon Edward West, as a chaplain of "The Most Venerable Order of the Hospital of St. John of Jerusalem."[17] The order looks back for its ideals and origins to the military brotherhoods that participated in the Crusades; its patron is the Queen of England and the prelate of the American Priory is the incumbent Bishop of New York. Today it focuses its efforts especially upon the St. John's Ophthalmic Hospital in Jerusalem and the treatment of eye diseases of native Palestinians in the Holy Land. Father Andrew's obvious commitment and infectious sincerity for this cause (he immediately began to wear its insignia over his vestments on Sunday mornings) inevitably attracted a number of the laity of the parish to the order's ideals. Father Andrew was elevated to the rank of sub-prelate on October 15, 1986, and he served with distinction as the provost of the order's American Society, as it was then called (later Priory), from 1990 to 1994.

The later years of the 1970s ushered in a period of acute controversy over churchmanship difficulties in both the diocese and the national church – especially regarding proposals for revision of the Book of Common Prayer and the ordination of women – from which neither Saint Thomas nor its rector were immune. In the midst of these arguments, and to his great credit, Father Andrew brought a steady hand and a remarkably irenic approach. His leadership was shown not in advocacy or angularity but in a calm objectivity and open-mindedness. In the early fall of 1976, he wrote:

> General Convention opens on Saturday, Sept 11th, and as an alternate deputy to it, I have to be there at least for a couple of days. There are two urgent matters to be settled: The admission of women to the priesthood, and the final revision of the Book of Common Prayer to be accepted or rejected. I have never used the Bulletin (at least, not intentionally) to air issues which can be contentious and which could divide the people of the parish and I do not propose to do this now. I want to listen to the arguments both for and against the moves which are proposed and my vote will go when I have considered the questions on their merits as they are argued in General Convention. Whatever happens in both these issues, there will be some who feel themselves so badly treated and hurt that they may want to leave the Episcopal Church. There is much emotionalism; more heat than light in some of the issues, I am sorry to say.[18]

After the Convention was over, Father Andrew expressed his "hope that if the Church is to have a revised Book of Common Prayer we should at least be able to keep the old Prayer Book which so many people find every bit as helpful to them as any new revision could be."[19] Indeed, so skillful was his handling of this controversy that parishioners and visitors on both sides of the Prayer Book question could continue to find a home at Saint Thomas. The 1928 American Prayer Book continued to be the book placed in the pews, and it remained in use because of the beauty of the Coverdale Psalter, a masterpiece of classical English verse that has been a constant ingredient of the Anglican Prayer Book tradition and is still a feature of Choral Evensong at Saint Thomas. The services themselves, however, came to be more and more drawn from the new American Prayer Book of 1979, skillfully adapted by the Rev. Gary Fertig, but this was not overly noticeable because around the same time laminated print-cards were introduced and distributed in the pews for virtually all the services. Overall, the dominant motif was the traditional language of Rite I, but at times Rite II was followed. This solution was not quite Archbishop Cranmer's original ideal of one people united around one book following "but one use," yet it was a masterful synthesis that kept most of the people happy and retained the priority of beautiful worship rendered superbly. The question of the ordination of women, decided by the Convention in the affirmative, did not come to public notice in the parish until several years later.

Pastoral sensitivity came to Father Andrew both by nature and by intention, and an analysis of the embellishments in worship that were achieved during his years shows how remarkably adroit the rector was in sensing what the parishioners would probably like, or at least accept, and then in leading them to want it and embrace it. Rather like Dr. Morris in this respect, he was inclined to make innovations in a non-controversial way. All this can be seen in the transition to eucharistic centrality as well as in the introduction of the Reserved Sacrament, incense, and icons. The transition to eucharistic centrality was accomplished in the early and mid-1970s, although the ideal was one that the parish had already known under the rectorate of Dr. Brown in the late nineteenth century. Saint Thomas already had a daily Eucharist in the early morning when John Andrew arrived, and his first move was to augment that service by another, daily at 5:30 p.m., for people finishing their day of work. Next, the Wednesday mid-day Eucharist was expanded to every day of the week at that hour. Finally, for the main service on Sunday mornings, the logical development was to shorten choral Morning Prayer and follow it immediately by the Eucharist beginning at the offertory. Other embellishments, hardly contested, included a certain elaboration of ceremonial, more elaborate vestments such as copes and chasubles, use of the traditional rites for Holy Week and Easter Eve,[20] and display of all the sacred vessels upon the altar at the feasts of Christmas and Easter (pl. XVIII, XXIV). These and still other changes were accomplished with a minimum of adversity and with as few vestry votes, as little public announcement, as possible. It was John

Andrew's hunch – and he was proven right – that the deepest religious longings of his parishioners already coincided sufficiently with his own that more could be done if less was said.

A similar approach made possible the reservation of the Blessed Sacrament, especially needed in view of the increase of eucharistic services and the concomitantly increasing desire of parishioners to receive communion at home or hospital when they were ill. Father Andrew early discovered that the large double-cupboard near the altar rail opening out to the side chapel had been constructed by Bertram Goodhue to be serviceable as an aumbry, so he had the direction of the doors changed to face only the high altar and an upholsterer to line the cupboard with linen. Then he commissioned a hanging silver lamp from Watts and Company of London, suppliers of all the parish's vestments and furnishings during his tenure. Watts also provided the thurible and boat for the incense, which was likewise introduced with little fanfare and little opposition (and at first in a very moderate amount!). To the few who did raise questions, Father Andrew later recalled that he replied: "It's a marvelous opportunity to express outwardly the worship to which we are already committed inwardly, but if you don't like it, if it doesn't work, I will withdraw it."[21] Of course he never did – because most people liked it and agreed.

The story of the introduction of icons to the walls of Saint Thomas Church is bound up curiously with the story of the mysterious disappearance of some rare French and Flemish tapestries of the sixteenth and seventeenth centuries that used to hang on the north wall of the nave. The tapestries had been there since the days of Dr. Stires, and there had been much debate as to whether they helped, or actually hindered, the acoustical properties of the church itself. In any event, they were sent out to be cleaned and restored in 1979 and then after Easter they were re-hung on the wall with velcro attachments. After they had been up again for only a few days, on the night of April 19 four of them were stolen, possibly by a diminutive thief who broke through a small window on the south side of the church near Fifth Avenue.[22] They have never been recovered nor the thieves apprehended, but there is common agreement that without them the acoustics have indeed improved! The church received some insurance money as a result of the theft, and, since the walls of the church were looking rather austere, Father Andrew decided to use part of the payment for the purchase of a large, splendid eighteenth-century Baltic icon (in the Russian tradition) depicting the face of the Savior. He found it with the assistance of Canon Edward West in a Russian shop in the lower East Village, and in 1981 it was placed on the northwest corner pillar just before the entrance to the Resurrection Chapel. Soon another icon, a good reproduction of a Greek icon depicting the Mother of God and her Holy Child, was donated anonymously and placed on the southwest corner pillar just at the entrance to the Chantry chapel. In both instances the icons were accompanied by appropriate votive lamps. Like the incense and other changes, the icons were introduced with little preparation and little objection and with no public service of dedication or blessing.

Anniversaries at Saint Thomas did not go unnoticed. In thanksgiving for his tenth anniversary as the rector, in 1982, Father Andrew gave his own silver chalice and paten to the service of the altar, and the same anniversary was also commemorated by a parish gift that completely refurbished the clergy sacristy in beautiful woodwork designed by the architectural firm of Gerald Allen and his associates. About the same time, there was placed on the sacristy wall an eighteenth-century Greek icon of "The Three Hierarchs" (Saints Basil the Great, John Chrysostom, and Gregory the Theologian, all known for their associations with liturgy in the Eastern Orthodox churches). The re-working of that room complemented nicely its earlier stained glass window which was part of the original construction of the church under Dr. Stires earlier in the century, and had been given in 1937 by Henry E. Felton to mark the 300th anniversary of the King James Version of the Bible (known as the Authorized Version, 1611).[23] That window, still visible in the clergy sacristy, depicts vividly the three English bishops largely responsible for its translation: Bishop Lancelot Andrewes of Winchester (d. 1626), Bishop Nicholas Felton of Ely (d. 1626, ancestor of the donor), and Bishop Miles Smith of Gloucester (d. 1624). Still later, Father Andrew himself would give to the church a silver communion flagon, embellished with his coat of arms, in memory of his mother, Ena Maud Andrew, who had died in 1993.

The year 1993 also witnessed what was probably the greatest public challenge to Father Andrew's pastoral sensitivity during his entire tenure at Saint Thomas, and it involved the practical consequences of women's ordination. This was a subject on which he had already shown an even-handedness and objectivity, coupled, however, with his reservations springing from his concern for Catholic tradition and his zeal for ecumenical *rapprochement*, particularly with the Church of Rome. The Episcopal Church's General Convention of 1976, however, had made its decision to allow the ordination of women, and Father Andrew believed the parish should support it. Under Dr. Morris, women at Saint Thomas had been given the right to vote at the annual parish election and to serve as wardens and vestry members, and Father Andrew in 1989 had made the decision to invite them to serve as members of the Corps of Ushers[24] and also as lay readers. Then, in 1993, he made the decision to hire the first woman curate on the staff, a daughter of the parish named Frances LeBlanc, who had been attested for ordination by the Saint

Thomas vestry. There was much more objection to this appointment than he had counted on, however, even from persons on his staff who were normally supportive of change. After a number of expressions of opposition he decided that he must encourage her to move soon, early in 1994, to another placement. Commenting in retrospect, he remarked: "It was the worst experience of failure in my years as the rector of Saint Thomas, a brave experiment that lamentably failed. I must take the responsibility for that, and I have regretted that failure ever since."[25]

The incident left no obvious mark upon the rector's relationship with the parish as a whole, however, and in thanksgiving for his continuing service to the parish, the congregation joined in a gift of singular choice and appropriateness: on the Eve of the Octave of Prayer for Christian Unity – January 17, 1991 – the statue of Our Lady of Fifth Avenue was dedicated (pl. XIX). Several images of St. Mary the Virgin already adorned the church since its earlier stages of construction, at least two being especially prominent: on the façade she appears across from St. John the Baptist, while on the reredos she stands in her traditional rood position, under the cross opposite St. John the Beloved Disciple. But until now no image or statue of the Virgin had stood alone in the body of the church. Even more significantly, there was no Marian shrine in any Episcopal church making the intercession of Mary, the Mother of Jesus our Lord and God, available under a title that had particular reference to New York City, where teeming multitudes regularly traversed what is surely one of the world's busiest intersections, at Fifth Avenue and Fifty-third. The interaction of church and world was underscored in the same service that evening, for it was also the very night after the United States first bombed the city of Baghdad in the Persian Gulf War, and many of the speakers made anguished references to that and to the role that the intercession of Blessed Mary could indeed have in the pursuit of peace. To dedicate a votive statue to Mary in such times, and to name her not after some ancient and far-away apparition, but "Our Lady of Fifth Avenue," was a bold and creative synthesis of the old with the new for which Saint Thomas Parish could be justly pleased.

The statue dedicated that evening was a work of art that continues to inspire devotion and prayer in the southeast corner of the church, to the far east of the Chantry altar, to the extreme left as one enters the church from the outside main entrance. Depicting the Blessed Mother with the child Jesus on her lap, it is an appropriate complement to the four pairs of Chantry windows that depict great women saints in the history of the church[26] and to the statues of the Lyon Memorial at the entrance just outside the Chantry doors. More Romanesque than Gothic in its general appearance, it is of the "Seat of Wisdom" genre, Mary's posture, her lap and throne, representing the Divine

Wisdom that has become incarnate in her Son.[27] This four-foot bronze statue was made by Mother Concordia Scott, O. S. B., of the Benedictine monastery at Minster Abbey in Kent, crafted by her to resemble the statue of Our Lady that she had made for the undercroft of Canterbury Cathedral.[28] In attendance for the dedication were representatives of several New York churches: the Right Reverend Richard F. Grein, Bishop of New York, His Eminence John Cardinal O'Connor of the Roman Catholic Archdiocese of New York, His Eminence Archbishop Peter L'Huillier of the Orthodox Church in America, and Father Arten Ashjian, representing the Primate of the Armenian Church of North America. All spoke on the role of the Blessed Virgin in their respective traditions, most with some reference to the anguish of the bombing of Baghdad that had just begun. The entire membership from both sides of the national, official Anglican-Orthodox ecumenical dialogue attended as well. Father Andrew's words from an earlier, and obviously preparatory, sermon are clear about the role he saw for the Virgin at Saint Thomas in particular and in New York City in general, a role that was finally inaugurated and proclaimed in reality on that evening:

> My task here on noisy Fifth Avenue is to see that a widely balanced, full-blooded, whole-hearted, generous and biblical faith is taught and practiced, stretching the intellect, demanding upon the time and the minds and the self-giving of those who love Jesus, in worship, in praise, in sacrificial works of mercy. We need all the help we can get. New York needs a shrine: this crazy city needs such meeting places, silent and hidden. . . . It may well be that a place the size of St. Thomas could do with a fine and austere representation of the Mother who gave Him to us, as a reminder of the love she carries for us all, as a symbol of patient waiting and contemplation, and as a place of quiet access and constant readiness to show Christ to the world of busy business. So perhaps Our Lady of Fifth Avenue is not out of place.[29]

The work of integrating the new shrine of Our Lady of Fifth Avenue into the life of the parish was already under way. A letter from the church's verger to the O'Shea Candle Company asks for "information you might have on candle holders for votive lights," a first indeed for Saint Thomas Church[30] and a far cry from the old days of so-called "novelties which disturb our peace." An addition to the signboard in front of the church – already open throughout the day for prayer and meditation as well as the daily services – now appeared, inviting passers-by to "Come in and pray at Our Lady's Shrine." This integration and synthesis continues, as the daily prayers of countless worshipers are outpoured.

The prominence of prayer for the unity of the church, sustained throughout Father Andrew's rectorate at Saint Thomas, had been at the heart of his preaching and teaching from the beginning. Invited to be the guest preacher for the Octave of Prayer for Christian Unity at St. Patrick's

Cathedral less than two months after he became rector, Father Andrew made explicit his ecumenical vision and commitment when he concluded:

> Pray God that the time will quickly come when all that obstructs our view, our sight, our discernment, our apprehension of the Divine Will and purpose for us as separate Churches will be done away. So that in common love and understanding for Him in our Blessed Lord, in common devotion, in common worship, in the fulness of sacramental unity, we may humbly and penitently offer and bring to a broken and divided world the secret of His will, our peace together, which will prove our final blessedness.[31]

His Holiness Pope John XXIII, the Bishop of Rome who called the Second Vatican Council and inaugurated a new era in the ecumenical life of the church, became the subject of a lancet in the far left of the last of the clerestory windows to be installed at Saint Thomas. It was completed by the Willet Studios of Philadelphia in 1973 and given by William and Shirley Burden in honor of their mother, Florence Vanderbilt Burden, who with her sons had given the first of the clerestory windows as a memorial to her husband and their father back in 1927.[32] Intended to depict those who have been leaders in spiritual matters, located in the north wall, and being the fourth clerestory window given by members of this same family, it was dedicated by Terence Cardinal Cooke, Roman Catholic Archbishop of New York, in January of 1974.[33] Three years later, Archbishop Jean Jadot, Apostolic Delegate to the United States, visited Saint Thomas Church on the Feast of Saints Peter and Paul in 1977.[34] Other distinguished clergy of the Church of Rome, such as the Secretary of State from the Vatican, Cardinal Casaroli, and Archbishop John Quinn of San Francisco, also came to Saint Thomas during these years, as did the entire Anglican-Roman Catholic International Commission on a Sunday morning in the fall of 1985. Likewise, Father Andrew's involvement in Anglican-Orthodox relations was worthy of note, and he served in 1994 and 1995, at the appointment of Bishop Grein, as the chair of the New York Episcopal Diocesan Russia Committee. At his invitation, the entire membership of the national Episcopal-Orthodox joint commission had earlier attended the dedication of the Fifth Avenue shrine to Mary. There were also important public visits of noteworthy Orthodox clerics to the Sunday morning worship from time to time.

The rector also served for some twenty years on the Anglican-Roman Catholic Commission of New York, and his good relations with the hierarchy of St. Patrick's Cathedral just a few blocks away continued under John Cardinal O'Connor.[35] Framed portraits of Cardinals Cooke and O'Connor and of Bishop Joseph T. O'Keefe, former vicar-general of the Archdiocese of New York, also hung in Father Andrew's office. The great outpouring of ecumenical prayer at the historic dedication of Our Lady of Fifth Avenue, then, was a culmination of years of work for the unity of the church, and not merely a momentary demonstration of good will among Christians.

One story in particular, related by Father Andrew in his own words, shows the degree to which his friendship with Cardinal O'Connor developed. On the evening of August 18, 1988, as Father Andrew was walking along Sixty-fifth Street from dinner towards the rectory at 550 Park Avenue, he was suddenly attacked by a robber wielding a seventeen-inch lead pipe who proceeded to smash his skull and his left arm, leaving him in a pool of blood and taking his money, watch, and signet ring. The police summoned an ambulance and he was taken to New York Hospital where he spent the night undergoing surgery upon his head. A nurse in his attendance informed him that no visitors would be allowed in his room, but, according to Father Andrew:

> she had gone only a minute when I heard a man's voice saying, 'Father John, I'm a No Visitor,' and through the doorway slipped the cardinal. . . He was on his way home to supper. He asked to say some prayers at my bedside and did so, and he asked if he could give me a blessing. I told him that I greatly needed his blessing, which he gave me very gently on the bridge of my nose, because all the rest was pretty well untouchable. . . . And then the cardinal said, 'Father John, what I need is a wounded priest's blessing.' And he promptly knelt at my bedside, and with my undamaged hand I traced the sign of the cross on his forehead and gave him a blessing.[36]

"The doctors thought I was going to die, although I didn't know that at the time," Father Andrew later recalled. He made an act of forgiveness in prayer on behalf of his attacker, and very soon afterward he began to get better and was eventually released. His assailant, unknown and never caught, remains forgiven.

A positive approach to death and eternity must be on the agenda of every Christian church, and such was not absent from Saint Thomas, where the original plans had vaguely envisioned a burial crypt under the high altar. That had never materialized, and eventually, thanks to the initial gift from an anonymous donor, Father Andrew in 1990 was able to announce the installation of a columbarium in the north wall of the Chapel of the Resurrection to the extreme right of the high altar.[37] Consisting of five hand-carved oak cabinets united by a finely carved Gothic canopy, all beautifully designed by Gerald Allen and Associates, the new provision opened in 1992 and made available a total of five hundred niches for the urns of baptized members or communicants of the parish in good standing and their immediate families. The unity of the church in heaven with the church on earth was signified by such an arrangement, the chapel itself now housing an extended host of silent but heavenly beings whose praises of God would continue to blend with the voices of the living in the chancel just a few feet away.

The possibility of disturbance, unfortunately, is always present in places of high public visibility such as Saint Thomas at Fifth Avenue and Fifty-third, and after one or two disruptions occurred during the services it was decided, beginning in 1991, to employ two off-duty policemen from the local precinct to work alternately on their Sundays off as plain-clothes guards. For security and protection, as well as for assistance in cases of sudden illness, it was a reasonable step to take. The solemnity of the music and worship was also safeguarded in this way.

Meanwhile, the Choir of Men and Boys continued its own work of beautifying and expressing in song the worship of the congregation. Under the guidance and direction of Dr. Gerre Hancock, and living in the cultural center of New York, the boys experienced the finest opportunities for learning while contributing to the worship at Saint Thomas Church on a regular basis.[38] Tours and concert series brought a significant number of people who might not otherwise have any contact with the church or with sacred music into intimate knowledge of both. Through recordings on records, cassettes, and finally the new medium of compact discs, the choir's music spread throughout the world, making the audience for their sound ever wider. To Gerre Hancock, Father Andrew would pay high tribute, describing him as a remarkable man and a superb musicologist, organist, and master chorister: "Gerre's hymn accompaniment is famous, as are his improvisations. It is not at all unusual for him to be visited by church musicians from the far corners of the world. His rapport with choristers is extraordinary; his partnership with his parish priest, in church liturgies, is looked upon by many as a role model for musicians and priests alike."[39]

Such praises came not only from the rector, for during his musical career Dr. Hancock, already a fellow of the American Guild of Organists, had also been made an honorary fellow both of the Royal College of Organists and of the Royal School of Church Music. He had received the honorary degree of Doctor of Music both from Nashotah House (in 1985) and from the University of the South (in 1999). Most important of all, in terms of the substance of his profession, Oxford University Press had published over fifteen of his musical compositions as well as his book entitled *Improvising: How to Master the Art* (1994). On March 14, 1996, in honor of his twenty-fifth anniversary as the parish musician, the Loening Memorial Organ in the east gallery was replaced and renamed "the Loening-Hancock Organ," its first public music being called forth at that time by Father Andrew with the words "Organ, you are summoned to the service of God"[40] (pl. XX).

Father Andrew's consistent advocacy of the music program and Choir School had its culmination, in one sense, in the years 1985-1987, with the construction of its new fifteen-story building on West Fifty-eighth Street (pl.

XXI) at comparatively little cost to the parish.[41] The move was handled with expedition. "The Choir School is an adjunct of the church," he wrote. "It cannot pretend to be a preparatory school first, and a supplier of singers for services, second. It exists as a living part of the church's task for evangelism and worship."[42] These remarks, uttered in 1996, echoed some earlier words he had written in 1982: "This is not simply a prep school with a demanding musical program; it is a school founded to service the liturgy."[43]

Father Andrew received prominent recognition on January 29, 1995, when he was made an honorary Canon of New York by the Rt. Rev. Richard F. Grein. No other incumbent rector of Saint Thomas had been honored in this way. As directed in the service leaflet printed for the occasion, Bishop Grein addressed the new Canon Andrew:

> We, Richard Frank, by Divine Permission Bishop of New York, do admit you, John Gerald Barton Andrew, as a Canon of this our Diocese of New York, with all and singular rights and privileges as appropriate both in this place and in The Cathedral Church of Saint John the Divine, so long as your life shall last. May you minister among the People as a Canon with justice and with sanctity. May God who is mighty increase your grace.

With his "Amen" to these words Father Andrew was linked by his honorary canonry to the cathedral church of a great diocese he had now served for nearly a quarter of a century. The author of this book, a longtime friend and himself one of the few other such honorary canons, preached at the service.

Within a year, the time of the rector's retirement would be near, and there would be many events and dinners to salute him. During the time of his rectorate Father Andrew had received honorary doctorates from Cuttington College in Liberia, Nashotah House in Wisconsin, the Episcopal Seminary in Kentucky, and the General Theological Seminary in New York. From the Queen of England, monarch of his native land, he received the high honor of the Order of the British Empire (O.B.E.) in 1995. An honor from his mother church was the Cross of St. Augustine of Canterbury, which was awarded him by Archbishop George Carey in the narthex of the parish church in May of 1996; a personal touch was the fact that Father Andrew himself had been the original designer of this award at the invitation of Archbishop Ramsey in 1963.

To summarize at the more material or fiscal level, in the year 1972 when Father Andrew first came to Saint Thomas, the parish records (excluding the Choir School) had shown an income of $683,786, and expenditures of $676,439. By the end of 1996, the year that he left, with a stock market that was rapidly becoming "irrationally exuberant," the records (again excluding the Choir School) showed total income of $4,881,773 (of which, however, just under $300,000 came from current collections and pledges) and total expenditures of $5,174,330. Because of the changing financial picture in the nation as a whole, these figures should not, of course, be taken in any absolute sense as affording a reliable comparison from 1972 to 1996, and in addition the accounting methods had changed considerably over the twenty-four years.[44] It remains true and a matter of public record, however, that throughout this entire period only a fraction of the parish's operating expenses was being met by current pledges or contributions from the congregation itself; as the Stewardship Committee was to report in the *Yearbook* for 1987, "more than half of the parish family are not pledging to the work of St. Thomas Church." For nearly a decade the parish had been regularly giving an impressive range of about three to five hundred thousand dollars annually to many and various needy and worthy projects and beneficiaries outside its own boundaries, but these monies came from its Lippincott Fund, an endowment established in 1948.[45] This was, however, still over and above a contribution of a million dollars to the Diocesan Capital Campaign, pledged in 1994 and fulfilled a few years later. In spite of the low level of active current giving, though, by the end of 1996 (when Canon Andrew retired) the total endowment of the parish was well over one hundred million dollars.[46]

Canon Andrew's last sermon as rector of Saint Thomas Church, preached at the annual graduation ceremony for the Choir School on Sunday, June 9, 1996, merits quoting at length for the self-portrait it paints of the man and his rectorship:

> The Saint Thomas Fifth Avenue song is over for me. It began in 1959, nearly 40 years ago, when I was 28 and on the third day of my first stay in the United States. I was shown into this place. The impact hit me like a physical blow to the face. I knew at that moment of wonder and joy that my life and the life of this place were somehow to be joined. It was a revelation, which I kept secret, even from myself. And when the day came and I was told I was to be the eleventh priest and rector of this place, I was scared. There was a lot to be scared about. But people were ready to help me and since I have never been frightened of choosing people better than myself at doing certain things, it meant that the work of this parish acquired a momentum and an energy that brought it into leadership, for which I thank God, as I thank him for the energy and the good health he has blessed me with over this past quarter century. Health and energy and the companionship of my colleagues and my large parish family have kept me going. I am a very happily married man. It has been a glorious marriage. I know exactly how Jacob of old felt. He worked for his future father-in-law seven years in order to win the woman he loved. The Bible tells us that those seven years seemed like one day, for the love he had for her. I understand how quickly the years pass if you are in love. I have been. With you all.[47]

With those words he also said farewell to the Choir School as well as to an entire congregation, his parish family of a quarter century. The attendance at the principal service back on his first Sunday at Saint Thomas (Morning Prayer, on December 10, 1972), as indicated in the parish records, had been

What Is Saint Thomas Fifth Avenue Supposed to Be Doing?[52]

Very possibly, four things. I submit to you that we are here to suggest, to remind, to invite, and to inspire.

For good or ill, we have taken our place among the riches of the world, the financially and economically powerful of the world, the top jewelers of the world, one of the foremost modern art collections in the world, to *suggest* that over mankind's creativity and grandest achievements and over superlative technical skills and the expressions of the artistic soul of humanity arches the judgment of God. Calmly and without ostentation, Christ on his cross looks down on Fifth Avenue from above our main great doors, his eyes surveying the glory of all that inventive and successful evidence of human possession. Beneath his feet the words in great letters: "*Thou Art the King of Glory O Christ.*"

All you need to do is to lift your eyes. Much lower than the skyscrapers and seemingly insignificant among the soaring buildings stands this suggestion to one of the busiest streets in New York, that there is another dimension to this world that has to be accounted for: the power of the love of God. The arms of Christ are outstretched, for us, in welcome.

The suggestion is given in the outstretched arms, in the open eyes, and in the words of homage from the *Te Deum* that triumph and failure, joy and pain, victory and death are not as widely spaced as some would like to think, that such things as suffering, betrayal, and human weakness are as much involved in the glory of Christ's sovereignty as success and power and "arriving" on Fifth Avenue. This suggestion of a wider dimension is emphasized in Christ's arms outstretched to embrace *every* fortune in the human endeavor, that

> Neither death, nor life, nor angels, nor principalities, nor powers, nor things present, nor things to come, nor height, nor depth, nor anything else in all creation, will be able to separate us from the love of God in Christ Jesus our Lord. (Romans 8:38-39, RSV)

Second, this place is here to *remind.* There is not one of us in the Christian family who does not need the memory jogged on occasion about who we are and whose we are. We have a heritage to acknowledge, a relationship to live up to. St. Peter makes this point with force in his first letter: "You are a chosen race, a royal priesthood, a dedicated nation, and a people claimed by God for his own, to proclaim the triumphs of him who has called you out of darkness into his marvellous light" (1 Peter 2:9, NEB). If any of us as Christians has an identity crisis, that is all we need to know. The heritage is noble. It is clearly stated: we are a chosen race, a royal priesthood, a dedicated nation, a people singled out with a vocation, with a proclamation to make, not an admission to be wrung out of us. We are called to make this proclamation as members of a priesthood,

and a royal priesthood at that, a priesthood of which sacrificial service and lifelong loyalty to people are integral parts. This priesthood calls for more than individual responsibility; it entails a corporate awareness, a family membership, and today's celebration of the feast of our dedication to St. Thomas is designed to emphasize it. We are not subscribers to a philosophy; we bear a divine tattoo, a family responsibility to people beyond our ranks, to bring God to them and to bring them to God with us.

And so the third task that we are here to perform is to *invite.* We need to evangelize, to attract and to convince people by the heritage we possess to join us. We need to uplift Christ so that people may long to know more about him, to know him and to love him, to love him and to serve him, to serve him and to live for him, to share our destiny in him.

Mere words recited won't achieve this. They never do. I am probably more wicked than most of you in feeling quite unmoved by men shouting at me on Fifth Avenue that my sins which are many can be washed away; the flailing arms and the Bible raised and haranguing tones do little for me. But a welcome, a smile can work wonders for me in a place like this when I come in to worship, to see what the worship is like. And a place like this must not only look beautiful, it must *be* beautiful in its reassurance to the new and shy and lonely that they will be welcome and that they are wanted. They have a right to know that this place is prayed in. I am convinced that if we persist in our struggle to get the worship right, so that the atmosphere of this superb place rings with the worshipful love of Christ and resounds with concern and patience and joy, then it will be the vessel for all our activities for others in this city and beyond its bounds that proclaim Christ's kingship over us. Souls will feel *invited* to belong to the Christian family of forgiven sinners.

Invited, then *inspired.* Inspired not merely by this wondrous place and what goes on officially in it but by what it has always stood for: sacrificial generosity. . . . The need to give did not stop after the money poured in to build this glorious place. The need is with us still, for God's work still has to be accomplished, and still we need to give seriously, sacrificially, steadfastly. It is when we are giving more than we thought we ever could, more than we think we ever should, that our heritage mysteriously displays its integrity; for an ungenerous Christian is a contradiction in terms. When we commit ourselves to this hard road, we are doing no more than following the steps of the one whose divine tattoo we bear, who gave of himself to the point of shedding his most precious blood for us and our salvation. This costly self-giving spirit of his, unselfconsciously seen in us, is what will inspire, for it is the real thing, the authentic ingredient in the life of a Christian community and in the soul of a Christian individual.

435 persons, whereas the same registers indicate that for the main service on his final Sunday morning (Choral Eucharist, on June 9, 1996) the attendance was 965. Of course the entrance to the Gate of Heaven cannot be measured in numbers or figures of any kind (pl. XXII), but the national directory of the Episcopal Church indicates that Saint Thomas showed the greatest number of communicants, the largest parish family, in Manhattan by the year that Canon Andrew retired.[48]

Canon Andrew later stated in retrospect of those twenty-four years that he wanted to be remembered for "bringing a quality of worship to Saint Thomas that made God real to the people there."⁴⁹ He succeeded magnificently. He had made the worship beautiful, and he had done so much more (ill. 47). Some twenty-four years of his restless activity in zeal for the kingdom of God and its proclamation on earth had markedly changed – even transfigured – the parish and its worship. In the period of John Andrew's tenure at Saint Thomas, the song of the people and the song of the priest had become one. He himself had good reason to sing for joy in 1998 as he felicitated his successor at the celebration of the parish's 175ᵗʰ birthday.⁵⁰

47. Father Andrew with creche and children at Christmas

Notes

1 VM 3 March 1972, p. 3. The Vestry Minutes for this period are not numbered consecutively; their pagination begins and ends at every meeting.

2 It was at this point, in June of 1963, that the present author first met this future rector, while the author was a young and newly-ordained deacon living in Lambeth Palace for the summer while doing research in the Library there.

3 John Andrew, *The Best of Both Worlds* (Grand Rapids: William B. Eerdmans Publishing Company, 1991), p. xii. Archbishop Ramsey had taught him "the faith of the Catholic Church as Anglicanism has received it, reverence for Scripture and tradition, and a lively social conscience in its application"; see John Andrew, *Nothing Cheap and Much that is Cheerful* (Grand Rapids: William B. Eerdmans Publishing Company, 1988), p. xvi.

4 In personal interview with the author on 10 August 2000, Father Andrew confirmed that this

impression should be dated to his third day in the United States, as recounted below on page 223, and not on the fourth day, as recounted in *Nothing Cheap and Much that is Cheerful*, p. xiii.

5 *Year Book* 1972, p. 14.

6 One gets the impression from the records that, just as in the time of his predecessor, Father Andrew found it still an uphill battle to transform Saint Thomas into a parish family. In 1982, for example, there was only a total of 47 pupils enrolled in the Sunday School, whereas in 1959, after much effort on the part of Dr. Morris, there had been only 122. (*Year Book* 1982, p. 10).

7 Saint Thomas Archives. *Sermons by the Rev. John G. B. Andrew*, volume for 1972-75: "The New Rector's First Sermon," preached on 10 December 1972, pp. 1-2.

8 John Andrew: personal interview with the author, Sunday 17 October 1999. See also "What is Saint Thomas Fifth Avenue Supposed to be Doing?," page 224, below.

9 "An Anniversary Salute" by John Andrew in Harold Grove, ed. *Saint Thomas Church.* (New York: Park Publishing, n.d. [1973]), p. 3. Grammar has been corrected in the third sentence.

10 John Andrew: personal interview with the author, Sunday 17 October 1999.

11 John Andrew, *Nothing Cheap and Much that is Cheerful, The Best of Both Worlds*, and *My Heart is Ready: Feasts and Fasts on Fifth Avenue* (Cambridge, MA: Cowley Publications, 1995).

12 See "Principles for Preaching at Saint Thomas," sidebar on p. 210.

13 *Year Book* 1974, p. 12.

14 Saint Thomas Archives, file: HM the Queen Mother. Service leaflet of 1 August 1990.

15 *Year Book* 1976, p. 11.

16 For the text of the Letters Patent and further information, see Appendix 3 at the end of this volume, and also plate XXVII.

17 *Year Book* 1975, p. 12.

18 *The Bulletin*, September 1976, p. 3.

19 *The Bulletin*, October 1976, p 1.

20 In this case, however, for such matters as the foot-washing, procession of the Blessed Sacrament to the Altar of Repose, lighting of the New Fire, the Paschal Candle, and the Exsultet, it was deemed pastorally advisable to publish explanations in *The Bulletin* for 1981 and 1982.

21 John Andrew: personal interview with the author, Sunday 17 October 1999.

22 VM 26 April 1979, p. 1; William Self, *Mine Eyes Have Seen the Glory* (Worcester, MA: Worcester Chapter of the American Guild of Organists, 1990), p. 177-79. Mr. Self describes the theft as "an event rarely considered a blessing, but in this case, perhaps, one sent straight from heaven" (p. 179)!

23 The parish owns copies of the first two issues of this Bible; see above, chapter 12, note 81.

24 In addition to the perennial "Women of Saint Thomas," there also existed, for at least two years during Father Andrew's rectorate, a group called "The Sodality of St. Catherine of Siena," that was "open to all women of the parish interested in spiritual growth." (*Year Book* 1981 and 1982, each at p. 9).

25 John Andrew: personal interview with the author, Sunday 17 October 1999.

26 They are, in order from geographical east to west moving towards the altar: Saints Helena, Elizabeth of Hungary, Agnes, Dorothy, Dorcas, Phebe, Elizabeth (mother of John the Baptist) and Mary (mother of Our Lord). The themes inscribed upon them – Meekness, Faith, Goodness, Gentleness, Longsuffering, Peace, Joy, Love – parallel closely the "fruits of the Spirit" that are the themes of the northern clerestory windows. (See above, page 164).

27 For the theological meaning, which reaches back into the patristic period of the early church, see Louis Bouyer, *The Seat of Wisdom* (New York: Pantheon Books, 1962), and for the artistic form and its expression, which comes from the Romanesque period in the Middle Ages, see

Ilene H. Forsyth, *The Throne of Wisdom* (Princeton: Princeton University Press, 1972). Also see above, pages 217-18.

28 The cost was around $15,000 (*Yearbook* 1987, n.p.).

29 Sermon entitled "Our Lady of Fifth Avenue," dated on the Solemnity of the Dormition of Saint Mary the Virgin, 16 August 1987, in Saint Thomas Archives, file: Our Lady of Fifth Avenue. Text printed in Andrew, *Nothing Cheap and Much that is Cheerful*, pp. 146-47. Subsequent to the dedication of the shrine at Saint Thomas in 1991, a facsimile cast of the same statue on Fifth Avenue was given by Saint Thomas Church to the convent at Minster in England that had originally produced it after a fire destroyed their own Lady Statue. Father Andrew was subsequently invited to bless the new statue after the restoration of the convent chapel.

30 Saint Thomas Archives, file: Our Lady of Fifth Avenue; letter dated 23 August 1990. A recovery of the place of Mary as the first of the saints in heaven who intercede for us at the throne of Jesus was not to be unexpected from a rector of Saint Thomas who had introduced the blessing at his service of institution on 3 December 1972 with the words "May Holy Mary the Mother of God. . ." (according to the memory of former vestry member William H. Wheelock: personal interview with the author, 5 December 1999).

31 Sermon entitled "A Hope Shared," preached at St. Patrick's Cathedral, 21 January 1973 in the Octave of Prayer for Christian Unity (privately printed), p. 4 . Saint Thomas Archives.

32 VM 26 November 1973, p. 3; Harold Grove, ed. *Saint Thomas Church.* (New York: Park Publishing, n.d. [1973]), p. 54. Its overall theme is "Temperance," seen as one of the fruits of the Spirit.

33 Featuring St. Paul in its central panel and celebrating persons who have been moved to do great things for God's world, this window also depicts Mahatma Gandhi, Eleanor Roosevelt, Adlai Stevenson, Ralph Bunche, John Muir, Albert Einstein, and Oliver Wendell Holmes in addition to Pope John XXIII.

34 His framed signature is in the Saint Thomas Archives, dated 29 June 1977.

35 Claudia McDonnell, "Interfaith Partnership: A friendship began on the steps of St. Thomas Episcopal Church," in *Catholic New York*, 10 March 1994 (not paginated).

36 McDonnell, "Interfaith Partnership." The length of the pipe was reported by the police.

37 The word comes from the Latin *columba* meaning "dove," and suggests a home with many small resting places rather like a dovecote. A few urns containing the ashes of deceased parishioners were already kept in this chapel.

38 Further on the music and the Choir School, see the first two appendices at the end of this volume.

39 Andrew, *Nothing Cheap and Much that is Cheerful*, p. 178.

40 John Andrew: personal interview with the author, 17 December 1999; further, see Appendix 1 at the end of this volume.

41 Further see Appendix 2 at the end of this volume.

42 "Unforeseen Remarks," delivered at the Seventy-seventh Commencement Exercises of Saint Thomas Choir School, 8 June 1996 (privately printed), p. 1.

43 *Year Book* 1982, p. 2.

44 These figures have been kindly supplied by Mr. James E. Marlow, Director of Administration, with the cognizance of Mr. John C. Sterling III, the parish Treasurer, and with the appropriate caution as to any interpretation that might be drawn from them. Published figures are found, for example, in the *Yearbook* 1986, pp. 20-21.

45 The impressive list of recipients of such charitable grants made during the last year of Father Andrew's rectorship included, for example, the Anglican Observer at the United Nations, Bailey House Program of Pastoral Care, Berkeley Divinity School at Yale, Episcopal Charities' Summer Programs for Needy Children, FOCUS Educational Programs, Ministry for AIDS

Sufferers, Holy Apostles' Soup Kitchen, Incarnation Camp Summer Youth Program, Interfaith Assembly on Homeless and Housing, Manhattan AIDS Project, New Life of New York City, the Battered Women's Legal Service Program, Canterbury Cathedral Trust, Life Skills for Young People, a minibus for the Diocese of Amritsar, rebuilding of the Rising Star Baptist Church in Alabama, education for clergy and disabled students in the Philippines, the Fifth Avenue Community Center of Harlem, a missionary family in South Africa, Urban Pathways for Homeless Adults, and the Women's Prison Association. *Yearbook* 1996, p. 15 (of pages unnumbered).

46 *Yearbook* 1996, p. 20. Another summary of the state of the parish at the material level that was made about this time was the *Insurance Appraisal of Property Belonging to St. Thomas Church*, completed in 88 pages by Christie's of New York and dated 10 June 1996, the day after Canon Andrew preached his last sermon as rector. Copy in parish archives.

47 Saint Thomas Archives. *Sermons by the Rev. Canon John G. B. Andrew*, volume for 1996: "Singing a New Song: The Rector's Last Sermon," preached on 9 June 1996, pp. 1-2.

48 At Christmas eve in 1977, by contrast, some 6,200 persons had tried to get into the Midnight Mass: *Year Book* 1977, p. 7; *The Bulletin*, December 1978. Father Andrew was aware of how difficult the calculation of such figures could be. In 1978, for example, he reported that Dr. Morris before retirement in 1972 had pruned the Saint Thomas membership list down to 1,225 communicants, that his own calculation in 1973 at the end of the first year of his rectorate had reduced the count to 1,147, and, further, that in June of 1978 he had revised that figure down to 1,074! (*The Bulletin*, June 1978, p. 3). Apparently, though, the communicant strength did steadily increase after that. The round-number reported in *The Episcopal Church Annual* for 1996, as still for 1997 and 1998, was 1,900 communicants, making Saint Thomas in those years the largest of any parish in Manhattan. (In earlier volumes of the same *Annual*, Saint Thomas had been recorded at the beginning of Dr. Morris's tenure in 1954 as the fifth largest, and at the beginning of Father Andrew's tenure in 1972 as the fourth largest, behind St. Bartholomew's, St. James', St. Philip's, and Trinity, but after All Saints had split off with an original 600 communicants). The "Parish Statistics" reported at the end of the New York *Convention Journal* for June 5-6, 1998, and presumably reflecting the situation of a year or so earlier, listed Saint Thomas with the second largest communicant strength in Manhattan (1,555), following St. Bartholomew's with "2,000" (p. 97).

49 John Andrew: personal interview with the author, Sunday 17 October 1999.

50 See below, Appendix 4 at the end of this volume. Father Andrew's priestly work in New York was not done, however. After a period of rest in his native England, he returned in the spring of 1999 to the United States and to the same city in which he had already spent no small portion of his life to take up a position as priest-in-charge at Grace Church in the City of New York, located at Broadway and Twelfth Street. As in 1866, when the homeless congregation of Saint Thomas Church under Dr. Morgan had taken refuge at Grace Church at the invitation of that parish during the period while its rector was in Europe [see above, chapter 5], so now the retired rector of Saint Thomas returned a similar favor to Grace in its own hour of need. "I am a New Yorker now more than I am English," he remarked in a personal interview with the author on 17 October 1999.

51 Andrew, *My Heart is Ready: Feasts and Fasts on Fifth Avenue*, pp. xv-xvii. Excerpt from the Foreword to the same book, published in 1995.

52 Andrew, *The Best of Both Worlds*, pp. 147-50. Originally a sermon, later published in 1991, no date of delivery given.

❧ CHAPTER 14

Epilogue by The Rector

ANDREW CRAIG MEAD
TWELFTH RECTOR, 1996-

Introduction by J. Robert Wright

I T WAS TO THE TUNES AND WORDS of "Christ, the fair glory of the holy angels" and "Ye watchers and ye holy ones" that the service of institution of Andrew Craig Mead (ill. 48) as twelfth rector of Saint Thomas began at the Holy Eucharist on Thursday evening, September 26, 1996. The Rt. Rev. Richard F. Grein, Bishop of New York, presided, and the sermon was preached by the Very Rev. Gary W. Kriss, Dean of Nashotah House in Wisconsin. Sung immediately before the induction was the hymn "Firmly I believe and truly" by John Henry Newman.

As the final chapter of this history of the great parish of Saint Thomas presses towards its summation, it is well to ask just what sort of person is this new rector whose ministry the people of Saint Thomas have now begun to hear and see and feel? What are the convictions about God and the Gospel and the Priesthood that have become fixed in his mind and heart over the five and a half decades since his birth in 1946? After my brief introduction of Father Mead, this final chapter will conclude with an epilogue in his own words, as he himself describes the story that he is already beginning to write at Saint Thomas.

48. Andrew Craig Mead, Twelfth Rector 1996-

More than seventy candidates had been considered in the search for Father Andrew's successor. The vestry's search committee notified the congregation of their final decision in an open letter to the parish dated April 19, 1996, under the signatures of Wardens G. William Haas and Joan E. Hoffman. The letter summarized carefully the qualities that were regarded as critically important: "a commitment to our liturgical tradition, where music is central to our worship, and the need to strengthen and renew parish life through emphasis on fellowship and new program offerings." In its letter, the committee highlighted several ideals listed by Father Mead in the self-description on his resumé that had been influential in their choice; in particular, they noted his description of himself as "a parish priest in the Anglo-Catholic tradition, providing pastoral leadership through teaching and preaching, sacramental devotion and nurture, spiritual counsel and pastoral care." Translating these words into their own, the committee proceeded to describe the rector-designate in the following terms: "He is committed to doctrinal orthodoxy in teaching and pastoral work, and has had long experience in the liturgical heritage of Catholic Anglicanism, grounded in the rubrics of the Book of Common Prayer. He has broad experience as a pastor in the urban environment of Boston."[1]

If these were the qualities deemed influential, what were the factual credentials behind them? Born on December 8, 1946, in Rochester, New York, one of two children of Gaylord Persons Mead Jr. and Margery Elizabeth Wootton, Andrew Craig Mead was educated in various public schools and then at DePauw University in Greencastle, Indiana, where he majored in history, served as editor-in-chief of the student newspaper and, in 1968, took his B.A. degree. He tells his story there in his own words: "At DePauw University I fortified my unwillingness to go to church with scepticism, beginning with objections to the church and ending with rejection of God himself. I became involved in the New Left politics of the sixties and was outspoken as the editor of my college newspaper. However, I was searching for ethical and philosophical anchorage. This quest was answered when, one night, I rediscovered our Lord Jesus Christ while studying for a quiz in a New Testament course. I had enrolled in the course to 'study the enemy'; a year later I was in seminary."[2] He graduated from Yale University Divinity School in 1971 with the degree of B.D. (later M.Div.), having served as seminarian assistant at Christ Church, New Haven, Connecticut. On the first day of the next year (January 1, 1972) he married Nancy Anne Hoxsie, a skilled florist and *summa* honors graduate in French and Art of the University of Rhode Island. Later, in retrospect, he was to say that meeting Nancy and discovering the Oxford Movement were the "two momentous developments" that occurred in his life at Yale. He was ordained Deacon on June 11, 1971, and Priest on December 18 of the same year.

Initially considering a teaching vocation, he soon went for further study to Oxford University where he affiliated with Keble College and also assisted in a local Anglo-Catholic parish; the priest there, Father Anthony Fletcher, was influential in convincing him to decide that his vocation lay not in academics but in parish ministry. He later recalled that he and Nancy "began our life together at Oxford University. I spent my days in various libraries; Nancy worked for a florist in the Oxford covered market." His thesis, for which he received the Oxford degree of M.Litt. in 1974, was entitled "A Critical Investigation of the Controversy between Newman and the Tractarians over the Development of Doctrine." It was also in Oxford that his daughter Emma was born in 1973; son Matthew came later, in 1976.

Back in the United States, after early ministerial responsibilities at St. Paul's, Wallingford, and St. John's, Yalesville, Connecticut, he then went to serve as curate to the famous and much admired Father John Purnell at All Saints, Ashmont, in Boston, an experience that confirmed his love for the parish ministry. Next came seven years as rector of the Church of the Good Shepherd, Rosemont, a suburb of Philadelphia, followed by eleven more years as the rector of the Church of the Advent in Boston, a tenure that was distinguished by his preaching, teaching, and social outreach, all from an Anglo-Catholic perspective. It was noticed and appreciated there that he and his wife frequently opened the rectory to the people of the parish.[3] In 1987 Father Mead was elected to the Board of Trustees of Nashotah House Theological Seminary in Wisconsin, and much earlier, in 1974, he had begun his series of summer commitments as a faculty member of St. Michael's Conference for young people in the Anglo-Catholic tradition. One of his most cherished possessions, which he wears sometimes when hearing confessions, is a purple stole given him by Father Purnell that had once belonged to the famous post-Oxford Movement priests Arthur H. Stanton and Alexander H. Mackonochie and been worn by them at the parish of St. Alban's, Holborn, in London in the late nineteenth century.

Although Andrew Mead had already become a "builder of parishes," emphasizing the parish family as a congregation much as Dr. Morris had earlier done, he also was clearly and openly an Anglo-Catholic priest, continually emphasizing the beauty and priority of worship that had been Father Andrew's special contribution. If we have so far given a factual description of his accomplishments leading up to his appointment at Saint Thomas – his "track record," so to speak – we may also logically ask how he thought of himself as priest and pastor on the eve of his arrival at his new church. What were the deeper thoughts, the fixed principles, that he had come to hold as he contemplated the history and sensibilities that would soon be entrusted to his care at Saint Thomas on Fifth Avenue? In his *curriculum vitae,* he enumerated the following as being among his commitments: "Biblical preaching within a Catholic liturgical framework, coupled with an evangelical concern for the hearer," "Classical standards of doctrinal orthodoxy in teaching," "the liturgical heritage of Catholic Anglicanism, within the rubrics of the Book of Common Prayer of the Episcopal Church," "Pastoral counseling and the hearing of sacramental confessions," "love for the 'care of souls'," "commitment to the tradition of Western Catholic theology and devotion," and "love for catechetical work."[4] These were the underlying principles that he would soon begin to blend into his new parish, as he began to make his own contribution to an even greater future, both continuous and unique.

This concludes our summary, and it now remains for Father Andrew Mead to write the epilogue that follows. Even now, the future is already present, and he himself is making his mark, taking his place, proving his mettle. It is too soon to write the history of his rectorship, but let us read his epilogue, his vision, in his own words. It is a pleasure to introduce him.

Epilogue by Father Mead

This epilogue, which continues in my own words the chapter about my rectorship of Saint Thomas thus far, is written with the advantage of a full reading of the texts of all preceding chapters as well as the appendices which follow. Canon Wright's commission was to write the history of Saint Thomas from its beginnings in 1823 to the completion of my predecessor's tenure in June of 1996. The occasion was the observance of Saint Thomas' 175th anniversary as a parish church. I requested that the author finish his history with my call as the twelfth rector in May of 1996 and my Institution by Bishop Grein in September of that year, together with the relevant background details of my life and ministry.

I join the special parish history committee in their warm assessment of Canon Wright's work, completed right on time, by December 31, 1999. American history and church history are my avocations. This is not only the best parish church history I have read, it is a first-rate resource for the use of Episcopal and Anglican church historians and a significant contribution to the history of New York City.

On October 10, 1999, just before Canon Wright submitted his finished text, Mrs. Hope Preminger, a vestry member of the parish history committee, presented the first public viewing of *The Gate of Heaven*, a 55-minute video of the history of Saint Thomas, commissioned by the vestry (along with this book) to mark our 175th anniversary. The showing of the film was in the auditorium of the Museum of Modern Art, our next-door neighbor on West Fifty-third Street. The matrix which gave birth to *The Gate of Heaven* was a combination of Canon Wright's history of *Saint Thomas Church Fifth Avenue* and a project to produce a short promotional video on Saint Thomas Choir School. *The Gate of Heaven*, which has been broadcast more than once on WLIW public television and has been offered for sale at Saint Thomas, was intended to dramatize and popularize, as movies do with books, this chronicle so thoroughly written by Canon Wright. The video, produced by Our Town Films, has already won national awards as a documentary film and is a candidate for international awards as well. The video and the book go hand in hand to tell the story of Saint Thomas. Many viewers of the film should be inspired to become readers of the book. But the book, which plumbs depths and details no movie can, is itself an arresting and readable narrative.

My first concern in asking the vestry to commission this book was to secure the as-yet underwritten stories of the tenures of Frederick Morris and John Andrew, a period stretching back nearly half a century to 1954. These were quite distinct rectorships which included the passage of Saint Thomas through the turbulent sixties and seventies. The community's living memory of Dr. Morris's leadership will soon be gone, and I myself am keenly aware of the swiftness of time to "bear all its sons away." As I write these words, I note that my own rectorship of Saint Thomas already has outlasted that of George Upfold and is closing in on Edmund Neville and Cornelius Roosevelt Duffie himself.

But the tenures of the last two rectors, Dr. Morris and Father Andrew, not covered in the previous history of Saint Thomas published in 1958, cannot be properly appreciated without a true perspective gained from a full review of all that preceded them. It was for this reason that we engaged the talents of one of the premier church historians in the Anglican Communion to provide us with this perspective. Canon Wright (now an honorary Saint Thomas clergy associate) has not only rewritten and corrected the earlier published history of our past, which was itself compiled with diligence, but has also, I believe, given us the true remembrance we need to spell out our mission for the future opening up before us in this new century and millennium.

We know what happens when individuals and communities suffer from amnesia. In George Orwell's great parable against twentieth-century totalitarianism, *Animal Farm,* the first thing the pigs did to tyrannize the other animals was erase their memories. From then on, anything was possible, to the ruination of the community. Churches can lose their way, and have done so, by forgetfulness and amnesia. Let it not be so with Saint Thomas Church Fifth Avenue. As I look back over the struggles, setbacks, and accomplishments of my priestly predecessors and of our ancestor "brethren, kinsfolk, and benefactors" in the congregation, I see the major pillars of the edifice of Saint Thomas' mission for the future firmly established in our 175 years of history.

In what follows, I will review under five headings what I see as the parish's pillars to which I have just referred. Canon Wright has frequently noted in this history of Saint Thomas the biblical image from the first Epis-

233

tle of Peter, that of the Church as a living structure built of living "stones" who offer their gifts and energies as sacrifices to God. Their sacrifices are acceptable to God because the organic building made up of these living stones is also the Body of Christ, the "one true pure immortal sacrifice" who has reconciled us to his Father and unites us, living and departed, in "mystic sweet communion and fellowship divine." Therefore, as we all gather week by week to fill and animate this magnificent Gothic edifice of white limestone at Fifth Avenue and Fifty-third Street, we can build our future on the gifts coming to us from God through our goodly heritage. More than that, we can take instruction from our forefathers in the priesthood and our ancestors in the congregation.

The five pillars of our mission, the fundamentals of our life at Saint Thomas, that I shall now review are our extraordinary location, our glorious Gothic church building, our heritage of classic Anglican worship and preaching, our unique music program and Choir School, and our generous social mission and warm fellowship.

1) THE LOCATION

Traditional church organization divides the visible flock into dioceses and parishes with fixed geographical bounds, but modern life for some time, especially in New York City and its environs, has not submitted to such neat limitations. Founded to meet the needs of an expanding population moving northward into the more rural areas of Manhattan Island, Saint Thomas Church in the City and County of New York has from early times been forced to be more than a parish church. From the start, Saint Thomas ministered to an aggregation of people drawn from beyond its immediate vicinity as well as to a parochial congregation. The first Saint Thomas Church at Broadway and Houston Street, a Gothic structure built to express the High Church principles so clearly taught by Bishop John Henry Hobart and his protégé Cornelius Roosevelt Duffie, drew people to its worship and to the attractive although brief pastoral ministry of our saintly first priest and rector. The celebrated pulpit eloquence and catechetical abilities of Francis Hawks, our third rector, drew great crowds and produced a children's Sunday School which staggers late twentieth-century imaginations. Saint Thomas Church had by then become both a *congregation* within the Episcopal Diocese of New York as well as an *aggregation* or mixture of regulars and visitors.

When perhaps the greatest strategist so far among our rectors, William Ferdinand Morgan, took up the reins in 1857, he saw that the location of Saint Thomas was impeding its ministry to both *aggregation* and *congregation*. The neighborhood was not only no longer residential; it was at best commercial and "surrendered to the purpose of crime." Not that Dr. Morgan ever neglected the poor; on the contrary, he established a chapel specifically to draw them in and care for them, a ministry which continued as the parish moved north to Fifth Avenue and Fifty-third Street in 1867. This extraordinary leader, supported by his vestry and people, gave us our present location, which enables Saint Thomas to draw the very large *aggregations* of visitors and friends we now see from all over the city, the nation, and beyond, as well as to invite many of them to join in the active participation of what is an enthusiastic and gifted *congregation* of regulars. What a street corner it has become, with our Roman Catholic brethren to the south at St. Patrick's Cathedral and our Protestant brethren to the north at Fifth Avenue Presbyterian Church. The official style of our name now, Saint Thomas Church Fifth Avenue, manifests the nature of our parish, both local and beyond. We are in the midst of what surely is the "world's mall," surrounded by Disney and Warner Brothers, Radio City and Carnegie Hall, with Elizabeth Arden and Brooks Brothers facing us across the avenue and the street. The Museum of Modern Art and, for the time being, the Gap, share the block with us. We have not only been on television and radio; we now have a web site on the internet, with tens of thousands visiting the church and Choir School via their personal computers. Flowing like a river (and sometimes, especially in the winter holiday season, overflowing) up and down the sidewalks of Fifth Avenue, from Central Park and the Plaza Hotel on our north to the Empire State Building on our south, many thousands of souls, as if siphoned off into a river weir, flow into our hushed and majestic sanctuary by climbing its Fifth Avenue steps. An enormous *aggregation* visits Saint Thomas each week, month, and year. And yet, from the side streets on the avenues of both the East Side and West Side of New York City, some hundreds of souls also come and stay, Sunday by Sunday and day by day, to be regular participants in the worship of the *congregation*. Our location uniquely positions us to be a witness for our Lord Jesus Christ in the center of the largest city of the most powerful and wealthy nation on earth. This is quite a challenge and a sacred trust from God.

2) The Building: The Gothic Idea

The first church building at Fifth Avenue and Fifty-third was a grand edifice, especially its bell tower. The architect Richard Upjohn greatly enhanced the Gothic idea as expressed by Saint Thomas' two predecessor churches at Broadway and Houston. The destruction of Upjohn's structure by our second fire (may God forbid any more) was widely viewed as a disaster, but out of the rubble came a far greater architectural triumph by two of the greatest masters of the Gothic Revival, Ralph Adams Cram and Bertram Grosvenor Good-hue. As a devotee (and, I trust, a true son) of the Oxford Movement and its attendant movements in ecclesiastical art and architecture, I believe I understand the spiritual impulses that led my predecessors to choose and prefer the Gothic style of building for Saint Thomas Church at each critical juncture in our history. It may be fairly asserted – as Pugin, Cram, and other gothicists have said – that pointed or Gothic architecture is an art form largely developed within, by, and for Western Medieval Christendom. The Gothic ethos uniquely expresses the central tenets of Western Catholic (and subsequently Anglo-Catholic) religion and impresses them upon the beholder. The mystical reaching up toward heaven by the pointed arches soaring into the vaulting; the tripartite sectioning of the nave, chancel, and altar sanctuary (corresponding to the Church Militant, Expectant, and Triumphant); the delicate stone tracery of the windows admitting the cool light through the stained glass; the silent testimony of the saints in glass and stone from the reredos to the front porch; all these are combined in Saint Thomas Church Fifth Avenue, raised from the ashes of 1905 and without question a masterpiece (pl. VIII, XXIV).

For nearly a century – longer than the combined eras of the three earlier church buildings – Saint Thomas' Gothic jewel has drawn countless souls to the mystery of God and the splendors of worship. The boldness of our eighth rector Ernest Stires inspired the vestry and people to make the leap of faith required to engage the demanding geniuses of Cram and Goodhue. There is a persistent story in the parish and within the Stires family that Dr. Stires, moved by the catastrophe of the San Francisco earthquake in April 1906, gave away a large amount of money from Saint Thomas' building fund to aid the earthquake victims. We have been unable to find, either in parish records or contemporary newspaper accounts, written evidence to confirm the story. But the story persists and has well-connected roots, and it may well be reflective of a courageous altruism and benevolence that was born of the same spirit that generated the parish's commitment to the cost of a magnificent new church in the contract with Cram and Goodhue. Perhaps the angel of generosity assisted in the putting up of the new church building, in this way attracting support from even beyond the Saint Thomas community.

In any case, who cannot feel the power of the Gothic synthesis as you read in this book Dr. Stires'145 145 own guided tour of the reredos? And who cannot be touched by the catholicity of Dr. Stires' vision, which surely influenced the cast of characters one sees in the church's statuary? The statuary and stained glass were later completed in the same spirit by Dr. Brooks, Dr. Morris, and Father Andrew. In the reredos, there are Our Lady and Saint John with Christ at the center; the great apostles, fathers, and theologians of the undivided Catholic Church of the first millennium; the saints of the ages, crowned by the Holy Innocents carried by angels at the pointed top. Branching outward, we see secular Christian leaders such as George Washington and William Gladstone, along with later Anglican and Episcopal saints and worthies. Carved beneath the pulpit, there are Henry Parry Liddon and John Henry Newman (in his cardinal's hat) to warm a high churchman's heart, alongside Phillips Brooks, John Wesley, and other great evangelical preachers. In the choir, I regularly greet both the puritan John Bunyan and the Tractarian Edward Bouverie Pusey, carved into the woodwork where I make my way to the rector's stall to lead Choral Evensong. All of these comprise the Gothic idea, as it gathers all reality and points heavenwards, and the Gothic idea, so masterfully embodied in Saint Thomas Church Fifth Avenue, manifests the transcendence and holiness of God, the majesty of Jesus' incarnation, life, death, and resurrection, and the mystery of the Body of Christ and Communion of Saints. The Gothic idea is central to the history of Saint Thomas and its ongoing mission, a spiritual and aesthetic concept equal to the challenge of its location at Fifth Avenue and Fifty-third, a beacon and a shrine that proclaims in its every stone "Thou art the King of Glory, O Christ."

3) Worship and Preaching: High Church and Low Church

I wish the terms "high church" and "low church" could be avoided, because of their implications of superiority and inferiority on one hand or of complication and simplicity on the other. But they are historic terms, and there they are in the story of the Episcopal Church and Anglican Communion, the Diocese of New York, and Saint Thomas Parish. Beginning with Cornelius Duffie in 1823 and continuing through John Wesley Brown at the end of the last century, all our rectors were high churchmen of one hue or other, New York "Hobartian" churchmen reflecting the theology of that greatest of all Bishops of New York. Bishop John Henry Hobart conferred with and deeply impressed John Henry Newman himself, who wrote an essay about Hobart's prospects as a leader of the "Anglo-American Church," as Newman called the still fledgling Episcopal Church in the United States. Some of our rectors, such as Henry John Whitehouse and John Wesley Brown, strike me as having been "advanced" high churchmen, Anglo-Catholics in substance with more overt ritual and ceremonial expression to their ministries.

But as Canon Wright so ably tells us, a section of the parish, together with some of the lay leadership, regularly swung against High Churchmanship, occasionally in the interims attempting to call quite protestant evangelicals as rectors. The tale of Dr. Morgan's hanging-on at the end of his tenure to secure a worthy High Church successor in Dr. Brown illustrates the dynamic of those nineteenth-century days. Then with Dr. Stires, a broad-minded Evangelical, and his "centrist" successor, Dr. Brooks, began an era, culminating in the protestant but strict aegis of Dr. Morris, which has popularly (and fairly) been called "Low Church" in Saint Thomas history, the period from 1901 to 1972.

My predecessor and friend John Andrew, like me, is a spiritual child of the Oxford Movement. The great influence on his life and ministry was the Archbishop of Canterbury Arthur Michael Ramsey, one of the greatest leaders and thinkers the Church of England has ever had, whose roots were planted deep in the Oxford Movement and Anglo-Catholicism. Father Andrew's gradual and sensitive transformation of the worship of Saint Thomas into a world-class showcase of High Anglican liturgy over his twenty-four-year ministry – during which both the aggregation and the congregation of Saint Thomas grew enormously (coinciding with a period of sharp decline for the diocese and national Episcopal Church) – is one of the great accomplishments in Saint Thomas history. In some ways, this was a reversion to the type of churchmanship developed at Saint Thomas during the nineteenth century, but it is much more than that. Father Andrew was supported by the lay leadership and congregation at large, as a result not only of his powers of persuasion but also of several important factors beyond the parish. First, the enormous atmospheric change wrought by the Roman Catholic Church's new ecumenical attitude, arising from the Second Vatican Council, had removed most of the poison in Protestant–Catholic and High Church–Low Church relations. Second, the political and cultural traumas of the 1960s and 1970s, together with the increasingly secular mindset of the intellectual and ruling elite in America, threw the contours of American Christianity into sharp relief and revealed with great clarity a new situation. Namely, the differences between Catholic and Protestant or High Church and Low Church, great as they once may have seemed, are small when compared with the differences between believer and non-believer, between Christian (or even theistic) faith on the one hand and materialism or meaninglessness on the other. Third, the ratification of a new American Book of Common Prayer in 1979, the product of two decades of liturgical ferment under the two influences just described, resulted in a settlement of churchmanship issues within the Episcopal Church that officially endorsed a great many of the central tenets of the Oxford Movement. As Father Donald Garfield, a former rector of the Anglo-Catholic shrine Church of St. Mary the Virgin near Times Square and a member of the Standing Liturgical Commission which first submitted the draft Prayer Book to the General Convention in 1976, wrote concerning the 1979 Book: "What do we do when we've won?" But as we shall see, if there is a spiritual war going on, it has shifted from issues of churchmanship to another battlefield.

In any case, when the vestry search committee came to consider me as a possible successor to John Andrew, one of their concerns was the preservation and development of the worship that had drawn such crowds to Saint Thomas and which inspired many to stay. The parish where for eleven years I was rector before coming to Saint Thomas, the Church of the Advent on Beacon Hill in Boston, is the historic Anglo-Catholic flagship in New England, a fact of which the Saint Thomas vestry was well aware. My own ministry had been almost entirely within parishes of Anglo-Catholic heritage. The vestry search committee knew all this and their leaders had observed it all at first hand (even the incense). Moreover, I made the clearest presentation I could for them concerning my convictions, which are not only what I would call traditional and orthodox in Catholic theology, but are also "conservative" regarding the issues which currently try the whole Anglican Communion and persistently divide leaders and members of the Episcopal Church. Every member of the vestry search committee did not necessarily agree with me on every issue; however, it was clear that they all appreciated my candor and straightforwardness. But three leading considerations, gathered from questionnaires distributed to the congregation, guided their thinking and decision-making. These were, in order of emphasis as reported by the questionnaire, the concerns of 1) worship and liturgy, 2) music, and 3) preaching and teaching.

These concerns are in fact the priorities, the fundamental content, of what happens at Saint Thomas on every Lord's Day. We have already seen that passionate adherence to the highest possible standards of Anglican sacramental life, centered in the Holy Eucharist as the principal service on Sundays, determines the worship of Saint Thomas. Connected to these standards, indeed an integral part of them, is biblical preaching with an evangelical concern for the hearer, revolving around the Person and Work of Jesus Christ. Finally, there is music, the handmaid of the liturgy, to which we will turn under the next heading. But before we do, a few more things need to be said.

People for the most part are no longer asking the questions of churches that were asked a century or even fifty years ago. High Church – Low Church questions, even Catholic – Protestant questions, no longer vex people's minds as they once did, because deeper, more drastic and radical questions are now in people's hearts. The seekers who come my way want to know what, if any, meaning and purpose there is to life, most especially to *their* lives. They want to know if there really is a compelling reason to live, to persevere, to endure to the end, in this frantic, driven, and distracted world we

239

now live in. They want to know whether "this is all there is." They wonder if they are, as they are told in the secular classrooms of our schools and universities, merely an accidental assemblage of matter and energy with a genetic will to survive. They want to know: Who am I? Do I have a soul? Is there Anybody (or Anything) there? What, if anything, is on the other side of death? Are there only oblivion and nothingness?

The Church must address these questions with intelligence and clarity. She must not stutter or stammer in making her response, and she has God-given resources at her disposal. She must say: Yes, your life matters. God made you. Each day is an adventure in God's Spirit and is of great significance for all eternity. Time is precious and is not to be wasted. God lives. More than that, Christ is risen! Christ reigns in his Church, and he is there for us, right unto death and most certainly beyond – just as he is pictured in the Saint Thomas reredos, rising above the high altar, just above the tableau of Saint Thomas the Apostle, the former doubter, who kneels before the risen Jesus and exclaims "My Lord and my God." If there is a war going on, one of the most important battlefields is the issue of whether the clergy and leaders of the Church esteem or set at nought the authoritative resources of Church worship and doctrine – the Holy Scriptures as the Word of God written, the catholic creeds and the wisdom of the evangelical and catholic tradition, the classic documents and title deeds of the Church, including those of Anglicanism. Whether in periods of High Church or Low Church emphasis, it has been clear throughout Saint Thomas Church's history where she stands, for there has been from the first day until now a golden cord of authentic teaching running through all twelve rectorships and firmly grasped by our flock in each generation.

The persistent preference at Saint Thomas for the classic liturgical texts of Anglicanism is a sign of more than merely conservative sensibilities (which are indeed characteristic of the temper of the parish in matters of worship). We adhere to the rubrics of Rite I in the 1979 Prayer Book as the standard for our principal services at the high altar. (We do use Rite II at the noonday Masses said in the Chantry Chapel, and have done so for two decades.) And we employ texts, especially for choral use, from the 1928 Prayer Book (especially for the psalter), and even from the old English Prayer Book. But this is not because we have been Prayer Book reactionaries. It is because of the precision and clarity of expression in these classic Anglican texts, virtues which appeal to the deep desire, both Evangelical and Catholic, to communicate with the deepest mysteries of the Christian faith (pl. XXIII). Somehow, these great prayers of English religion express the same thing as the majesty of Saint Thomas' Gothic arches and vaulting: "All glory be to thee, Almighty God our heavenly Father, for that thou, of thy tender mercy, didst give thine only Son Jesus Christ, to suffer death upon the cross for our redemption. . ." (pl. XXIV). The comforting solemnity of the eucharistic rite and the majestic phrases of Cranmer's prayers attract both large aggregations and faithful congregations to the worship of God and the hearing of the Gospel of Christ. The liturgy, in a word, lives up to the Gothic building.

4) The Music and the Choir School

"Some to church repair, not for the doctrine, but [for] the music there," wrote Alexander Pope in 1711. In Saint Thomas' case "some" are very many, and who can doubt that the music here is our greatest ministry of outreach to the wider community of New York? Music also evangelizes. People continually come to Saint Thomas to hear the music and stay to worship "the Muse," who is none other than God himself. One of the chief accomplishments of John Andrew's rectorship, and one of the main reasons for his success in attracting such greater numbers to Saint Thomas, was the provision, by the more fully developed liturgy and schedule of services, of a proper format for the talents of our Organist and Master of Choristers, Gerre Hancock. Awarded two honorary doctorates in music for his leadership in the Anglican choral tradition and his contributions to church music in the United States, Dr. Hancock unites the highest artistic standards to the timely charm of the popular touch. His standards are certainly comparable to those of his now distant but still illustrious predecessor Dr. T. Tertius Noble and, many would agree, he is the best today at what he does. Certainly, no one in the United States surpasses Gerre Hancock at improvisation or in leading a choir of men and boys.

"Uncle Gerre" was called by Dr. Morris and is now with his third rector. Given his youthful spirit and the prospects of good health, my hope is that he will be with us for a good while yet. He will need another decade even to equal the retirement age of Dr. Noble! With the arrival of Gordon Roland-Adams in 1997, coming from Westminster Abbey Choir School to be our Choir School's new headmaster, we have a school leader who takes a vigorous interest in the choirboys' musical performance (as well as their scholastics, athletics, and general welfare) and who actively supports Dr. Hancock's ministry. Mr. Roland-Adams has brought a new harmony to the close relationship between church and school. At Saint Thomas, the rector, the Organist and Master of Choristers, and the Headmaster need to be a "trinity" who closely work together day by day, communicate and confer with ease, and trust each other implicitly. This is what the three of us have been and, by God's grace, what we shall be for a long time.

Thus the mission of Saint Thomas is bound up with the music of Saint Thomas and the work of Saint Thomas Choir School. I should add that the forty boys whom the Choir School houses, nurtures, and educates receive an extraordinary school experience. They perform music at professional levels that would tax seasoned adults. Their academic performance reflects the virtues learned by this discipline. They receive the Anglican Church's tradition of teaching and pastoral care through theology classes, a regular chaplain from the Saint Thomas clergy staff, and the ongoing worship. Boys from outside the Episcopal Church are not proselytized; their traditions are respected. But all applicants are aware that Saint Thomas Choir School is indeed a parish church school where the students are clearly exposed to Anglican Christianity.

Recently a Choir School mother told us that her young son telephoned their home in Baltimore while she and her husband were waking up with coffee at 6:00 a.m. "Hi, Mom," chirped the voice, while the mother took a breath wondering what had happened. "Do you know Sheppard?" the boy asked. Asked by Mom whether he meant sixteenth-century John Sheppard or twentieth-century Richard, the two artists she knew of with roughly that surname, the boy replied that he wasn't sure which, but his music had voices magnificently "tumbling all over" and was "awesome." When a nine-year-old boy near the end of the twentieth century calls his mother at 6:00 a.m. to say that a sixteenth-century polyphonic composer's music is awesome (it was John), we are accomplishing something wonderful at Saint Thomas Church and Choir School. It is the handing on of this heritage that is at the heart of our mission.

As Dr. Hancock notes in his Appendix below, my own preferences are with sixteenth and seventeenth century polyphony, and with the Anglican composers (Gibbons and Weelkes, for examples) of Jacobean and Caroline England. But let us also reach back to Gregorian Chant and Medieval Masses and forward to Britten and Locklear and even to Schuller and Susa. More than that, polyphony is still being discovered, from Francisco Guerrero in Spain to Juan Gutierrez de Padilla in South America (you can almost hear the castanets in his *Gloria in excelsis*). Let us hear it all, to the glory of God. The repertoire is old and new, broad and deep in the treasury of sacred music. The offering of this music, in union with good liturgy and biblical preaching, is central to the history and mission of Saint Thomas (pl. XXV).

Any look at the music of Saint Thomas would be incomplete without mention of the rendering of the psalter in the chants of the Church. On Sunday mornings, the chanted psalm follows the first biblical lesson, normally from the Old Testament, and precedes the Epistle, in the Choral Eucharist. But it is at Choral Evensong, on Sundays and on Tuesdays and Thursdays when the Choir School is in session, that the glories of the classic Coverdale

Psalter are united with dexterity to the melodies of Anglican Chant, so that a very large portion of the Psalms of David are sung within the Saint Thomas portals as they are nowhere else in North America. The English cathedral tradition of chanting the psalter for Choral Evensong is truly a gem in the life of Saint Thomas and is a principal means of outreach to our wider family of friends and visitors. How many souls, tired from a day of work in the bustle of the city, have found peace and solace at 5:30 p.m. on a Tuesday or Thursday by stepping into Saint Thomas from Fifth Avenue? And Sundays at 4:00 p.m. is one of the largest missionary services in New York, ministering the holiness of beauty in Choral Evensong to an average of at least three hundred people per week. This schedule of Dr. Hancock, his assistants, and the Choir of Men and Boys must be one of the most rigorous schedules of services and rehearsals in America!

5) THE SOCIAL MISSION

Saint Thomas made remarkable efforts in the nineteenth century to minister to the poor, to the sick, and to children. As Canon Wright has recounted, these efforts even pre-date the story of the Saint Thomas Chapel on the East Side. The twentieth century has seen great changes. Gone are the days of no annual budgets and *ad hoc* appeals for money, and we are emancipated from the constrictions of pew rents. But Saint Thomas, in spite of its reputation hanging over from the Gilded Age of the 1890s, has no single great benefactors. We have many highly successful and gifted business and professional people in our flock, but Saint Thomas could not exist on their yearly contributions, in spite of the comparatively large size of our congregations. The annual Every Member Canvass, born in Dr. Morris's time, supports, at just over $600,000, about ten percent of the annual budget of Church and Choir School (at the present time of writing).

The endowment fund of Saint Thomas, begun in Dr. Brown's rectorship and developed under his successors (special credit goes to Dr. Brooks), has kept us alive. This is a legacy for the most part of many modest, rather than of one or two great, bequests. The Church and Choir School have been seen as an attractive heritage to remember in one's will, and the vestry, to its great credit, has managed that trust with both courage and prudence. The growth of the endowment is one of the great stories of Saint Thomas history. In the early 1970s, the wardens and vestry leaders, concerned about the conspiring effects of high inflation and a stagnant American economy ("stagflation"), decided to commit most of our invested funds, then about $25 million, to investment in stocks rather than fixed annuities. The 1980s and especially the 1990s have seen a prosperous economy and stock market, but it has often

49. The clergy as of the year 2000. Front row, l-r, Father Andrew Mead, Rector; Canon Harry Krauss, Senior Curate. Back row, l-r, Father Robert Stafford, Assisting Priest; Father Joseph Griesedieck III, Curate; Father Park Bodie, Curate

taken courage for the vestry to stay the course of its investment strategy. This courage has been rewarded over the past thirty years. The Saint Thomas investment portfolio has been valued at over $100 million since 1997. The generosity of our benefactors in their wills and legacies, together with the "bull market," keeps Saint Thomas Church and Choir School, with their combined annual budget of now over $6 million, going, and it has allowed us to continue the social mission of the nineteenth century in other ways.

Saint Thomas gives one million dollars each year to church work outside the parish, including the diocesan assessment. We are surely one of the strongest supporters of the Bishop and Diocese of New York. We have just completed payment over four years of a pledge of one million dollars to the Diocesan Capital Campaign. Beyond the Diocese, we support two Episcopal seminaries; New York hospices and soup kitchens (including our own at the Choir School); domestic and foreign missions, hospitals, and schools; emergency appeals from parishes and other institutions; church youth camps; and special ministries to children, AIDS sufferers, and the homebound. The Archbishop of Canterbury has frequently received our support for special appeals for the mission of the worldwide Anglican Communion, the Lambeth Conference of Bishops, and his own ministry. Canterbury Cathedral knows us as a generous supporter of projects such as its new Canterbury Education Centre. The Vestry Grants Committee is one of the most active groups in the parish, making on-sight visits and responding to the appeals that come to the rector every week of the year. It is because of the endowment fund, the ongoing gifts of our "brethren, kinsfolk and benefactors," that this mission continues.

I have mentioned the Every Member Canvass, which has seen encouraging increases in recent years, currently approaching six hundred pledges to Church and Choir School. More important to our mission than the money itself is what it represents: the active engagement of the congregation. When I was called to be rector, the development of the life of the congregation was one of the major elements of my call. To assist with this task, I called a cherished friend and esteemed priest colleague, the Rev. Canon Harry E. Krauss, who joined me in 1997 as Senior Curate, leaving a highly successful rectorship of nearly twenty years at All Saints Church, Wynnewood, Pennsylvania. A strong clergy team with a joyous *esprit de corps* (ill. 49) is crucial to the spirit reflected in our large lay staff in both Church and Choir School as well as in our dedicated vestry and in the congregation at large. As I write, we are particularly blessed in this regard in our two Curates, Fathers Park McD. Bodie and Joseph E. Griesedieck, and in our Assisting Priest, Father Robert H. Stafford. A vigorous program of Christian education led by Canon Krauss and taught by the clergy (and some lay teachers) on Sunday morning and on three nights of most weeks; suppers and fellowship events for each parish group; regular offerings of hospitality at the rectory and in the parish house; outings and retreats – all these endeavors, combined with conscientious pastoral work by our team of clergy, have begun to renew the life of the congregation – including the Choir School – and enrich its sense of being a family.

Hardly a thing is written of the wives of my predecessors in this history, because, unfortunately, hardly anything about them survives in the records. We know how bereft Mr. Duffie was as a widower and how his loss drove him to find refuge in his faith. He and his wife and child still lie buried in Green-Wood Cemetery with no proper home in the church he founded. I had the joy of visiting, with my wife Nancy, the graves of Dr. and Mrs. Morgan in Portsmouth, Rhode Island, where we prayed for this *Pastor fidelis* and his faithful spouse. I am told that Dr. and Mrs. Brooks reared their grandchildren in the rectory. I had the pleasure of meeting Mrs. Morris with Dr. Morris in Connecticut in 1997, the year before they died. I cannot speak for them and their life together at Saint Thomas, except to recount how Dorothy Morris told me that she and her husband spent many happy years in the parish and wished me and my family the same happiness. John Andrew, a celibate priest, had the loving assistance of parishioners in his ministry of hospitality.

I want to conclude this epilogue by setting down the fact that my own wife Nancy, the mainstay of my life and ministry for nearly thirty years as I write this, has blessed the Saint Thomas fellowship with the zest of her creative and aesthetic gifts, hospitality, and charitable work. Designer of flower arrangements, creator of a new parish garden, hostess of rectory receptions and dinners for nearly one thousand souls each year, regular volunteer at the Saint Thomas Soup Kitchen, she has provided light and life and strength to the fulfillment of my calling as priest and rector. Father Andrew introduced her with gracious words as he announced me as his successor. She is my beloved wife, and she is mother and friend not only of our two grown children Emma and Matthew but also to the parishioners of Saint Thomas Church and to the boys and staff of its Choir School. If anyone has aided me in the mission of bringing many from our great aggregation into the warm activity of the congregation, it is she. She brightens and energizes the reality of the Christian family at Saint Thomas.

So concludes this epilogue, which is a review of our history, an assessment of our present position at the turn of a century and millennium, and a mission statement for the future. Our mission, as I say as frequently as I can, is to present the Gospel of Jesus Christ with intelligence and clarity, using all the gifts at our disposal. The five pillars of our spiritual edifice – 1) our extraordinary location, 2) our glorious Gothic church building, 3) our heritage of classic Anglican worship and preaching, 4) our unique music program and Choir School, and 5) our generous social mission and warm fellowship – these continue to be the fundamentals of our life.

Notes

1 Saint Thomas Archives. File on Father Andrew Craig Mead, Twelfth Rector.

2 Saint Thomas Archives. File on Father Mead.

3 Betsy Hughes Morris, *A History of the Church of the Advent* (Boston: Church of the Advent, 1995), pp. 122-31.

4 Saint Thomas Archives. File on Father Mead.

APPENDICES

APPENDIX 1 ❧ MUSIC TODAY AT SAINT THOMAS CHURCH

BY GERRE HANCOCK

Aℒℛℰ𝒜𝒟𝒴 with the completion of the splendid third church in 1870 there had begun a *crescendo* in the music program of Saint Thomas; it continues to the present day in the fourth church. The importance of music for liturgy was established at last, as the history of the parish demonstrates, and this integral relationship is continually being developed within the parish. There is a dual purpose in the music program of Saint Thomas that is now pursued daily and with fervent industry: music as art which enhances every public act of worship, and music as art which becomes in extra-liturgical events an outreach to the wider community.

From the birth of the parish up to the later nineteenth century, the position of Organist and Choirmaster saw a procession of incumbents whose average tenure was rather brief, perhaps not more than two or three years. This fact may indicate a certain lack of musical consciousness on the part of the parish in those days.

George William Warren, whose work here began in 1870 and lasted a full thirty years, quite possibly became the first musician to set a tone of professionalism in the music program of the parish. His reputation for seriousness of purpose is impressive. One remembers that the music in Episcopal churches of his day was often more operatic than ecclesiastical in nature, and his music, in fact, is not without an occasional reference to those hit composers of the day, Gilbert and Sullivan. If Dr. Warren's music occasionally reminds one of the theater, the skill of craft and sincerity of spirit that his music embodies is nonetheless striking. The fact that his compositions are performed in churches to this day gives some indication of their quality. George Warren's work as the active chief musician at Saint Thomas Church ended at the close of the nineteenth century, bringing to completion a career rich in creativity.

Like many of his successors, Dr. Warren was influential within his profession, both here and abroad. Within a younger circle of musicians who emulated him was William Macfarlane, who in 1900 succeeded his mentor. Mr. Macfarlane was the first who dreamed of a vested choir of men and boys for Saint Thomas Church that would sing the Anglican liturgies of the day on Fifth Avenue. It is well-known that he worked tirelessly to try and establish a boy choir; however, the time was not ready or right, and it befell his successor to develop the joyous work of the choral foundation as we know it today. Will Macfarlane was nevertheless a dazzling organ virtuoso and an imaginative composer whose works are widely performed even to this day. The idiom of his composition is perhaps a bit ripe by today's less sentimental standards; still, his music is compelling and rather exciting in its spontaneous and joyful nature. Like his predecessor, Mr. Macfarlane enjoyed popularity and admiration.

His departure in 1912 set the stage for an epiphany in music as worship, the advent of a musician who would help change the face of church music in America. Thomas Tertius Noble of York Minster, already a legend in his day, accepted the ringing challenge of the parish's beloved rector, Ernest Milmore Stires: to come to Saint Thomas Church and build a music establishment more worthy of the church's ambition in its worship and outreach by setting performance standards more in keeping with the nobility of the new building's architecture. Dr. Noble made clear to his new rector that, in order to build and maintain what he called a proper music program, a choir of men and boys was exactly suited to the Anglican Church and her liturgies. In order to build such a choir, a choir school was required to house and educate the boy choristers; since the early Middle Ages at Canterbury, Dr. Noble was fond of pointing out, such a practice had been standard both in England and on the continent. Dr. Noble was the subject of some wonderment and not a little scorn amongst his colleagues in Britain, for they were startled to think that a man of his stature would leave one of the prime posts in the Anglican Communion to come to the United States, a country better known for its cowboys than for its choirboys. One is impressed that, in his late forties, Dr. Noble would undertake such a move. The outcome of this transplantation is history, and today's present music foundation at Saint Thomas Church is entirely to his credit, the result of his vision.

Like Dr. Warren, Tertius Noble enjoyed a long tenure of some thirty years. During his days, the choristers could be seen trooping down the Avenue of the Americas, heading toward the NBC Studios, for example, where they performed with *maestro* Arturo Toscanini and his NBC Symphony, or up Seventh Avenue to Carnegie Hall, where they sang under the baton of the likes of Bruno Walter and the New York Philharmonic Orchestra. Here was begun a tradition which extends to this very day. Saint Thomas Choristers have sung with other orchestras and *maestri* as well, performing also at Lincoln Center with such orchestras as the Pittsburgh, the Los Angeles, the Cleveland, and the Brooklyn Philharmonic. Leonard Bernstein and Robert Shaw were especially fond of the choir, inviting them to join their orchestras in works new and old.

A strict disciplinarian, Dr. Noble was a compassionate choirmaster, committed to his younger charges and their welfare. He thought it all of a piece: discipline and conscientiousness provided their own rewards. Few of his lads who still return to the Choir School refrain from offering him tribute and thanks, all after more than half a century.

Succeeding Dr. Noble was another English-born musician of great accomplishment, T. Frederick H. Candlyn, a musician and pedagogue well-known throughout America as an outstanding conductor, composer, and trainer of boy choirs. His work in Albany was uniformly recognized with admiration. He built on the monumental work of T. Tertius Noble, and his Saint Thomas boys were thought to produce a beautiful tone. Such was his reputation that colleagues came from many corners to observe and work with Dr. Candlyn.

After almost ten years service to the parish, Dr. Candlyn retired, chiefly because of rapidly failing eyesight. In fact, his vision was so poor that he played most of the hymns, chants, canticles, and accompaniments for virtually all the church's services entirely from memory. What he lacked because of his poor sight, he more than made up for by his ability to keep very careful track of his choristers. His ability to toss a hymnal across a rehearsal room and barely miss, but entirely shake up, a hyperactive boy chorister is celebrated in legend to this very day. He too was regarded with much affection.

Acting as an interim organist at this juncture in the parish's history was an assistant organist and assistant headmaster whose glowing influence is still felt, Edward A. Wallace, now Organist and Choirmaster at the Church of Saint Michael and Saint George in St. Louis. Other prominent assistant organists served over the years, young musicians who enjoyed brilliant careers as musicians in the church. In fact, Will Macfarlane began his association with the Church as an assistant to Dr. Warren. G. Darlington Richards, assistant to Mr. Macfarlane, went on to serve at Trinity Church-on-the-Green in New Haven. Andrew Tietjen and Grover Oberle, assistant organists to Dr. Noble, enjoyed robust careers, serving prominent parishes in New York, Boston, and Norfolk. Dr. Noble's last assistant, Frank MacConnell, performed an exemplary service for half a century at Saint James' Church in Lancaster. One of Dr. Candlyn's assistant organists, Frederick W. Graf, has built much-admired music programs at, among other places, the cathedral in Bethlehem, Pennsylvania.

Dr. Noble, like his predecessors and successors, was in much demand as a teacher. Perhaps the most famous of all Dr. Noble's pupils was the internationally-known composer and conductor Gunther Schuller. Dr. Schuller began his musical life as a chorister in the Saint Thomas Choir School. He is fond of relating that he became a professional musician precisely because Dr. Noble became a mentor to him during the early days of his boyhood; he claims that he first began to learn the music literature of the Western world by turning pages at the organ console for "his musical father," as he affectionately remembers Tertius Noble. Another celebrated pupil, Paul Callaway, began his career at what is now All Saints Church in New York, then named the Chapel of Saint Thomas Church; a few years later, he became the *titulaire* at Saint Mark's Church, later a cathedral, in Grand Rapids, Michigan. The pinnacle of his career was the position of Organist and Choirmaster of Washington National Cathedral, where he established the superb music tradition at that hallowed place.

Yet another of Dr. Noble's supremely accomplished pupils is the composer, organist, choirmaster, and conductor, M. Searle Wright. Mr. Wright came to New York as a teenager for the express purpose of studying organ and composition with Tertius Noble. He went on to become the Organist and Choirmaster of what was then the Chapel of the Incarnation, now the Church of the Good Shepherd; perhaps the climax of his career was his tenure at Columbia University as University Organist and Master of the Music at St. Paul's Chapel, an Episcopal foundation in those days. He premiered many works, old and new, never before heard in this country. After the disturbing days of the late sixties on that campus, Mr. Wright went to Cincinnati, where he became Organist and Choirmaster of Christ Church Episcopal, now a cathedral. His so-called "retirement" finds him in his native town of Binghamton, where he is active as usual in church and university circles, still composing, still teaching, still spreading musical good cheer. Few teachers in this century, it is clear, have influenced the practice of church music to as great a degree as Dr. Noble, and none has been a stronger force for helping younger colleagues.

Of not a little interest is the number of boy choristers each of these musicians felt was required by the rather dry acoustic of the church at that time. In order to provide a good balance with the boys and with the countertenor, tenor, and bass sections of the choir, and to ensure a good projection of the choral sound throughout the nave, Dr. Noble began with twenty boys, but gradually increased the number to twenty-five and then to thirty. Dr. Candlyn thought thirty a good balance, but his successor believed the building's acoustic needed at least forty or maybe even as many as fifty boys to do the job. The issue was ultimately resolved only by extensive work on the ceiling of the church some years later.

From a distinguished career in Worcester at All Saints Church came William Self. His choir in that venerable parish had been touted and celebrated under his administration. He was in addition an active consultant to builders of pipe organs, working in close cooperation with G. Donald Harrison of the Aeolian-Skinner Organ Company in Boston. It was with Mr. Harrison that Mr. Self designed and built at Saint Thomas Church one of the more deeply admired pipe organs in this country, known as the Arents Organ after a generous parish family which not only supplied most of the contribution towards its cost, but also endowed its upkeep and maintenance to this very day. This miracle was accomplished within the third year of Mr. Self's tenure at Saint Thomas, an accomplishment which speaks loudly of his leadership and the parish's commitment to church music. Later altered radically, the original 1956 instrument is still renowned in the profession, its immortal sounds preserved on recordings for all to hear. This instrument, in its present incarnation, still sounds brilliantly with some original pipework from the Ernest M. Skinner Organ which Dr. Noble helped to design (even before his arrival on Fifth Avenue), some pipework from the G. Donald Harrison Organ, and much superb work by Gilbert F. Adams of Brooklyn, an alumnus of the Aeolian-Skinner firm. Daring in design, this instrument of more than 120 stops is actually two instruments, contained within the chancel of the church, playable from one console, the shell of which harks back to the inspired drawing-boards of Ralph Adams Cram and Bertram Grosvenor Goodhue. There are two major divisions of French design and two matching divisions of German-American design, all voiced with Swell and Pedal divisions to match; this instrument displays amazing virtuosity and flexibility and has served as a model for many instruments in this country and in Britain as well. The Brooklyn firm of Mann & Trupiano undertook the most recent and thorough-going restoration and refurbishment of this historic pipe organ; recently modern technology has been added to the instrument without changing its basic integrity.

A great lover of the French tradition in organ construction, William Self also had a keen interest in building an instrument that would play the great literature of the French Baroque; to this end, with his vestryman and friend, Edward C. Weist, he commissioned Mr. Adams to build such an instrument, the first of its kind in America at that time. This Loening Organ, named after the generous family who gave it, grew in scope from a small "French toy" of some sixteen stops to one of the *Grands Orgues* of more than fifty stops. Its virtues were enhanced by its location in the gallery of the liturgical west end, the place God must surely mean such instruments to reside within His Holy Church. Thus the organ spoke commandingly and sang right down the nave. To this day, lovers of organ music speak glowingly of this instrument.

A quarter of a century later, this instrument was replaced with a pipe organ of an entirely different style, and of a more modest specification, by the firm of Taylor & Boody Organbuilders of Staunton, Virginia. Unlike its French predecessor, this instrument of twenty-one stops finds its inspiration in models of organs in the Netherlands of the late seventeenth century. In fact, in *The New York Times* review of the dedication concert played by Frederick Swan (published on May 25, 1996), reference was made to the fact that the good burghers of New Amsterdam would find the sounds which this organ makes quite familiar to their ears, just as present New Yorkers delight in the sparkle and energy of its flutes and diapasons. This marvelous instrument plays all sorts and conditions of music, but the pipes produce the sound in works composed before 1800 or after 1950 with authenticity and verve seldom heard elsewhere. The instrument was re-christened the Loening-Hancock Organ, a name combining the names of the original donor and the present Organist and Master of Choristers, in commemoration of the latter's twenty-fifth anniversary as parish musician.

While Dr. Warren and Mr. Macfarlane were celebrity organists, Dr. Noble, an artist of equal if not even greater repute, began the tradition of presenting organ music on Sunday evenings after Evensong. Many a music-lover delighted in his playing of literature for the organ and, most remarkably, in his transcriptions of orchestral and operatic works which he played from full and open orchestra score. There are those who still relate their ecstatic experience of hearing him play his version of Wagner's Good Friday music from *Parsifal* on Palm Sunday afternoon. Thus began the Organ Recital Series which continues to this day. Additionally, for varying occasions and in concert, great musicians from around the world have performed in this series. Joseph Bonnet, Marcel Dupré (who also recorded here on the 1956 organ), E. Power Biggs, Maurice Duruflé, and a host of other organ virtuosi have all played the highly touted Saint Thomas instruments.

After a tenure of seventeen remarkable years, Mr. Self began a series of retirements which led him to leave his unmistakable mark in parish churches in Utica, Rye, and Worcester. Ever loyal and dedicated to Saint Thomas Church and its Choir School, Mr. Self is missed by parishioner and alumnus alike. Under him the choir had visited West Point, Annapolis, and the Metropolitan Opera, and had sung at the installation of Presiding Bishop Hines and at the seventy-fifth birthday of Igor Stravinsky.

Mr. Self's first assistant organist was, as we have noted, Edward Wallace. Following him were George Decker, who became chief musician at the cathedral in Syracuse; Arnold Ostlund Jr., who succeeded to the post of organist of the Plymouth Church of the Pilgrims in Brooklyn; and Frederick Grimes, who succeeded to the post of Director of Music at the Lutheran Church of the Holy Trinity in New York. Bradley Hull left Saint Thomas Church to become organist at Grace Church in Brooklyn Heights.

Thus did the tradition continue whereby the parish sent out into the world young musical apostles who bear the mantles of Warren and Noble, in what was by then widely recognized as "the Saint Thomas Tradition."

I was called in 1971 by the tenth rector, the Reverend Frederick M. Morris, to become its twentieth Organist and Choirmaster. A mild curiosity prompts the observation that musicians early in the history of Saint Thomas enjoyed an average tenure of about seven years while that average tenure during the last century and a quarter has been more than twenty years. What all this means is open to interpretation by numerologist and philosopher alike – dare one conjecture an increased seriousness of purpose coupled with the space of years required to work toward ever-increasing goals? But this is a question for theologians and musicologists to ponder during the next 175 years! Dr. Morris was a rector for whom one wanted to achieve the very best in music and the very highest in musical standards. While he professed musical ineptitude, his modesty disguised a sensitive ear for the vocal and organ contributions to the parish worship. He brought out the very best in his staff.

During my many years at Saint Thomas, my associates and I have made every effort to build the music ministry here upon the great foundations laid by those master musicians from 1870 onward. For example, one of the first tasks at hand was to increase the repertory of music available for the choir to sing, adding works from an even broader and wider historical and liturgical range of musical expression.

Immediately in this endeavor, extensive attention was given to developing the chant, both Anglican and Gregorian; this musical form, unique to the Christian Church, is the very bedrock of the Church's music. From here the quest for an ever-growing repertory naturally looked toward the music of the Renaissance, both continental and British, Roman Catholic and Anglican. During the early days of Dr. Noble's career on Fifth Avenue, for example, he regularly inspected new gifts and acquisitions of old manuscripts to the New York Public Library, just arrived from Europe, transcribing them for performance in Saint Thomas Church long before they were published or even thought suitable for modern congregations. Inspired by this example, every new publication now is greeted with the same enthusiasm and with the ever-present hope that such music, old and new, might enhance the worship of Almighty God, be it Tallis or Tippett, Byrd or Britten, Purcell or Parry, Bach or Brubeck, Brahms or Bernstein, Stanford or Stravinsky. Provided the music suits that one-and-only sound, the unchanged boy soprano's voice, and that one-and-only moment, the very presence of Our Lord in His Church, new works are assayed; some remain, others are replaced during the passage of years.

The parish's enterprise in commissioning new musical works from outstanding composers has borne much fruit during the past few decades. Of course, some of the parish musicians have themselves composed works for the church. As we have seen, Warren and Macfarlane left us solid works which are frequently performed, and Noble and Candlyn were prolific writers of music for the church. I have composed many works for choirs, brass instruments, organs, and orchestras far and wide. In celebration of the Choir School's Fiftieth Anniversary, Randall Thompson was commissioned to write a delectable work for treble voices, "The Place of the Blest." During the past few years, Gunther Schuller, about whom we learned earlier, and Conrad Susa each composed stunning settings of the Evening Canticles for the choir. Ned Rorem has written two works on commission for Saint Thomas Church.

All this flurry of activity has led quite naturally to recording projects which have been completed at the rate of about one album per year, no less than fifteen of them being in print at this time. The choir and organs of Saint Thomas have been featured on discs – recorded by the American firm of Gothic Records, the American/Austrian firm of Koch International, and the British firms of Decca/Argo and Priory Records – which exemplify the repertory of our liturgies in chant and canticle and anthem. Joining artists of other styles, such as opera stars Leontyne Price and Jessye Norman as well as singing star Judy Collins, in recording projects has been a treat not available to many choirs.

An intriguing piece of work with the composer and singer Carley Simon was created in the late eighties. Miss Simon was asked to compose the score for the Hollywood film *Working Girl*. Having visited Saint Thomas Church for Evensong on several occasions, she fell in love with the sound of the choir and wrote some very beautiful songs for the film especially intended for the quality of its voices. The final result in the movie was altered somewhat from the original sound track, but that recording retains the Choir's singing as she intended. In fact, the most popular song from the picture, "Let the River Run" (also known as "The Wall Street Hymn"), won the Oscar that year for Best Song Composed for a Film.

With the express purpose of extending the parish's outreach to a wider community, a Concert Series was begun in the early seventies. Works that are just right for the time-honored choral forces of men and boys, the historical precedent of which is abundant and, indeed, the norm until relatively recently in Western music history, have been featured. From settings of the Passion of Our Lord by the Renaissance and Baroque composers such as Schütz and Bach to the celebrated and always-popular *Messiah* by Handel, masterpieces by Purcell, Fauré, Bernstein, Walton, Stravinsky, and many other composers have been performed within the exquisite architectural setting of Dr. Cram's edifice – the sort of setting, visual and acoustical, for which these works were intended. The list of works performed with such distinguished instrumental ensembles as the Orchestra of Saint Luke's and with period or early instrument groups such as Concert Royal and The New York Collegium would be of considerable length. Performed regularly are the afore-mentioned Passion settings by the great Cantor, Johann Sebastian Bach, of both Saints Matthew and John, as well as that master's *Mass in B minor, Magnificat in D*, and numerous cantatas and smaller Mass settings. George Frideric Handel (the German spelling of whose middle name I retain) is also represented by his stirring *Coronation Anthems* and his compelling oratorio *Israel in Egypt*. Also important are works of the woefully-neglected English composer Henry Purcell, which find pride of place in any Anglican musical community; here have been performed the *Ode for Saint Cecilia's Day, Te Deum, Jubilate Deo*, and *Coronation Anthems*, performed, as were the previously noted Baroque works of Bach and Handel, with Concert Royal. *Requiem* settings by such diverse composers as Victoria, Michael Haydn, Mozart, and Fauré are

50. The Choir singing with Placido Domingo in 1985

heard several times, as are the classic settings of the Mass by composers of the Viennese school, including the Haydn brothers, Mozart, Schubert, and Beethoven. Holst's *Hymn of Jesus,* Britten's *Saint Nicholas,* Stravinsky's *Symphony of Psalms* and *Mass,* and Walton's *The Twelve* were all given energetic readings by chorus and orchestra alike. More recent works of such composers as Susa and Schuller were premiered as a part of the Concert Series. Financial support for the Series has come entirely from outside the parish's music budget; indeed, contributors to its Friends of Music number in the hundreds of faithful, appreciative, and devoted music lovers throughout the metropolitan area, followers of what is thought by many to be, as Father Andrew so succinctly put it, "a civilizing influence in a great city."

Visiting choirs from Britain such as those of the Chapels of King's College and of Saint John's, Cambridge; Westminster Abbey; Westminster Cathedral; Saint George's Chapel, Windsor Castle; and the cathedral choirs of Canterbury, Norwich, and London have all performed at Saint Thomas Church. The Vienna Boys' Choir, the *Tomanchor* from Leipzig, the *Kreuzchor* from Dresden, and the Copenhagen Royal Chapel Choir of Denmark have all sung here. The Saint Paul's Cathedral Choir sang daily services here in the year 2000 as part of a choir exchange with the Saint Thomas Choir, which had earlier sung daily services at their cathedral in London.

A world premiere which garnered international attention took place at Saint Thomas Church in 1985. The famous composer Andrew Lloyd Webber, known principally because of his works for the theatre, had just composed a colorful and moving setting of the ancient words of the *Requiem.* The composer requested that the Saint Thomas Choir perform alongside the Winchester Cathedral Choir, together with Placido Domingo (ill. 50) and the Orchestra of Saint Luke's, in singing and playing this exciting work in concert. The British Broadcasting Corporation sent a large crew from London to film and telecast this glittering occasion. Mr. Webber's father had been one of Britain's finest church musicians; commemorating Mr. Webber's father in this fashion in New York was indeed a moving occasion which commanded wide press coverage and afforded boy choristers from both sides of the Atlantic an opportunity to work together in a mighty venture.

The interest of the BBC was quite serious, for the Saint Thomas Choir was broadcast by means of live recordings throughout their world-wide network, beginning in Great Britain and Europe. Two services of Choral Evensong, with the Office sung by Father Andrew, were recorded each year live at the church for broadcast over many years.

Beginning in the mid-seventies, an annual workshop for church musicians was instituted at Saint Thomas. Each spring, during the post-Easter lull, a British musician with expertise in the training of boys' voices and in building ensembles with men's and boys' voices is brought to work with the Saint Thomas Choir in the presence of other choirmasters and organists who attend the workshop. The idea is primarily to learn by observing a master English musician work with American boys, all within the acoustical and liturgical setting of Saint Thomas Church. Luminaries from abroad who have led the conferences include, among others, Sir David Willcocks, Sir David Lumsden, Dr. George Guest, Dr. Stephen Cleobury, Dr. Christopher Robinson, and the very first director, Dr. Barry Rose.

International tours became a significant feature of the choir's life in the early 1980s when the choristers journeyed to England to participate in the Aldeburgh Festival at the invitation of Sir Peter Pears. At the same time, an invitation to sing daily services of Choral Evensong in the incomparably beautiful chapel of King's College in Cambridge arrived, marking the first time a choir from the United States was so honored. A few years later the choir returned to Cambridge, this time to be one of the spotlighted choirs for the Fourth International Congress of Organists; a concert in that same chapel was given, and afterward the choir remained in residence at Westminster Abbey, where the choristers sang services of daily Choral Evensong in that venerable place. Other appearances included singing at Saint John's Chapel, Cambridge, the "other Abbey" in Saint Alban's, and an appearance at the King's Lynn Festival. In the early nineties, the choir toured Italy and Austria, singing in the great cathedral churches of Venice, Trieste, Salzburg, and at the Augustinian Church in Vienna. A concert and a service of Festival Evensong were sung at the 1992 International Music Festival of Dublin, in the presence of the President of Ireland; the setting was the awe-inspiring Cathedral of Saint Patrick. These tours provide learning experiences for students of all ages, and, even more importantly, the opportunity to sing God's praises in churches in many places and for many audiences and congregations.

Several domestic tours have taken the choir to venues in great American cities. The Saint Thomas Choir was the choir-in-residence at the Third International Congress of Organists in Philadelphia; the choir also appeared at national conventions of the American Guild of Organists in both Washington and New York. At the time of the nation's Bicentennial celebrations, the choir sang in the presence of Queen Elizabeth II and President Ford in Washington Cathedral. Other tours have taken the singers to perform in concert in such cities as Boston, Hartford, Springfield, Charlotte, Orlando, Tampa, Sarasota, Naples (the Floridian version), Cincinnati, Houston, Denver, Los Angeles, San Francisco, Chicago, Detroit, Kansas City, Little Rock, and, of course, Lubbock, as well as in many other lovely halls and churches in the New Jersey, Connecticut, and New York regions. Many friends are cultivated on these colorful and educational sojourns.

At the present, besides offering a full annual concert series with orchestra, the Saint Thomas Choir of twelve men and eighteen selected boys sings at six weekly major worship services of the parish, preparing an astounding four hundred pieces of sacred music a year. The Gentlemen of the Choir are professional singers, and the boys attend the Saint Thomas Choir School, the only church-related residential choir school in the United States and one of only four similar schools remaining anywhere in the world.

During the course of almost every school year and liturgical season, the Saint Thomas Choir is invited to appear either on the radio or on television, usually on one of the major networks such as ABC, CBS, NBC, and Public Television and Radio. This is a true delight for the young musicians whose eyes feast on all the electronic equipment, lighting techniques, and interesting show folk. Rising before dawn to appear for makeup sessions seems not to bother in the least choristers of all ages, proving that the role of the performer is inherent in each and every one of them. The networks have come often to Saint Thomas Church to film and telecast live Services of Lessons and Carols and the thrilling Mass of Christmas Eve, when the irresistible Charpentier *Messe* for that mystical service is performed with an orchestra of period instruments, evoking the majesty of Notre Dame or the chapel at Versailles.

51. Gerre and Judith Hancock at the Arents Memorial Organ

Judith Hancock's brilliant playing of the accompaniments and the literature for the organ has throughout the years been an inspiration to countless worshipers and recital-goers (ill. 51). She has, as Associate Organist and Master of Choristers, set the standards in the organ field on this very same corner of Fifth Avenue. The excitement she brings to the music in transferring it from off the page, by means of the keyboard or the singers' voices, is well-known and admired by all. She strayed from this fold for a spell, taking charge of the music at two churches of St. James, one on Madison Avenue and the other (that of -the-Less) in Scarsdale, where she performed with her usual energy and dedication; this represents the very best in music for the church, and it is no secret that the parish owes her an incalculable debt, even though her work is usually invisible but joyfully audible.

Still other assisting musicians from the recent decades of Saint Thomas also enjoy conspicuous and influential successes in their various callings and places of worship, for all have become, like so many of their predecessors, leaders in the field of church music in America. Michael Kleinschmidt presides at the Church of All Saints, Ashmont, in Boston; Peter Stoltzfus, himself a successor to Mr. Ostlund, that former assistant organist of the parish, leads the music in worship and in concert at the celebrated Plymouth Church of the Pilgrims in Brooklyn; and Patrick Allen is Organist and Choirmaster of Grace Church Broadway in New York. The brilliant Thomas Bara now serves with enthusiasm and artistic grace as assistant organist on the music staff. The parish has been extraordinarily fortunate in sharing the worship of Our Lord in the context of such gorgeous music.

The music is enhanced by its acoustical environment, often called by experts "the most beautiful voice in the choir" or the "most important stop on the organ." This gift had to be claimed, if not wrenched, from the very stones of Saint Thomas Church, however. Dr. Cram had used light-weight and virtually indestructible tiles built by

Rafael Guastavino to construct the ceiling of the church's interior. Those tiles, enormously porous, absorbed both spoken and musical sound most efficiently, so that there was little reverberation within the building; in other words, the building did not sound as it looked. In less cultivated circles, Saint Thomas Church in those days was even described as "dead as a door nail" or, less elegantly still, as a "pillow factory." By fits and starts, experimental work was done from the mid-fifties in an attempt to seal the countless little pores in each tile. After the fortuitous discovery of a set of light fixture holes in the ceiling, occasioned by an earlier move of the chandeliers, suspended scaffolding operated by hydraulic lift was able to be used, which made this vast project literally within reach of skilled craftsmen in the early 1980s. In this way for the first time the glory of sound was created within this glorious church. Its acoustics are now widely admired in the world of music.

For twenty-four of the past twenty-nine years just described, the Reverend Canon John Andrew was the guiding light for music as worship at Saint Thomas Church. It was his vision, aesthetically and musically, which provided the inspiration for the effort to build upon the earlier visions of Dr. Stires and Dr. Noble and their successors. Father Andrew was fond of reminding his staff that he would never let them off or let them down, a stance which proved to be true through the decades of his leadership. No musical venture was too bold, no note too high or too low, no language too exotic or too plain, no work too long or too short, no organ chord too soft or too loud, for him to discourage. You who read these words are hearing this from his "Organgrinder" of many years, toward whom he showed such patience and appreciation and affection. One cannot help but observe that any rector who requests Stanford and Parry must be as great a rector as one could pray for, and that rector's name was John Gerald Barton Andrew.

This being said, one does not wonder at the anxiety caused by Father Andrew's departure. But, as the saying goes, God must surely love Saint Thomas Church very much, for He sent to us still another rector whose energy, imagination, wisdom, and style are carrying us onward in search of ever higher standards and new songs in what often seems a strange and barren land, this glorious and maddening and challenging and wonderful phenomenon called New York. Father Andrew Mead has already shown in a short time the depth, breadth, and width of his commitment to Saint Thomas Church and to its Choir School. Much has been accomplished with gratifying and startlingly refreshing results. The music of the parish has reflected these marvelous changes and is indeed enhanced by a Choir School supportive of its choir and its mission. Gordon Clem's distinguished tenure as headmaster brought academic and administrative respectability and renown to the School. Headmaster Gordon Roland-Adams, previously for ten years the headmaster of Westminster Abbey Choir School and brought to Saint Thomas by Father Mead, has given us new insight into the very nature of a choir school and indeed into why so much time, energy, and money are necessarily and happily given to such a monumental place and cause. Already in such a short time, Andrew Mead's rectorship looms bright and exemplary. Together with his wife Nancy, whose artistic gifts are remarkable, they are gladly received and much loved in this place. After all, any rector who requests the music of Gibbons and Weelkes must also be as great a rector as one could pray for, and that rector's name is Andrew Craig Mead.

APPENDIX 2 ❧ THE SAINT THOMAS CHOIR SCHOOL

BY KENNETH A. LOHF

IN COMPANY with such venerable religious institutions as Westminster Abbey, St. Paul's Cathedral in London, and King's College in Cambridge, Saint Thomas Church on Fifth Avenue in New York today supports one of the most distinguished choirs of men and boys in the Anglican world. The school's fifteen-story facility, designed by Harold Buttrick and completed in 1987, is in the heart of Manhattan. The only totally residential church choir school in North America and one of only four similar schools remaining in the world,[1] Saint Thomas Choir School now educates each year forty boys from the ages of eight through fourteen in the traditional academic subjects as well as in sports, and trains them as singers for services in the church for nine months of each year beginning in September and ending with graduation in early June. While theirs are rewarding lives, the boys maintain daily schedules that are full and busy, rising at seven in the morning and continuing with studies, classes, athletics, and rehearsals until nine in the evening. The music repertoire totals more than four hundred works each year, ranging from anthems and motets for each service to the *Messiah* sung at public concerts during the Christmas season. Why was the school founded and how has it developed into such a remarkable institution? It is necessary first to situate the founding of the Choir School within the total history of the parish.[2]

From the time of its founding in 1919, it has taken eight decades to bring the school to its present level of excellence. The two earliest Saint Thomas Churches at Broadway and Houston Street, among the first Gothic structures in New York, were modest by present-day standards. There was an organ in the gallery facing the altar, solo singers, and eventually a choir of men and women to sing at services. Despite rebuilding and repair, debts and mortgages, the church by the 1850s was providing funds for the music program approaching approximately one-fifth of its entire annual budget, an indication of the growing importance of music to the parish. After the congregation outgrew the second church building, Dr. William F. Morgan preached the final service in the church on Houston Street on Easter Day, 1866, and the homeless congregation was invited to worship at Grace Church while a new location was sought farther uptown.

The rector and the vestry finally decided on a large lot on the corner of Fifth Avenue and West Fifty-third Street. Because much of this area was on the verge of development for residential and, later, for business purposes, the selection of this site was an act of faith. A temporary chapel was constructed in the center of the area that was to become the nave of the new church, the cornerstone was laid on October 14, 1868, with appropriate ceremonies by the Rt. Rev. Horatio Potter, Bishop of New York, and on October 6, 1870, the church was opened for divine worship. This third Saint Thomas Church, an imposing structure designed in neo-Gothic style by Richard Upjohn (who had also designed Trinity Church), was situated at one of the best locations in the city at the time, and its monumentality suggested a cathedral rather than a parish church. The organist appointed for the new church, the accomplished Dr. George William Warren, was a strong indication that the rector, Dr. William F. Morgan, and the vestry had determined to have in their new church the best music obtainable. Dr. Warren carefully selected a quartet of professional soloists and a volunteer double chorus of some forty men and women and brought the music of the church to new heights. A collection of forty-seven hymn tunes with texts, *Hymns and Tunes as Sung at St. Thomas's Church, New York*, written by Dr. Warren, was published in 1888. Dr. Warren also taught singing to the boys and girls in the Sunday School, and one can conclude that their rehearsals were the very beginnings of the movement toward the full choir of men and boys for which Saint Thomas was to become well-known, even famous, in the next generation. Much beloved and respected, Dr. Warren, after thirty years of service, retired in 1900.

The achievements that the third Saint Thomas Church inspired were short-lived. In the summer of 1905 a large fire virtually leveled the church building that so many parishioners and friends had, by their contributions and hard work, brought into being. The William F. Morgan altar, the John La Farge murals, and the statuary of Augustus Saint-Gaudens were all destroyed. Dr. Ernest M. Stires, rector since 1901, and a committee appointed by the vestry to investigate the damage and to make a recommendation for the future of Saint Thomas concluded that an entirely new church constructed with more suitable stone should be built. Dr. Stires never wavered in his conviction that the new church should be built on the old site. It was to be a great building which would stand in the midst of fashion and commerce, an enduring witness to the faith of the Gospel. Designed by Ralph Adams Cram and Bertram Grosvenor Goodhue in the Gothic style, an impressive new edifice began to rise in 1911. The cornerstone was laid on November 21, 1911, and the first service was held in the fourth Saint Thomas Church on October 4, 1913.

As early as 1902, Mr. William C. Macfarlane, a highly respected concert organist who had served as assistant organist at Saint Thomas under Dr. Warren and been appointed to succeed him, expressed the need to establish a choir school to provide stable choir membership and thereby gain the adequate rehearsal time needed to attempt a fuller repertoire of Anglican church music. Mr. Macfarlane had established a vested choir of men and boys in 1902, leading him to comment:

> the feeling that the choir should be put on a permanent basis by the founding of a Choir School is becoming stronger. At present the boys are gathered from all parts of the city, and a number of boys consume from two to three hours to come and go. This makes impossible frequent rehearsals. Young minds and voices need daily attention, regular and frequent hours of study should be provided.[3]

Moving beyond the Victorian church music favored by his predecessors, Mr. Macfarlane introduced the choir to the music of the early twentieth century. In the autumn of 1912, however, the year before the new church was opened for worship, Mr. Macfarlane, Organist and Choirmaster for fifteen years, resigned to take a position as municipal organist in Portland, Maine.

An opening for this position now gave the vestry, in its search for a notable successor, the opportunity to think in large terms commensurate with the developing grandeur of the soon-to-open new church. A fortuitous circumstance presented itself. One of the great organists and choirmasters of the day, Dr. T. Tertius Noble, happened to be in the United States to give a series of organ recitals. Members of the vestry contacted him and the rector then invited him to come to St Thomas for a meeting. Shortly thereafter, Dr. Noble was called to become the organist at Saint Thomas Church, and he accepted. Dr. Noble had studied composition with Sir Charles V. Stanford and served as his assistant at Trinity College, Cambridge, before becoming Organist and Choirmaster of Ely Cathedral and then York Minster. The musician with this impressive experience arrived to take up his duties at Saint Thomas in May of 1913.

Dr. Noble's tenure as organist at York, one of the major cathedral institutions in the British Isles, and his reputation for developing a superb choir of men and boys, made him well suited to face the challenges that lay ahead at Saint Thomas. The rector and the music committee of the vestry were elated with his acceptance. The rector, Dr. Stires, wrote: "It is not too much to hope that [Dr. Noble's] coming to St. Thomas's will mean not only the uplifting of our hearts by his great ability and splendid spirit, but that it will mean almost as much for the cause of church music in the United States. Indeed, many organists and choirmasters in this country have with utmost generosity already expressed this belief."[4] Brought up in the English Cathedral tradition of church music, Dr. Noble did, indeed, raise the level of the church's music to a high peak of excellence. In writing of Dr. Noble's appointment, the rector was also justifiably optimistic: "His intelligence and energy, coupled with a real understanding and sympathy, will soon produce a remarkable choir. His methods are quiet and thorough; they are certain to be crowned with great success. . . ."[5]

Noble was considered one of the foremost composers of church music, and it was not long before the choir of some forty boys and twenty-five adults was singing Noble's anthems and masses at Sunday services, as well as those by William Boyce, Henry Purcell, C. V. Stanford, and S. S. Wesley, along with Brahms, Handel, and Mendelssohn, among others. His achievements were highly admired because, in the words of Dale L. Adelmann, Noble

> was more than a consummate musician. He was acutely aware that music in worship is a means to a higher end, and that music ought to function in harmony with the other arts to achieve that end. At the outset of his tenure at Saint Thomas he wrote, "it will be my earnest endeavor to make the service not only beautiful from a musical standpoint, but above all devotional and spiritual." Upon his retirement he summed up his basic belief thus: "The purpose of church music is to stimulate a truly devotional attitude in the congregation; and this can be achieved only by creating a more than ordinary quality of beauty."[6]

The library of the choir was growing significantly as huge quantities of new music were added to the repertoire. Through more intensive rehearsals Dr. Noble raised the singing of the choir to a high level of excellence. He became readily known for bringing the English cathedral tradition to Saint Thomas, and this has remained the style and the purpose of music at the church ever since. After only two years of Dr. Noble's work, the rector wrote that he was "rendering service beyond our power adequately to praise. His ability, his fine spirit and the beauty of his compositions have endeared him to the parish, and it is a deep satisfaction to know that he feels as though we have belonged to each other always."[7]

Responding to the many suggestions that Saint Thomas found a choir school, Dr. Stires in 1913 pointed out that, of the three key geographical areas for the Episcopal Church in Manhattan, both the Cathedral of St. John the Divine and Grace Church had established such schools. Dr. Noble added his strong opinion to the need frequently expressed for regular daily rehearsals and stability in attendance, and in 1915 he wrote: "There are many difficulties which face us. The chief one is obtaining sufficient rehearsals for the boys. As far as I can see, there is only one solution of this difficult problem – a Choir School. Once this is secured, and I sincerely trust that my hopes will soon be realized, work will be very much easier, and the results far better."[8] At the time of his appointment, Dr. Noble had made it clear that a choir school would need to be established to achieve the musical standard that all concerned wanted for the parish. The rector and vestry had assured him that he would have such a school. At a vestry meeting in 1918, the rector and three members of the music committee were appointed as a special committee to investigate the possibility of establishing a choir school. The committee's decision was positive but contingent on finding thirty parishioners each of whom would provide a scholarship of $500 every year for five years. The vestry would then assume responsibility for the rent of a suitable house to contain the school. Happily, this was accomplished.

In the school's archive there is an undated draft of a letter written by Dr. Noble to prospective parents in which he outlines several of the advantages to being a student at the school which is shortly to open: the boys will be divided into small classes to ensure that special attention is given to every student; the teaching staff will consist of a headmaster and an assistant master, chosen because of their accomplishments and experience in teaching boys of ages ten to fifteen; the moral and physical training will be "thoroughly looked after" so that there is a "symmetrical development" of each boy; the headmaster's wife will act as house mother; the boy's musical education will be thorough, with at least an hour each day "devoted to singing, elementary theory of music, and solo work; this department will be in the hands of the Choir Master and his assistant;" and, last but not of least importance, "This thorough scholastic and musical education will be given in a homelike atmosphere, in a charming house situated on West Fifty-fifth Street, where the same principles of good manners and good breeding, that you would insist upon at home, will be carried out."

On March 3, 1919, the Choir School was officially opened at 123 West Fifty-fifth Street with an enrollment of twenty-one boys, fourteen of whom were boarding pupils. "Those who have visited the school know what a beautiful home it is," wrote Dr. Noble, "and I am sure must have noticed what a happy set of boys we have. I need not say what an enormous advantage it is to our music in having the school for I am able to teach these children daily and I find that the more they sing, the more they love it."[9] The school was administered by the Music Committee of the vestry, chaired by

Charles Steele and also including Robert B. Dodson and William H. Truesdale as members. Mr. Clarence Jack Smith was chosen as the first headmaster.

In the early years there was a modest staff consisting of two resident teachers, a house mother, and Dr. Noble. The house on West Fifty-fifth Street was soon found to be too small and cramped for twenty boys and the teaching and maintenance staffs. Consequently, within a short time there were appeals from the Music Committee and the vestry for additional space, a permanent endowment, and facilities that would allow a more logical organization for educational purposes. Dr. Stires summarized the situation in 1922:

> The opening of the Choir School four years ago has been fully justified. Not only has our music reached a higher level, but those who are in frequent contact with our choir-boys have observed their steady gain in all good qualities. The School has lived in a rented house, 123 West 55th Street, all too small for twenty boys, two masters, house-mother and servants. Moreover, for the proper rendering of the music in our large church we have found it necessary to enlarge the number of boys in the Choir School from twenty to thirty. Two serious problems confronted us: the necessity of more room for the School, and the need of ten more scholarships for the support of the new boys.[10]

These needs were also much in the mind of the rector and the vestry. With the approach of the parish's centenary, which would occur in December of 1923, they were seriously addressed.

Solutions could not have been found so quickly and easily without the extraordinary work of three individuals. Already mentioned were the forceful commitment and leadership of Dr. Stires and the sensitive insights and organizational skills of Dr. Noble. However, of equal importance in this trio was Charles Steele, an astute railroad lawyer and business associate of J. P. Morgan, for it was his keen interest and support that inspired each of the planning stages in the founding and early development of the school (ill. 30). A member of the vestry from 1905 to 1915 and a warden from 1915 to 1939, Mr. Steele served as chair of the Music Committee which initially administered the school, and it was he who purchased for the use of the Choir School and presented to the parish the two houses at 121 and 123 West Fifty-fifth Street. He underwrote the costs of remodeling those buildings to make them effective for school use and donated the ten additional scholarships for boys needed to bring the choir up to full quota. When these gifts were tallied in the early 1920s it was found that he had given the single largest gift of funds that had been made to the parish up to that time. Moreover, in 1925 Mr. Steele wrote to the vestry to inform them that he was turning over securities valued at $275,000 as an endowment fund for the school. The gift was gratefully accepted and appropriately named "The Charles Steele Foundation." Dr. Stires, Dr. Noble, and Mr. Steele are to be remembered and honored as the true founders of this Choir School.

The commemoration of the centenary of the parish was held in the week of December 2-9, 1923. The theme in the words of the rector was the "duty of St. Thomas Church to lay deep foundations for the extension of our work for the city, for the nation and for the cause of God in all the world."[11] The importance and value of the work of the Choir School was undoubtedly in the thoughts of Dr. Stires as he wrote those words. Dr. Stires resigned from his position as rector in 1925 and was consecrated Bishop of Long Island. The following year the Rev. Roelif H. Brooks, who had been serving as rector of St. Paul's Church in Albany, was elected rector. His parish in Albany had been known for its missionary outreach and the quality of its musical services, both of which would serve the new rector well at the church on Fifth Avenue.

During the next several years the school curriculum was revised and the list of subjects offered was extended. By 1926 the boys were, in addition to the traditional subjects, taught penmanship, typewriting, mechanical drawing, and manual training; by 1930 physiology, ancient history, general science, and art were also included in the curriculum. A weekly school paper, titled the *Pioneer*, was started, and the school baseball team became part of the league that included the Cathedral School and Grace Church School. In 1927 the Saint Thomas team won the championship of the league. It should also be noted that the boys worked on the weekly newspaper, took hikes, performed in dramatic productions, attended Philharmonic concerts and Broadway shows, and, of course, enjoyed themselves at numerous parties hosted by the clergy and school staff. In spite of all these extra-curricular activities, there was also a marked improvement at the scholastic level, and on graduation the boys were accepted into such venerable schools as Trinity, Taft, Hotchkiss, and Kent, among others. Many of the graduates would become clergymen, lawyers, doctors, dentists, and business men, among other professions, and it must be noted that in the Second World War seventy-eight graduates served in various branches of the country's military services.

On March 15, 1931, Dr. Noble celebrated his fiftieth anniversary as an organist, and at all services on that Sunday the music consisted entirely of his own compositions. Dr. Brooks in his sermon spoke of the importance of music in worship and paid tribute to Dr. Noble's contributions to the cause of ecclesiastical music. The rector also announced that the vestry, in honor of Dr. Noble's fiftieth anniversary, had decided to raise a fund for the purpose of erecting a stained glass window in the north clerestory above the oak-carved organ screen. A year later, on February 28, 1932, at Evensong some seventy graduates joined the choir of fifty voices to sing at the unveiling of the stained glass window devoted to the subject of Music in honor of Dr. Noble's services with the Church of England and in America during the past half century. Placed over the organ screen where it still may be seen from the organ bench, the window was made possible by the rector and many good friends who contributed to this "glorious gift."[12] Designed by James Hogan, the various stained glass panels commemorated the music of, among others, St. Cecilia, Perotin, St. Gregory, Jan Sweelinck, Henry Purcell, Pierluigi da Palestrina, St. Ambrose, Johann Sebastian Bach, and George Frideric Handel. By letter the Archbishop of Canterbury informed Dr. Noble that he had been selected to receive the honorary Lambeth degree of Doctor of Music, and at Evensong on February 28, 1932, it was conferred upon him by William T. Manning, then Bishop of New York.

Funding for scholarships was always needed, so it was a great pleasure for the school to receive in 1933 a bequest from the late Miss Margaret Crane Hurlbut, as well as gifts establishing the Harold L. Gibbs Memorial Fund, the income from both of which was designated for scholarship aid in preparatory school and college to exceptionally deserving graduates of the Choir School. It was noted at the time that these funds represented a great step forward in the school's history of providing aid to able and ambitious boys to continue their educations. The receipt of these bequests caused Headmaster Charles Mead Benham to reflect on the school's aims in educating the current generation of students:

> Much is heard at the present time about the "aims of modern education," as though the fundamentals of a good education had greatly changed in recent years. Should not these aims still be, very briefly, to make "gentlemen and scholars" and to awaken in the individual the desire to be a useful member of society? It seems almost self-evident that if the spirit of religion and the welfare of our country are to be preserved, it must be through the inculcation in the very young of sound habits of thought, generous and humane impulses and a desire to aid in the work of the world.[13]

Headmaster from 1928 to 1942, Mr. Benham was closely involved in the placement of graduates at Phillips Exeter Academy, Williston Academy, and Choate School, among others, and in the planning for the erection of the much-needed addition to the school.

It had become apparent by the mid-1930s that the school buildings on West Fifty-fifth Street were inadequate to accommodate the growing student body, and the teaching staff had been suggesting a more extensive curriculum that would require greater space. The rector, the vestry, and Mr. Steele agreed on the need for larger quarters, and in 1937 the vestry voted to erect an addition on a lot facing West Fifty-sixth Street behind the existing buildings. For this purpose they were permitted to use the Kate L. Adams Fund for a fully equipped gymnasium that would occupy the largest space in the new structure. In addition to the gymnasium, the new building would contain a study hall and three classrooms. This new facility would also allow enlarged dormitory space in the old building for the forty boys who now made up the student body. The building was completed by March of 1938 and occupied soon thereafter. Mr. Steele, who had been presenting funds to the Choir School since 1918, made substantial additional gifts to complete and furnish this third building.

The late 1930s saw a series of changes in the cast of individuals whose concepts and support were responsible for the founding and dynamic growth of the school. On April 26, 1938, Dr. Noble completed his twenty-fifth year as Organist and Choirmaster and as teacher of music at the school, an event which was celebrated by a dinner given by the rector and vestry in his honor at the Union Club, and he openly expressed his wish to retire. His contributions to the music programs at the church and the school were of such high caliber that he had come to be regarded as one of the most distinguished figures in the history of the parish. On the occasion of his retirement in June of 1943, Dr. Noble expressed his gratitude: "I am more grateful to all who have done so much to make my life here such a happy one. I shall ever remember the affection of my boys and men who have stood by me loyally through these thirty years, happy years, which I shall never forget as long as I live."[14] The vestry adopted a resolution of appreciation for Dr. Noble's long service, appointed him "Organist emeritus," and voted him a pension. Dr. Brooks expressed the gratitude of the church and the choir school: "Too much credit cannot be given to Dr. Noble for the fine work he accomplished at St. Thomas – a work which has given the Parish a world-wide reputation for good church music."[15]

On June 23, 1943, the former rector, now Bishop Stires, wrote to Dr. Noble: "In America you were soon recognized as the Dean of ecclesiastical musicians and composers. This made me very proud. Indeed, during our twelve years of happy association, a great privilege for me, you were an infinite comfort to me in every part of my ministry. Your quick, sympathetic understanding; your reverent and radiant, strong and masterly spirit made your organ a truly celestial choir. We shall not hear the like again from any other person."[16] To this day Dr. Noble's hymn *Ora Labora* ("Come, labor on"), to words by Jane Laurie Borthwick, is traditionally sung in church on graduation Sunday. Moving and heartfelt, the hymn has set the tone for the graduates and the congregation of Saint Thomas in their study, their responsibility, and their worship.

The death of Charles Steele in 1939 was also a great loss, not only to the parish but especially to the Choir School, for it was his gifts of encouragement and support that were of critical importance in making possible the founding of the school. He continued his benefactions into the late 1930s, and at his death the vestry passed the following memorial minute: "As patron of music, he gave in 1922 the buildings which house the Choir School, and endowed the school; he caused another building to be erected in 1939 and increased the endowment, and in his will he made a further addition to its endowment, making his gifts to this object over a million dollars. More than once did he refer to the school as the best investment he had ever made. He called the choir boys his dividends."[17] Mr. Steele was often described as kindly in counsel, faithful in service, and noble of character. To this day his oil portrait hangs prominently in the school's dining hall to commemorate his extraordinary affection and loyalty (ill. 30).

Shortly after Dr. Noble's retirement, his friend and fellow Englishman Dr. T. Frederick H. Candlyn, was called to succeed him. Dr. Candlyn had been organist at St. Paul's Church in Albany, where he had served under the Rev. Roelif H. Brooks. Dr. Candlyn had built a nation-wide reputation there as organist, choirmaster, and composer. He also served as head of the music department at the State College for Teachers in Albany. This background in music and teaching would make him an ideal Organist and Choirmaster in the succession of distinguished musicians at Saint Thomas. He carried on the style of choral repertoire as it had been under Dr. Noble, and he introduced to Saint Thomas the church music of Ralph Vaughan Williams as well as his own compositions and his hymn and plainsong arrangements. The same rehearsal schedule as had existed under Dr. Noble was maintained, with additional singing lessons each week for boys new to the choir.

During Dr. Candlyn's tenure the choir became more active outside the church, appearing frequently on television and radio and at Carnegie Hall. The interest of the public in the choir helped maintain the church's reputation in the vanguard of fine church music. In 1948 an issue of *The New York Herald Tribune* carried a lengthy article on the choir devoted to their recent changeover to Elizabethan collars (called "modified cavalier ruffs," still the style of today) from the traditional Eton collars, a change made because the new sort was more comfortable and easier to launder. As Dale L. Adelmann remarked about this change, "Saint Thomas was a sufficiently fashionable parish that even the most trivial matters were observed with interest."[18]

The twenty-fifth anniversary of the Choir School occurred in 1943 during a period of change. In the academic year 1943-44 the Rev. James O. Carson Jr., who taught English and linguistics, served as headmaster, and for the period following, 1945-49, Mr. Leon D. Phillips was appointed to head the school. The country had emerged from the depression and, although the Second World War had affected the school, enrollment was increasing once again. The first issues of a new school paper, called "*Ioneer*," were printed and distributed, and a hobby club, a school band, and a student council were organized. On May 5, 1945, the birth date of founder and benefactor Charles Steele was marked with the first celebration of Founder's Day.

Because of increasing applications from prospective students, standards for the selection of students were discussed and revised in the mid-1940s. The ninth grade was dropped from the curriculum; the span of grades would now be from the fifth to the eighth grades, a change that lessened the spread between youngest and oldest age groups by one year. Some of the boys' voices at age fifteen were now no longer capable of singing soprano parts. The new standards noted that applicants for the boy choir were selected on the bases of voice potentiality, educational achievement, and personal maturity, qualities that, in general, remain the criteria for selection to the present day.

Modern methods were introduced in several courses in the late 1940s. The science teacher, Mr. Douglas A. Reed, planned a science course in which laboratory techniques were taught and used by the students. Mr. Reed also acquired educational films for the library collection and he and other faculty screened them in their courses. At the time, these teaching aids were relatively new for boys in the grades being taught at the school. Some military training on a voluntary basis was recommended in the immediate post-war years, and, since the boys were not able to attend a military school, a junior cadet corps, known as the Knickerbocker Greys, was established at the school in 1950 to teach elementary military training to twenty-nine boys who registered for the course. The following year the entire student body was enrolled in the Greys.

A significant modification in the curriculum occurred in 1951 when courses in art under the instructorship of a professionally trained artist were introduced. In addition, the library was being enlarged through gifts from parents and alumni, more than two hundred carefully selected new and used books were added to the stacks, and the cataloguing of the entire library was completed under the direction of the librarian and a student committee. The purpose of the school, that the students should excel in academic work as well as in music, remained firm. The headmaster, Mr. Henry B. Roney Jr., who taught mathematics and history, summed up the school's obligation in his 1951 annual report: "We firmly believe that it is the obligation of private boarding schools to justify their independence through careful, thoughtful leadership in establishing standards of excellence in all aspects of school life."[19]

At a special service of thanksgiving, the twenty-fifth anniversary of the rectorship of Dr. Brooks was celebrated on October 7, 1951. The Bishop of New York, the Rt. Rev. Horace W. B. Donegan, delivered the sermon and blessed the magnificent processional cross of gold, silver, and precious stones, given by the parishioners in gratitude for the rector's twenty-five years of faithful ministry and service. During this anniversary year school needs were discussed relating to the possible construction of another school building to provide space for a refectory and dormitories for forty boys. Property was subsequently purchased adjoining the existing school buildings on West Fifty-fifth Street and plans for the new structure were formally developed.

On September 30, 1954, Dr. Brooks, who had served Saint Thomas for twenty-five years, retired and was succeeded as rector on October 10 by the Rev. Frederick M. Morris, who had been serving as Dean of St. Mark's Cathedral, Minneapolis. In Dr. Morris's first annual report he outlined the difficulties that had been encountered in constructing the new building for the Choir School. The demolishing of the old school buildings at 121 and 123 West Fifty-fifth Street and of the two houses at 117 and 119 West Fifty-third Street was accomplished without incident, but a strike of building supply drivers halted work for more than two months during the summer. In spite of these labor difficulties, the education of the boys continued without interruption in the remaining classroom building on West Fifty-sixth Street. Fortunately, the Great Northern Hotel opposite the classroom building housed and fed the boys until the students, faculty, and staff were able to move into the new quarters in March 1954. The new building was dedicated by Dr. Brooks on May 26 of the same year.

Because of increasing infirmity and ill health, Dr. Candlyn, after serving for ten years, retired in 1953. In the summer of 1954, shortly after the new building was completed, Mr. William Self assumed the duties of Organist and Choirmaster. A well-known choir conductor and organist, as well as composer and teacher, Mr. Self had formerly served for twenty years at All Saints Episcopal Church, Worcester, Massachusetts, and had taught music at Clark University. The vestry was eager to appoint an Organist and Choirmaster who would lead the choir to the level of its former glory. Mr. Self had deservedly become known as one of the nation's outstanding experts in the training of boys' voices, and in Mr. Self's early years at Saint Thomas there was a notable rebirth in the tone and vigor of the boys' singing. Drawing from his previous music experience, Mr. Self introduced to the repertoire Russian and French anthems and other varied choral works.

The current enrollment included students from Louisiana, Georgia, Pennsylvania, Massachusetts, Rhode Island, Connecticut, New Jersey, and New York. There was no longer a restriction to accept only applicants living within commuting distance of New York City. With this change, the school now began to operate on a seven-day basis, which conformed to the schedule policies of other independent boarding schools. Headmaster Roney wrote that the Choir School "with its intensive religious program, excellent musical training, high academic standards and small classes, financial aid to students from families of moderate income, and the close association between students and faculty, offers a unique educational experience to the students who are selected for admission."[20] With the ratio of students to faculty now approximately four to one, it became possible for each student to benefit from working closely with faculty members, not only during classes, but in study assignments and extracurricular activities.

Concluding his fifth year as headmaster, Mr. Henry B. Roney Jr. resigned in 1955, and Mr. Robert H. Porter, who taught geography and history, was appointed to replace him. The new headmaster spent the summer months acquainting himself with the school's routines and concerns, much of his time being taken up with interviewing prospective faculty members and recruiting new students. When the thirty-sixth academic year began in September there was a full complement of forty boarding students and one day-boy, that number of students being the average that emerged as ideal for the school. An educational consultant was added to the staff and an experienced arts and crafts teacher came in weekly to give instruction. Also new was a testing and advisement consultant, a trained psychologist who would assist in the selection of boys to be admitted. Two additional masters took up residence, bringing the number of faculty up to ten. One of the new teachers was Mr. Gordon H. Clem, listed as science and mathematics teacher and director of athletics; he would eventually become headmaster in 1967.

To ensure that a high standard of academic excellence was being maintained, tests published by the Educational Records Bureau were now administered twice yearly to the boys. The results were tabulated and each boy was compared on a countrywide basis with other students in public and private schools. Also, each faculty member visited at least two independent schools to judge for himself the effectiveness of his own work and to discuss with those teachers new skills and techniques. In addition to a formal athletic program and participation in intra-mural sports events, the students increasingly benefited from the city's many cultural advantages, among them museums, parks, historical sites, and other field trips. The purpose of such a varied program was to achieve a constructive balance among class time, rehearsals, athletic events, and recreation, all of these programs planned with the advice of the rector and the Choir School Committee of the vestry.

The organization of the educational and social life of the school became more formal and active during the latter years of the 1950s. Entrance examinations continued to be thorough. Science was taught in all grades, and mathematical studies were in advance of most public school curricula. A full year of algebra was given in the eighth grade. Each boy was instructed in sacred studies, English, history, geography, French, and Latin. Because of endowment funds and contributions received from the church, the tuition was kept at a minimum. The 1957 annual cost for educating each boy was $2,000, while the portion of that cost charged to parents was only $400. This modest charge helped to assure that no boy of promise was excluded for financial reasons.

Faculty advisors were available to each boy at all times, and parents were informed of school activities through newsletters issued four times each year, improved and more detailed report cards and comment sheets, and personal letters. Following each marking period parents were invited to a tea at which time they were able to consult with faculty members concerning their boy's progress. Finally, an open house was held for parents and friends in February of each year at which there was a basketball game, displays in the classrooms, opportunities for conferences with faculty, dinner, and dramatic productions. And, of course, there were the usual classes and exams for the boys, daily choir rehearsals and occasional public concerts, a full round of athletics and extracurricular activities, and the abundant cultural life in the heart of Manhattan. An exhaustive life for boys aged nine through fourteen, it was a program that developed each one's character and won some scholarships at some of the finest independent schools in New York and along the east coast. In summation, Headmaster Porter wrote to the parish: "Today, the Rector and the Choir School Committee of the Vestry are dedicated to the task of guaranteeing that this school provide for the proper care and nurture of boys committed to our charge. The faculty is devoted to the task of assisting each student realize the very limits of his academic potential. May I urge you to be glad concerning the manner in which this school has fulfilled its responsibilities and to be proud of this vital institution within the life of St. Thomas Parish."[21]

On March 3, 1959, the Choir School reached the age of forty. During this anniversary year the school plant was enlarged by completing interior construction of the new building's fourth floor, which added rooms for the student council, administrative offices, faculty apartments, and redesigned and re-equipped kitchen and storage areas. These changes, it was believed, would provide adequate space for facilities required for the 1960s. The forty-second academic year opened with forty-four boarding students, the optimum number of boys that the enlarged quarters would now accommodate. The redesigned quarters, affecting the musical and academic programs significantly, brought the school to the same level as the most prominent choir schools in England and on the continent. As Headmaster Porter noted, "Here, all sing in the choir, all live at the school and all receive a rigorous classical education."[22]

In 1963, the assistant headmaster, Mr. Edward A. Wallace, guided the school during the illness of Mr. Porter, and Mr. Gordon H. Clem, who assisted in the running of the school, was appointed senior master in 1963 and assistant headmaster the following year when Mr. Wallace resigned. For the fifth year, the Men's Council sponsored the school's annual Gilbert and Sullivan operetta, a production of "The Gondoliers," an event which added a sizable sum to the Council's scholarship fund and provided at least two full annual scholarships. Most importantly, in 1964 the evaluation of the school by the Evaluation Committee of the Department of Christian Education recommended that the Choir School now be certified as "A School of the Diocese of New York." The Bishop of New York took the final action and signed the documents that accredited the school. The report of the Evaluation Committee expressed the impressions made on its members during its review:

> One of the outstanding impressions which the Committee gained from the visit
> was the quality of sincere religiously oriented community life within the school
> itself. The unselfconscious relationship between masters and pupils, and the
> family effect on the school of the married families living within the school all
> impressed us favorably. Added to this was an active prayer life within the school
> itself. The grace at table, varied and beautiful, the devotions in the dormitory,

conducted by the boys and masters, provided a very real religious activity for the students.[23]

Fifty boys registered at the school when it opened in September of 1964, forming the largest body of students ever recorded. Twelve of the boys were classified as "very superior" based on the accepted intelligence quotient. In 1965, the last year of Mr. Porter's tenure as headmaster, several important changes were made. The library was completely reorganized, with reference and related books shelved in the classrooms, and the very best fiction housed in the original library which now functioned as a reading room. To guide the student to think inductively and to develop his sense of reason, the science classes now had equipment and facilities that enabled the individual student to learn by personal experimentation. The Women of Saint Thomas provided funds to strengthen the library holdings, while the Fathers Club made it possible to send the boys and faculty to Incarnation Camp in Ivoryton, Connecticut, for two weeks in the spring and one week in the fall. Mr. Porter exclaimed that the boys, some for the first time, "swam, rowed, farmed and sang, sang, sang!" There were, of course, classes and an outdoor chapel service by the lake or at campfire "with heart-felt devotion to our good God." At camp, the students moved closer to a Christian community than ever before.

Mr. Porter resigned as headmaster at the end of the academic year in June of 1966 to become headmaster at St. Peter's School, Peekskill, New York, and the assistant headmaster, Mr. Gordon H. Clem, who had been at the school for twelve years, was appointed to succeed him on July 1, 1967. "I am sure," Mr. Porter wrote on the occasion of his own departure, "that Gordon Clem will provide inspired leadership and that he will blaze new trails of creative activity in the on-going life of this school."[24]

In the first year following Mr. Clem's appointment, a number of major changes were made in the academic program. An elective program, offered during the evenings, was initiated to augment the standard curriculum. Subjects taught were recreational mathematics, bridge, chess, art, calligraphy, astronomy, creative writing, wrestling, public speaking, Russian, stagecraft, and private instrumental work in piano, organ, violin, guitar, trumpet, trombone, and drums. Evening study halls were eliminated, and extended class periods were substituted which allowed faculty the option of assigning homework that could be done in the classroom when faculty would be available to help the student. A system of contracts (student projects, assigned or suggested by the student) was initiated. Classroom teaching was also reorganized so that, rather than using textbooks, students would learn from original sources, lectures, and discussions. Finally, a laboratory approach was employed in the teaching of mathematics. Also offered was a reading course for parents entitled "The Care and Nurture of the Intelligent Parent," and to keep abreast with current learning methods the school sought assistance in acquiring teaching-calculating machines and video-tape recordings. The headmaster and the faculty began to work with the Private School Scholarship Program, for which office space was made available at the school. The purpose of this program was to administer the placement of talented, disadvantaged youngsters in private schools.

In 1969, the church celebrated the fiftieth anniversary of the founding of the school with a service on Sunday, March 2. On this occasion a cantata for treble voices and chamber orchestra entitled "The Place of the Blest," commissioned and composed for the anniversary by the noted American composer, Randall Thompson, was sung. This anniversary offered the rector, headmaster, and vestry the opportunity to study the school and its services to its students, and from this study the headmaster reported that the school "resolved to move into the 70's with a commitment to excellence in our current program and to expand services to the musical community and to the people of New York City. It is our feeling that the production of glorious music and educational excellence can be effectively combined with community service."[25] Added to the elective courses this year were ceramics, welding, photography, film study, film making, cooking, oral interpretation of literature, museum trips, African-American literature, and play reading.

After seventeen years of commendable service as Organist and Choirmaster, Mr. Self retired in 1971 with the title "Organist emeritus." During his tenure the Loening Memorial Organ was installed in the east balcony of the church. Given in memory of Mrs. Albert Loening by her sons, the organ was dedicated on Sunday morning, November 23, 1969, with Bishop Donegan presiding. Mr. Self called it a brilliant instrument, one that would supplement and augment the Arents Memorial Organ in the main chancel; he foresaw that the two instruments together would make a major contribution to the musical world of New York. Dr. Morris commented: "The newer organ, although designed as a classical French instrument, has a quality which speaks to the preferences of modern youth and it has been interesting to see how many have been coming into the church to hear it."[26]

The departure of Mr. Self was an event of sadness to the parishioners, for his life at Saint Thomas was remembered with much affection and gratitude; he was devoted not only to the music program but also to the welfare of the entire parish. Mr. Self nominated his successor, Dr. Gerre Hancock, with strong enthusiasm. Dr. Hancock, who came to Saint Thomas from Christ Church, Cincinnati, brought to Fifth Avenue a brilliance at the organ keyboard and a genius on the choir podium. His knowledge of music covered a broad spectrum, but his special affinity for and understanding of the English church music repertoire began to transform, from the start of his tenure, both organ and choir music in the great space of Saint Thomas. Dr. Hancock's wife, Mrs. Judith Hancock, whose energy and ability lay in interpreting the impressive twentieth-century church music of France, was appointed assistant and later associate organist. They brought to the church the broadest range of music that it had ever known, and as a result the music program grew and flourished as it had during the era of Dr. T. Tertius Noble.

Within the first few years of his tenure at Saint Thomas, Dr. Hancock stated that his goals were to provide music of the highest quality and to extend the church's ministry of music into the community at large. This new choirmaster introduced into the many services the music of the rich and beautiful heritage of Anglican music from the seventeenth through the twentieth centuries. The second goal was realized through the number of public choir concerts that were given in a variety of venues, not only at Saint Thomas but also in such places as the First Presbyterian Church in New Canaan, Connecticut; at Carnegie Hall with the Pittsburgh Symphony Orchestra directed by William Steinberg; and on television and radio in New York. The choir's public face was definitely becoming known among New Yorkers.

In the spring of 1971, the vestry approved the formation of a Choir School Advisory Committee to assist the headmaster to guide the school in broadening the social life of the boys and to assist in the recruitment program. Membership of the committee was comprised of the rector, three members of the vestry, three parents of boys in the school, three alumni, three parents of alumni, and other concerned persons. The headmaster reported that the committee, which would meet four times a year, was to serve as a useful sounding board in evaluating present and proposed programs. This Advisory Committee was related to the Choir School Committee of the vestry through the several members who served on both bodies, thus facilitating communication and planning for the school. During this year the school expanded its program of sex education by offering a coeducational course in human sexuality, given to the boys of Saint Thomas Choir School and to the girls from the Spence School, also located in New York City. Using materials developed by the Unitarian Universalist Association, the course was led by two parents of the Choir School, the Rev. and Mrs. Neal Fawcett.

Before the end of 1971, a committee was formed to select and call a successor to the position of rector. Father John Andrew, who possessed a deep love for the music of the Anglican cathedral tradition, was chosen and came to Saint Thomas as rector shortly after the Hancocks, forming with them a dynamic music team. They illustrated the harmony of clergy and musicians working together to bring renewed life to the patterns of worship within the heritage of the Anglican Communion.

The 150th anniversary dinner, commemorating the founding of Saint Thomas Church, was held at the Plaza Hotel on October 17, 1973. More than five hundred guests attended, Bishop Paul Moore and Dr. Morris delivered talks, and the new rector observed that this anniversary gathering was sure testimony of the family feeling that produced such a remarkable atmosphere. On the Sunday before Christmas, the "Festival of Lessons and Carols," performed by Dr. Hancock and the choir, was filmed, and on Christmas day it was televised nationwide over the ABC-TV network.

In April of 1973, the Choir School was for the first time evaluated for accreditation by the New York State Association of Independent Schools. Chaired by Mr. David Hume, headmaster of St. David's School in New York City, the evaluation team spent the first three days of April visiting classes and consulting with students, faculty, vestry, and parents. The conclusion of the report was enthusiastic: "The Choir School is an extraordinary institution in every way. The curriculum is contemporary and well carried out. The faculty members relate to the boys with great respect and understanding. The quiet professionalism of the young choristers is enormously impressive. The faculty and boys are a rare example of a Christian community."[27]

The rector in his 1974 annual report praised the choir on the popularity of its

Christmas record which completely sold out and had to be reordered. "The Christmas record has gone all over the world," he wrote, "and we have had letters in from every place saying how beautifully the music on it was sung. Mr. and Mrs. Hancock and Mr. Gordon Clem and the faculty of the Choir School deserve our heartfelt gratitude."[28] A custodian on duty at the midnight Christmas Eve Eucharist reported that he lost count after the first four thousand worshipers were recorded, so there were doubtless immense crowds at Christmastime who heard the choir boys in the church itself as well as on the record.

Mr. Sidney H. Stires, Dr. Gerre Hancock, and the music committee of the vestry planned and launched a series of annual public concerts to be held on four Tuesday evenings in 1974 and 1975. This first series, "Bach at Saint Thomas," included the German composer's religious music sung by the boy sopranos and the choir accompanied by a Baroque chamber orchestra in a church setting for which the music was composed. Capacity crowds attended each concert and the press was encouraging; the concerts' initial success assured that the annual series would become a permanent part of the choir's schedule, as indeed it has been up to the present day. In 1975 a handbell choir was formed at the school, and an enthusiastic group performed during the Christmas and Easter seasons on handbells given to the school by a parishioner, Mrs. Grace Powers. Another popular recording, *Service of Lessons and Carols from St. Thomas*, was made by Dr. Hancock and the choristers and sold "briskly and profitably," as reported by the choirmaster.

During 1975 the school planned a promotional film about itself to be used for recruiting and fund-raising purposes the following year. Entitled "Sing Joyfully," the film was produced by Peter Rosen and shown in 1976 on television and to school and church groups throughout the country. A sensitive and moving film about the school, it met with considerable critical acclaim, earning a Cine Golden Eagle and being entered in international film festivals as the American representative in the documentary category.

In his report for 1976, Father Andrew praised with special forcefulness Mr. Clem and the "splendid flavor at the Choir School, an atmosphere of happy freedom and discipline which serves well to make the young gentlemen at the School into good students and leaders."[29] A request in the spring of 1976 to Father Andrew from the Dean of the National Cathedral in Washington, the Very Rev. Francis B. Sayre, asked if the young gentlemen of the choir, along with adult members, could come to that cathedral on July 8, a few days after the celebration of the American Bicentennial, when the American President and the Queen of England would visit there during Her Majesty's state visit to this country. The boys did indeed sing at the National Cathedral on that impressive day, and the rector commented: "The event, when it took place, was wonderfully happy and it is not immodest to say that the St. Thomas choir took a good deal of the burden of the music on that memorable day, with two solos being sung by our choristers, one adult and one boy soprano."[30]

The school was evaluated once again in 1977 by the New York State Association of Independent Schools, and, as in 1972, the comments were very positive and accreditation was granted. The Visiting Committee in its report found that "nowhere did we see students as passive recipients of information, but rather as active young men pursuing well defined educational goals."[31]

In his 1978 Rector's Letter in the *Yearbook*, Father Andrew noted the continuing excellence of the music at Saint Thomas and its standing on both sides of the Atlantic. He went on to praise Dr. and Mrs. Hancock for achieving in eight years "the transformation of the field of Anglican Church music in this country." The single area that was reported as troubling to the rector and vestry was the rising cost necessary to maintain the admirably high standards of teaching and music performance, a cost that because of inflation had gone beyond what might be safely budgeted without going into debt. He finally warned: "The School could go under. It is a horrifying thought and it must never happen." The headmaster, in the report that followed the rector's, announced that the church had retained the firm of Carl Shaver, Inc., to prepare a plan to raise funds for the Choir School and the music program of the church, and he pointed out that many parishioners had already given "generously of their time and their money to support the work of the Choir School." Within the year the parish's Treasure Chest (the gift shop in the parish house) and the Women of Saint Thomas sponsored fundraising events on behalf of the school. Approval was also granted to the school by the Internal Revenue Service to receive matching grants from corporations as an educational institution and as an arts institution.

The year 1980 was memorable for the choir because it was during this year's exciting concert tour in England that the boys and men of the choir sang a week's engagement of Evensong at the legendary and magnificent Chapel of King's College, Cambridge. The week held special significance for the Saint Thomas Choir since it was the first American choir invited to be in residence there. Father Andrew remarked with much pride that one of the greatest acknowledged choir directors in the world had said that "he considers our choir to be among the six top church choirs in this present decade."[32] The tour also included concerts at the Aldeburgh Festival of Music (responding to an invitation from Sir Peter Pears); St. John's, Smith Square, London; St. Alban's Cathedral; and Westminster Abbey, all of which were recounted in detail in the Saint Thomas Choir School's news sheet, *Cantate*, in an article written by one of the students, Nicholas Brownlow. Another honor can be mentioned: in 1982 the choir became the first choir outside of Britain ever to be broadcast live by the BBC to Europe.

During this period the school continued to host conferences and workshops for teachers of other schools, and the headmaster served on the boards of several education associations and conducted workshops in mathematics for the National Association of Independent Schools and the National Council of Teachers of Mathematics, among other organizations. Of singular importance in 1983 was the bequest received from the estate of Margaret W. Forshay of more than five million dollars designated for the benefit of the choir school. The income from this splendid endowment helped greatly to ease the immediate financial needs of the school, and in appreciation of the bequest a Margaret Forshay Memorial Concert was performed by the choir at the church in October of that year.

In the expanse of the eighty years during which the Choir School has existed, the 1980s must be viewed as a period equal in importance to the years of its founding. Before the 1980s the school was in a constant state of development, especially in the selection and growth of the student body, the securing of a motivated and talented faculty, the organization of the curriculum, the rehearsal for and the performance of the church's music, the enlargement and furnishing of the premises, the special musical responsibilities, and the life together as a family. The needs for each of these features were all considered in the major project of the decade, the design and construction of the school building that would become the choir's permanent home for many decades to come. And, once again, three individuals played key roles in this daunting project – Father Andrew, Mr. Clem, and the architect, Mr. Harold Buttrick.

Father Andrew announced in 1985 with much feeling and decisiveness that "1985 will be known as the Year of the Choir School. A decision was made to accept an offer by a firm of developers: to sell the site of the present school upon being offered an alternative site and a new school. . . . It has been an anxious but most deeply interesting time for your Rector and for the Vestry who had to make difficult and at times rather dangerous-seeming decisions."[33]

As will be remembered, the school buildings in 1985 were located on West Fifty-fifth Street. Until recently, the school had been comprised of three separate buildings joined together, and, because of the pressing need for additional space, the two buildings on West Fifty-fifth Street were demolished and a single four-story modern structure erected and connected to the remaining third building. Space for the library and the science and computer laboratories was still inadequate, the rooms for the boys were crowded, and apartments for the senior staff and faculty were insufficient to fulfill current needs. Many solutions had been suggested but no funds were available to make any major change. Possibilities seemed at a dead end until the Fisher Brothers offered to purchase the entire school site on West Fifty-fifth and Fifty-sixth Streets, to become the site of an office building. This purchase provided an alternate site for the construction of a new school on West Fifty-eighth Street between Broadway and Seventh Avenue, three blocks north and two blocks west. Quite simply, a piece of land would be provided and a new building constructed at virtually no cost to the church. The rector convinced the wardens and the vestry; the headmaster was delighted by the prospect of designing space for a modern school and braced himself for the issues and complexities that would arise during planning and construction; and the firm of Buttrick, White & Burtis was chosen as architects with Mr. Harold Buttrick, the father of a former Saint Thomas chorister, as the partner in charge. An architect practicing in New York since 1963, Mr. Buttrick had designed numerous buildings for educational and religious organizations, and continues to do so to this day.

The team was in place by the winter of 1985, and the much anticipated project began, with completion and the move-in time scheduled for August of 1987. Preparation of the site began in the winter of 1985, the site was ready for construction in June of 1986, and the school staff began to move from West Fifty-fifth Street to West Fifty-eighth Street in August of 1987 (pl. XXI). When the choristers returned from their summer holidays in September, it was to the new quarters where, having been assigned their rooms, they unpacked their bags. The spacious common rooms may have seemed strange at first, but were soon admired as handsome, efficient, and welcoming for study and singing.

Approaching this school building today, one is immediately aware of an unpretentious structure to the east, a traditional gray apartment building, and to the west a shabby red brick structure with dingy skylights. In the center between these two buildings is the Choir School, a sleek fifteen-story structure with limestone and gray-brick trim that rises six stories from the sidewalk before stepping back in a tower that culminates in a gabled roof housing the chapel in its crown. Architectural features include an "oculus" in the gable-roofed chapel and, lower down, the stylized, multi-paned "oriel" in the center of the street façade. Architect Harold Buttrick stated that the goal was to design "a Modern building that exhibits a tension between current technology and the humanist traditions of an English choir school."[34]

The building's setbacks reflect the purposes of the several components of the school: The first four floors contain the major components of the school, including the entry vestibule and main stair hall, recreation room, music practice rooms, school offices, parlor and dining hall, classrooms, and library. Floors five through seven house dormitory rooms and faculty apartments, linked in the center of the building by a three-story-high "great hall" which provides a family and community atmosphere situated in an urban setting. Floors eight through thirteen house apartments for clergy, headmaster, and choirmaster. The fourteenth floor is devoted to the chapel and storage space, and the basement and lower mezzanine levels house the gymnasium and exercise rooms. At the north end of the gymnasium is the rehearsal stage where the choir rehearses early each morning. The gymnasium was designed by the architect to have a resonance similar to that of the stone vaulting at Saint Thomas Church – which causes Dr. Hancock to sigh with satisfaction, "The acoustics are heavenly." The rector summed up the major living spaces: "The School has everything from a gymnasium to a chapel, with beautifully designed classrooms, themselves a tribute to the extraordinary sensitivity of the headmaster, as he cooperated with the architects. . . . It houses not only all the resident faculty and the domestic staff but the students and master of choristers with his wife and three clergy besides."[35]

The oak paneling chosen for the walls and wide-plank floors of the common rooms and the wooden trim throughout the entire building give the interior of the 80,000 square-foot structure a decidedly comfortable, mellow atmosphere. The paneling, the interior staircase, the setback façade and the architect's sensitivity have given the building a personality which the headmaster described as a unifying force, providing "a combination school and home."

The dedication of that new Choir School building was held on January 14, 1988, in the great hall. Father Andrew described the ceremony:

> The year began on a resounding note. We were visited by no less a person than the Archbishop of Canterbury who came to dedicate the new Choir School on January 14. Dr. Hancock had written a special setting for *Ecce Sacerdos Magnus!* – "Behold a Great High Priest!" – which the choristers sang to him as he appeared

on the balcony in the atrium with Bishop Paul Moore. The Senior Warden greeted him as did Andrew Zurcher, a senior chorister. Graciously and easily the Archbishop addressed Andrew in reply and we all were privileged to overhear the response. It was a superb beginning. . . .[36]

At this time in the proceedings Senior Warden Sidney Stires invited the Archbishop to dedicate the Choir School, which he proceeded to do with a prayer. Miss Anne J. Exline, Junior Warden, then thanked the Archbishop for his visit and, after remarks by the headmaster, the rector, and the chaplain, the Archbishop gave his blessing.

Now that the students, faculty, and staff had moved into the new school building on West Fifty-eighth Street, it was necessary to refine lines of communication between the school and the church and to consider administrative changes mandated by both the new premises and budgetary concerns. Mrs. Arnold Zurcher was appointed to the staff with the responsibility for student recruiting. Mrs. Judith Hancock resigned to accept the position of Organist and Choir Director at St. James' Church on Madison Avenue; as replacement, Mr. Michael Kleinschmidt, a recent graduate from Oberlin College and the University of Rochester, was appointed to succeed her at the beginning of 1990.

Early in October of 1992, Mr. Clem's many long years of service to the school were recognized. The rector wrote: "He is a deeply caring, fatherly, Christian man who has a vocation which he glorifies by living himself: to make truth, accuracy, and decency important to young souls. For that any priest should give unfeigned thanks to God, who has the privilege of working with someone like Gordon."[37] To celebrate the seventy-fifth anniversary of the school, which occurred in 1994, a series of recitals, concerts, and colloquia was held throughout the academic year, the climax of which was, according to the rector, "a magnificent celebration dinner and fund-raising event in November when a good sum of money was added to the Choir School funds. Much needed."[38]

The year 1995 became another one of great change. First, the vicar and chaplain to the school, Fr. Gary Fertig, after eighteen years at Saint Thomas, resigned to accept the post of rector at the Church of the Ascension in Chicago. Then, after graduation ceremonies in June, the headmaster of the school, Mr. Clem, retired and returned to his home in Massachusetts. As acting headmaster, Mr. Murray Lawrence was appointed for a two-year period until Mr. Clem's permanent successor could be selected by the wardens and the vestry. Finally, there was the momentous announcement from Father Andrew that he planned to retire as rector in June of 1996; he had given the announcement of his intentions a year in advance of his retirement so that the wardens and the vestry might have sufficient time to select a successor. One bit of good news was the appointment early in the year of Dr. Patrick Allen, a specialist in early church music, as the new associate organist. Dr. Allen would also assist in rehearsal, conducting, and teaching assignments.

Before the Choral Eucharist on Sunday, April 21, 1996, Warden Joan E. Hoffman, reporting for the search committee, announced to the congregation that the Rev. Andrew C. Mead had been voted by the vestry as the next rector of Saint Thomas Church. An advocate of high standards in the Anglican choral tradition from earlier periods, Father Mead had been rector for the past eleven years at the Church of the Advent in Boston where he had gained a wide reputation as a faithful priest. In his first Rector's Letter he wrote forcefully of "the beginning of a new day of closer collaboration between the Choir School and the Church"[39]

Among Father Mead's earliest decisions was the appointment of Mr. Gordon Roland-Adams as headmaster-elect of the school (ill. 52). Mr. Roland-Adams, who himself had been a boy chorister at Worcester Cathedral, had just finished a decade of distinguished leadership as headmaster of the Westminster Abbey Choir School, often called "our school's unique twin across the Atlantic." Quite by accident, Mr. Roland-Adams, during the Abbey Choir's concert at Saint Thomas, had heard of the church's search for a new headmaster. Shortly thereafter, he phoned the rector of Saint Thomas and had a meeting with him before leaving New York. Mr. Roland-Adams was called back to New York to meet with the search committee for a formal interview. After his return to London, Mr. Roland-Adams was offered the position.

52. Gordon Roland-Adams, Headmaster of the Choir School 1997–

Shortly after his appointment as headmaster, Mr. Roland-Adams selected Dr. Gregory Blackburn as assistant headmaster. Formerly head of the lower grades at the Browning School in New York, Dr. Blackburn moved to the school early in the summer of 1997 and began his work familiarizing himself with school records, discussing classwork and responsibilities with individual faculty members, and preparing for the fifth-grade English class that he would soon be teaching in addition to his administrative duties. Mr. Roland-Adams moved from London to the school in mid-August of 1997, and the administrative and teaching staffs were at full strength and in place in time for the opening of the fall semester.

Over the summer and in early autumn several significant proposed changes began to take form. After several years of construction, the need to continue and maintain the high standards of the education program was paramount. First of all, new faculty were added to strengthen several of the basic subject fields. It was also necessary to re-examine current recruitment practices and to devise new methods to make the school and its program better known to prospective students. Teaching schedules were studied so that time could be found for additional choir rehearsals early each day and on Saturday mornings. Because many boys' voices now tend to change earlier, it was essential to consider planning for the addition of a grade four to the current grades five through eight; this came to fruition in September of 1998 when the first grade-four class came into being with six students.

The evaluation committee of The New York State Association of Independent Schools visited Saint Thomas Church and School in April of 1998 and met with the rector, wardens, members of the vestry, and the Choir School Committee. Later in the year word was received from the Association that the school accreditation had been renewed for a ten-year period with an interim visit from the Committee to be made in five years. The Evaluation Committee's report, in concluding, commended the boys and the faculty for their "relaxed and purposeful attitude – as relaxed as it can be in the demanding and disciplined environment that a world class choir demands."

A world-class choir in a world-class city! New Yorkers and visitors to the city are known for their hurried and detached lifestyle, but there is one event on Sunday mornings and three times each week at which even New Yorkers become curious passersby (ill. 53). They quietly stop, stand aside, and stare in wonder and admiration. It is the procession of forty choir boys and their headmaster, each in a black cloak with the crest of the Saint Thomas Choir School on the left breast, walking briskly and with purpose in procession across West Fifty-seventh Street on their way to Saint Thomas Church to sing for the choral service. They are freshly-washed, bright and cheerful, and intent on their urban pilgrimage. Like their predecessors, they know that their presence in the choir stalls wearing cassocks of Royal Scarlet[40] and singing Byrd or Britten will help fulfill the glory of worship for themselves, their parish, and their God.

53. Choir boys walking along the street from school to service, led by their Headmaster

Notes

1 Other church-related residential choir schools are to be found at Westminster Abbey in London, Vienna in Austria, and Montserrat in Spain.

2 For the purpose of presenting a reasonably complete and continuous historical survey of the Saint Thomas Choir School here, some details of the broader history of the parish and its musical tradition are repeated in this essay. For the history of the Choir School in general, see the autobiography of William Self, who was Organist and Choirmaster from 1954 to 1971: William Self, *Mine Eyes Have Seen the Glory* (Worcester, MA: Worcester Chapter of the American Guild of Organists, 1990), especially chapters 34 and 35.

3 *Year Book* 1943, p. 9.

4 *Year Book* 1912, p. 9.

5 *Year Book* 1913, p. 11.

6 Unpublished master's thesis, "Music and Musicians at Saint Thomas Church" (Yale Institute of Sacred Music, May 1986), p. 24; copy on deposit in Saint Thomas Archives.

7 *Year Book* 1915, p 15.

8 *Year Book* 1915, pp 32-33; E. Clowes Chorley, *Manuscript History of St. Thomas Church* (unpublished manuscript in Saint Thomas Archives, 1943), p. 483.

9 *Year Book* 1919, p. 29.

10 *Year Book* 1922, pp. 11-12.

11 *Year Book* 1923, p 9.

12 *Year Book* 1932, pp. 32-33.

13 *Year Book* 1934, p. 31.

14 *Year Book* 1942, p. 47.

15 *Year Book* 1943, p. 10.

16 Saint Thomas Choir School Archive, Unpublished Memoirs of T. Tertius Noble, p. 275.

17 *Year Book* 1939, p. 15. See above, chapter 11, at note 30.

18 Unpublished master's thesis, "Music and Musicians at Saint Thomas Church," p. 39.

19 *Year Book* 1951, p. 55.

20 *Year Book* 1954, p. 43.

21 *Year Book* 1958, p. 37.

22 *Year Book* 1961, p. 40.

23 *Year Book* 1964, pp. 39-40.

24 *Year Book* 1966, p. 43.

25 *Year Book* 1969, p. 37.

26 *Year Book* 1969, p. 14.

27 *Year Book* 1973, pp. 50-51.

28 *Year Book* 1974, p. 10.

29 *Year Book* 1976, p. 12.

30 *Year Book* 1976, p. 12.

31 *Year Book* 1977, p. 13.

32 *Yearbook* 1980, p. 8. The title changed to the one word *Yearbook* in 1978.

33 *Yearbook* 1985, p. [3].

34 *Architectural Record*, November 1987, p. 116.

35 *Yearbook* 1987, p. [2].

36 *Yearbook* 1988, p. [1].

37 *Yearbook* 1992, p. [1].

38 *Yearbook* 1994, p. [1].

39 *Yearbook* 1996, p. [1]. See also Betty Hughes Morris, *A History of the Church of the Advent* (Boston: The Church of the Advent, 1995), pp. 122-31.

40 This color can be worn at Saint Thomas because it is not under English royal jurisdiction.

APPENDIX 3 ❧ HERALDRY AT SAINT THOMAS CHURCH

BY CANON HARRY E. KRAUSS

ONE OF THE FIRST THINGS visitors ask after they have begun to take in the splendor of the Great Reredos which graces the west wall of Saint Thomas Church is this: "Who are all of those figures?" Most can easily identify Our Lord and Our Lady, some quickly pick out General George Washington. But the identity of the remaining eighty-odd figures from the Bible and church history remains a mystery until the visitor picks up one of the charts that provide a key to the vast backdrop.

Yet there is another way in which the many divines can be identified, namely, by reading the heraldic shields that are near many of the figures just as if they were captions identifying the illustrations found in books or journals. In fact, in addition to other architectural features, subtleties, and splendors, the vast display of heraldry which is part of the fabric of Saint Thomas Church is not only remarkable, but it is also unique in the United States. The many shields that are immediately visible and the many which are tucked away in obscure corners are a major component of the dramatic decorative program of the building. It has been observed by F. R. Webber in his book *Church Symbolism* that "Among the many churches where we may find good use of symbolism in sculpture, wood carving, stained glass and murals one might list 'Saint Thomas's Church Fifth Avenue' in New York."[1] Such comments no doubt must have pleased the original designers, Bertram Grosvenor Goodhue and Ralph Adams Cram, for the latter once remarked: "Minor symbols coalesce into a great symbol, and so life is made richer, its significance and potentiality more clearly revealed."[2] Perhaps Dr. Cram intended his comment to apply to the symbolism that Goodhue lavished upon Saint Thomas Church.

Before we look more closely at the program of heraldic symbols which the architects created for this building, we ought to take a look at the origins and some of the particulars of heraldry itself, paying special attention to ecclesiastical heraldry, so that we can more fully appreciate the program to be seen at Saint Thomas Church. It has been observed that heraldry is both an art and a science,[3] involving not only principles of design and color but also regulations and orderly concepts developed through observation and experiment. Few societies down through time have not used some form of heraldry. While we in the West might be vaguely familiar with medieval shields decorated with various symbols, geometric designs, and colors, similar emblems have also been used for centuries in the East. The whole system of Japanese samurai devices called *mon* developed independently of western heraldry, in fact, but is of the same importance in Japanese society. The devices are found on early banners and field curtains, seals, and other property.

In the secular world, "heraldry," that is, the use of symbols as a means of identification, is thought to have had its genesis in the coming together of three ideas.[4] The first is the use of a device or emblem by an individual for identification. The children of Israel, the Romans, the Greeks, and the Egyptians, for example, used such means of identification. Next came the decorative idea of identifying ownership by the use of some kind of emblematic seal. Seals were of course used by kings and rulers on official decrees and documents, and the images on them came to have great significance as signs of power, authority, and influence. Lastly, the necessities of the battlefield made their contribution. Anyone who has been on a battlefield, even in modern times, knows how very difficult it can be in all of the confusion to determine to what fighting unit you belong and perhaps on what side you ought to be! A knight in battle array needed to be identified by some kind of device painted on his shield or on other equipment. Eventually, banners and guidons were made which also helped clarify who belonged where and to whom. The Garter Principal King of Arms in Great Britain, Peter Gwynn-Jones has pointed out that one of the earliest and most intriguing examples of heraldry is the famous Bayeux Tapestry which shows us the activity of the Norman Conquest of England in 1066.[5] Not only do we see knights bearing shields on which various emblems and designs are shown, but we also see lance flags similarly decorated. The presence of these items on the tapestry does not necessarily signify the birth of heraldry, but it certainly gives some hint of what was yet to come. The first generally accepted instance of heraldry in western Europe comes to light in 1127 when King Henry I invested his son-in-law, Geoffrey Plantagenet, with a blue shield charged with little lions of gold. Geoffrey's tomb at the cathedral at Le Mans even shows this early heraldic device.[6] In ways such as this, the three ideas for using symbols as means of identification came together and a system was born which worked rather well. Soon heraldry was used to identify personal property of all sorts.

At the same time, a particular and peculiar heraldic terminology developed. As a result, reading a grant of arms can be quite a challenge, for such grants are described in words of medieval and obscure origins. An everyday word such as "blue" becomes "azure," while "red" is "gules." A "pile" is not a heap of something but a rectangular shape issuing from the top, base, or sides of the shield. "Barry" is not a man's name, but an even series of horizontal bands. Customs, rules, and strict laws were created to govern the choosing and use of symbols and "the granting of arms" became the privilege of the monarchy or of institutions such as colleges of arms which existed at the pleasure of the monarch. The establishment of the College of Arms in England in 1484 was an effort both to ensure the proper use of arms and to ensure that such arms would be under royal authority. In fact, the rules and regulation of heraldry became a matter of international concern, as similar developments took place on the continent. Although it commands rather limited interest in our own time, heraldry still surrounds us and we are better educated when we know something about it. It actually embodies some principles which are not only contemporary, but are also respectful of modern ideas of property and of individual rights. "It is the birthright of any human being to bear names and signs which distinguish him from another person. This right is limited by the corresponding rights of others, and it is clearly inadmissible for someone to appropriate the emblems of rank, office or dignity to which he is not entitled."[7]

Because Saint Thomas Church is located in the United States, it seems right that some reference ought to be made to the place of "regulated heraldry" on these shores. It began with a probable grant to the City and Corporation of Raleigh in Virginia in 1586,[8] only rough drafts of which seem to have survived. By 1662, a seal for Virginia was issued. The first petition for a grant was received from a resident in North America, Francis Nicholson, "Captain General and Governor in Chief of Their Majesty's Province in Maryland," in 1693-94. In 1705, a Carolina Herald was appointed. There is a brief though rich history of grants of arms in the seventeenth century, but not surprisingly the story slows down considerably after 1775-76. For the purpose of this essay, we pick up the story with a series of honorary grants, which are the only sort allowed by the American Constitution and which began to occur in the 1960s. These were probably the result of anniversaries being celebrated in the South in areas which were once British colonies. The grant to Saint Thomas Church in 1975 is at the forefront of renewed interest in this form of symbolism and identification and we will look at the details of it shortly.

We turn now to ecclesiastical heraldry. Its origins are the same as those of secular heraldry, but it is interesting to note that as early as A.D. 312 the Emperor Constantine required that the Chi-Rho monogram for Christ be painted on the shields of his soldiers going into battle at the Milvian Bridge. The emblem soon appeared on the imperial standard, on coins, and elsewhere. Thus one commentator has named Constantine the father of ecclesiastical heraldry.[9] There seem to be two types of ecclesiastical heraldry. The first is personal arms. Armorial bearings, that is, the use of emblems according to heraldic principles, began to appear on bishops' seals and banners. Such coats of arms are distinguished by the presence of the mitre, the crosier, and the ecclesiastical hat. One of the earliest such forms is thought to be the arms of the Bishop of Chichester which are derived from those of Bishop Siegfrid who lived at the end of the twelfth century. The second variety is impersonal arms. Such, for example, are the arms of the diocese in which a bishop serves. We might also include in this type the use of devices which mark theological concepts such as the Holy Trinity or Holy Baptism. Both types of arms found their way into use in exquisite embroidered form on vestments or in carvings on wood or stone. Both types and both uses are well represented in Saint Thomas Church.

There can be no doubt that the architects of Saint Thomas readily appreciated not only the historical significance of heraldry, but also its decorative attraction. There is evidence that both Ralph Adams Cram and Bertram Grosvenor Goodhue had already used heraldic devices in various contexts before they embarked on the Saint Thomas project. Of the two, however, it was Goodhue who was principally responsible for the decorative scheme of Saint Thomas. He took wonderful advantage of the opportunity to develop a stunning program of decoration and symbolism, no small part of which involved the use of heraldry. Cram says in his autobiography:

> "All the exquisite detail, and the placing of this detail, was [Goodhue's] work, and in its originality, delicacy, and charm, and in the justness of its placing, it would, I think, be hard to beat. Later, and after the dissolution of our partnership, he alone designed the great reredos for the high altar together with all the other chancel furniture, fittings, and embellishments, all of it work of singular originality, richness, and charm."[10]

At this point, we should note how often coats of arms appear in designs that Goodhue created for other purposes. One example can be found in a book he helped design for the famous Merrymount Press of Daniel Berkeley Updike. Entitled *A Description Of The Pastoral Staff Given To The Diocese Of Albany* and commissioned by the donor of the staff, the book is replete with decorations which Goodhue devised in addition to the opening pages and the binding. The book is described in a catalogue of an exhibition which marked the one-hundredth anniversary of the Merrymount Press as being "the Press's last blast of gothicizing Arts and Crafts style, far more congenial now to the church architect Goodhue than to Updike."[11] The borders of each page are profuse with wonderfully rendered symbols and coats of arms, both personal and impersonal. Further evidence of Goodhue's interest and facility in coats of arms can be enjoyed by leafing through his *A Book of Architectural and Decorative Drawings.*[12] The bookplates, title pages, and printers' devices in it show many coats of arms, all handsomely drawn and handled with grace. In this same spirit, Goodhue embellished Saint Thomas Church in a singular and appealing way with arms of all sorts.

But before we turn to any consideration of the many arms represented in Saint Thomas Church, it is appropriate to note the various emblems the parish has used in an heraldic way since its incorporation in 1823. The first certainly makes reference to elements found in the traditional coat of arms for Saint Thomas himself. The initial emblem is enclosed within a roundel embellished with foliage bearing the label "ST. THOMAS CHURCH, NEW YORK." There is an open Bible on which is written the famous declaration Saint Thomas uttered before the risen Christ, "My Lord and my God" (John 20:28), and across the Bible is laid a spear. Also within the roundel is written "Let us also go, that we may die with him" (words of Saint Thomas in John 11:16). These devices, including the texts, remind us that Saint Thomas was the first explicitly to confess the divinity of Christ, and further, that our patron was a missionary who preached the Word in India, as tradition would have it, and that he was martyred at Mylapore near Madras by being run through with a spear. Iconographically, Thomas is usually shown as an old man holding a lance or pierced by a lance. Perhaps the most easily seen version of this emblem is on the wooden carved southern overdoor at the Fifth Avenue entrance, although it also appears on the original Communion silver and in many publications from the earliest years of the parish.

It seems, however, that from the time of the construction of the present building, and no doubt under the influence of its architects, the standard, traditional coat of arms for Saint Thomas came to be used. Described in non-heraldic terms, this consists of a shield on which a Latin cross is charged or overlain. In the upper left-hand corner there is an open Bible, in the upper right-hand corner a builder's square, and overlaying the Latin cross there is a spear. The significance of the builder's square is that the saint was thought to have been a builder by trade and that he may have built a church in India. We see this form of the arms in many places here, on the wooden carved northern overdoor at the Fifth Avenue entrance and in plaster relief on the ceiling of the Priests' Vestry, for example. It must be noted that the form of arms for almost any of the early personalities in church or secular history can vary in details. The standardization of such arms happened rather late and is founded in popular usage, not in registration at such institutions as the College of Arms.[13]

When Canon Andrew became rector of the parish in 1972, Saint Thomas Church gained a resident expert and enthusiast of heraldry.[14] He soon saw to it that the College of Arms in London, the official institution of the royal household which issues coats of arms in behalf of Queen Elizabeth II, would create a particular arms for the parish. There is no doubt that while the Richmond Herald, Mr. J. P. Brooke-Little, was the herald who conveyed the arms to the parish, the rector himself was the principal designer of the new arms (pl. XXVI).

Drawing inspiration from the so-called traditional coat of arms for the saint already described, it uses some of its elements, the cross and the spear, but, rather than an open Bible and a builder's square in the upper corners, it displays in each corner of the shield four closed red books charged with a cross, representing the four Gospels. This shield, by itself, can be seen in full color behind the rector's stall at the left and front of the choir area just above the parapet. The current arms is also meant to be more particularly indicative of this parish and not just of our patron in a general way, and it is obvious that the large roles which music and the Saint Thomas Choir School play in the parish have become definitive in the new design. The crest boldly sets forth these themes, for while a standard silver and red wreath forms the base, a celestial golden crown adorned with five fanwise silver trumpets tops it off. The trumpets certainly refer to the rank of *trompettes en chamade* on the rear wall of the nave just below the rose window, linked to and played from the Arents Memorial Organ, but they also refer to the importance of musical instruments in the worship of God Himself. In addition, this particular arms is grandly distinguished by "supporters" in the form of two choirboys (one blond and one brunet, for whom there were no human models). The boys are dressed in vestments typical of Saint Thomas Church choristers in more recent decades: a cassock of the Royal Scarlet over which is a white surplice, with a modified cavalier ruff being worn at the neck . Each chorister holds a black book.

The Letters Patent also grant the use of a badge, which can be used independently as a sort of shorthand heraldic symbol of the parish. It is derived from the arms and displays eight golden trumpets conjoined at the mouthpieces and interlaced with a golden ring. Though the arms can be seen in many places in the church, the badge has been displayed sparingly. There is, however, a dossal sometimes hung behind the cross on the high altar which stunningly bears this badge. Finally, there is the motto "O God My Heart is Ready," although it is not a part of the grant of armorial bearings because no authority is needed to use a motto.[15] The arms serves both the church and the choir school, as does also the motto.

In May of 1976, with no little ceremony, the colorful and lush patent which authorizes the use of the arms and gives a full and proper description in correct heraldic terms was presented to the parish by the Richmond Herald. The text of the Letters Patent, which hangs proudly in the parish house, reads precisely as follows (pl. XXVII):

We Sir Anthony Richard Wagner, Knight Commander of the Royal Victorian Order, Garter Principal King of Arms, John Riddell Bromhead Walker, Esquire, Member of the Royal Victorian Order, upon whom has been conferred the Decoration of the Military Cross, Clarenceux King of Arms and Walter John George Verco, Esquire, Commander of the Royal Victorian Order, Norroy and Ulster King of Arms, having been requested by John Gerald Barton Andrew Clerk in Holy Orders, Master of Arts of the University of Oxford, eleventh Priest and Rector of SAINT THOMAS CHURCH in the City and County of New York in the United States of America on behalf of the Rector and Wardens and Vestry of the said Church and with the consent and approval of the Governor of the said State of New York to devise for Saint Thomas Church such Armorial Ensigns as We may deem suitable to be borne and used for SAINT THOMAS CHURCH on Seals or otherwise have devised the Armorial Ensigns following that is to say, for Arms: Or on a Cross formy throughout Azure between four closed Books saltirewise Gules garnished and each charged with a Long Cross a Spear Or headed Argent and for Crest: On a Wreath Argent and Gules Issuant from a Celestial Crown Or five Trumpets fanwise Argent garnished Or Mantled Azure doubled Argent; and for the Supporters: On either side a Chorister vested in Red Cassock with White Surplice and Ruff proper holding in the exterior hand a Book also proper bound Sable; and for the Badge Eight Trumpets conjoined at the mouthpieces gyronwise Argent garnished and interlaced by an Annulet Or as are more clearly depicted in the margin In witness whereof We have subscribed Our names and affixed the Seals of Our several Offices at the College of Arms in London this First day of December 1975.

[signed] Anthony R. Wagner, Garter
[signed] J. R. B. Walker, Clarenceux
[signed] Walter J. Verco, Norroy & Ulster

At the time of the presentation, Saint Thomas Church was the first parish church in over half a millennium to receive a grant of arms from the College of Arms in London, though now several others enjoy this distinction. The Cathedral Church of the Advent in Birmingham, Alabama, is one such. The creation of the current Saint Thomas arms thus seems to be merely a natural progression from the heraldic tradition that was so heartily encouraged by Goodhue and Cram in 1913.[16]

The Saint Thomas Choir School also uses arms designed in 1963 by the Reverend Canon Edward N. West, late of the Cathedral of Saint John the Divine. This arms has been used by the Choir School on various publications and otherwise since that time. It is described as "azure on a spear palewise proper surmounted by an open book displaying the text, Cantate Domino."[17]

At first look, the present Saint Thomas Church seems to be lavishly decorated with coats of arms, especially in the more intricately designed areas of the building. It may seem that these are just decorative. After a closer look, however, themes or patterns emerge by which the arms help define the areas in which they appear. The most obvious place in which the arms appear is in the reredos, mentioned above, where they are used to label and identify each statue. In the choir, however, they are more decorative and commemorative. At various places in the stalls they seem intended to punctuate the general decorative scheme of random devices; the Brooklyn Bridge, Fulton's steamboat, the telephone, the arms of Canterbury. The chancel floor shows another arrangement of coats of arms, which calls to mind the theme of the place of the church within the community, both locally and nationally. Five mosaics there show the arms of the Parish, the Diocese of New York, the City and State of New York, and the United States itself. But in the delicate canopies over the rear stalls we see a series of arms used commemoratively to indicate all of the dioceses of the Episcopal Church, domestic and missionary, at the time of the construction of the stalls. On the reverse sides of these shields, still more arms are visible in the ambulatory on the south and in the Resurrection Chapel on the north.

Again, we see arms used commemoratively at the First World War Memorial at the southeast corner of the nave. There sixteen beautifully painted arms of the Allied Forces fill the upper portions of the paneled doors at the center of the memorial. These arms call to mind that in addition to the many parishioners who served in the Great War countless others from many parts of the world also served and were sacrificed. In addition, there is a series of colored shields above the door which delineate the various branches of the military services. The arms in this case seem to describe the scope of the conflict. The same approach can be seen in the Second World War Memorial in the narthex, even though the cast of players in the Allies' roster has changed somewhat. Some visitors, for example, still find it offensive that the arms of the Soviet Union are allowed to remain in mosaic form in the narthex pavement! There are also some places for which arms were obviously planned, but which have yet to be realized. One such, to be seen above the entrance to the south gallery, is a blank vesica (a shape formed by the intersection of two equal circles, each of whose circumference passes through the center of the other) which would usually be completed with a diocesan arms.

On the exterior of the building, arms are used in exactly the same ways. The Fifth Avenue elevation with its vast number of statues has arms as captions for those formidable figures. Yet the four faces of the Bell Tower each have fourteen blank shields and crests awaiting carving. On the Fifty-third Street elevation at the bottom of the turret that carries an interior stair up to the rector's office, the personal arms of Canon Andrew have been carved. His own arms here are impaled, that is to say, arranged side-by-side in one shield divided with those of the parish. This sort of arms is often used to show the arms of a husband and a wife or, as in this instance, of an office and the office-holder. At the top of the turret just above the windows each face is decorated with a shield, most of which can no longer be read due to the weathering of the stone. Also on the Fifty-third Street façade we see the traditional arms of Saint Thomas over what is now the entrance to the parish house. Finally, at the third floor level an empty niche is captioned with an arms.

The listing of all of the coats of arms to be found in and on Saint Thomas Church has proven to be a desirable but impossible task at the present writing. There are arms both outside and inside. They embellish the reredos, the chancel carvings, various accouterments such as candle standards and chalices, stained glass windows, and plaster relief ceilings. There have been two partial listings,[18] but no complete record of all the coats of arms seems to have been kept. Whenever it is compiled, a complete listing of all heraldic devices (that is, symbols on shields only) will need to be made, first of those found in the interior of the church, then of those on the exterior, and finally of those on items such as muniments and other noteworthy objects.

Notes

1 F. R. Webber, *Church Symbolism* (Cleveland: J.H. Jansen, 1938), p.24.

2 Webber, *Church Symbolism*, p. iii.

3 James-Charles Noonan Jr., *The Church Visible* (New York: Viking, 1996), p. 187.

4 *The Catholic Encyclopedia*, "Heraldry, Ecclesiastical."

5 Peter Gwynn-Jones, *The Art of Heraldry* (New York: Barnes and Noble, 1998), p. 11.

6 Gwynn-Jones, *The Art of Heraldry*, p. 13.

7 Bruno B. Heim, *Heraldry in the Catholic Church* (Gerrards Cross: Van Duran Publishers, 1978), p. 19.

8 Thomas Woodcock and John Martin Robinson, *The Oxford Guide to Heraldry* (Oxford: Oxford University Press, 1988), p. 156.

9 Eckford DeKay, *Heraldry in the Episcopal Church* (San Jose: Acorn Press, 1993), p. 6.

10 Ralph Adams Cram, *My Life in Architecture* (Boston: Little, Brown, and Company, 1936), p. 117. See above p. 128.

11 Martin Hutner, *The Merrymount Press* (New York: The Grolier Club, 1993), p. 7.

12 Bertram Grosvenor Goodhue, *A Book of Architectural and Decorative Drawings* (New York: The Architectural Book Publishing Company, 1924).

13 Thus we see, for example, an alternate form designed by Ellwood Post in George E. DeMille, *Saint Thomas Church in the City and County of New York 1823-1954* (Austin TX: Church Historical Society, 1958; Publication no. 47), p. 18.

14 At the time of this writing, he was still known in heraldic circles of the most official sort as "the Manhattan Herald"!

15 On the origins of this motto, see chapter 13 above.

16 For many other examples of heraldry in American Anglican ecclesiastical institutions, see DeKay, *Heraldry in the Episcopal Church*, and J. Robert Wright, "Heraldry in the Anglican and Episcopal Tradition," *The Anglican* 26:3 (July 1997): 17-21.

17 For the origins, see *The Saint Thomas Church Bulletin*, November 1963, p. 6.

18 Ernest Peixotto, "St. Thomas's and Its Reredos," *Architecture* 42:1 (July 1920): 193-202, reprinted in [Frank Le G. Gilliss], *A Short Description of the Reredos, Wood Carvings and Other Objects of Interest in Saint Thomas Church New York City* (New York: Gilliss Press, 1927), pp. 6-9; and [Harold E. Grove], *St. Thomas Church* (New York: n.p., 1965).

APPENDIX 4 ❧ THE 175TH ANNIVERSARY CELEBRATION

At the University Club, New York City, on Thursday evening, 29 October 1998, the one hundred and seventy-fifth anniversary of Saint Thomas parish, 1823-1998, was celebrated in the context of a gala dinner for some 400 persons. The following addresses were given.

ADDRESS BY THE REV. CANON JOHN G. B. ANDREW, RECTOR EMERITUS

I am happy to be here. At my age, as George Burns used to say, I am happy to be here at all.

I have a bit of a feeling of *déjà vu* about tonight. Memories of a quarter of a century ago flood my mind as I remember the 150th anniversary dinner, when I was young and considered promising. This is a family get-together to enjoy our identity as a very special parish on a very special City Avenue. The Episcopal Church is suspected by many of suffering from a crisis of identity. I don't think Saint Thomas suffers from that. I'm reminded of an incident in London, in Fortnum & Mason on Piccadilly, where a young sales clerk was having difficulty with a pompous man making life unpleasant about a delivery. The man said, "Do you know who I am?" The youngster lifted up his voice around the store; "There's somebody here who doesn't know who he is. Can anybody help him?" No identity crisis for Saint Thomas.

Gratitude, yes. For blessing far beyond our deserving through the years. Generosity unheard of when in 1905 the church burned down and the rector on his own volition sent money raised from insurance and a restoration fund campaign to the Mayor of San Francisco for the victims of the earthquake, and ten days later the fund stood higher still: all New York had responded to his reckless unselfishness. . . . To create a church of astonishing beauty and integrity which we are lucky enough to enjoy and be proud of. To have one of the finest choirs in the world, and one of the musical world's characters in its Organist and Master of Choristers. To have a man of distinction as Head of the magnificent Choir school. To enjoy an unrivaled strategic location. To be in a Diocese with a learned and gentle Bishop like +Richard. We thank God for all this generosity of good things. As we should, for a young and devoted rector, our twelfth, and a distinguished one, too. And my friend. Andy, the Lord has set your feet in a large room! (As the psalmist says. . .)

You cast a beam over the quarter century since the last celebration in 1973 and what do you see? A strong liturgical direction taken; an intensity of worship which has structured my own life and the lives of many of us. You see remarkable liturgies—my own sister Ann was converted by the *Tenebrae* a decade or so ago—when the power of the Holy Spirit was felt; I recall one extraordinary Christmas Eve, about which a young man in prison later wrote to me. He had been there and wrote most movingly of the strength of the Holy Spirit's presence. What else? I remember that the pledge totaled $88,000 in 1972. Now it is over half a million, thanks to enormous and imaginative effort of our campaign chairmen. What else? Ecumenical involvement, not merely by us but by our friends made in Churches other than ours. It has been a quarter century of friendships made and shared, the pulpit often occupied by friends from the Archdiocese and beyond and work undertaken together outside our walls, in the community. How can you speak of an occasion like this without a kaleidoscope of the characters who crowd a quarter-century? Colleagues in the priesthood, from beloved Douglas Ousley onwards, with his wife Mary; the gentle Tom Greene from Canada; the tall Ron Lafferty, the great Gary Fertig, the supreme Stuart Kenworthy, not to speak of the latter-day saints like Stafford and Sellery and both the Altons who made my life such fun? And yours, too. Oh yes! Jim Marlow and Robbie and Larry the cops who kept me and all others (for the most part) on the right side of the law, and Morgan Holman and later Addison Keim, on the right side of the liturgy. And Lonnie Bell Gay, the ineffable Lonnie with a large heart, a large smile, and a frighteningly large talent in the kitchen at 550.

And the noble army of unforgettable individuals who have loyally tied their colors to the Saint Thomas Parish mast. I mention only one: the fierce old lady who regularly got hold of the wrong end of most sticks: who raged at me when the roof was being accoustically sealed in the 70s for my philistinism in having a flat roof put in, 40 feet lower than the arches. Who always turned her hearing aid off into a squeak as I was about to preach. . . .

They are for you and for me a great cloud of witnesses to life in this place and parish; a cloud of many colors, a cloud of many joys.

Let me finish with something I've noticed about a parish where the life of the Spirit soars. Being lively isn't the same as having life. It's not that everyone is busy, busy, busy, for the sake of being busy. Activism can be a curse, and it is the lighted fuse to burnout. There is a partnership of the quiet ones, who wait upon the Lord to renew their strength, who "tarry the Lord's leisure" as the Psalms say, *and* those whose involvement means their active time as well as their talents; a partnership of the individual who is less gregarious, who doesn't enjoy the coffee hours, with the extrovert who does. It is not an either/or situation in a parish where the waters of the Spirit run deep, so much as a both/and. Self-giving has many faces.

There is *cooperation. It's obvious to any observer.* A friend of mine desperately wants, no doubt for the best possible reasons, to win the Lottery. Her prayers are fixed, and she barnstorms Heaven like the lady in the commercial who sings "O Lord send me a Mercedes Benz": "Lord I do my best for you at Saint Thomas. I pledge. I help with the Baroque Fair. I pour at Coffee Hours. Let me have a nice win!" No win. More prayers. No win. More prayers—and then the clouds parted, and a great bearded face looks down and says, "I've heard all of this. I'm sympathetic. Let me meet you half way. BUY A TICKET. . .".

I am so pleased to be part of this 175th Anniversary Celebration of Saint Thomas' Parish and to share this podium with your rector and Canon Andrew, the former pastor of this great parish.

Ever since I received the letter from Father Mead inviting me to say a few words at this banquet, I have been thinking and searching for just the right theme. Something that in a succinct way might capture some of the true character of Saint Thomas'. Or at least the thing that expresses what I think is so important about this wonderful church. And, I have settled on this: It has something to do with vertical religion. And by that I mean those expressions and acts of our religion that draw us upward. Jacob's experience at Bethel would be a good example of vertical religion, that ladder connecting heaven and earth, angels ascending and descending. There he encounters God. But, let me begin with the description of a painting which also portrays this notion of vertical religion, and at the same time something of why it is so necessary for those who believe.

Raphael's last and possibly greatest painting was of *The Transfiguration*. It is a sizable work that was painted in a competition for an altar piece. It's an unusual painting of the Transfiguration in that it includes both the scene at the top of the mountain where we see Jesus with Moses and Elijah, and the three disciples, Peter, James, and John; and, the scene at the bottom of the mountain: the nine disciples left behind attempting to heal the epileptic boy. Raphael intended that this painting should be an expression of his own profound faith. He died just before it was completed so the finishing touches were added by people from his workshop. At his funeral it hung over his casket.

Let me describe the painting in some detail. At the top we see Our Lord floating above the mountain top suffused in brilliant light. Clearly, the incarnate expression of the glory of God. Beside him, also floating in the air and reflecting the brilliance of the light, are Moses and Elijah. Below him on the mountain top, Peter, James and John lie prostrate. Hands shielding the eyes from the bright light, they are in awe, frightened by what they experience.

At the base of the mountain, Raphael has painted the other scene. Here, if one recalls the story, the nine disciples that were left behind are approached by a father whose son has epilepsy. He asks for healing. At the center of the lower scene we see the father holding the son, rigid in seizure and the mother kneeling beside them pleading with the disciples to heal the boy.

This lower scene by contrast to the bright light at the top of the mount is held in gloomy darkness painted with harsh hues which suggest ambiguity, discord, despair and conflict. It clearly expresses the situation, for the disciples are unable to work the miracle of healing. We see them gathered around the boy and his parents in a variety of smaller groupings. One disciple in the forescene has a Bible open and seems to be looking for some answer there. Behind the boy and the father, we see a couple of disciples who seem to be saying to one another, "Let's stay out of this, it's none of our business." In the background on the other side, we have two whispering to one another, possibly saying something like, "What are we to do, He is not here to help us?" These can all be seen as various expressions of the church at any given moment of its history — bewildered and helpless in the face of the world's plight.

At the very center of this scene, we see a little cluster of five disciples, one pointing to the lad and the other to the top of the mountain. These two pointing disciples connect the top and the bottom of the painting and are an expression of Raphael's faith. One pointing disciple seems to be saying, "here is the problem." The other pointing upward to the transfigured Christ as if to say, "there is the solution." Without the top of the mountain, the world below remains dark and ambiguous. But with that transcendent transfigured Christ, which is from above, we see our hope. And, in our story you will recall that Christ does come down the mountain and heals the boy, bringing the light of the Transfiguration to the dark world below.

This painting not only expresses in a clear way what I mean by vertical religion, but it states unambiguously why it is necessary. To believe in God requires a belief in a transcendent realm of being which exceeds our human powers to grasp on our own without revelation from God. And, while we have no power to invade this realm or control it, because we believe in it we can invoke it, aspire to it, long for it, sing and dance before it. These are all acts by which we point to that which is beyond us in every way. In this we are like the disciple in the painting who points upward to the top of the mountain toward the Transfigured Christ. And even though he cannot see the top of the mount, somehow what he believes and what he does by that gesture connects him with that transcendence which is beyond him. And this is what I mean by vertical religion – those activities of prayer and worship which by faith recognize and point to the transcendent in such a way that one knows God is God.

Well, what does this have to do with Saint Thomas'? First of all, one cannot enter the church without being drawn upward by that magnificent reredos — Christ in glory, the orb in hand as He gives us His blessing. But what is so important here is that the worship is consonant with the beauty of the stone. The matchless music with liturgical ceremonial to go with it. This is worship expressed with as much beauty, dignity and reverence as is possible to give. Such devotion to the worship of God can never be too good or done too well. And what this is about is not simply the perfection of religious ceremonial but rather the expression of our interior longing for God. It is an outward sign of our faith or else it would be empty. By gesture, song, and prayer we seek to show forth our aspirations, invoke the heavenly, and call down the divine presence. For we know God is our only hope.

I have an old priest friend who after each especially good liturgy would say, "Weren't you just transported?" That is it, isn't it? Worship done well transports us spiritually – lifts us to the heavenly. And while it is also true what the Psalmist says: "Be still and know that I am God," yet we can know God in the quiet, in the emptiness. But in the kind of worship that transports us, faith seeks the holy through the use of symbols.

Two years ago my friend Archbishop Sergei, the Chancellor of the Russian Orthodox Church, was with us for Easter liturgy at the Cathedral. After, he said to me, "Today I got to heaven." That was a great compliment. Getting to heaven is the object of Orthodox worship. And, it is I believe, what worship at Saint Thomas does for so many of us.

Closing Remarks by The Twelfth Rector, The Rev. Andrew C. Mead

I am going to make a few "Rector's Remarks" before we have a closing prayer and then I ask the Bishop to bless us on our way.

First, I want to thank one person, Hope Preminger. She is the chairman of our 175th Anniversary in all its various activities.

Our 175th anniversary occurs early enough in my rectorship and close enough to the commencement of a new century and millennium, so that this is a fitting moment to state a mission for the future. We cannot, however, look to the future without appreciating our history, without *memory*. It is in aid of this corporate memory that we have commissioned the writing of a serious parish history, the first such since 1954, by one of the Church's premier scholars, the Rev. Canon Professor J. Robert Wright.

When rectors look to their parishes' past, they do well to honor and bless their predecessors in their priestly faithfulness. We stand on the collective shoulders of our pastoral predecessors; we build on their accomplishments.

We are a work in progress. Our locations and building reflect this progress: the large room at Broome Street and Broadway, the church on Houston Street, the churches on Fifth Avenue and 53rd (may God long preserve our present glorious temple). The developing expressions of our liturgy and churchmanship reflect this progress: the nineteenth-century staunch high churchmanship inspired by Bishop Hobart, the orthodox broad churchmanship of two long twentieth century rectorships, and since 1973, the spirit of the Oxford Movement and of classical Catholic and Anglican liturgy. We are a work in progress, but it is fair to say, so far, that we have proven ourselves to be both conservative and broad-minded—high, broad, catholic, classical. We recapitulate our history. Just look at the saints in the reredos and you see what I mean, from St. Paul to George Washington, to our Lady to William Ewart Gladstone.

We cannot predict or control the future, but we can have a clear sense of who we are. This includes how we want to grow and what we want to become.

God has given Saint Thomas such great gifts and resources: a goodly heritage of worship, a history of movement, mission and building, even of death and resurrection amidst apparent calamity. Now we have a glorious temple at the center of one of the greatest cities in the history of the world. We have a liturgy and music uniquely upheld by the 80-year heritage of the Saint Thomas Choir School, worship which powerfully animates that architecture as the temple of the living God. We have had the generosity of many benefactors and the faithful stewardship of our leaders to endow and preserve these costly gifts. We also give away a great deal, at home and abroad. The clergy strive within this setting to preach and teach, with intelligence and clarity, the Gospel of our living Lord and Savior Jesus Christ. What then? What next, as we mark this auspicious turn of the calendar? What do we do with what has been entrusted to us, this goodly heritage?

One of the best developments this century at Saint Thomas (and in much of the rest of the Church) has been the recovery of the Holy Eucharist as the principal and central act of worship on the Lord's Day. This mystery has superlative expression in our Sunday morning liturgy and music, week by week. There, at the heart of it all, is the Body of Christ. But it is not only the consecration of the sacramental bread and wine that we speak of. It is also the congregation.

I believe our mission now is to become ever more visible as a *congregation* of faithful people. I heard this mission as part of my call to be your priest and rector. This mission has been confirmed to me more clearly, month by month (now year by year), as I get to know this flock. As the Prayer Book in the Articles of Religion (number 19) puts it: "The visible Church of Christ is a congregation of faithful men, in the which the Word of God is preached and the Sacraments be duly ministered according to Christ's ordinance." A *congregation*, of men, women, and children!

We are the body of Christ and members of one another. As we pray, after receiving Holy Communion, we are made "very members incorporate in the mystical body of thy Son, the blessed company of all faithful people." We attract large numbers of individuals, great crowds at times, to Saint Thomas. Let us strive to bring as many as possible into that full mystery of Christ. Let us bring people from passive attendance to active participation; let us make more of the aggregation into a congregation. Let us have more and more communication, education, fellowship, hospitality and friendship, more corporate service and witness.

This nearly 21st century world, which New York City supremely illustrates, urgently needs community. The Christian Church, in order to be authentic, must by definition *be a community*. Let us become, more and more, that living, active, visible congregation of faithful people, the Body of Christ at Fifth Avenue and 53rd Street. That, dearly beloved, is our mission. I finish with the apostle's words: "Now you are the body of Christ and individually members of it. . . . If one member suffers, all suffer together; if one member is honored, all rejoice together." (I Cor 12: 27, 26).

CLOSING PRAYER

Almighty and everlasting God, who dost govern all things in heaven and earth, we thank thee for the goodly heritage of Saint Thomas Church and Choir School; and, we beseech thee, mercifully hear our prayers, and grant unto this parish family all things necessary for its spiritual welfare: teachers to educate thy people in thy faith and fear, ministers to labor in this portion of thy vineyard, a church main-

*tained in the beauty of holiness. Strengthen and increase the faithful; visit and re-
lieve the suffering; turn and soften the wicked; rouse the careless; recover the fallen;
restore the penitent; remove all hindrances to the advancement of thy truth; and
bring us all to be of one heart and mind within the fold of thy one, holy, Catholic
and Apostolic Church; through Jesus Christ thy Son our Lord, who liveth and
reigneth with thee and the Holy Ghost, ever one God, world without end. Amen.*

APPENDIX 5 ❧ PERSONNEL

SAINT THOMAS CHURCH 1823-1999[1]

THE RECTORS

Cornelius Roosevelt Duffie	1823-1827
George Upfold[2]	1828-1831
Francis Lister Hawks	1831-1843
Henry John Whitehouse[3]	1844-1851
Edmund Neville	1852-1856
William Ferdinand Morgan	1857-1888
John Wesley Brown	1888-1900
Ernest Milmore Stires[4]	1901-1925
Roelif Hasbrouck Brooks	1926-1954
Frederick Myers Morris	1954-1972
John Gerald Barton Andrew	1972-1996
Andrew Craig Mead	1996-

ASSISTANT CLERGY AT THE PARISH CHURCH

James A. Bolles	1833
Joseph H. Price	1833
Pierre P. Irving	1836
Charles H. Halsey	1839-1840
Isaac Pardee	1840-1843
J. A. Spencer	1856-1857
Nathaniel T. Richardson	1862-1867
John Frederick Butterworth	1867-1868
John Brainerd Morgan	1868-1873
Christopher B. Wyatt	1870-1871
Frank L. Norton	1872-1874
Joseph Firth Jowitt	1874
Mytton Maury	1875
John Anketell	1875-1877
Frederick Courtney[5]	1876-1880
Alexander Mackay-Smith[6]	1880-1887
James B. Drysdale	1884-1885
Alexander B. Carver	1886-1887
Reuben W. Howes	1887
Charles R. Treat	1887-1888
Reginald Heber Starr	1887-1889
Henry Martyn Kirkby	1889-1893
Charles Edward Spalding	1893-1894
John Huske	1893-1901
DeWitt L. Pelston	1900-1904
William Henry Owen Jr.	1901-1908
James Biggar Wasson	1905-1910
George Ashton Oldham[7]	1906-1908
Frank S. Cookman	1908-1911
Wilbur Larremore Caswell	1910-1916, 1923-1925
Haywood L. Winter	1911-1912
Andrew F. Underhill	1912-1913
Henry V. B. Darlington	1913-1914
W. Strother Jones	1914-1918
A. Wolford Brooks	1917-1918
Floyd Swallow Leach	1918-1923
Walter Charles Bihler	1924-1927
Joseph Haas Titus	1926-1927
Harold L. Gibbs	1927-1933
John Stephen Willey	1933-1935
Otis Radcliffe Rice	1933-1938
George Johnson Hall	1936-1941
Lauriston Livingston Scaife[8]	1938-1942
Sturgis Lee Riddle	1941-1945
David McAlpin Pyle	1945-1948
Lesley Wilder Jr.	1945-1948
John Durham Wing Jr.	1948-1951
James Hart Morgan	1948-1955
John Castles Francis	1951-1953
Howard S. Hane	1953-1956
Harry L. Thomas	1955-1956
Carroll Eugene Simcox	1955-1958
George Zabriskie II	1956-1959
Sidney Lanier	1958-1962
John Dyson Cannon	1959-1963
William Alan Sadler Jr.	1960-1961
Thomas Dorgan Byrne	1961-1965
Wilbur Henry Tyte	1963-1969
James Lawrence B. Williams	1965-1967
Charles Jackson Minifie	1966-1969
Charles Howard Rowins	1969-1971
Henry Albert Zinser	1970-1975
Paul Conrad Christopherson	1971-1972
Thomas M. Greene	1973-1977
John Douglas Ousley	1973-1978
Samuel Bancroft Bird Jr.	1976-1978
Gary P. Fertig	1977-1995 Vicar 1983-1995
Ronald Lafferty	1978-1982
Gordon Hayes Duggins	1983-1985
Dorsey W. M. McConnell	1983-1985
Robert Holmes Stafford	1985-1991, 1996-
Stuart Albert Kenworthy	1986-1991

Howard Stringfellow	1986-1993
Duane W. H. Arnold	1991-1994
Daniel G. G. Ade	1992-1994
Frances A. T. LeBlanc	1993-1994
Richard Charles Alton	1994-1996
David Forster Sellery	1994-1999
Harry Edward Krauss III	1997-
Park McDermit Bodie	1997-
Joseph Edmund Griesdieck III	1999-

HONORARY ASSISTANTS

Leslie John Alden Lang	1974-1990
Stanley Frederick Gross	1979-1980
Gordon-Hurst Barrow	1981-1982,
	1984-1995
James P. Nicholls	1985-1986
Ivan Weiser	1991-1993
Harold Ransom Landon	1996-
William Andrew Norgren	1996-
John Robert Wright	1997-

VICARS OF THE CHAPEL

Ralph Hoyt	1858-1859,
	1867
Frederick Sill	1859-1867
J. B. C. Beaubien	1868
John J. Roberts	1869-1874
Robert C. Lowry	1874-1889
William Hawks Pott	1889-1900
Robert R. Claiborne	1901-1910
Frederick Widmar Cornell	1910-1912
Claudius M. Roome	1912-1913
Daniel Wilmot Gateson	1913-1917
James Sheerin	1917-1918
John Sylvanus Haight	1918-1924
Richard Marquedant Doubs	1924-1930
Paul Stevens Olver	1930-1933
Frederick Swindlehurst	1934-1941
Harold Earl Towne	1941-1944
Paul Curry Armstrong	1944-1959
George Augustus Trowbridge	1960
R. DeWitt Mallary Jr.	1960-1965

CHAPEL ASSISTANTS

Roland Ernst Grueber	1882-1893
William Hawks Pott	1887-1889
Alfred Brittain	1893-1894
Nathan A. Seagle	1894-1900
Robert William Cochrane	1901-1910
George Frederick Bambach	1907-1909
William G. Thompson	1910-1914
Walter Williams	1913-1917
Claudius M. Roome	1913-1921

Donald Schuman	1917-1918
Harold Lyman Smith Johns	1918-1920
Charles Jeremiah Mason	1920-1921
John Herman Feringa	1922
George McKinley	1922-1923
Edward Alfred Evans	1922-1924
Nigel S. MacEwan	1926-1927
Frederick Swindlehurst	1927-1934
John L. Williams	1928-1931
John Oliver Ferris	1931-1933
John Stephen Willey	1935
Myles A. Vollmer	1935-1936
Robert Noel Rodenmayer	1935-1936
Archibald Dixon Rollit	1945-1946
Edward Chandler	1948-1950
Johann Schenk	1951-1953
Meredith Mendenhall Calvert	1954-1956
William John Fisher Lydecker	1956-1958

CHURCH WARDENS

Isaac Lawrence	1823-1839
Thomas Mumford Huntington	1823
David Hadden	1824-1856
Morris Robinson	1839-1850
William Neilson	1850-1851
Mark Spencer	1851-1859
Lyman Denison	1857-1877
Edward M. Willett	1859-1877
Daniel Taylor Hoag	1878-1899
George McCulloch Miller	1878-1917
James C. Fargo	1901-1915
Charles Steele	1915-1939
William H. Truesdale	1918-1932
Robert B. Dodson	1932-1938
Lancaster Morgan	1938-1946
William Adams Kissam	1939-1950
Lewis Gawtry	1946-1954
George Arents	1950-1960
Alfred H. Townley	1954
Walter C. Baker	1954-1971
George A. Wilson	1960-1967
John C. Pierson	1968-1973
John E. Merow	1971-1978
Sidney H. Stires	1974-1989
Francis Robinson	1979-1980
Anne J. Exline	1981-1990
John B. Hoffmann	1990-1993
G. William Haas	1991-
Joan E. Hoffman	1994-

VESTRY

David Hadden	1823-1824
William Beach Lawrence	1823-1826
John James Lambert	1823-1826

Charles King	1823–1827	Charles Vandervoort	1861–1866
Murray Hoffman	1823–1832	Abraham M. Cozzens	1862–1864
John Duer	1823–1840	John S. Williams	1864–1875
William Backhouse Astor	1823	Daniel Taylor Hoag	1867–1878
Richard Oakley	1823–1831	George Kemp	1867–1872
Benjamin M. Brown	1824–1828	John Hall Watson	1868–1901
John Smyth Rogers	1824–1828	Allen J. Cumming	1868–1874
Morris Robinson	1826–1839	James C. Fargo	1871–1901
Oliver H. Hicks	1826–1827,	William I. Peake	1872–1881
	1831–1832	William H. Lee	1873–1894
Robert Gracie	1828–1850	George MacCulloch Miller	1874–1878
William H. Jephson	1828–1839	Joseph M. Cooper	1875–1877
C. N. S. Rowland	1828–1832	Jacob Halstead	1875–1883
William C. Rhinelander	1829–1833	Robert S. Hone	1878–1883
Richard C. Auchmuty	1832–1838	Charles Short	1878–1886
William Nielson	1832–1850	Henry H. Cook	1878–1905
John Rogers	1833–1840	Joseph W. Harper Jr.	1881–1896
Benjamin McVickar	1833–1836	Roswell P. Flower	1883–1892
Daniel Oakley	1836–1838	Hiram W. Sibley	1883–1887
Thomas L. Servoss	1837–1844	Fessenden N. Otis	1887–1891
Jonathan Amory	1838–1843	Frederic Gallatin	1887–1891
Fanning C. Tucker	1839–1844	Harris C. Fahnestock	1891–1914
George Gibson	1839–1844	William Seward Webb	1891–1901
Jeremiah Van Rensselaer	1840–1842,	John T. Atterbury	1892–1898
	1843–1852	George L. Gillespie	1894–1903
Frederick Prime	1840–1841	James T. Woodward	1900–1910
Bernard Rhinelander	1842–1844	Alexander M. Hadden	1901–1942
Samuel W. Moore	1842–1844	Darius Ogden Mills	1901–1912
Peter Lorillard Jr.	1844–1845	Clarence M. Hyde	1901–1908
Samuel I. Bebee	1844–1846	Charles H. Stout	1901–1928
Charles M. Leupp	1844–1845	Anson R. Flower	1903–1909
Luther C. Carter	1844–1845	Charles Steele	1905–1915
Walter Rutherford	1844–1845	Albert B. Boardman	1909–1918
William Burgoyne	1845–1848	William H. Truesdale	1911–1920
Jasper Grosvenor	1845–1851	Robert Scoville	1913–1934
Richard L. Schieffelin	1845–1848	William P. Clyde	1915–1918
Galen Carter	1845–1850	Robert B. Dodson	1915–1932
Matthew Maury	1846–1851	William Fahnestock	1916–1936
Mark Spencer	1848–1851	H. D. Babcock	1917–1918
Lyman Denison	1848–1857	Samuel W. Fairchild	1918–1927
A. Bleecker Neilson	1850–1851	Lancaster Morgan	1918–1938
John C. Zimmerman	1850–1854	William Adams Kissam	1920–1939
Edward M. Willett	1850–1859	George E. Fahys	1920–1953
Evert A. Duyckinck	1851–1868	John V. W. Reynders	1927–1944
Thomas J. Leslie	1851–1854	Lewis Gawtry	1928–1954
Archibald Russell	1851–1854	Harris Fahnestock	1933–1939
Charles H. Clayton	1851–1854	George Arents	1934–1960
George C. Collins	1852–1875	Ernest Fahnestock	1934–1937
Revo C. Hance	1854–1862	William C. Breed	1936–1951
Alfred Wagstaff	1854–1857	Charles E. Dunlap	1936–1959
Elihu L. Mix	1854–1872	Gerald M. Livingston	1936–1950
Fulton Cutting	1854–1867	E. Victor Loew	1936–1950
George D. H. Gillespie	1857–1868	J. William Kilbreth	1936–1953
C. A. Berrian	1857–1861	Charles C. Paulding	1936–1938
John Tappan	1859–1871	Robert Goelet	1937–1959

Harry Payne Bingham	1938-1955	G. William Haas	1979-1984,
Walter B. Duryea	1938-1954		1987-
Francis B. Davis Jr.	1939-1956	Keith R. Johnson	1979-1984,
William Walker Kennedy	1942-1959		1986-1991,
William M. V. Hoffman	1943-1947		1994-1995
Alfred H. Townley	1944-1954	Charles Wormser	1979-1984
Samuel R. Fuller Jr.	1946-1955	Elizabeth Burr	1980-1985
Walter C. Baker	1947-1971	Mary T. Dailey	1981-1986
William DeForest Manice	1950-1961	Jeffrey Lawrence	1981-1986,
George Leal Genung	1950-1959		1989-1994
C. Douglass Green	1951-1953	Stephen F. Ambrose Jr.	1985-1988
George A. Wilson	1952-1967	William M. Barnard	1985-1987
Samuel Milbank	1953-1966	Robert P. Arzberger	1987-1992
Medley G. B. Whelpley	1953-1964	Martha Dodge	1987-1992,
William Francis Gibbs	1954-1967		1994-99
Robert E. Strawbridge Jr.	1954-1964	Ellen D. Beschler	1989-1994
Walter Wilds	1954-1960	John C. Sterling III	1989-1994,
Herbert E. Twyeffort	1954-1963		1997-
Broderick Haskell	1955-1960,	Theodore R. Gamble Jr.	1991-1996
	1962-1969, 1971-1977	John M. Neiswanger	1991-1996,
Max D. Howell	1956-1964		1998-
Thomas A. Ennis	1958-1965	Robert H. Gutheil	1992-1996
Sidney H. Stires	1961-1967,	Nancy Nielsen	1993-1998
	1970-1989	Hope B. Preminger	1993-1998,
John C. Pierson	1964-1973		2000-
Edward C. Weist	1964-1971	William E. Davis	1995-1996
Henry W. Manville	1965-1967	William H. A. Wright II	1995-
Cornelius DeF. Howland	1965-1971,	James T. Parkinson III	1996
	1972-1980	Jean Cameron Grainger	1997-
James M. Cannon III	1965-1971	Kenneth A. Lohf	1997-
Carroll L. Cartwright	1966-1972,	Kazie Metzger Harvey	1999-
	1983-1988	W. Michael Margolin	1999-
Thomas W. Phelps	1967-1972, 1973		
John E. Merow	1967-1978		

PARISH CLERKS[9]

J. L. Earle	1827-1831
Thomas Thornton	1831-1832

CLERKS TO THE VESTRY

Murray Hoffman	1823-1831
Robert Gracie	1831-1850
A. B. Nielson	1850-1851
Evert A. Duyckinck	1851-1868
Allen J. Cumming	1868-1871
James C. Fargo	1871-1874
John H. Watson	1874-1901
Charles H. Stout	1901-1928
Alfred M. Chapman	1928-1930
Franklin A. Plummer	1930-1945
William Walker Kennedy	1945-1958
Thomas A. Ennis	1958-1965
John E. Merow	1966-1971
James M. Cannon III	1971-1973
John D. Shultz	1974-1975

The remaining first-column entries:

Karl R. Bendetsen	1968-1972, 1973
Charles S. Mitchell	1968-1972
William Bradford Banks	1971-1973
Carl F. Greenway	1971-1973
William H. Wheelock	1971-1975
William M. Weilbacher	1972-1973
Wilbur C. Barth	1973-1978
Anne J. Exline	1973-1978,
	1981-1990
Jean J. Rousseau	1973-1979
Louis M. S. Beal	1974-1979,
	1980-1982,
	1985-1990,
	1997-
Joan E. Hoffman	1974-1980,
	1983-1988,
	1990-
Francis Robinson	1974-1980
John B. Hoffmann	1976-1993
J. Gary Burkhead	1978-1983

Frank Rykowski	1976-1980
G. William Haas	1981-1982,
	1984, 1989
Stephen F. Ambrose Jr.	1983, 1985-1988
George J. Moeschlin III	1990-

TREASURERS

Richard Oakley	1823-1831
C. N. S. Rowland	1831-1832
Oliver Hewlett Hicks	1832
John Rogers	1832-1839
Thomas L. Servoss	1839-1844
Jeremiah Van Rensselaer	1844-1852
George C. Collins	1852-1861
Elihu L. Mix	1861-1869
John Tappan	1869-1871
Allen J. Cumming	1871-1874
James C. Fargo	1874-1915
William H. Truesdale	1915-1932
Lewis Gawtry	1939-1951
Walter C. Baker	1951-1965
Edward C. Weist	1966-1971
William Bradford Banks	1971-1973
Robert I. Hume	1974-1978
John B. Hoffmann	1979-1989
G. William Haas	1990
Joan E. Hoffman	1991-1993
John C. Sterling III	1994, 1997-
John M. Neiswanger	1995-1996

ORGANISTS AND CHOIRMASTERS

Thomas S. Brown	1826-1827
Charles Willson	1827-1830
Thomas Hall	1830-1831
William Taylor	1832-1833
Richard B. Taylor	1833-1837
F. C. Unger	1838
Charles Wilkins	1839
John Dunderdale	1840
Austin L. Phillips	1841-1845
J. L. Northam	1847
A. M. Van Nostrand	1848
Daniel P. Lyon	1848-1851
George W. Morgan	1854
John F. Huntington	1856-1864
George William Warren	1870-1900
William C. Macfarlane	1900-1912
T. Tertius Noble	1913-1943
T. Frederick H. Candlyn	1943-1953
William Self	1954-1971
Gerre Hancock	1971-

ASSISTANT ORGANISTS

P. Auguste Schnecker	1878
Richard Henry Warren	1884
William C. Macfarlane	1887-1900
Gordon Darlington Richards	1902-1913
Daniel R. Philippi	1913-1920
Maurice Garabrant	1921-1926
Andrew J. Tietjen	1926-1935
Grover J. Oberle	1935-1942
Frank J. MacConnell	1942-1944
Richard W. Harvey	1944-1946
Frederick W. Graf	1946-1952
Edward A. Wallace	1952-1964
George Decker	1964-1967
Arnold Ostlund Jr.	1967
Frederick O. Grimes III	1967-1970
Bradley L. Hull	1971-1972
Judith E. Hancock	1971-1989,
	Associate 1997-
Catherine Burrell	1989
Michael Kleinschmidt	1990-1993
Peter Stoltzfus	1993-1995
Patrick Allen	1995-1997,
	Associate 1997-1998
Thomas Bara	1999-

CHAPEL ORGANISTS

Frank A. Warhurst
William J. Craft
Frederick Maurice Michell
William G. Goldsworthy
W. LeRoy Raisch
Cyril G. Laub
Maurice Garabrant
Rupert Sircom
Paul Smith Callaway
Andrew J. Tietjen
Wesley Irving Steele
Clyde A. Newell
Charles D. Walker
Walter R. Rye
Samuel B. Stribling Jr.
James L. Palsgrove III

HEADMASTERS OF THE CHOIR SCHOOL

Clarence Jack Smith	1919
Raymond Wallace Gauger	1920-1922
Herbert H. Hannan	1923-1925
Clair J. Smith	1926-1927
Charles Mead Benham	1928-1942

The Rev. James O. Carson Jr. 1943-1944
Leon D. Phillips   1945-1949
Henry B. Roney Jr.   1950-1955
Robert Porter   1955-1966
Gordon H. Clem   1967-1995
Murray Lawrence   *Acting* 1995-1997
Gordon Roland-Adams   1997-

DIRECTOR OF ADMINISTRATION

James E. Marlow   1983-

SEXTONS

William Purcell   1824-1827
James C. Dugan   1827-1846
Wilson McLean   1846-1858
Benjamin W. Williams 1858-1910
Edmund M. Speer   1910-1935
Francis D. Connell   1935-1967

William Anderson   1983-1984
Selvyn McLean   1987-1988

SEXTON-ADMINISTRATORS

Robert C. Jones   1968-1974
James E. Marlow   1975-1982

VERGERS

Morgan Holman   1984-1997
Addison J. Keim   1997-

Notes

1 Names and dates are compiled from the parish *Year Books*, Vestry Minutes, other sources in the Saint Thomas Archives, and the national *Episcopal Clerical Directory*, not all of which agree with each other. Where discrepancies have been found, the most reasonable guess has been made. I am especially grateful to Mrs. Joan Hoffman for her assistance with dates of wardens and vestry.

2 Later, second missionary and first diocesan Bishop of Indiana, 1849-1872.

3 Later, second Bishop of Illinois, 1852-1874 [Coadjutor, 1851-1852].

4 Later, third Bishop of Long Island, 1925-1942.

5 Later, fifth Bishop of Nova Scotia, 1888-1904.

6 Later, sixth Bishop of Pennsylvania, 1911 [Coadjutor 1902-1911].

7 Later, third Bishop of Albany, 1929-1949 [Coadjutor, 1922-1929].

8 Later, seventh Bishop of Western New York, 1948-1970.

9 The duty of the Parish Clerk, in accordance with Anglican custom, was to lead the congregation in the responses. Saint Thomas Church abolished this office in 1832.

❧ LIST OF ILLUSTRATIONS

Most illustrations are taken from the collections now in the Saint Thomas Church Archives.
Particular gratitude is noted in the credits that follow

❧ INDEX

Whenever possible, churches outside New York City are identified by location. Color plates have been indexed by capital roman numerals in italics. The unpaginated commentary following color plate V has not been indexed, nor have the serial listings of Personnel in Appendix 5.

SET IN CASLON, TRAJAN, AND GOLDEN COCKEREL
TYPES. PRINTED BY THAMES PRINTING.
DESIGN AND TYPOGRAPHY BY
JERRY KELLY.